/lea
av
in

$
V
W
W

ww

79 307 681 X

Lesley Blanch

Also by Anne Boston

Wave Me Goodbye: Stories of the Second World War (editor)

Lesley Blanch

Inner Landscapes, Wilder Shores

ANNE BOSTON

JOHN MURRAY

First published in Great Britain in 2010 by John Murray (Publishers)
An Hachette UK Company

I

© Anne Boston 2010

A CIP catalogue record for this title is available from the British Library

ISBN 978-0-7195-6037-8

Typeset in 11.5/14 Bembo
by Servis Filmsetting Ltd, Stockport, Cheshire

Printed and bound by Clays Ltd, St Ives

John Murray policy is to use papers that are natural, renewable and recyclable products and made from wood grown in sustainable forests. The logging and manufacturing processes are expected to conform to the environmental regulations of the country of origin.

John Murray (Publishers)
338 Euston Road
London NW1 3BH

www.johnmurray.co.uk

For Richard

Contents

Illustrations

Picture Acknowledgements: photography by Ulf Andersen/Gamma/ Eyedea, Camera Press London: 14 below. © Eve Arnold/Magnum Photos: 13 above. © Apis/Sygma/Corbis: 13 below right. Author's collection: 1, 8 below, 10 below. Courtesy of Don Bachardy. All rights reserved: 10 above left. Courtesy of Anne Bretel: 8 above left and right. © Henry Clarke, Coll. Musée Galliera, Paris/ADAGP, Paris and DACS, London 2009: 15 below. © Condé Nast Archive/ Corbis: 3 above right. Ernest Daniels © Royal Shakespeare Company: 2 below. © Getty Images: 3 above left, 5, 10 above right. © Keystone, France/Eyedea, Camera Press London: 12 below. © Eamonn McCabe/Guardian News & Media Ltd 2007: 16. © Lee Miller Archives, England 2009. All rights reserved. www.leemiller.co.uk: 3 below, 6 below, 7 above right. Courtesy of John Murray: 7 left. © Norman Parkinson Archive: 6 above. © Popperfoto/Getty Images: 15 above. Private collections: 2 above, 4, 9, 12 above right, 13 below left, 14 above. © Sam Shaw/Rex Features: 7 below right. Société Nouvelle Cinématographie/Productions Georges de Beauregard/ Imperia/BFI: 12 above left. LADY L. © Turner Entertainment Co. A Warner Bros. Entertainment Company. All Rights Reserved: 11.

Every reasonable effort has been made to trace copyright holders, but if there are any errors or omissions, John Murray will be pleased to insert the appropriate acknowledgement in any subsequent printings or editions.

The story of a life is a very informal party; there are no rules of precedence and hospitality, no invitations.

Muriel Spark, *Loitering with Intent*

And what Russian does not love fast driving? How could his soul . . . not love it? How not love it when there is something wonderful and magical about it? . . . Oh, you *troika*, you bird of a *troika*, who invented you? You could only have been born among a high-spirited people in a land that does not like doing things by halves, but has spread in a vast smooth plain over half the world, and you may count the milestones till your eyes are dizzy . . . The driver . . . has only to stand up and crack his whip and start up a song, and the horses rush like a whirlwind, . . . and the *troika* dashes on and on! And very soon all that can be seen in the distance is the dust whirling through the air.

Is it not like that that you, too, Russia, are speeding along like a spirited *troika* that nothing can overtake? . . . What is the meaning of this terrifying motion? . . . Russia, where are you flying to? Answer! She gives no answer. The bells fill the air with their wonderful tinkling; the air is torn asunder, it thunders and is transformed into wind; everything on earth is flying past, and, looking askance, other nations and states draw aside and make way for her.

Nikolai Gogol, *Dead Souls*

Admittedly the truth about a man lies first and foremost in what he hides.

André Malraux, *Antimemoirs*

Preface and Acknowledgements

Lesley Blanch died in 2007 at the age of 102, leaving behind her twelve highly distinctive books and an insistent buzz of rumour and speculation. Had she been able to eavesdrop, this would probably have amused her, since she herself had been the source of much of it.

Those who knew her mourned a grand eccentric, a compelling conversationalist whose house of treasures reflected her adventurous travelling life. To the world at large she has remained surprisingly hidden for one who was such a vivid presence to meet, and who wrote with such impassioned vitality. She was somehow iconic but obscure. People who are unfamiliar with Lesley Blanch's writings sometimes mistake her for a romantic novelist, especially when her name is coupled with the title of her best-known book, *The Wilder Shores of Love*. More than once I was asked if her name was invented. After her death some obituaries speculated likewise about her early history, without drawing conclusions.

As all her writings reveal, however, Lesley Blanch *was* irrepressibly romantic: a scholarly romantic with a sharp debunking wit. Discriminating in her choice of subject matter, she had a rare story-teller's gift for animating and adding lustre to past events. She wrote with enthusiasm and verve about people, buildings, landscapes and, above all, about countries. Her taste for the exotic pervades her books, which range over travel, history, biography, memoirs, fiction – and food: she savoured the aromatic pleasures of meals in far places with the sensuous recall of an English Colette.

The Wilder Shores of Love was her first book. The elegant, racy 'brief lives' of a quartet of nineteenth-century heroines who galloped away from their domestic fetters to find love and fulfilment in the Middle East, it became a runaway international best-seller and bequeathed a new phrase to the English language. The work that fully tested her claim to scholarship was *The Sabres of Paradise*, her epic, prescient history of Imam Shamyl, the nineteenth-century warrior-prophet who led the Muslim mountain tribes of Daghestan and Chechnya, through thirty years of bloody resistance, against massed Russian armies bent on imperial conquest.

Lesley Blanch had found her exotic subject and terrain through her driving obsession with Russia. This, she insisted, had directed her life and defined her fate since the age of four, when she fell ardently in love with a mysterious Russian friend of her parents, known only as the Traveller. *Journey into the Mind's Eye*, her seductive, original memoir, followed the transformation of her childhood adoration for their Tartar visitor into the flowering of the young woman's grand passion; then eventually, after the loved one was lost to her, into a lifetime's fixation with a nation and its people. Thanks to the subtle layering of the narrative, you reach the end of her life's story to find you have also read an atmospheric portrait of Russia. Then again, it was the making of the myth of Lesley Blanch.

Journey into the Mind's Eye was subtitled 'Fragments of an autobiography'; but the French translation, published in 2003 months before Lesley's hundredth birthday, is described on the cover as 'autobiography, travelogue and tragi-comic novel'. If Lesley's imagination turned always to the nineteenth century, and her ornate language verged on the baroque, her attitude towards image and identity was decidedly modern. She was brilliantly adroit at telling the world exactly as much as she wanted to reveal about herself and no more. She was Pinter's equal for 'secrecy and gap', as Rose Baring put it. She preferred question marks to explanations as her legacy – a preference that raised unsettling dilemmas for me in relation to this project. Her books beckon insistently towards the life of their creator, but the urge to know more leads to a door labelled No Entry. Do you fall back, or push on?

Lesley Blanch was one of the legends of my life, to borrow her phrase. I first read *The Wilder Shores of Love* at an impressionable age and never forgot it; later I fell under the spell of her 'Siberian book'. The mystery of the Traveller combined with a palpable lack of information about the author sharpened my curiosity. Living abroad, she was invisible to her readers and her books had fallen mostly out of print. Looking for Lesley Blanch became a hobby, fitfully pursued in second-hand bookshops and press cuttings. She flitted through the memoirs, letters or journals of Marie Rambert, Lee Miller, Cecil Beaton, Nancy Mitford, James Lees-Milne and other more visible figures.

This project might never have materialized without the encouragement of the late Lady Lancaster (Anne Scott-James), a *Vogue* colleague, wartime flatmate and friend of Lesley Blanch who knew of whom she spoke. Her enthusiasm and her sparkling pen portraits of Lesley and her second husband Romain Gary fired my interest. She suggested several valuable contacts, notably the late Audrey Withers, Lesley's editor at *Vogue* during the war, who confirmed the already powerful impression that the woman, like her books, was *sui generis*. Even they encouraged more than they revealed. Years passed before it became remotely feasible to consider the possibility of writing about Lesley Blanch.

When it did, the problems that I confronted didn't at all conform to conventional stereotypes of the solitary, sedentary woman of letters. Lesley neither set out to be a writer nor lived to write. By the time her first book was published she was fifty, and had already restlessly discarded as many lives as a cat, letting her past vanish behind her. She dismissed a decade of high-profile journalism as *Vogue*'s roving features editor as 'just something I did' (while remaining a revered contributor). She was elusive about her family antecedents; an only child, she lived to a great age and had no known direct descendants. Few contemporaries survive from her early years. She was intriguing but evasive concerning her amours, and vague on her tally of husbands. After her marriage to the diplomat-writer Romain Gary she embarked with him on a succession of foreign postings, and following their divorce she continued to live abroad. When she was ninety her house on the French Riviera burnt down, reducing to ashes many papers along with the rest of her possessions.

Sightings were scattered and contradictory. Lingeringly as Lesley evoked Russia and the Caucasus as the 'landscapes of her heart', how often did she actually go there? Her wayward trajectory led me not as I expected to Richmond, Russia and the Caucasus, but to Brentford and Chiswick public library, the London Theatre Museum, the London Library's Special Collections, repeatedly to Paris, and eventually to Bulgaria, New York and Los Angeles. Gaps remained, leaving scope for guesswork which may not always have been inspired, for which I ask the reader's forbearance.

There were compensations, however. Living abroad for so long, Lesley became a prolific letter-writer. Jock Murray, her mentor, published her first five books and in the 1980s his successor published her second cookbook. To John and Virginia Murray I owe a major debt of gratitude for allowing me access to the Lesley Blanch archive at 50 Albemarle Street, although because this biography is unauthorized I am not able to quote at length from Lesley's unpublished letters. Her correspondence with Collins, her subsequent publisher, could not be traced, but Philip Ziegler, who edited *Journey into the Mind's Eye* and her biographies of the Shahbanou of Iran and Pierre Loti, compensated by recalling his working relationship and friendship with Lesley.

My special thanks are due to the late Lady Lancaster for permitting me to quote from her pen portraits of Lesley; also to Michael Henry Wilson for permission to consult and quote from the unpublished journals of Hélène Hoppenot. Thanks respectively to Maureen Cleave, and to E. Glass Ltd, executors of the Rodney Ackland Estate, for permission to quote from their works; and to the editors of *Slightly Foxed* for allowing me to recycle my own. I thank Deborah, Dowager Duchess of Devonshire, for making available to me letters from Lesley to Nancy Mitford, and Mrs Patricia Creed for Lesley's letters to her. I thank Don Bachardy, Rose Baring, Patricia Creed, Valerie Grove, Jane Moore, Diana Murray, Barnaby Rogerson, Nabil Saidi, Philippa Scott and the late Audrey Withers for talking to me about Lesley Blanch, and Victor Borovsky for information about Feodor Komisarjevsky.

Lesley's second husband, Romain Gary, has become a *monstre sacré* of French literature, more famous since his suicide in 1980 than in his lifetime, though scarcely remembered in Britain. He left a fine character portrait of Lesley in his novel *Lady L.*, and 'a wife-shaped void' in his memoirs. 'In the biography of this man subjected for thirty-five years to the glare of public life, there exist vast zones of shadow,' I read with dismay, in the first of several interpretations – sometimes conflicting – of his life and work.

I should like to thank Professor Yves Agid, René Gatissou, Pierre Louis-Dreyfus, Jean-François Hangouët (founder of 'Les Mille Gary', the Romain Gary appreciation society in France), Nancy Huston and Raoul Coutard (cameraman on *Breathless* and director of Jean Seberg's last film project) for talking to me about Lesley, Romain and/or Jean Seberg. Translations from French interviews and texts are my own unless otherwise stated.

Trying to pierce the fog around the origins of Lesley's husband, I made a flying visit to Vilnius, Lithuania. On my last morning, a chance meeting at the State Jewish Museum of Lithuania brought contact with Genrich Agranovsky and Galina Baranova, whose definitive research established Romain Gary's family history.

I am grateful to the Society of Authors Foundation for two awards that assisted with my travel expenses. I owe special thanks to Nadia and Graham Marks, who not only travelled with me to Los Angeles but chauffeured me on its boulevards and freeways; also to Peter Graham for lending me his perch in Paris.

I am grateful to Jacques Bourdis, Véronique Bourdis-Gispalou, Jeremy Bugler, Rachel Bugler, Judy Cumberbatch, Jonathan Fenby, Renée Fenby, Matthew Hamilton, Jean-François Hangouët, Ben Hopkins, Toby Hopkins, Eeva and Peter Lennon, Sharon Morris, Judith Ravenscroft, Amanda Schiff, Ralph Schoolcraft, Lucinda Smith, Deirdre Stirling and Professor Ginette Vincendeau for valuable advice, research, new material, practical assistance and/or help with translations. At John Murray (Publishers), I thank Roland Philipps, Celia Levett and above all Caroline Westmore for her guidance and discreet efficiency.

I should like to thank the following institutions and their staff for access to their collections: the British Library, London Library, Carolyn Hammond of Brentford and Chiswick Local History Society at Chiswick Library, Chelsea Public Library, Holborn Library local history department, the Condé Nast Library in London, the Bibliothèque Littéraire Jacques Doucet and the Bibliothèque Nationale in Paris (special thanks to technicians at Inathèque), New York Public Library, UCLA Arts Library Special Collections, and the Academy of Motion Picture Arts and Sciences' Margaret Herrick Library in Los Angeles (George Cukor and John Huston Special Collections). Thanks also to Editions Gallimard and Mercure de

France, publishers of Romain Gary and Emile Ajar respectively, for allowing me access to their files of press cuttings.

I am indebted to Gail Pirkis, who always believed in this book. The late Richard Boston's comments on early chapters were salutary. Katharina Wolpe and Tess Jaray, both Blanch enthusiasts, offered valuable insights. Amy Burch listened and endured. Without Penny Phillips, who read and commented on both drafts, I would never have finished.

Prologue

As she approached her hundredth birthday and her books began to come back into print, I wrote to Lesley Blanch to ask for a newspaper interview. We spoke at length on the phone but she was discouraging about a meeting. Months passed, until suddenly the call came to meet her in early January 2003. The timing was tremendously inconvenient, snow in London caused flight delays and I arrived at Garavan, the last railway station on the Cote d'Azur before the Italian border, famished and exhausted. But at the hotel an invitation, or rather summons, came from Lesley to call on her immediately.

Subdued lighting fell on a small commanding figure with a clear gaze, important nose and short grey hair in a Julius Caesar cut, chic in a black tunic and cut-off trousers with a soft crimson stole flung over her shoulders. Lesley served neat vodka poured over ice and lemon, and cocktail blinis. Her clipped speech and old-fashioned accent ('profeels', 'orf') evoked another, earlier world. She denounced the unseasonal cold, her new French translator who tried to call in unexpectedly (she had rebuffed him), and mafiosi developers whose gross new apartment buildings blocked her sea view. She expressed a violent dislike for children. The prospects for a cordial interview the following day looked dismal.

Next morning she stood at the top of the steep steps through the garden, in excellent spirits. Sea-facing windows cast wintry rays of sun over the interior. Lesley's home surroundings and her possessions were enormously significant to her, intrinsic to her identity in fact. By then the house was not what it had been, for one April night in 1994 the villa and its mass of rare and precious contents collected over a long lifetime went up in flames. Lesley, trapped in her bedroom, escaped in her nightdress just before the roof fell in. At the age of ninety-plus she had rented a flat, laboriously replaced the bureaucratic paperwork and supervised the house's reconstruction over the ashes of the old one. Then she had risen to the challenge of disguising the new building's botched proportions, and coaxing style from auction salvage and garden furniture. She was still painting and moving things around in her ninety-ninth year.

Near the front door was her round dining table, symbol of a central pleasure: 'Thank God, I have all my life been able to eat what I want when I want. Even now I can eat Christmas pudding at midnight.' Oriental divans were heaped with cushions against two walls, a Turkish brass *mangal* set on a low round copper table; her desk stood in a book-lined alcove. On the walls, Persian rugs and fine Arabic calligraphy here, diamond-paned garden trellis hung as wallpaper there, glittering strips of mirror (a Persian decorative detail called *einé khari*) to hide an awkward corner: 'that finial is a painted glass decanter top'. Propped against a samovar were some scorched remnants of her lost library of rare oriental books, rescued and rebound by Lesley. The terrace out-side was curtained by an orange-flowered creeper to make a shady workplace in summer, with the steep jungle of garden beyond. 'Leaves I mind about very much. I conduct the house on that principle, you can see the greenery in that vase.'

'I still enjoy a lot of things,' she said. The company of friends, for instance: her previous visitor had been her godson Morgan, James Mason's son, who supplied her with Westerns on video. Her daily routine started at eight and she worked every morning, usually to music: Bach, Bob Dylan or reggae, which she found soothing. For concentrated listening she enjoyed the Russian composers and opera, especially Wagner. Food was still important ('a wasted meal is a wasted moment in life'), requiring due ceremony; she mixed oil and vinegar in a painted Russian spoon balanced across the salad bowl, a sleight of hand which looks easy but isn't.

She inveighed against the time lost to household crises and legions of requests for her memories of the recently departed: 'I tell them I met everyone and knew no one.' Her quick decisive voice would launch into a burst of gossip, then make a practised retreat when it came to specifics about herself. Her past came out like an album of snapshots. 'I seem to have lived so many different ages,' she said, 'always happiest when travelling.

2

'It was Dr Johnson who said the object of travel was to regulate the imagination by reality. Well, I think that's losing a great deal of quality. I've always regulated reality by imagination, or rather by going back in my imagination. I'm all for travelling with ghosts. I couldn't see a landscape that I didn't want to people with history. Even in the most desolate places in the Sahara you feel the presence of people – what made them go?'

Charm is a quality that vanishes on the page. Anticipating romantic excess, you met resourcefulness and panache: dry wit, forceful views, sudden flights. After that meeting I was convinced that I *had* to write at length about Lesley Blanch. But she had always been biographobic, and when the subject was broached later she made it clear that the project would not be authorized. She wanted to be left to the portrait that was more true than real, which no one could do better than herself. Except of course for Romain Gary, who had bequeathed her that in his novel *Lady L.*

My account is more real than true, in the manner of conventional biography. If the facts as far as I could find them thin the mystery that she gathered around herself, I hope that they enhance the achievements in a century of adventure, colour, emotion, farce and tragedy that amply fulfilled the saying she used to describe her heroine of *The Wilder Shores of Love*, Aimée Dubucq de Rivery: Character plus opportunity equals fortune.

The Traveller was a fixture in all her hundreth-birthday interviews and profiles, including my own. For years he hovered like a malign seductive djinn over my research. He exerted a terrific gravitational pull in the writing of this book. Everybody, Lesley above all and myself included, wanted him to be true. I felt like the character in V.S. Pritchett's story 'The Spanish Bed': 'the faculty of uttering facts had left him. He was adrift in her imagination.' Finally there was nothing else for it: the Traveller must open the story of her life. Then he must disappear until she conjured him into it.

The Traveller

*A*LMOST FROM HER *first memories the Traveller dominated her thoughts, whether present or not. Whenever he was in Europe he would visit her parents and come to see Lesley in the nursery. Nanny would cluck disapprovingly as he lounged in his fur-lined greatcoat, inflaming the little girl's imagination with stories of his snow-covered homeland while she crouched by the fire making toast for their tea.*

He said he was from Moscow, but the slanting eyes and amber skin tautly drawn over his bald skull betrayed Tartar origins in deeper Asia. He had long double-jointed fingers and wore one little fingernail unnaturally long in the Chinese fashion. He padded past the stuccoed terraces of west London in soft leather boots from Irkutsk with an upturned blunt toe, leaving footprints that looked the same going backwards or forwards. In his pocket he kept an agate spoon for eating caviar, which he sometimes presented to Lesley's mother.

Lesley was possessed by the Traveller and his Russia. He transfixed the child with a jumble of images: of his niece's birthday feast of stuffed sturgeon; fairy tales of a lucky hump-backed horse called Konyiok Gorbunok; the Mongols' legendary marmot Tarbagan Bator who shot down suns with his bow and arrow. He taught her how to count to ten in Cyrillic while she was recovering from measles. Above all, he told her about his journeys on the Trans-Siberian Railway stretching five thousand miles across Asia: the great locomotive steaming across the steppes, its front carriages equipped with grand pianos, brass bedsteads and an Orthodox chapel; coupled to the back were prison trucks crammed with convicts in chains on their way to a freezing exile in Siberia. She begged him to take her with him ('Children under ten travel free'), chugging through whirling snow into a white horizon – his horizon. But he teasingly called her Stupidichka and Numskullina, and taught her instead to spirit herself away to anywhere she wanted in the parallel dream world of the Run-Away Game.

From his travels he sent the ardent schoolgirl a Muslim chaplet, her first samovar, and most romantically unsuitable of all, an inlaid Caucasian cigarette case which she hid in her satchel. His nicknames now were fond in a different way: Rocokoshka, Poussinka moiya. On her first visit to Paris with her governess when she was seventeen, the Traveller took her to Easter midnight mass at the Russian cathedral, then to listen to gipsy music in a louche night-club. Finally, leaving a barely adequate note of excuse, they escaped on an overnight train to Dijon, a stand-in for the Trans-Siberian, on which she eagerly learnt to love him 'properly'.

Her parents sent her to an Italian convent to be 'finished', then were unwisely persuaded by the Traveller to let him take their daughter to Corsica for a family summer holiday with his Montenegrin Aunt Eudoxia, two moody illegitimate sons hardly younger than herself, Kamran and Sergei, and a Mongolian sheepdog called Hondof (the Baskervilles). Between tumultuous Slav uproars and Mediterranean storms, she escaped with the Traveller to Gallantry Bower, an amorous grown-up version of her hiding place on child-hood holidays. As summer turned into autumn they travelled back via the Côte d'Azur, dallying by the French-Italian border at Menton-Garavan.

They were secretly engaged. She dreamt of a golden-crowned wedding cere-mony when she reached twenty-one. But for her birthday the Traveller sent her a prayer rug folded round an icon and an empty notebook with a page torn out, on which he had written a farewell letter. She never saw him again.

The infatuation with Russia that had seized her in early childhood now turned into an obsession. She lived in London, but her heart and mind were filled with the land and the culture he had known. She devoured nineteenth-century Russian literature compulsively. She met its artists and émigrés, learnt its history; she embraced everything Slav, in paintings, plays, food and folk songs. He had taught her to value beautiful things; now she collected anything small and fine that seemed remotely connected with him, or with his country.

She was convinced that somewhere or somehow her fate was bound up with Russia. Only Slavs would do for her lovers. Meeting Kamran again, she tried to exorcize her passionate nostalgia for his father. The Traveller had told her that a woman should marry three times: the first time for love, the second time for money and the third time for pleasure. In that, too, she would follow his advice.

And one day she would make the journey on the Trans-Siberian and learn what had happened to the man who had taught her to view the world through his eyes.

I

The Run-Away Game

1904–1930

Conceal thy tenets, thy treasure and thy travels.

Arab proverb

ALL HER LIFE Lesley Blanch had a passionate relationship with the places she inhabited. Architecture was a dominant thread; it was as if she had been born with bricks and mortar in her genes. The first time she married was for love of a house. Her supreme statement of self-expression was arguably the Aladdin's cave she created for her husband Romain Gary and herself out of a ruined medieval tower and huddle of animal huts perched high above the Ligurian coastline at Roquebrune. In her writings, buildings are often as important as her characters or even become protagonists: *Pavilions of the Heart*, the least known of her twelve books, traces the architecture of romance, 'settings for lovings'; and one of her four heroines in *The Wilder Shores of Love* was hardly more than an excuse for Lesley to write about Topkapi, the Seraglio in Istanbul, whose cruel history and fabulously intricate decoration held lifelong fascination for her. At ninety she supervised the rebuilding of her little villa at Garavan after fire had gutted the old one, taking everything in it.

The same super-sensitivity to her surroundings that made her such a potent travel writer left her nostalgic for her birthplace. She loved and often returned to the West London of her childhood, to the great meanders of the Thames with its honking wildfowl and seething tides, overlooked by the graceful eighteenth-century terraces of Richmond and Strand on the Green, and the Thames-side reaches of Hammersmith and Twickenham, Barnes and Kew.

When it came to describing where she was born and brought up she was more elusive. Forty-six Grove Park Gardens, Chiswick, is not at

7

all Lesley's chosen era or style: an uncompromisingly late Victorian semi-detached family house with bay windows at the front, solidly brick-built and tile-hung in now mellowed ox-blood red. From the rear upstairs windows the nearby Thames could then be glimpsed glinting between the Georgian waterfront houses of Strand on the Green. A front garden, now a car bay, distanced the bow windows from the long straight suburban road lined with late Victorian and Edwardian villas and semi-detacheds. Today's quiet back-street neighbourhood would have been still partly countryside, though increasingly disrupted by the mess and noise of housebuilding. Trains puffed down the nearby track, carrying commuters from Weybridge to Waterloo and the city.

'Culverden', one of the first houses in the road, was less than a decade old when Walter and Mabel Martha Blanch moved in after their marriage in July 1900. Its three spacious reception rooms on the ground floor and five bedrooms were more than ample living quarters for the couple and a live-in maid, pointing to the assumption that they intended to start a family. But by Lesley's account her arrival nearly four years later on 6 June 1904 was a mistake, her father having been against the idea of having children, and no younger children followed her into the nursery.

Lesley Stewart Blanch might herself have been a deterrent, for she never brooked competition. She looked like a little blonde cherub, but the angelic appearance was deceptive: the first memory she could summon from her childhood was of banging her head in frustration against the nursery floor 'because I couldn't get my own way'. Both her forenames could apply to either sex: perhaps her parents had hoped for a boy. Later Lesley changed the spelling of her middle name to what might be considered the more distinguished Stuart.

It was a household of three determined individualists in which only Martha was prepared to compromise. She was in her late twenties, fourteen years younger than Walter, when her daughter was born. Lesley was extremely fond of her mother and leaves the impression of a talented, charming, domestically creative woman who passed on her gifts to her daughter, while lacking the fierce self-belief that became Lesley's motivating force.

Lesley was as reticent about her forebears as she was about the house where she was born, and her survival to great age meant that she outlived her contemporaries who might have remembered the family when she was small. She never tells us how her mother and father met, or anything about their wider family backgrounds, remarking only that as far as she was concerned they could both have been orphans – which could have been a statement of her own preference.

Her voice and bearing in later life were such that her interviewers invariably awarded her an upper-middle-class upbringing, especially in France where the stereotype of the eccentric English lady traveller assumed a well-bred and affluent start in life. In fact her parents came from modest backgrounds and were never well off, while her paternal and maternal grandfathers were both working men in a skilled trade: the one a builder and the other (her step-grandfather) an engineer.

Her mother had been brought up to a role of duty and responsibility, as the first in a family of nine children. Mabel Martha Thorpe was born in Hackney, her younger brother John in Hornsey, and her sister Jenny in Islington; so many changes of address in poorer areas suggest that the family was hard pressed. Their father died shortly before Jenny was born in 1880 and soon afterwards the widow married William Jackson, an engineer two years younger than herself. Mabel Martha, the eldest daughter, would have become a hard-worked second mother to the new family of six brothers and sisters who arrived in quick succession.

Marriage to Walter must have offered her the sweet prospect of escape from the cramped noisy family home at 67 Petherton Road, Hackney, into comfort, privacy and security (which alas, would not last her lifetime). At their summer wedding at St Augustine's church, Islington, Martha was given away by her mother and stepfather. If the entire tribe of younger siblings had come along, her side of the aisle would have hardly needed to invite outside guests.

Walter Blanch was a bachelor of thirty-eight when he married Martha. Until then he had been living with his elder sister Rhoda and another sister, Emily (sixteen years older than Walter, and probably a half-sister), in rented premises at 26 Baker Street, Marylebone. Their comparative prosperity was recent and seems to have been due to Rhoda. Since the death of their father, James, she had built up a lucrative business buying up property and letting out rooms in the back streets of Holborn where they were brought up.

James Blanch was a builder who ran his business from a warehouse off Theobald's Road, a few yards from the house where he lodged with his wife Ann and their family. It was a good trade to be in during the massive expansion of Victorian London, and his yard was well placed on the edge of Bloomsbury, close to the great termini of Euston and King's Cross. Over twenty years he had worked his way up from junior builder in the 1860s when Walter, the youngest, was born, to master builder. Nevertheless the family still lived modestly at 30 East Street (now Dombey Street), sub-letting the house next door to boarders. At nineteen Walter was out at work, toiling as a lowly mercantile clerk.

In 1883 James Blanch died, leaving Rhoda in charge of the household (Alfred, the eldest of their three children, had left home). She proved to be an extremely capable businesswoman, gradually investing in more properties close by in the best Monopoly-board tradition, so that by the turn of the century she had prospered enough to move to Baker Street with Walter; Emily came too, from her separate lodgings in Holborn. Eventually Rhoda was collecting the rent from ten or more multi-occupied houses in and around Dombey Street. Thanks to her, by 1900 Walter had been transformed into a man of independent means, an antiquarian who could afford to marry and rent a new house in the far reaches of west London for himself and his bride.

The couple's decision to move west to an unfamiliar, upwardly mobile semi-rural neighbourhood suggests they intended to distance themselves from family spheres of influence. Walter was used to being looked after by his sisters, and no doubt wanted his wife to do the same for him. It wouldn't do for Martha to live near her old home, where her mother would miss her presence around the house and would continue to depend on her for help if given the chance.

Lesley's maternal grandparents were both still alive when she was a child, and she had eleven uncles and aunts plus a growing entourage of their spouses and children. But without the will to maintain links families can quickly drift apart. Decades later, when Lesley was living abroad and her mother was old and ailing, none of those relatives came forward to look after Martha, who depended on Lesley's friends to visit and care for her.

Whatever contacts remained with the extended family, Lesley made it clear that they didn't interest *her*. Huguenot ancestry implied by her surname was her only concession to family history; if her passion for architecture was inherited from her grandfather James Blanch, it wasn't acknowledged. She followed her parents in being more interested in escape. After her memoir was reissued in 2001, her publishers were approached by a cousin of Lesley's who wanted to contact her: 'a bit of a Gradgrind', he mentioned a foundry making ships' boilers on the Kent/Essex borders, which might have belonged to William Jackson, the engineer who was Martha's stepfather. Lesley roundly told her publishers to have nothing more to do with him.

Before Lesley's third birthday, the family moved a few hundred yards down the road to Burlington Court, Spencer Road, a solidly built new block of mansion flats designed by a local architect for rental and completed in 1902. This four-storey painted brick building with a central arched entrance and stairway is an oversized oddity in the neighbourhood, like a seaside hotel surprised to find itself looming over Chiswick railway station. Next door, on a street junction, was a public house with rooms to let. Flat 8, Burlington Court was on the fourth floor, without a lift; the Blanch family might have had a balcony, but no garden.

The family house at Grove Park Gardens was apparently beyond Walter's means. A major virtue of their new apartment was its rent and rates (the rateable value was £32, down from £38 for Culverden) which were lower than those on the floors below although it was one of the largest flats, occupying half the top floor. Even so, the decision to retreat to a sort of high-rise existence beside the railway instead of waiting for one of the more modest houses then being built in the neighbourhood seems perverse in an area whose virtue lay in being still semi-rural. The Duke of Devonshire had relatively recently released the fields bordering on the Chiswick House estate for housing development, with the stipulation that public access to the river and green space for sports fields must remain priorities. Just conceivably, the family transferred there partly to escape the commotion of housebuilding that was turning the fields into residential streets all around.

Whatever the reasons for the move, this must be what Lesley meant by 'the horrid caged-in Victorian life' endured by her mother. For the wife and housekeeper, Martha's new home was frustrating and inconvenient. All the shopping and domestic supplies had to be lugged up four flights of stairs, even if most of the carrying were done by the maid, leaving aside the question of where to store the pram (Lesley was only two when they moved). Worse for an active young woman who loved fresh air and being out of doors, Martha was cut off from her surroundings, and had lost the treasured access to a private patch of garden for her family.

Moving house, then, was one of Lesley's first memories, and her first significant setback in life. No more grassy space where the family could sit outside together, or where an energetic little girl could run out to play with her pets whenever she wanted. (What happened to the beloved black-and-white pet rabbit Ermyntrude? In old age Lesley hinted darkly at a loss that had never been forgiven, maybe victim to the move.) From now on 'going out' became an expedition that entailed being buttoned and tied into coat, boots and bonnet for a formal walk accompanied by an adult. They could still walk to the river nearby, but they could no longer see it from home.

Lesley inherited her mother's love of al fresco meals, and left memories of fast-cooling lunches devoured outside on chilly grey days, muffled in coats and rugs. The ghost of their lost garden makes Martha's insistence on eating out of doors 'on a balcony, or wherever the sky was all around' whenever the weather allowed, and Lesley's lifelong relish for picnics, more poignant.

If her bedroom was at the back, from now on the little girl was woken and lulled to sleep by the sounds of arrivals and departures: carriage doors slamming and the guard's whistle at the station, the whoosh of express trains steaming down the track.

A note of impatience crept into Lesley's voice when she spoke of her father. She described him as a man with 'a very brilliant brain which he completely wasted. He would talk about anything almost.' He read widely, and dabbled in buying and selling antiques, specializing in oak. But she couldn't forgive him for not making more of himself and the modest capital he had brought to his marriage.

In her writings, Walter appears as an ironic, misanthropic figure shrouded in tobacco smoke in his dressing room, shaded by a Moorish screen across the window. (The Latakieh tobacco and *moucharabia* are as telling of Lesley's own tastes as of her father's.) He seems to have believed that the world owed him a living, and to have existed in a state of perpetual dissatisfaction. Was his discontent partly to do with their social mobility, which left him feeling displaced? He was antisocial, and had a temper which Lesley inherited. As a child she watched her parents come home one evening: her father, in a rage, tore off his dinner jacket and threw it on the fire, vowing that he would never go out again. Her mother burst into tears.

Walter had inherited his father's interest in architecture and passed it on to Lesley. When she was small he used to take her, sometimes with Martha, from Chiswick station (so close it could have been their personal stop), to look at the Wren churches in the city. Religion was not the motive and he was less interested in going inside than in studying the exterior proportions, the stonework, the details of archi-traving. Or they spent hours at a time roaming the museum galleries, which were second homes to him. Avid with curiosity, the little girl trotted beside her father, stopping with him to peer at buildings and treasures, her round blue eyes absorbing, assessing, comparing.

Home was Martha's domain. At the time when Lesley was writing her 'memoir' she was dining out with the upper crust in Paris, a con-text which could have encouraged her to add a cook and nanny, family retainers to her childhood. But only one young general domestic serv-ant lived in with the household at Burlington Court, and Lesley said later that her mother 'did almost everything' in the kitchen. This was labour-intensive, time-consuming work, especially with suet puddings often on the menu. A skilled and creative homemaker, Martha passed on to her daughter a robust and questing attitude to food and a flair for visual display. Lesley dedicated her first cookbook to her mother, 'whose tray meals I enjoy more than other people's banquets'. These 'tray meals' were a staple in the Blanch household. It was standard practice for each family member to breakfast alone: Lesley in the nur-sery, tea and toast for her mother in bed, her father downstairs nibbling some nuts with strong black coffee which he brewed himself. Reading was part of the ritual: Daniel Defoe's *Journal of the Plague Year* to con-firm Walter's pessimism, Martha dabbling in *The Times*, Beatrix Potter and the Koran. (Or is this vignette a late fancy of Lesley's, remembered in *From Wilder Shores*, written in her eighties?)

Martha might have travelled if her circumstances had allowed. Instead she read Pierre Loti's *fin de siècle* novels and travelogues, and passed on her enthusiasm to her daughter. The great escapist's evoca-tive accounts of his passionate 'lovings and leavings' in faraway places left a lasting influence. In the 1980s after Lesley's biography of Loti was published she said she had written it for her mother, 'who could only travel through Loti'.

Martha subscribed to the art journal *The Studio* and collected art books; Lesley learnt to read at her knee as they sat poring over pages of paintings and illustrations. Books were all-important to both parents and the little girl was soon experimenting with whatever reading matter caught her fancy. In *Who's Who* she described her education as 'by reading, and by listening to conversations of elders and betters'. Nonetheless, by the age of six she was attending kindergarten school. In *Journey into the Mind's Eye* she was taught by the Misses Peeke, among other things to waltz, wield Indian clubs and sew a red flannel bedjacket called a Nightingale (which she loved for its Crimean/Russian connection). Family holidays were spent on the Sussex downs or by the sea in Cornwall. At birthday parties she and other little girls tucked into jam sandwiches and éclairs. Special occasions were marked by tea at Buzzard's of Oxford Street whose windows were filled with dazzling displays of wedding cakes and other sugary glories.

From her solitary, bookish upbringing Lesley developed an only child's solipsistic vision of the world, and the unshakeable conviction that she could arrange things as she chose by force of will. Martha soon realized that once her angelically pretty daughter's mind was made up, nothing could make her change it. Between Walter's detached cynicism and Lesley's fierce determination, Martha generally steered a pragmatic course, bending with the strongest wind.

Just as striking as Lesley's obstinacy was the way that as far back as she could remember, her inner life ruled her outer life. Of course this is far from unusual in a small child, but most children grow out of it. She never mentions feeling lonely or neglected during the long hours she spent alone or with her mother or her minder in the nursery. Instead her solitary childhood fed the wishful thinking that was always her dominant trait. She was too self-engrossed to wish to be some*one* else, but she was always longing to be some*where* else. She had a second reality running parallel to her suburban surroundings. On the one hand there was suet pudding for lunch and a daily dose of fresh air on her constitutional walk. On the other was the view from high windows, and trains thundering past, and the Run-Away Game, where you wished yourself elsewhere so hard that you could almost, nearly, as good as find yourself there.

Her escapism left her perpetually dissatisfied and yearning for some other far horizon; yet it also made her self-sufficient. Secretive, too. Like Loti, forever finding love and leaving it in ports of call between his long voyages, Lesley was always *elsewhere* in her head, an elsewhere more real to her than the here and now. And this was odd because, far from being vague or dreamy, her presence had a most definite stamp and left an extra-emphatic impression, like a strong dark outline in a sketch. By her own account the young Lesley was a changeling who sprang into the world with the urgent and fully formed desires that would nourish and direct her from earliest childhood through half her life. 'But to make everything that you will see and hear in your life stem from your first childhood memory is a literary temptation,' as Italo Calvino, a rigorous writer of fantasy, cautions.

Lesley was born into the Edwardian decade when the last shreds of Victorian mourning were being cast off and every social convention, every traditional art form was being challenged. Bohemia, that 'country of the mind', was in the air, urgent and miasmic. Whoever it touched became avid for colour, flavour and sensation. Foreign influences swept in, bombarding the senses with the fresh and the new, the more exotic (the Latakieh tobacco, the *moucharabia*) the better. Impressionism, post-Impressionism, Modernism transformed the arts and filtered down into fashion and designs for living. From conforming and keeping up, the great thing now was to 'free the spirit', to give vent to personal tastes and individual style through one's choice of clothes and home surroundings.

The corduroys-and-sandals style of painterly bohemian circles was not for Walter and Martha, who liked everything to be good quality: handmade shoes, silk umbrellas, which was all very well for as long as Walter's income matched their expensive tastes. Instead of seeking her inspiration in travel, Martha searched for it in books and paintings, and found ways to express herself as best she could in the domestic sphere. For Lesley, both a child of her era and intensely individual, the new thinking would pervade her entire way of life, to embrace especially the romance of travel and an insatiable appetite for everything foreign and ethnic. It would spill over into her voracious reading, the way she dressed, what she ate, her flamboyantly inventive surroundings at home. Later it would influence her choice of friends and the landscape of her heart.

Left to her own devices, the determined little girl seized on the subjects that interested her most and shaped them to her imagination. Above all, she caught the mania for all things Russian that was sweeping across Europe.

> Compared with the imperial territories of India, Africa and the Far East, Russia was still relatively unknown to the British traveller. The excitement of discovery was palpable. The glamour of Droshkies and moujiks, the Bolshoi and the Nevski Prospekt seemed boundless. Bohemia was intoxicated by Russian literature, Russian cigarettes, Russian clothes, and of course the Russian ballet.

Lesley was by no means the only small girl who caught the fever. Frances Partridge, four years older, remembered finding everything Russian 'fantastically moving': reading the novels newly translated by Constance Garnett, meeting a Russian prince, seeing a Diaghilev ballet – the overpowering influence of the Ballets Russes's first appearance in London in 1911 can hardly be exaggerated.

In Lesley's case the contagion set in quickly, initially perhaps through exposure to her parents' books. The giants of Russian literature were then arriving in the West freshly translated: in the year she was born Tolstoy was alive and still writing, and that autumn Gorky's play *Summer Folk*, staged by the legendary muse of Russian theatre, Vera Komisarjevskaya, caused riots at its première in Moscow. The plays of Chekhov, who died within a month of Lesley's birth, were as yet unknown in England; it would be twenty years before they were directed to sensational effect for London audiences by Vera's younger brother Feodor Komisarjevsky, who would influence Lesley so profoundly as a young woman.

Martha's art journals were full of the cultural cross-currents between France and Russia. Before Diaghilev turned to ballet, he brought eleven exhibitions of Western paintings to Russia in less than a decade and in 1906 took Paris by storm with his Russian Season at the Grand Palais. Soon Bakst and other avant-garde Russian artists he had fostered would be creating spectacular new designs for the revolutionary Ballets Russes.

The new Trans-Siberian Railway added to the Russian mania,

opening up to the intrepid traveller the epic prospect of the world's longest train journey. From 1904 a passenger could buy a ticket in London and travel all the way to Vladivostok by train – though they would not lightly embark on the easternmost stretch from Chita to the Sea of Japan on the Chinese Eastern Railway, which ran through Chinese territory infested with brigands and marauding Boxer troops. The Amur section, a great 1,200-mile loop that took the train from Moscow to Vladivostok entirely on Russian soil, was not completed until 1916.

A troika harnessed to galloping horses – or a great engine ploughing through snow drifts, dragging its tail of carriages – was speeding across the *taiga* to Lesley's nursery bedside. The infant Russophile's passion was ablaze. Her nursery cupboard began to fill with trophies, proudly displayed to visitors together with her library, ranging from a study of Siberian leper colonies to Atkinson's graphically illustrated *Travels in the Regions of the Upper and Lower Amoor* (1861). Her pocket money was recklessly spent on Russian 'things', a samovar here, a glowing icon there, acquired by poking about with her father in salesrooms and junk shops.

What began as a childish affectation, amusing the grown-ups, became entrenched. Images of a vast snowy region filled her dreams and threatened to blot out her daily English existence. Martha was shocked when Walter gave Lesley Dostoievsky's *House of the Dead* to read, hoping that its morbid despair would put her off, but it only fed the flames. She steeped herself in the great nineteenth-century writers long before she could understand them, pounced on tales of sleigh-bound travellers lost in blizzards, learnt barbarous Russian folk tales off by heart. Her father trod in a saucer of Sunday lunch that Lesley had put by the front door to placate the Domovoi, a gnomish house sprite. Her mother helped her with a Russian makeover of Lesley's dolls' house, which acquired onion domes of painted clay and a bright blue façade to show up against the snow.

Lesley was still a little girl when she came across an early naive picture of Imam Shamyl, the warrior-prophet who had led the Caucasian rebels against Russia. In Victorian England during the era of the Crimean War Shamyl was a folk hero, a sworn enemy of the Tsar and his armies, and British ships smuggled guns out to his followers. Lesley was mesmerized by the cheap coloured print of the moustachioed hero with a curved dagger in his belt, looking sideways out of the picture. The caption read 'Shamyl the Avar'. She never forgot it.

In the autumn of 1915 Lesley was enrolled as a day pupil at St Paul's Girls' School. This came as a profound shock to the clever, cosseted little girl and possibly to the school as well. In the school archives her file contains just one anonymous sentence: 'By the time she was sent to St. Paul's her nature was too set to acquire team spirit, and she was not a success.'

Well connected to the prestigious boys' school, the school opened in west London in 1904 and soon set the high academic standards that have lasted to this day. For an annual fee of £24, it attracted upwards of 400 pupils from middle- and upper-class families whose daughters were beginning to expect a secondary education. Perhaps they might never marry; they might even want to work, for their self-respect if not for their living.

Many Paulinas looked back on their schooldays as a privilege. Anne Scott-James, a friend and colleague of Lesley's in the 1930s and 1940s, had glowing memories of school; but then Anne was good at games, which suited St Paul's emphasis on hearty sports. This was disastrous for Lesley, already possessed of forceful views and loathing all athletic activity. Her sole consolation was that Miss Volkhovsky, the Callisthenics mistress, was rumoured to be the daughter of Felix Volkhovsky, a Russian writer who had been exiled to Siberia, and Vera had been smuggled out of Siberia dressed as a boy. Even her glamorous past wasn't enough to compensate for the discomfort she caused Lesley, hanging upside down and scarlet-faced in the gym.

The music department was outstanding; its head was the composer Gustav Holst and classes were taught by a student of Clara Schumann. But the art teaching was a serious disappointment for a gifted child who had been taught to 'muddle with brushes' for as long as she could remember and had absorbed the language of painting at her mother's knee.

Art evidently rated low on the curriculum and the art department was in a state of flux when Lesley was a pupil. In autumn 1917 the chief art mistress left; then her part-time assistant went on sick leave for a year, so her junior had to fill for both of them. Even so, Lesley's sole recorded concession to school activities was to join the Junior Drawing Club. That year she won a bronze star for 'an original composition in colour' and even briefly became Secretary of the Junior Drawing Club whose president was the formidable High Mistress, Miss Grey. Next December Lesley Blanche (as she was listed) was singled out for 'some very nice pencil drawings', while 'Eunice Wallis presented her work in a very careful and dainty manner' (the reports speak volumes for prevailing aesthetic standards). After that, apart from visits to art galleries and museums Senior Sketch Club reports are limited to some dull debates.

School reports described her as moody and secretive. She refused to be confirmed along with her classmates; only Orthodoxy would do. Her agile intelligence remained stubbornly disengaged, except by Russia: a Literary Society discussion on aspects of Russian Literature, possibly, or a Musical Society recital of Borodin and Mussorgsky accompanied by a paper read out on 'Russian Music', when 'Some Folk-Songs were also sung by a few members who aspired to singing in Russian!' It's tempting to imagine twelve-year-old Lesley Blanch among them, singing lustily.

At school Lesley was appalled to find her freedom to read was cramped by 'a library you had to ask to get into'. Stuffing a copy of Jules Verne's *Michel Strogoff* into her tunic bodice, she hid in a lavatory cubicle and read until she was found out. At home, all her pocket money went on books on Russia or, preferably, Siberia. Her bedside reading was *Murray's Guide Book for Russia, 1893*. When she was persuaded to take a different tack, she dismayed her elders by devouring bawdy, blood-soaked Restoration dramas with unfeminine gusto. (She always displayed the Romantic's love for the gory and macabre; not long before her hundredth birthday she remarked that her bedside reading was usually military history, whose violence she found soothing.) Her mother was alarmed by the skew of Lesley's education; but Walter refused to intervene, declaring that his daughter should be allowed to choose her own subject matter.

In February 1919 the school administration agreed that half of Lesley's fees, paid the previous term, should be transferred to the following one. The great influenza epidemic, then at its peak, was probably the reason for Lesley's absence. She left St Paul's in 1920 when she was sixteen, by which time the sulky schoolgirl had developed into a devastatingly attractive, dangerously intelligent young woman who was well beyond her parents' control. The one area they met on was books; otherwise she admitted that she was a very difficult daughter.

She had a best friend, Edna, younger than herself, whose dark hair and complexion offset Lesley's English rose colouring. Edna was pretty, clever and artistic like Lesley; but whereas Lesley's humour was naughty or mischievous, Edna could be malicious and was treated with caution by their friends. Three decades later Edna Fleming developed a talent as a naive painter under the pseudonym Eden Box, and Lesley wrote up her friend's success.

Lesley was next sent to Florence, where her parents knew the owners of a *pensione* for girls, to be 'finished'. Violet Paget, alias Vernon Lee, that unfashionable writer Lesley later came to admire, lived close by on the hills above Florence and the girls often passed the house on their daily walk. As a little girl Lesley had already been intrigued by a red chalk portrait of Vernon Lee in an old copy of *The Studio*; she couldn't make out whether the face belonged to a man or a woman. They never did call in to see 'Miss Paget' – Lesley suspected their chaperone was frightened of her – but years later, when Lesley was writing her Siberian book, she wrote her essay in appreciation of Lee, whose 'elective affinity' to Italy made Lesley identify with Lee's emotional geography.

Meanwhile Lesley's blonde curls and wide blue eyes promising both innocence and mischief made her a magnet for Italian males, who hardly needed encouragement. She was soon in deep trouble for flirting with officers from the nearby Fortezza and was asked to leave, along with her friend Piggy who had to leave too.

> Things were always made out to be so much worse than they really were. We were escorted home by a governess and came back through Paris. She wanted to take us to visit Notre Dame cathedral, but we staged a rebellion and absolutely insisted on going to Galeries Lafayette. We became quite hysterical and rushed about the place spraying scent on ourselves. I bought a red leather fan – what on earth I thought I would do with it I don't know.

In October 1921, back in London, she enrolled for a Fine Art Diploma at the Slade, where Rex Whistler and Oliver Messel were among her contemporaries and the social life might be expected to absorb her. Yet she left after only two terms of drawing classes, before she was eighteen.

The reason she gave for abruptly leaving the Slade was that the family finances had crashed (though judging from their move to Burlington Court, a similar misfortune had already struck them earlier). Lesley said that Walter and Martha had invested in Russia, and blamed it on the Traveller; she might even have persuaded them to do so herself. Continuing this conjecture, possibly they had put their savings into Russian bonds and, like so many other small investors, lost everything when the Russian economy imploded in the chaos of the Great War, revolution and civil war. Tsarist Russia had routinely raised money for public investment projects by issuing bonds which helped to finance ports, building developments and 40,000 miles of railtrack, including the Trans-Siberian (whose fundraising promotion was one reason why the great railway was so well known). During the First World War French and British investors were encouraged to buy Russian bonds to support their ally in the war effort. But the Bolsheviks refused to honour the agreements, which were later revoked by the Soviet Union.

Walter's inability to keep the family afloat must have been especially galling in comparison with his sister Rhoda's fortune, amassed from the modest assets she had inherited from their father. By 1922 she had become a tycoon, reaping the rents from nearly a dozen houses and commercial properties in the streets where they grew up.

From her childhood on, Lesley never lost her fear of financial insecurity. After she left school money, or the lack of it, became a constant anxiety and in times of stress the fear of destitution haunted her. She always respected the power of money, even if she sometimes lacked business sense.

She was still living mostly at home with her parents, her room stylishly crammed with plants, pictures, 'the shawlery' (an enormous collection, some crocheted by herself) and unlikely treasures acquired from Russian charity bazaars and auction salesrooms with her father, or coaxed from friends. Growing up in an era dominated by the electrifying influence of the Ballets Russes, she embraced a crowded version of the Slav/Art Deco look parodied by Osbert Lancaster as 'First Russian Ballet Period'. She and Martha adored the vogue for bold colour: waiting until Walter had gone to bed, they would prise open the paint pots and work through the night, going round furniture that was too heavy to move; next morning he would come downstairs to find the whole room pink, or violet. All her life Lesley would be distracted by doing up her living quarters, just as she enjoyed dressing up herself, loving the displacement activity while agonizing over the time it stole. She was still painting and rearranging furniture in her hundredth year.

Lesley's mother was her greatest ally, encouraging and interested in everything. 'She . . . was quite remarkable, managed to be gay and charming, a very feminine woman. My young men spent hours with her, she knew how to talk to them. They used to say, You're not a patch on your mother.'

Lesley was outrageously pretty, if not conventionally beautiful; admirers hovered about her like bees around a honeypot. Why hadn't she found a husband? Determined not to be a war victim, she avoided the fate of so many girls of her age who committed themselves to a fighting man and were left shattered by his death. Nevertheless she was indirectly a casualty, by the historical accident of belonging to a generation that lost its young men in the trenches of Flanders and the Somme. Lesley was, in fact, largely impervious to the attractions of callow English youth, but she had never expected the alternative, which came as a lasting shock to her: she was going to have to earn a living for herself and her now precariously placed family.

The school Walter and Martha chose for Lesley had encouraged its girls to anticipate an independent wage-earning life. Beyond that she was hugely creative, with a restless intellect and intelligence that demanded to be challenged. She wasn't someone to be satisfied with a little light sketching and flower arranging, although she excelled at both when she chose. However she might chafe at the daily drudge of work (and she did), Lesley had the temperament and the drive of an artist. The question was in which direction her multi-faceted talent would lead her.

Painting and drawing were a natural first choice, being as expressive of herself as her slanting copperplate handwriting. Lesley designed her own Christmas cards; she illustrated her own books, stitched gros point pictures of her favourite places and overpainted Victorian portraits with the faces of her adored pet animals and birds. After leaving the Slade she transferred to a commercial art college for a course in graphic arts which gave her a professional training in book design and jacket illustration.

Her professional illustration was light, feminine, mischievous, embellished with rococo curlicues. It was controlled by a strong sense of composition, the central subject often contained in a frame forming part of the picture. She made deft use of collage, sticking snapshot faces on a painted background.

The London Library has a copy of *Racecourse and Hunting Field*, a limited-edition centenary account in doggerel verse of the 1830 Doncaster St Leger and 'Melton in 1830', illustrated by Lesley. On the cover a saucily demure Britannia in a plumed helmet, her bust barely draped by a Union Jack, holds a laurel wreath over a jockey, while huntsmen and a dog, all with prim little mouths, look on. The frames and drapes, cherubs, china dogs and (surely?) borzois in these tongue-in-cheek pastiches quite subvert the conventional English sporting genre.

Lesley designed a lot of book jackets; a poster for London Underground; whatever came her way. She worked quickly, her illustration was able, clients seemed pleased, but the wage slave's routine was never part of her self-image. She wanted to make money and then go out and enjoy herself.

Her two role models came from a different mould. They were neither artists nor feminists, but impudent chancers more inclined to *la vie horizontale* than the work ethic. Becky Sharp from *Vanity Fair* was her favourite heroine in literature, and there was more than a touch of Becky in Lesley. Thackeray's pretty, unscrupulous social climber wasn't interested in 'nice'; she was ambitious for a life which offered her airs and graces, glamorous clothes and a good time in the very best masculine company. Becky knew she was top quality, more than equal to the privileged circles she chose to infiltrate. But at heart she was like her father, an artist and a gipsy, who if she fell off *Debrett*'s ladder could make herself at home with a glass of wine in a boarding house.

Later, Lesley liked to present herself as a femme fatale with a mysterious history. Highly selective in the glimpses she allowed into her own past, she was often most revealing about herself when writing about other people. This is true especially of her introduction to *The Game of Hearts* (her edited version of Harriette Wilson's memoirs, 1957), where her voluptuous description of the courtesan's way of life assumes a close affinity with this high-living creature of the Regency demi-monde, who gleefully chose and threw away men's favours. Though not beautiful, Lesley conceded, 'she was herself, like no one else, and her immense vitality, her wit and lively interest in many things, combined with her independent, take-me-or-leave-me terms, brought her to the top of her profession.' Lesley breaks off to muse on how Harriette learnt from some of the greatest minds of her time:

> Harriette . . . was born witty; but *I think* she acquired a considerable culture, the art of conversation and letter writing, and a philosophic way of thought which she did not owe to her family background but rather to those men who were her protectors – men who, *one might say*, came to sleep but stayed to dine; men who, probably unconsciously, paid for their entertainment with more than a mere fee. [my italics]

And here is Lesley as she remembered herself: 'I was very pretty, I will say that, and I had a swarm of men round me always. And I was terribly bored with them because I wanted something *much* more exotic . . . I've been very spoilt, I had a lot of interesting men when I was very young who took an interest in me.'

Her father's antisocial habits offered little help with introductions. She found society for herself, probably at parties. Mr Berry the wine merchant, from the famous wine shop in St James, took her out, ostensibly with the aim of educating her palate. Was Berry her companion on a picnic in Cornwall worthy of Harriette Wilson? Pasties featured, and a bottle of vintage claret which Lesley had to warm against her nicely rounded bosom. When the wine was suitably chambré they were ready to picnic – but alas! They had forgotten the corkscrew.

She cultivated men whose knowledge interested her, and learnt quickly from them, while realizing early on that it was better not to reveal how clever she was. Her mentors were invariably men. Philip Ziegler, her editor at Collins who worked on *Journey into the Mind's Eye* with her long afterwards, said Lesley was 'the most completely feminine person' he had ever known in his life, 'and she used her femininity ruthlessly'. She met musicians, writers, poets. Among them was Peter Quennell, a good-looking young Oxford aesthete the same age as Lesley, who frequented the 'smart arty set' that twenty-two-year-old Cecil Beaton told his diary he 'must get in with'; later he helped her more than once in journalism. Did they meet at a party? He set the scene in his memoirs:

> The mid-1920s was an age of extravagant parties, held in ball-rooms, night-clubs, studios, or even in the Westminster Public Baths . . . Fancy

dress was almost always worn; and Cecil Beaton has described a period of his life when, for eight or nine days at a stretch, he never once assumed his ordinary clothes, but would discard a fancy dress on going to bed and assume a new travesty before he again left home. There were fashionable parties, too; and such a party, under the Sitwells' auspices, I remember observing at a Georgian house in Chelsea. Our hostess was Mrs Somerset Maugham; her guest of honour was a Royal Duke . . . Around him circled some seductive young women, curtseying to him with an agreeable mixture of gay familiarity and loyal deference.

The season's high point was the Chelsea Arts Ball at the Royal Albert Hall, where fancy dress was de rigueur and emperors, belly dancers, bathers in swimsuits struck attitudes on the dance floor. Artists and art students excelled at special effects, Lesley among them. She was addicted to dressing up, usually *à l'orientale*, all her life: three weeks before her hundredth birthday she was carefully reviewing what to wear at the celebration.

She was a first-rate partygoer, pretty, opinionated, comic and entertaining. Her ability to charm her way through any social milieu was exceptional. Her natural affinity was with raffish creative types but she had no qualms about infiltrating chilly country houses, though she preferred the breakfasts of kedgeree and grilled kidneys served from silver-domed dishes, to the red-faced Guns who devoured them.

During the 1920s, Edith, Osbert and Sacheverell Sitwell staged an energetic assault on the English arts through their own work, fiercely promoting their idols and protégées and attacking their enemies. Peter Quennell was a Sitwell acolyte; another, Harold Acton, a fellow aesthete, was nearly lynched by Oxford hearties for reciting Edith's poems through a megaphone from his college window. Lesley was strongly influenced by Sacheverell, the younger brother, whose writings about art and travel championed neglected areas of European architecture, painting and sculpture. His *Southern Baroque Art* (1926) has dated badly, but when it appeared was controversial and influential and would confirm Lesley's lifelong preference for the baroque and rococo as opposed to Renaissance orthodoxy. His radical approach to travel writing, blurring the boundaries between travelogue and art history and jump-cutting across countries and continents to illustrate a theme, impressed the youthful Robert Byron on the eve of his travels; it was Sitwell's penchant for gore and grotesqueries, Sitwell's drifts between fact and fancy, that influenced Lesley's *Journey into the Mind's Eye* decades later. He exoticized the free nomadic life of the Roma, the Travellers, and the oriental Jews' long-settled communities in the Middle East and beyond. His enthralled digression into the Sultan's Palace in Istanbul, dwelling on heaps of skulls at the entrance to the inner splendours of Suleiman the Magnificent's room, helped to ignite her obsession with the seraglio.

Quennell, Constant Lambert, 'Sachie' Sitwell, Lord Berners and Nancy Mitford were all part of a coterie that Lesley began to dip into in her late twenties. The Sitwells shared her passion for Diaghilev's Ballets Russes, which symbolized everything vital and outrageous in the arts; for Lesley the ballet was *Russia* in all its incomparable exoticism. Marooned in Europe since the Russian revolution, the company now languished at the Coliseum, the Alhambra and the Empire in London when not wintering in Monte Carlo. 'Sachie' Sitwell, who worshipped Diaghilev, worked with him and Gerald Berners on *The Triumph of Neptune*, staged in 1926; Lambert wrote a score of *Romeo and Juliet* for the impresario. Either production could have given Lesley her chance to stand in the wings and encounter the great man – yet she would meet him not in England, but in Paris.

Despite the partying, there was a dark side to Lesley's twenties. Her parents had fallen on hard times and she struggled to keep the household solvent. Marriage was a route to prosperity that she had to consider.

Conceal thy tenets, thy treasure and thy travels: the Arab saying that Lesley liked to quote might have been, indeed was, hers. Why do the shadows fall most thickly over these years when she followed life and movement so avidly? She never liked to dwell on unhappiness. It was probably during her headstrong twenties that she had the hidden misfortune which she accidentally revealed many years later to her friend and ally, Hélène Hoppenot. A woman who invited confidence, Mme Hoppenot also meticulously kept a journal over several decades. On the afternoon in question Lesley confessed to her that she had once had a baby and given it away. They were speaking of the lack of maternal instinct in some women; Lesley blurted out that she had experienced none at all and denied having any regrets for the daughter she had given up. Hélène Hoppenot hid her shocked reaction to what she saw as Lesley's refusal to take responsibility for her actions.

An unwanted pregnancy could have been the reason why Lesley left the Slade so suddenly in 1922 and why she so urgently needed to earn her own living afterwards. It could have happened later, during her party-going twenties, or even after her marriage in 1930. Whenever it occurred, she buried the event and her unhappiness as completely as she could. She might have gone abroad to have the child, or registered the birth under another name. Going to term with a pregnancy and giving up the baby for adoption at birth was far more common then than it is now, not surprisingly given the alternatives. An illegal abortion abroad was a life-threatening and costly operation, while the stigma of an illegitimate child put an end to freedom and ambition for most single women. Afterwards Lesley was ruthlessly consistent on the subject: she was inclined to claim that she disliked children and personally knew people who had been 'ruined' by starting a family. This was deliberately provocative, for she could be charming to the young and was cherished by the children of family friends.

Unhappiness might have sharpened her desire to travel. She had already been to Paris and Italy, of course. She toured Europe with a woman friend who owned a car. Prague stirred her interest, but she quickly tired of places close to home and Europe on the whole left her dissatisfied. Her sights were on far more distant horizons – or fiercely fixed on her home surroundings.

Lesley was twenty-five; it was the start of a new decade; marriage was what one did. It was the conventional solution to nagging money worries and her mother's concern that she ought to 'settle'. It failed to anchor her for she was soon, if not already, deeply involved in a relationship whose influence on her was galvanic and lifelong.

On 17 January 1930 Lesley married Robert Alan Wimberley Bicknell, an advertising agent, in Richmond Register Office. He was thirty-six, eleven years older than his bride, and their witnesses were Lesley's parents. She soon knew the marriage was a mistake and moved on, emotionally if not physically. In *Journey into the Mind's Eye* she dismisses the episode as a brief early mistake without gracing her husband with a name. But her flippant dismissal of the marriage ('outside the charmed Slav circle') compares cruelly with her lovingly intense description of the place where they lived. In *Mind's Eye* the house has moved to the foreground, pushing its owner aside. Even today, with a busy road in front and Heathrow air traffic whining overhead, its romantic allure is tangible.

The early Georgian façade of number 57 Petersham Road, Richmond, last but one in a roadside terrace, is handsome enough; approached from the Thames towpath at the back, the building is exquisite. Weeping-willow fronds half hide a Rapunzel-like rounded bay running up four of its five storeys, whose tall windows overlook a walled garden leading down to the river. It was the first of Richmond's Paragon houses, built in 1720, pre-dating the white stone arches of Richmond Bridge. Inside, the original curved sash windows and shutters, fireplaces and wall panellings are still intact. From the back door a path wound through the garden to a gate opening on to the towpath, where Lesley walked her dogs. To the right, downstream, was Richmond Bridge and the road to town, to the left the shady path followed a sweeping curve of the Thames to the open fields of Petersham Meadows, still grazed by cattle. In the distance Richmond Hill rose from the meadows, with the promise of Richmond Park's great green expanse beyond. Within yards of the house London had vanished, and waterbirds treated this stretch of the river as their own.

Lesley was profoundly susceptible to place, as we have already seen, and could become just as attracted to *things* as to *people*. When drawn in this way to possessions she was unstoppable. She *had* to have them, believing that they were owed to her. She wasn't a gold-digger in the sense of cultivating the company of rich men – looking back she rather regretted this, it would have made the practicalities of living much easier for her – but her unerring eye for perfection made her passionately acquisitive. She claimed a mystic unity with things that became somehow part of her individual essence. Many were the stories of friends clinging desperately to objects that Lesley coveted; in the end they always went to Lesley. In a less attractive personality this aspect could put one off for life, yet somehow her charm allowed her to get away with it. Her friends mourned their lost quilt, or inscribed first edition with marbled endpapers, but forgave her and remained friends.

She had always loved riverine west London and was irresistibly drawn to this atmospheric place. My suspicions that Bicknell's house was his primary attraction were confirmed when she confessed in an interview in 2004 to a marriage that had been '"naughty" – solely to gain possession' of the house in Richmond. But Lesley's new husband was not the owner of 57 Petersham Road. Robert Bicknell was its tenant, and didn't move there until 1930, or at least after *Kelly's Directory* for 1929 was published, when it was unoccupied. When Lesley joined him in Richmond, Bicknell was possibly as new to the lovely house as she was. What was more, his wife brought with her both her parents, who moved out of Burlington Court and into Petersham Road when she did.

Once again, one can only speculate. A kind of ruthless loyalty to herself and her own seems to have been at work here. Bicknell offered a solution to several pressing problems. Lesley wanted a better home for herself and her parents, especially her father who was now nearly seventy and ailing; the stairs at Burlington Court were too much for him and burdensome for her mother. She passionately desired the house on Petersham Road and allowed her desire to be fused with the man who could offer it to her. Had she noticed that number 57 was to let in the local paper or while walking her dogs by the river? Did she persuade Bicknell to take the house, and her parents, as a package if she agreed to be his wife? Was the marriage even a lightning manoeuvre on Lesley's part after he moved there in late 1929? However it happened, her order of priorities is clearly established by the fact that by 1932 Bicknell had left, and Mrs Bicknell – Lesley – is listed as the household head, along with her parents, another couple called Sydney and Harriette Clarke, and Elizabeth Wilson, probably the maid. She had shed her husband, but kept the house and Walter and Martha still living with her.

Her insistent associations in *Mind's Eye* lend a Russian tinge to the lush green landscape, recalling a scene from Turgenev, or Herzen who lived in Richmond during his years in exile. For even in that house, *especially* there, Lesley's eyes were set on the 'radiant unreal horizon' she longed to reach. By her own account she drooped about the house in a gown from Bokhara, engrossed in obscure Russian memoirs and neglecting the washing up. In one of those slanting passages carrying her off into a past world, Lesley imagines herself in a scene from Aksakov's *Chronicles of Bagrovo*, as a young bride arriving at her husband's homestead in early summer. Plump cattle graze the fields, trees are reflected in the nearby stream, the wooden house is full of wedding guests. She is greeted by her parents-in-law and turns to find her husband, 'but his face is shadowy . . .'.

Which of course tells us nothing about Robert Bicknell, but nicely illustrates the sleight of hand by which Lesley drew a veil across the past. The imaginative empathy that made her historical works so persuasive could also be used to magic her out of an unhappy episode. Not liking what she saw there, she pasted another layer, a picture from past Russia, over her own – like the faces of her pets that she used to paint over portraits in Victorian photographs, or her collage illustrations.

Who or what had made Russia colour her vision again so suddenly, so intensely, even though her outer existence was clamped to London? From her bifocal viewpoint her world of the Run-Away Game would be temporarily eclipsed by the urgent demands of everyday life. Then her long-distance focus would reassert itself and she would have to extricate herself from the inconvenient present. So it was with her marriage: no sooner had she settled in Petersham Road than the siren call of Russia became overwhelming.

Marriage had freed her from the grind of earning her keep and had given her the house of her dreams, in that it was the perfect place to dwell in them. During the brief spell when her material needs were taken care of, she focused all her enthusiasm on the performance arts and found her way into their charmed circles. Her childish games with Pollock's toy theatres as a little girl had evidently fostered bigger ambitions. Ardently attracted to creative energy, she now made serious attempts to break into stage design. The three opportunities that she seized all had Russian connections. A fervent balletomane and friend of Marie Rambert (a former dancer in Diaghilev's Ballets Russes), Lesley designed a 'chamber ballet' for the tiny Mercury Theatre where Rambert staged her Ballet Club productions. In 1934 she did the set design for a brand new ballet danced by the revived Ballets Russes at Covent Garden. Crucially, two years before that, in 1932 she was embroiled with the prodigiously gifted Russian-born director Feodor Komisarjevsky on set and costume design for a Shakespeare production at the new theatre at Stratford-upon-Avon.

Lesley was irresistible when she set herself body and mind to it. Komisarjevsky was notoriously attractive to women and never allowed an existing marriage to deter his advances. No mere Englishman, an advertising man at that, could stand a chance against so titanic a rival. Lesley fell ecstatically, agonizingly in love.

2

The Promised Land

To live with the wolves you must howl with the wolves.

Russian saying

IN A NATION that worshipped its performing stars, Feodor or Theodore Komisarjevsky was born into a family of theatrical divinities. His father, one of Russia's greatest tenor singers, had an insatiable appetite for life and art and existed as if he made no distinction between them. His half-sister Vera – she whose production of Gorky's *Summer Folk* had inflamed Moscow the year Lesley was born – was a stage legend whose Nina, in an early production of *The Seagull*, had made Chekhov weep with joy. Feodor, also awesomely talented, trained as an architect and worked with his sister in the theatre she founded before becoming artistic director at Moscow Opera House. He left Russia after the revolution, not because of political disaffiliation but because the conditions of civil war made theatre production impossible. Komisarjevsky went first to Paris, arriving in England in 1919.

During the 1920s and 1930s his productions electrified the English performance arts and profoundly influenced the actors who worked with him, among them John Gielgud, Alec Guinness, Peggy Ashcroft and Charles Laughton (who addressed him in letters as 'Dear Master'). To define his influence on British theatre as avant-garde would be to limit him. Multilingual, culturally internationalist, he saw the stage as a temple and was savagely rude about most of the entertainment that passed for drama in London. As a producer, or *régisseur* as he preferred to regard himself, he achieved his revolutionary effect by letting actors find their own way while orchestrating a kind of symphonic control around them, exploiting then-neglected aspects like lighting and sound to heighten the spectacle.

His one-time students told Victor Borovsky, Komisarjevsky's biographer, that 'he entered the room and the air changed. He had a quiet disposition, not very verbal, but people felt he was omniscient.' He had a bewitching ability to bend people to his will when he chose. 'Mysterious and cynical, with a perverse and impish sense of humour', as John Gielgud remembered him, Komisarjevsky was hypnotically attractive to women. Edith Evans, one of few who remained unscathed, nicknamed him 'Come and Seduce Me'. By 1937, Komisarjevsky had notched up nine officially registered marriages, almost always to women involved in the theatre. Ruthless and pathologically secretive, he severed the last to make way for the next with cruel finality. Few of his wives knew about the others or about the many children he fathered and consistently neglected.

In 1929, 'Komis' was already tiring of his fifth marriage. By 1934, he was living with Peggy Ashcroft, who divorced Rupert Hart-Davis in order to become his eighth wife. That autumn, while he was staging a production in New York, he met Ernestine Stodelle, an unknown young American dancer whom he instantly decided must be his life's partner. In 1935, he went through with the marriage to Peggy Ashcroft, then left her. Two years later, while still officially married to Ashcroft, he celebrated his union with Stodelle, who had already borne his first child, in the Russian Church in Geneva. His last productions in England were in 1938–9; when war was declared he was in Switzerland and wanted to return to England, but Stodelle persuaded him to go with her to the United States, where he remained until his death in 1954.

Who was the shadowy figure by Lesley's side in the wings of a Paris theatre, watching rehearsals of a Diaghilev ballet in the late 1920s, not long before the great man died? Why should it matter? Only that if her companion was Komisarjevsky, then conceivably Lesley's secret affair with him began *before* she married Robert Bicknell. She might even have decided to marry out of desperation after yet another of Komis's lightning replacements of one wife with another – why couldn't he marry *her*, if she was available?

Lesley says she met Komisarjevsky in Paris. She also says she treasured a long friendship with him, in which case it would have outlasted several of his marriages. That would explain why she was often in Paris, to meet him secretly. Only a Russian of his eminent status could have taken her to Rachmaninov's house in Rambouillet to join the audience of friends who heard him play. Only such a Russian could have chatted on equal terms with the *basso profundo* Chaliapin, the Russian entertainers Nikita Balieff and Vertinsky, and the great seducer of the silent screen, Ivan Mosjoukine.

Komisarjevsky had everything Lesley prized most highly: genius; the theatrical circles which were home and family to him as an exile; his innate familiarity with the distant nation that she had been trying so hard to make her own. The slant of his features and semi-bald Asiatic skull added to his elusive charisma. His dark mesmeric eyes seemed to see into her soul. He alone understood the extent of her Slav obsession, while to him, ever the foreigner in England, she must have been a novelty – someone who fancied herself more Russian than he was himself. He teased her for flirting with Orthodoxy at the Saturday Russian mass, knowing that what she really enjoyed was the theatre, the robes and the ritual. He was amused by her attempts to relive in Richmond the Russian provincial life that she knew from genre paintings and obscure nineteenth-century novels. When she bewailed the lack of serfs to do the washing up, he slyly observed that she pictured herself as the *Barinya*, the lady of the manor.

Everything she could have wished for was tantalizingly almost hers: a delectable house, financial security and the chance to embark on a demanding artistic career. Now she had the attentions of a man of myth who surpassed all her exacting standards. But all the desired elements were tormentingly disjointed and confused. Never the time, the place and the loved one together, as she would sigh. She should have been blissfully happy at home, dreamily watching the Thames flow by from the open window where wisteria tumbled over the wrought-iron balcony. If only she knew when she would see him next . . . The secrecy and conspiracy added to the intoxication of their clandestine meetings, at least to begin with; but it was a dangerous liaison which scattered acceptable codes of behaviour like so much chaff in the wind. As time went on Lesley, who was used to getting what she wanted, was tortured by the way he came and went without a word of explanation. There was nothing she could do: he was all she craved, yet always out of her reach. Her emotions soared and dipped terrifyingly.

The affair must have been at its height in June 1932, when Lesley had the vertiginous experience of collaborating with him on *The Merchant of Venice*, a prestigious production launching the first Summer Festival at the newly built Shakespeare Memorial Theatre, Stratford. The programme credits 'The Settings designed by Komisarjevsky and Lesley Blanch' and 'The Costumes under the direction of Lesley Blanch' – a rare collaboration, for Komis usually designed everything himself. Only Shylock, played impressively by Randle Ayrton, was in Elizabethan dress; as Portia, Fabia Drake (another of Komis's victims) was dressed in toyshop-doll mode. Komisarjevsky and Lesley went out of their way to provoke Stratford's conservative audience by changing the text, erasing the period and staging *The Merchant* as a masquerade complete with Pierrots in false noses. In addition, they were trying out the theatre's new state-of-the-art machinery whose traverses slid across the stage 'too slowly and too often'. Traditionalists were shocked, 'but there is invention, and it is the invention of a true theatrical artist', the *Observer* concluded. The production was a much-needed box office success for the new theatre in spite of mixed reviews, and was well enough received to be revived the following year.

Komisarjevsky's biographer tells us that his personal upheavals almost invariably coincided with a crisis in his professional life. 'Just as a new theatrical idea and its practical use in performance wore out, so the unique object of his affections, which was recently so desired, ceased to be a source of inspiration.' His greatest passion was the stage, and if a relationship no longer added to what he was trying to achieve there, he finished it, which was very likely what happened to Lesley.

She had sensed in him the comfortless melancholy of the perpetual exile. In England his seven languages and cultural range were no advantage, he was always made to feel a foreigner, however long he stayed. It seems that he eventually found refuge in his marriage to Stodelle partly because he felt at home with her in America, as one immigrant among many. As Borovsky put it, he was 'the vagabond of Schubert's songs . . . always looking for his ideal'. The concept of compromise was equally alien to him in his art as in his private life, as it had been to his father and his half-sister, both of whom left emotional chaos in their wake. The extreme temperamental climate which Lesley saw as essentially Slav had drawn her to him as a meteor to a planet. Komisarjevsky personified the Russia of her imagination; and later, that was how she immortalized him. Other traits might be borrowed and added from another original; but his Asiatic features, the bewitching presence, the erudition, the tantalizing mystery and secrecy about his past (as well as his present), his offhand introduction of two sons, his sudden arrivals and djinn-like final vanishing – all would be reincarnated decades later in Lesley's Traveller.

Later in life Lesley liked to recall the Traveller's dictum that 'Every woman should marry three times', implying that she had followed it. After her house burnt down in 1994 she insisted that among the few things she saved were her three wedding rings, while declining to be drawn on the identity of the first two husbands. In her late nineties she said that Bicknell (or rather, the owner of the lovely house) was her second husband, which would fit in with the Traveller's advice: marry the second time for money. Yet when she married Romain Gary in 1945, only her divorce from Robert Bicknell was cited on her marriage certificate. Given Komisarjevsky's incorrigible impulse to marry, and Lesley's single-minded passion for him, was there a secret ceremony? If so, it would almost certainly have been bigamous. Had Lesley known this, it might not have shocked her – her desire was ruthless and she hoped to win him completely in the fullness of time. Possibly the ring was a token of intent, never fulfilled.

Emotionally, Komis had embodied the perilous extremes that so attracted her in her Russian friends, though she admitted they led her far out of her depth. The manners and morals of a well-brought-up English miss were hopelessly inadequate in equipping her to deal with this elemental, cruelly changeable Slav spirit. When at last she understood from the lengthening silence that her lover had gone and she would never hear from him again, her desolation had to be as secret as her happiness had been. She was devastated, yet yearned for more. She would find aspects of him in other men, but after Komisarjevsky she must have acquired a certain callousness as a means of self-protection. Lesley hated being a loser and always rejected the role of victim, at least in the face that she showed to the public. The episode made her fall back on herself, emphasizing her self-centredness, 'which is the outward form of self-sufficiency', as another only child she came to know well, Peter Ustinov, pointed out.

Soon she hid her loss behind another grief. In November 1933 she watched her father die of a cerebral thrombosis and cerebral atheroma at the house in Petersham Road. There was no will and little money. Lesley's feelings towards her father were complex and hidden. Though fond enough of Walter to bring him to live with her and to care for him until his death, she was not tender about him in retrospect: in her late nineties she remarked that he had had a first-class brain, adding that it was a pity he had failed to use it. Devoted as she was to Martha as she had never been to Walter, from then on she would feel the weight of her mother's dependence. They stayed on at 57 Petersham Road, where 'Mrs Bicknell' headed the list of residents while tenants and domestics came and went. Lesley and Martha were still listed at 57 Petersham Road in *Kelly's Directory* and the electoral register in 1940, when local records stopped for the war's duration.

Although Komisarjevsky had left her, as he left every other woman except Stodelle, he had confirmed in her many of her most deeply held convictions: about the supremacy of the arts, and the preciousness of objects; about her love of exoticism and far places. His disappearance sharpened her need for stimulation.

Her craving for beauty, spectacle and excitement found its apotheosis in 1934 when a glorious new incarnation of Russia overtook London, in the form of Colonel de Basil's ballet company. Almost overnight, balletomania was reborn. Colonel V. de Basil, a former Russian army officer (whose real name was Voskressinsky), reunited choreographers and dancers from the original Ballets Russes who had scattered after Diaghilev's death in 1929. De Basil's company added new ballets to the repertoire and its barely teenaged 'baby ballerinas' were launched to great sensation as new stars. Lesley became familiar with their cramped billets in dingy Bloomsbury hotels, cluttered with trunks (and often with their mothers, who chaperoned and fought their battles for them). When the company left for Monte Carlo at the end of the season, Lesley's Russophilia had to move on from 'love and *entrechats*'. Hints of romance trailed by Lesley led questionably to Colonel de Basil himself. Writing in *Vogue* about him as one of several 'limelight dodgers' in 1938, Lesley said she had known the enigmatic impresario for years and slyly referred to a 'florid Caucasian' supper that he had cooked behind locked doors, in between pulling off last-minute financial deals and tamping down backstage hysterics.

In fact she had other pressing reasons for witnessing behind-the-scenes uproars at the Ballets Russes. She was working on a stage design that had its première towards the end of their summer run at Covent Garden between the opera season and the proms. She and 'Freida' Harris designed the decor for a new short ballet, *Les Imaginaires*, created by David Lichine: a 'Euclidian drama' in which 'the love of a Circle for an Isosceles Triangle follows a course which an evil Star and a tyrannical Blackboard, Chalk and Sponge do not allow to run smooth'.

The Ballets Russes devised five or six new ballets every year, mostly ephemeral. The response to this one was at best lukewarm. A review by the rambunctious Constant Lambert was headed 'Nought + Nought = Nought' and mauled every aspect – Lichine's concept and choreography; music by Georges Auric – except the dancers themselves. As to the costumes, 'Anything more genuinely sickening, both spiritually and indeed physically, than Count de Beaumont's use of colours and textures I have never seen', though the scenery was 'comparatively harmless. Simple geometric patterns, kabalistic symbols and some gauzes that didn't work, the whole executed in discreet pastel shades. Nothing to please and nothing to offend (except negatively).' Lambert warned de Basil not to rely on revivals and to give his dancers new material worthy of them. Impressively, Lesley forgave Lambert; a few years later she wrote generously of his work with Ninette de Valois in establishing British ballet at Sadler's Wells. Nevertheless, the failure of *Les Imaginaires* must have been especially wounding in contrast to the company's otherwise sensationally successful visit. In its honour Covent Garden had been kept open until mid-August for the first time in living memory, and the *Observer* claimed that the London Season 'may now be said to end when Col. De Basil's troupe leaves London, and not before'.

After this, on top of the mixed notices for *The Merchant of Venice*, Lesley turned her back on stage design. Her aspirations had been pinned to the glittering world of spectacle, only to be cruelly, publicly dashed. She had worked only for the best, with her idols – Rambert, Komisarjevsky, Lichine – but even they carried no guarantee of success. In that stratosphere she had invited comparison with Picasso, Braque, Marie Laurencin, Derain and Miró, all of whom designed for the ballet. Lesley had had the courage, even foolhardiness, to aim high, but she was unknown, had little professional experience, and lacked the insatiable ego and drive of the artist colossi. The Stratford episode stabbed her with memories of Komisarjevsky. The experience was lacerating enough for her to erase all mention of her stage design from later accounts of her life (although she didn't refuse further opportunities: in 1940 she became involved in some decor for a film and again in Hollywood, in the early 1960s, she worked for George Cukor on his film version of Romain's novel *Lady L.*, which yet again was dogged by bad luck).

In retrospect, in her journalism and in her memoir, she painted a charming, decorative image of amours and intrigues over the less satisfactory background of creative struggles that failed to match up to her hopes. Love among the scenery flats of Covent Garden was the way she preferred to remember the Ballets Russes.

That autumn Lesley paid her first visit to the promised land. According to her memoir she owed this first trip to Russia to an English benefactor, who hoped perhaps that seeing Soviet life in the raw would blast her romantic vision of Russia out of her system once and for all. At any rate, the cure did not work; quite the reverse, in fact, for the country that she yearned to encounter had now come to stand in for the loved one who represented the Russian destiny that she was convinced was hers. Since he had abandoned her she was desolate. Her familiar surroundings no longer felt like home. The only way she could express her anguish was by transferring her longing to the places *he* had come from. Her grief became an overwhelming homesickness for somewhere she had never been. Only by reaching the world that had once been his, it seemed, could she become herself and learn to live again.

She made the trip with a group organized by the British Drama League, and invited her friend Marie Rambert to go with her. Rambert (born in Warsaw of Jewish descent, and a fluent Russian speaker, which to Lesley made her authentically Slav) was already a moving force behind English ballet; with her husband, the playwright and drama critic Ashley Dukes, Rambert turned an old church hall in Notting Hill into the little Mercury Theatre, where they took turns to stage drama and Ballet Club (later Ballet Rambert) productions. A backdrop by Lesley survives for one of Rambert's 'chamber ballets', which were specially scaled to fit the tiny stage.

Their voyage to Leningrad, on a boat called the *Sibir* (*Siberia*), took five or six days, travelling via Kiel, along the coast of Sweden. Conditions on board were unbearably cramped, but the food was good and they gorged on caviar for breakfast. Approaching the port in the pearly evening light they saw Peter the Great's massive creation swathed in sea mist, as though one day it might sink back into the swamp on which it had been built.

Later, after supper, they decided to try to find Pushkin's house. They stopped to ask for directions from a workman, who said he would walk there with them. They asked him about housing conditions and were chastened by his reply that he was not 'badly off . . . I have part of a room for my wife and myself – and when it comes to doing my studies there are communal work rooms with large tables and good lights. It's all made easy for us.'

Visiting Soviet Russia in the 1930s was less of an adventure than it had been a decade earlier, when grass grew in the streets of Leningrad, but tourism was still in its infancy, so fixed itineraries were not yet obligatory. British visitors consisted mostly of communists who wore their workers' clothes like a badge for their beliefs, leftist politicians, questing journalists and adventurous tourists in search of novelty, aside from balletomanes like Marie Rambert and Lesley. The rest of their Drama League party spoke no Russian, were suspicious of everything they were told and thoroughly disapproved of the conversations that Lesley and Marie conducted in Russian with their hosts.

After only a day in Leningrad the party entrained to Moscow, 'the real blood and bones of Russia'. Lesley gazed ecstatically at the Kremlin's stocky, solid, four-square buildings, epitomizing Old Russia, topped by onion domes and pinnacles 'come like strange birds to rest on the roof'.

The guides were perplexed by her lack of interest in Soviet achievements, even while admiring them. Her love of Russia was coloured by nostalgia for a past before she was born, that had been enacted in places where she had never been. During their day in Leningrad she skipped the more famous collections at the Hermitage for the neglected narrative paintings that spoke to her of Old Russia. Her mind was crammed with images etched by the writers whose works she had absorbed since childhood: Pushkin and Dostoievsky in Leningrad, Tolstoy in Moscow; Lermontov, Griboyedov. She sought ghostly presences in the houses where they had lived and the places they described. She became suddenly eager to visit a Soviet day-nursery on hearing that it was housed in Prince Kropotkin's childhood home. She wandered round Novodievitchi Convent, and the cemetery where Chekhov and her Decembrist heroes were buried. She was seized by melancholy at the sight of jars of Tolstoy's favourite pickles and preserves, stored in the house in Moscow he had shared so unhappily with Sonia. She saw what she wanted to see, yet was fully aware of the self-delusion which allowed her to fuse fact and fiction into 'the eternal Russia' that for so long had been her inner landscape.

Lesley saw *Lady Macbeth of Mstensk* at the Mariinsky Theatre in Leningrad, and recognizing Shostakovich on the stairs, introduced herself to him. Her chutzpah was rewarded by an invitation to the green room with the singers after the performance. After their Russian visit Lesley co-wrote with 'darling Mim' a chapter on the ballet for *Playtime in Russia*, a collection of essays by various writers about Soviet life outside work. 'Some Impressions of the Ballet in Russia – 1934' was based on their visit to a Bolshoi performance of *Swan Lake* at the State Theatre in Moscow, and to the ballet school to watch classes taught by the great Chekriguine. Their account, served up with authentic Blanch sauce, tells how they tripped late in their high heels over the cobbles across Sverdlov Square to the theatre and were ushered to what had once been the Tsar's box. They were impressed by the enormous orchestra, the expensive sets and costumes, the fine technique in the corps de ballet, the cult of the *prima ballerina assoluta*, the virtuosity of the performers. Almost the most fascinating aspect for them was the shabbily dressed audience in the packed theatre, devoid of trappings of wealth and privilege and including a posse of small boys and girls who were embryo balletomanes, all engrossed in the perform-ances and applauding ecstatically. After struggling not to express dismay that the production seemed stuck in time, the authors finally came out with it in a quotation by Arnold Haskell from *Balletomania*: 'It was a step into the past, the result of a whole generation who knew neither Fokine nor Massine . . .'

How many times did Lesley *really* visit Russia? She said she made two more visits to the Soviet Union after that, though the only definite evidence I found was of her Trans-Siberian journey in the early 1960s. In *Mind's Eye* she implies that she travelled by steamer along the Volga from Kazan to Astrakhan, but the picture is too faint to convince. Lesley was a successful journalist by that time, yet no account of such an exotic journey appeared in her writings, either then or later; almost certainly this was a voyage in the mind's eye.

Whether she went again to Russia or not was almost immaterial to *her*, in that her Slav obsession continued undiminished. In 1942, when the Russians' heroic stand against the invading Germans was the Allies' chief hope for survival, she wrote a panegyric, 'Some of All the Russias', in *Vogue* which summed up the shape of her prejudice. She said she was often asked whether her admiration for Russia took the form of nostalgia for the old regime, and the exoticism of that vast country where East met West, or whether it was for the visionary plans and strenuous achievements of the Soviets. But surely, she argued, each emerged from 'the Russian character, each an aspect of "all the Russias" over which the Tsar ruled; "all the Russias" which are now the U.S.S.R.' Lesley believed that her sympathies lay with the poor and dispossessed and she was too intelligent to disregard completely the politics of the here and now. But her devotion was to a nation and its people, not the state system. Defending Russian culture in her piece, she listed all the loves – paintings, music, literature, ballet, film – that she had already absorbed so hungrily into her cosmos and that would be shimmeringly evoked decades later in *Journey into the Mind's Eye*.

Lesley returned from Russia with all her Slav convictions intensified. She was still officially living at Petersham Road, where Mr and Mrs Clarke were replaced as tenants by Frieda Harris, her collaborator on stage design for the sad story of the circle's love for a triangle. (Could this artist *possibly* have been the Frieda Harris who befriended the notorious occultist Aleister Crowley and designed the Crowley Thoth deck of Tarot cards with him? As so often in the byways of Lesley's life this seems both improbable and likely. Lesley was an inveterate collector of curious people with esoteric interests, and was always influenced by card readings and astrology.) Yet restlessness and probably a new lover led her to take flight and move into two attic rooms in Albany, just off Piccadilly. She was seduced by the history and location of 'this modish cloister', a Regency development of seventy sets of chambers tucked behind Savile Row and Burlington Arcade. Once the bachelor residence of Byron and 'Monk' Lewis, it had kept a slightly rakish masculine reputation, although Lesley was not the only woman living there. Nor was she the only unofficial tenant lodging upstairs in the cramped and unmodernized servants' quarters, which had to share bathroom facilities with official residents. Nevertheless, the address had cachet: 'Live in an elegant building (even if you're in the cellar),' in Onassis's dictum.

She continued to 'collect' and cultivate Russian friends and acquaintances from among the émigré and artists' communities in London and Paris. She could speak a smattering of Russian with them, though never enough to satisfy her; despite her sensitivity to language, Lesley was not a linguist. She haunted the Academy Cinema's Russian film seasons and followed Russian music and stage productions with fanatical loyalty. She delighted in shows like the Habima Players, a Jewish theatre group from Russia imported by the impresario Charles Cochran in the 1930s, returning to the theatre night after night to watch *Uriel Acosta* and *The Dybbuk*. The season was a commercial failure – English audiences failed to appreciate plays in Yiddish – but she remembered it as 'great theatre, great art', and shared their *Schalète* (apple and raisin cake) after a performance.

Now that she was single again, earning her living became an urgent priority. Illustration paid poorly, while her efforts at stage design had left her badly buffeted. Around this time she began to switch to journalism. At first she supplied both words and pictures. Her first piece, for *Harper's Bazaar* in June 1935, was a single-page counterblast against the tyranny of beige imposed by Chanel's ubiquitous influence. Headed 'Anti-Beige', it called on women to revolt against biscuit, café-au-lait and oatmeal in favour of all shades of scarlet, even at mealtimes when she championed rare beef and strawberry jam over boring beige 'slimming Nordic biscuits'. *Vogue* too was impressed. Other commissions followed. 'Then,' she recalled, 'the manager [the managing director, Harry Yoxall] asked: "Where are you mingling?"'

Several of Lesley's features appeared in Brogue, as the UK edition was known, in 1936. The following year she was asked to join the staff. As she remembered it, 'They threw me into it like that one morning. I'd sold them some piece of writing and they'd asked me for something else, and then one day they said, well, you'd better come in and be feature editor. I hadn't the slightest idea what to do. But they gave me a secretary and of course she did everything. And she typed anything I did.' Lesley never learnt how to type and all her life filed copy, wrote letters and composed all her books in longhand.

Audrey Withers, Brogue editor for twenty years from 1941, was managing editor when Lesley arrived, and had to teach her the nuts and bolts of journalism. Lesley would bring in four or five photographs, expecting to fit them plus 2,000 words all into one spread. She had to learn about layouts, how to tailor her words to a line, a column or a caption, and which pictures were most effective. 'She got the hang of it quite quickly of course, but it was *completely* strange to her.'

By this time Lesley had developed into a considerable personality. For Audrey Withers, who dealt with some memorably gifted people during her time at *Vogue*, she was 'the most completely individual character that you could meet in a lifetime. She was a free spirit, really, in a period when it wasn't at all as easy as it would be now. She was uninfluenced by anybody, let alone anybody's opinions.'

As St Paul's had shown, Lesley was emphatically not a team member and she was far from a *Vogue* stereotype. But her writing and illustrations – and her thinking – were fresh and original, with a rare light touch. She was witty, inquisitive, knowledgeable and opinionated; what was more, she knew how to 'mingle'. She was fearless and undeterred by social strata. Above all, the most determined resistance fell in the face of her charm – true charm, unfeigned and irresistible.

Whatever Lesley's ambitions, they were not conventional. In later years she laid no great claim to her early achievements, dismissing her 'glossy magazine' work as just 'something I did'. She moved on restlessly from illustration and stage design to journalism, film criticism, travel writing, and later on again to books. In old age she reflected on her move from visual to verbal creation: 'With illustration I did what I had to do because I had to earn, for me and for all of us. I had to get by somehow. But I was never in any way satisfied by the work. It was sometimes quite able. But when I began to write the thing would come out how I meant more or less.'

Anne Scott-James (the late Lady Lancaster) was ten years younger than Lesley, a tall, willowy beauty of cutting intelligence who went on to become the distinguished columnist, broadcaster and writer. Having left Oxford after two years with an Honour Mods First in Latin and

Greek, eager to make her way in journalism, she joined *Vogue* in 1934 as assistant to the knitting editor. She began her illustrious career by reknitting grotesquely deformed garments sent in by distraught readers who had followed patterns in a *Vogue Knitting Book* that had been translated, unchecked, from French. During her seven years at *Vogue* she became a sub-editor, then beauty editor, before moving on to *Picture Post* as women's editor. She got to know Lesley well as a *Vogue* colleague and personal friend; they shared a flat in Swan Court, Chelsea for a while in wartime when Anne found herself bombed out and homeless.

Anne wrote two vivid pen-portraits of Lesley, in her novel *In the Mink* and here, in her autobiography:

> She was a bohemian, a nomad, an artist, deeply romantic, widely travelled, a spirited writer and caricaturist and a brilliant raconteuse . . . [she] looked like a baroque angel. She had an oval face framed in a halo of honey-gold curls, a rounded figure, an expression of experience combined with innocence . . . Lesley had a feverish manner of talking, extravagant in praise of friends, vitriolic about enemies, and she lived in a whirl of melodrama – something as trivial as a missed bus became a black tragedy. She wore exotic clothes of Russian ballet inspiration and moved in a nimbus of veiling, often topped with a fur shako, to the accompanying music of jangling bracelets. She had the sweetest of smiles. She never seemed to have a penny. She was devoted to cats and burst into a storm of tears when told by a skin doctor that she had a cat allergy. Her favourite country was Russia, and she claimed to have visited its remotest districts with a Russian admirer at some unspecified time in the past. Siberia, Samarkand, the Caucasus were as familiar to her as Piccadilly or Chelsea.

Vogue in the 1930s had a tiny staff compared with its battalions today. There was a society editor who dealt with the *ton*, and a features editor (Lesley) who covered cultural events and people so that society could talk about them. Lesley's title did not mean she commissioned or edited anything. Happily she had been hired to do what she was good at: use her excellent contacts to infiltrate every area between celebrity and the bohemian demi-monde, and to write snippets about forthcoming films, exhibitions, plays, ballets and books. She followed her own inclinations, ignoring what was fashionable in favour of what interested her most. She wrote about her friends, loyally reviewing their output;

conversely she had no truck with Bloomsbury which, judging from her column, might never have existed. Her Christmas round-ups show discrimination and an almost faultless ability to pick future classics. She regularly enthused about 'Sachie' Sitwell's new works which appeared with factory-line speed, and raved about his *German Baroque Sculpture*, photographed by Anthony Ayscough. She also contributed features on whatever off-beat subjects took her fancy: the launch of the liner *Queen Mary*, the lost art of narrative painting, animal portraits . . . and always, on any excuse, anything about Russia.

Lesley soon found her writing voice and a maverick role as *agent pro-vocatrice*. She deftly handled the third social category (after 'society' and 'celebrity') featured in *Vogue*: the 'little man' or 'treasure' on whom 'Mrs Exeter', the archetypal *Vogue* reader, depended to supply every need and generally make life acceptable. Lesley, who throve on disaster and made it her own, enjoyed tossing bombs into this pool of complacency. Her contribution to a series about cooks ('My Cook is a Russian', etc.) was headed 'My Cook is a Catastrophe'. Nimbly, flirtatiously, she bit the hand that fed her. 'First Night Hocus Focus', illustrated by her own full-page collage of celebrity figures stuck on to a painted backdrop of theatre boxes and stalls, pokes fun at first-night addicts who felt like social out-casts if they missed a première.

In her 'Vogue's Spotlight' column, Lesley refused to follow the usual policy of featuring only what was praiseworthy. An early column attacked the summer tradition of open-air theatres: shivering actors, 'sodden scenery and programme girls hiring out rugs (why not hot-water bottles too?)' On the same page she also savaged Vivien Leigh's performance in *The Dark Journey* (though she made friends with Leigh later), and the 'tubby tenor' Richard Tauber's miscasting as rake-thin Paganini, which she deemed disastrous.

She was equally forthright in her approval and left no doubt where her loyalties lay. Her first signed column – a 'Slavonic Rhapsody' – managed to link a batch of new ballet books to Marie Rambert, and thence to Komisarjevsky's production of *Antony and Cleopatra* starring Eugénie Leontovich. Russia was her motif, her trademark: even a piece on Crufts Dog Show mentions that one of the tsars sent his finest borzois from the imperial kennels. Her editors must sometimes have despaired at the wayward beam of Lesley's spotlight. Her three 'Women of Achievement' in March 1937 were Dr Charlotte Wolff,

German-born psychologist and palmist to all London; Madame Karinska (Russian of course), a dramatic costumier; and Nadia Benois, a French-Russian-Italian painter. The last was the wife of I.V. Ustinov, journalist, antique dealer, cook and raconteur, and mother of the precocious, omni-talented Peter – Ustinov *père*, *mère* and *fils* often appeared in Lesley's column.

Still she hankered after Slav company. After a round of professional socializing at a publishing launch, a new exhibition or a restaurant opening, she would jump on a bus to the far reaches of Islington or Hoxton, where her Russian émigré friends, penniless intellectuals or exiled aristocrats, had washed up in dingy lodgings reeking with the lingering odour of cabbage soup. On the long bus rides she buried herself in Herzen's memoirs and looked forward to emotional dramas and vehement arguments about Russian poets which were far more enticing, to her, than the 'good-gracious living' she wrote up for her paymasters.

While Lesley adored glamour and was more than equal to dealing with celebrity, she was less interested in fame *per se* than in how people earned it. A craftswoman herself, she was as fascinated by costume as by the star who wore it and appreciative of the creativity behind successful stage and screen decor. She was allowed masses of space for her pieces on ballet: after financial wobbles the Russian Ballet was reborn in spring 1938 under the clumping title of United Art Incorporated. It was then the height of chic, dressed by Schiaparelli with sets designed by Matisse and Dali. Lesley wrote up its Easter debut in Monte Carlo, where it was celebrated by France's *crème de la crème* in a riot of parties, led by Chanel wearing trousers, sweater and pearls.

Lesley's subjects were often called into the studios to pose for one or other of *Vogue*'s stable of portrait photographers. There she learnt the secrets behind the flawless visions of elegance and wealth that breathed glamour from the pages. Beaton, then *Vogue*'s star photographer, deified beauty and described his job as 'to stage an apotheosis'. Lesley saw how he did it, surrounding his sitters with frames and backdrops and costumes (she herself often drew frames round her illustrations, or made framed pictures part of her composition). She saw, too, how performance and presentation were used to manipulate reality into images of fantasy. Like Beaton, she was another adventurer in high places who became part of the *beau monde* that she was paid to observe. Also like him, she adored theatrical presentation and regalia, hence her weakness for the trappings of royalty and Orthodox Church ritual, as well as for the satin radiance of screen gods and goddesses. In 1942 he memorably posed Lesley, wide-eyed and demure in a cowl headdress in the role of *bariniya*, for a Russian apotheosis owing nothing to fashion.

She was fascinated by his phenomenal output, reassessed her early verdict on him as a 'coloratura photographer' and 'spotlit' his latest exploits. Her most revealing sketch, an admiring hatchet job, was dashed off for her weekly *Daily Mail* column in 1945, when she no longer worked for *Vogue*. She explains how Beaton's 'witty, extraordinary' portraits became the rage in the 1920s, demolishing and reconstructing faces and figures by ruthless retouching, all for the highest fees. His fashion photography in London, Paris and New York made him 'a virtuoso of the lens'. The war, she wrote acidly, brought 'even him into contact with reality', and he published two well-written travel books. 'He combines the energy of a shock-worker with the ruthless social drive of an ambitious hostess,' she remarked, noting his 'endearing sense of humour when not directed at oneself'.

Observing the spread of his talent into costume and set design for film and stage, she perceptively concluded that he was 'happiest designing Edwardian elegance. Plans to launch such nostalgic, seductive clothes for women who have money and opportunity to wear them. Personally I think they're only for fancy dress or the theatre. But Beaton's a theatrical figure, anyhow: his whole personality and achievements are a triumph of production.' In 1950s Hollywood she would find him in his element, designing elaborate period costumes just as she predicted.

Of course appearances were paramount on the magazine. For Lesley dressing up was part of her identity. She clothed herself with confident originality, adapting modish and ethnic themes to her looks and personality. Her copy occasionally sniped at the fashion department's slavish loyalty to the Collections – 'Unaccustomed as I am to write upon any subject with deep feeling (I leave that to the Fashion Staff)' – which didn't prevent her from knowing the best dressmakers.

She was still living at Albany when she started working at *Vogue*. Later she returned to Petersham Road where her mother was ensconced with Frieda Harris. Colleagues remembered her living again in Richmond and that Harry Yoxall, the managing director, lived nearby. This was awkward for Lesley, as he could keep an eye on who she spent her time with; she said herself that she lived continually in an atmosphere of passionate intrigue. When fuel shortages and the black-out were imposed in 1940, commuting became difficult for Lesley and they gave up the lovely house with its blue gate opening on to the tow-path by the river. Later she rued her decision, regretting the loss of her own small paradise. Martha transferred to a more modest address nearby at 4 South Lodge, Ham Common, and Lesley moved back into town.

Wherever she was she regarded her home surroundings as an exten-sion of herself and dressed them accordingly, causing first-time visitors to fall back in amazement. Her idiosyncratic decor appeared at least twice in fiction. In Anne Scott-James's novel *In the Mink*, Lesley is 'Amy Sweet' and the first sign of things to come is a Persian scimitar for a door knocker:

Amy herself let me in, wearing an exotic *déshabille* consisting of flimsy Turkish trousers, a short embroidered velvet jacket and masses of jan-gling gold bracelets. Her hair was hidden under an enormous Russian fur hat, with blonde curls escaping here and there . . .

I squeezed into the narrow hall, nearly smashing a blue Victorian lustre with my right shoulder which stood on a rickety empire pedestal in the corner. Having negotiated this hazard, my left elbow banged into a china jardinière holding a castor-oil plant which sprouted to the ceil-ing. My head just grazed a small chandelier which hung from a hook, and the feather on my hat tickled a row of china jugs hanging on a shelf on the wall.

'I'm so sorry,' I said, as I snaked into the sitting-room; 'I seem very clumsy today.' . . .

'I'm afraid it all looks very bare and streamlined,' said Amy, taking off her fur hat and placing it, like a cosy, on one of the teapots, 'but I've just moved in and I've made a clean sweep. My last flat was just like a junk shop – crammed with stuff. But I've lent a lot, and sold some, and now, as you see, it's absolutely *functional* . . .'

'I should like to have seen your last flat,' I said with truth, looking for somewhere to sit down. I marked down a fairly empty-looking rocking chair which had only some knitting, a trumpet and a pile of prints on the seat, and as I could see nowhere to move them to, I sat down on the lot. By working the trumpet into the small of my back, I made myself quite comfortable.

Lesley kept her own room at her mother's, too, done up in her inimitable fashion. Two decades later it would be reconstructed, with all its bizarre contents, by Romain in his novel *Lady L.*

Since her father's death Lesley was protective of her mother and Martha became a favourite with *Vogue* staff, especially with Jane Stockwood. Jane, who joined the magazine in 1938 as a sub-editor, became a lifelong friend and devoted disciple of Lesley. During the war they would go to stay with Martha at Ham Common, to get a break from bombing raids on the city centre. When Lesley moved abroad after the war Jane became one of Martha's regular visitors in her old age.

As war loomed some women's magazines managed to avoid the subject completely, but *Vogue* hit a patriotic note from the start. Its January 1940 editorial launched a defiant defence of fashion, as 'no surface frivolity but a profound instinct . . . fashion is as essentially rooted in civilised life as architecture and decoration – and indeed leads rather than follows these other arts'. Rather admirably, in fact, the magazine maintained this attitude as the hostilities deepened. When France fell, English designers and the few French ones in London – Worth, Paquin (Molyneux, despite his name, was Irish) – took on the mantle of Paris couture. All their prestige and their best efforts went into tailoring home-grown wool and Harris tweeds for export to the US, to earn dollars for the war effort.

The Ministry of Information enlisted *Vogue* to mobilize women's contribution to the war. From autumn 1940, Lesley wrote a series of reportage features about the Wrens, the WAAF, the Land Army, etc. – mostly models of enthusiasm, although the best she could say about the ATS recruits' mass dormitories was that they were better than slave labour camps. They appeared with pictures by the American photographer, Lee Miller. Both women were bold, determined and unbiddable. Lesley followed her own inclinations. Miller, a former top model for Condé Nast and muse, torment and photographic apprentice to the surrealist Man Ray, joined Brogue after some of its regular photographers were enlisted for war work. She quickly revealed her versatile talent.

Audrey Withers was promoted to editor in 1941 when German U-boats made the Atlantic crossing too dangerous for the American editor of Brogue to return from the United States. In many ways she was a surprising choice for *Vogue*, temple of fashion, being far less interested in clothes than in features and preferring the role of office anchor for self-motivated hunter-gatherers. This worked well with her two mavericks, from whom she extracted fine results. Unusually for *Vogue*, all three also shared leftish political views, though Lesley was apt to comment that she never believed politics referred to *her*.

Lesley stayed at the magazine until late 1944 when she became film critic on *The Leader*, a new weekly journal for which she wrote some of her best journalism. Lee Miller, blocked by British bureaucracy which refused to allow women photographers near the front line, eventually got accreditation as an American war photographer with the Allied invasion in France. *Vogue* published her superlative picture-and-word reportage of the troops, month by month, as they moved across Europe into Germany. She sent back her photographs of Dachau and Buchenwald with the telegram: I IMPLORE YOU TO BELIEVE THIS IS TRUE. *Vogue* published them. 'I felt that Lee's features gave *Vogue* a validity in wartime it would not otherwise have had,' Audrey Withers wrote.

In 1940, after the shattering collapse of the Low Countries and France, followed by the evacuation of British troops from Dunkirk, Britain's lonely refusal to surrender to the Nazis attracted a stream of refugees from the occupied territories of Europe. They straggled in, singly and in small groups, after tortuous journeys and feats of endurance, hoping to fight in whatever way they could. London became weirdly polygot, its blacked-out streets now host to strange uniforms and languages: Dutch, Norwegian, Polish, Czech, French. Gradually they sorted themselves into small fighting forces and, on leave, entered the mêlée of the capital's nightlife.

Lesley remembered the atmosphere in the capital as '*boiling* at the time. Marvellous tempo.' After the Battle of Britain was fought across clear summer skies, the Blitz set in with the coming of winter, and her columns became models of brave, daft frivolity. In 'Living the Sheltered Life' she reported breathlessly that lemons were becoming as rare as caviar and sugar as precious as cocaine: 'Cinemas now flash *All clear! All clear!* across the screen, regardless of the picture. It looked wonderful scrawled across Lillian Russell's 1880 bust, the other night.' While the East End 'took it' night after night, Lesley's front line was subterranean

West End restaurants like Hatchetts, where crowds crammed in, oblivious to mayhem above ground, to hear Arthur Young and the Swing Sextette jamming with Stephane Grappelli. The theatres closed but she noted the bistros in Soho, which were enjoying a heyday: Père Louis and the Escargot in Greek Street, the Etoile and Quo Vadis.

Meanwhile one discussed whether or not to take shelter during a raid. Then one had to consider whether to evacuate one's treasured possessions to a safe place, or whether one shouldn't keep them about oneself to defy the bombs. Lesley loved and lost. A prized golden sofa was lost to a smoke bomb: 'There were these oil bombs which spread dark purply-red oil everywhere, which ruined everything and you had to throw it all away.' Then she remembered having supper one evening in Notting Hill with Ashley Dukes and Marie Rambert, and going home to find her house was a heap of rubble. (She was almost certainly overdoing it in claiming that she had been bombed out three times, though. She didn't leave Swan Court as a result of bomb damage, because Anne Scott-James stayed on there after Lesley left.)

Brittle as this stiff-upper-lip stuff was, Lesley remained exacting about the arts and took her job of previewing entertainment seriously: 'Lightness is too often triteness, and does not, in itself, spell entertainment any more than profundity spells boredom,' she argued. 'We do not necessarily have to be *amused* but we must be *enthralled*.' She cited Bob Hope, Shostakovitch and boxing at the Queensberry All-Service Club ('housed in the old London Casino') equally as first-class entertainment.

Ballet was eclipsed by wartime exigencies and she transferred her allegiance to film, the great escapist mass medium of the day, on which she wrote well. Its fusion of diverse talents and disciplines fascinated her and she was familiar with its artists, designers and musicians. Always susceptible to creative impresarios of exotic origins, the more chaotic the better, in early 1940 she fell under the spell of Gabriel Pascal, a chunky Transylvanian-born film director who was filming George Bernard Shaw's play *Major Barbara* at Denham Studios. Her exuberant profile describes how he arrived unshaven off a cattle boat to ask the irascible Shaw for film rights to his plays. Told to show the colour of his money, he produced 2s 7d from his pockets and within an hour the deal was struck. Just as filming started in 1940, the war began in earnest: phones broke down, fuel ran out and Wendy Hiller, Rex Harrison, Robert Morley and Sibyl Thorndike had to doss down in pubs and cycle to work. Lesley was allowed a month's leave from *Vogue* to decorate the walls of a children's nursery for an 'important scene' – but surely she didn't need to ask his advice *quite* so often as the profile implies?

'Pascal lives nomadically. Sometimes I ran him to earth at Alexander Korda's house where they would be discovered playing poker for their month's petrol ration.' Or scouring the countryside for a farmhouse to buy, or wandering in the lobbies or lounges of grand hotels, or dictating to a secretary from his bath. Once she found herself in a tiny hall hemmed in by a crowd of women, half of whom were waiting to audition for a film, while the rest were applying to fill a vacancy for a Hungarian cook. Lesley elbowed her way through the throng to learn that startled candidates for the part of Mog, 'the converted tart', had been told to recite the Lord's Prayer. 'Alas, so few of them seemed to know their lines.' (Audrey Withers told this story about Komisarjevsky, but must have misremembered.) Lesley accepted at face value Pascal's improbable background – running away with gipsies, then being adopted by a princely family and taught by Jesuits – which added to the attraction of his 'peculiar, excruciating, lucid English: "Nonn! For me, not happy conception. I spit on it . . . . My dear childrens – must I hypnose you?"'

Lesley's nursery, painted with musician mice, 'giraffes in prams, harlequin cats and pantaloon dogs', was the barely visible background to an early scene in Shaw's timely drama about the Salvation Army heiress, her armaments-manufacturer father and her sceptical fiancé. Pascal left a good deal of the direction to David Lean. Despite running grossly over budget, *Major Barbara* was a box-office hit in 1941, but Pascal's career crashed with Shaw's *Caesar and Cleopatra*, a catastrophic and expensive flop in 1945, after which he produced only one more movie.

Lesley flitted like an imp in and out of interlocking circles, yet left remarkably few traces in contemporary memoirs (possibly partly because she wasn't interested in English men). Among the literati were Heywood Hill, who owned the famous bookshop in Curzon Street, where Nancy Mitford worked; Sacheverell Sitwell and his caravanserai when in town; James Lees-Milne; Lord Berners – Lesley had a soft spot for his whimsical conversation and pastel-dyed doves, and respected his talents as a painter and musician; and Peter Quennell, appointed as editor of John Murray's resuscitated *Cornhill* magazine in 1943.

The imaginary panel of thinkers she chose for the hugely popular *Brains Trust* radio broadcasts consisted of (among others) Rebecca West, Raymond Mortimer, Cyril Connolly and Edward Sackville-West. She was loyal to her favourite talents: Feliks Topolski, Polish officer, war artist and socialite; the 'tragic wag' artist-illustrator Ludwig Bemelmans; writer-translator-actor-producer Peter Ustinov; and playwright and director Rodney Ackland. She featured witty, thought-provoking cartoonists: Osbert Lancaster the dandy, David Low, and Giles, chronicler of the People's War (whose cartoons, she informed readers, were hugely popular in Russia). As always she took liberties, suddenly throwing in a paean to the great Russian director Sergei Eisenstein's new book about the cinema before reverting to her proper subjects: Clark Gable (posted to England as a USAAF gunnery officer), Beaton's travels, two Polish artists and a set designer who had caught her fancy.

Lesley was not known for her accuracy and overwrote to the point of verbosity, but her writing, though ephemeral, was maturing. By inclination she was an essayist; her feature on the cinema, in September 1942, was an assured review of contemporary film-making that showed understanding and judgement of form and technique. She wrote equally perceptively on British ballet and was generously critical. She preferred the analytical, descriptive profile to the quote-laden interviews of today. She was specially chosen by *Vogue*'s US editor to tail and talk to Bob Hope, 'the World's Comic No. 1', over the July Bank Holiday weekend of 1943; she and Lee Miller did eventually track him down. She met Lord and Lady Louis Mountbatten at Broadlands after his appointment as Viceroy to India. Her piece about Noël Coward in his new role as film director (*In Which We Serve*, *This Happy Breed*) mused on how precisely his plays had followed the evolution of the national consciousness through cynicism, brittle humour and nostalgia to coalesce gradually into a spirit of unity. She followed the goings-on at the studios at Denham, near Watford, and at Shepherd's Bush, both of which functioned throughout the war.

Lesley extolled the ground-breaking Crown Film Unit documentaries that so tellingly evoked the wartime atmosphere, especially Humphrey Jennings's film about the no. 1 song of the war, 'Lili Marlene'. Like Jennings, she saw a glamorous subject that captured the imagination. The song had become a German broadcast fade-out signature tune by accident in 1941 and was loved by both sides. According to Lesley, Goebbels banned it and all entertainment for German troops after the disastrous defeat at Stalingrad in 1943 (by which time Lale Andersen, the German singer who made the song famous, was in disgrace because of her friendship with Jewish artists. Lesley mis-reported that Andersen was in a concentration camp). She watched Jennings's unit filming in dockland, urged her readers to see the film and prayed that it would not be ignored by distributors interested only in major stars and Hollywood glamour.

In 1943 she was renting a flat in Swan Court, Chelsea when Anne Scott-James (by that time working at *Picture Post*) was bombed out and homeless. Even in that featureless modern block, Lesley had transformed her room into 'a stage set'; she offered Anne the spare room and they shared the place amicably enough, rarely seeing each other because both were so busy. But Anne happened to be in the flat when Lesley turned up with a new young man. 'He was wearing battle dress with enormous boots and was about six foot three high, and the only telephone was by my bed – he used to lie on my bed with these muddy boots.' This was Vadim Komisarjevsky, whom Lesley had introduced to *Vogue* readers in 'Spotlight' in November 1942: 'An old and famous name in the theatre and one new to films, is Komisarjevsky . . . Now his son, Vadim, is working here on the technical side of pictures. He came from Hollywood, served two years in the army, and, invalided out, has just completed his first documentary script *Soho Travelogue*.' In the photograph 'this stormy and single-minded young creature' looks eager, bashful, sensitive; his consuming ambition, he told her, was to direct films with the artistry that his father had shown on the stage.

Vadim would have been twelve to fourteen years younger than Lesley. The romantic reunion in *Journey into the Mind's Eye*, when she catches sight of the Traveller's son Kamran through the crowds at the Easter service in the Russian Orthodox cathedral in Paris just as her candle sets fire to her lace décolleté, must be reluctantly rejected. She describes elsewhere how a charming pastry-cook extinguished her flaming décolleté, then taught her the Cyrillic alphabet in icing-sugar letters. The affair with Vadim was intense if short-lived. She must have known from the first meeting that there was no future in it, but how headily it chimed with her past . . .

By 1943, thirty-seven London theatres were open; new small clubs (Bon Viveur, 500) came on the scene; the old ones were still packed and behaviour was louche. 'It was their total lack of charm, elegance and even the most commonplace amenities that gave these war-time night-clubs their attraction . . . The atmosphere was dim and dense – so dense that, towards the end of the night, one felt that it was becoming semi-solid; and the entertainments they offered were strikingly monotonous,' Peter Quennell wrote. Crowded restaurants served Spam as 'ham Americaine', rabbit as chicken, charged too much and closed at midnight. Journalists and actors met at the Savoy Grill, politicians at the Dorchester. US 'dough boys' were everywhere and so were their dollars. Bus clippies allowed General de Gaulle's Free French troops to travel cut-price or free. On Bastille Day 1943, Gallic exiles were moved to find that Londoners had hired a dance band and decked out the area in St James's outside Le Petit Club Français (the only place in London where you could eat decent steak and chips) for a *fête champêtre*.

One did one's best. But the overlapping cliques were small and tired, and London was cut off from the countryside by fuel rationing and transport difficulties. The claustrophobia was intense. Picture Blanch and Miller, dispatched on a story about the Wrens swarming down rope ladders and being useful on boats off western Scotland, raging about the impossibility of contributing anything serious, of being *part* of big events, in the fatuous context of hand-knitted stockings and Utility tunics. Their ambitions, though, lay in totally opposite directions. Lee Miller could not rest until she reached the front, where from the moment she walked into the heart of the battle at St Malo she would scoop the world's press for *Vogue*. Lesley's front line, though she would surely never have expressed it so pompously, was to guard artistic integrity in the face of total war. This took courage and tenacity of a different kind. Cyril Connolly, editor of the prestigious journal *Horizon*, wrote that 'art occupies in society the equivalent of one of those glands the size of a pea on which the proper functioning of the body depends, and whose removal is as easy as it is fatal'. The work of artists and intellectuals in wartime could always be dismissed as inessential and secondary, and the gland, in Connolly's simile, removed. Lesley's job was to see that it was not, which in its small way was vital. Maintaining the strength and unity of civilian morale had become as crucial to Britain's stand against the Axis powers as the military effort.

Although dauntless about staying in London through the Blitz and in her writings about the war effort, she ached to get away. After the heavy bombing of 1940–41 the capital returned to (relatively) normal, but gas and electricity were often cut off, phones worked intermittently, and the cold and constant cheeseparing were depressing. 'Escapism takes many forms,' she wrote – the Run-Away Game, again. 'There is the study of elaborate cookery-books; Rita Hayworth; re-trimming retired hats; reading old love-letters; writing new ones; philosophic arguments; bridge. . . . Collectively, it's frittering, but individually, it's a life-giving oasis, and a psychological "breather".' Chafing against restrictions that made 'abroad' virtually impossible for civilians, she chose travel books, the more exotic the better, as her magic carpet out of damp, dreary London. Or, taking shelter during air raids, she amused herself with Harriette Wilson's racy memoirs, identifying with her devil-may-care attitude to life, men and mores.

Meanwhile Lesley added to her wages with odd freelance commissions. She did the line drawings for a book about making the most of kitchen-garden produce by Constance Spry, the doyenne of flower arranging and the Elizabeth David of her time. And early in 1944 she persuaded Michael Foot at the *Evening Standard* to take a piece about Pushkin – 'the apotheosis of the Russian spirit' – pegged to the 107th anniversary of his death. Since Germany had invaded the Soviet Union in June 1941, Russia had been recast as hero of the Alliance, and for months on end – years, now – the newspaper front pages had been reporting on the Eastern front, where the Soviets' appalling sacrifices were shifting the balance of the war.

By the spring of 1944, Londoners' nerves had become frayed to snapping point by five gruelling years of war. After a lull the bombing raids had started up again in February and March over central London.

By then the city had become the Free French capital. At a party given for Free French forces men, Lesley noticed a sombre-looking man in air force uniform, who kept himself apart from the chatterers. He had a long face like a Russian icon, padded round the room as if scenting food, and eventually lay on the floor, monopolizing a bowl of rare olives until the hostess confiscated them, whereupon Lesley heard below the buzz of French 'a strangled groan of protest'.

In that deep growl of complaint Lesley was certain she recognized a Russian voice. Intrigued, she was introduced to its owner, and as they sized each other up she remarked that he looked very like the portraits of Nikolai Gogol; *Dead Souls* was her bedside reading, she explained. Surprised but determined not to be impressed, he brusquely retorted that reading it in translation didn't count. In her best pidgin Russian she agreed, adding slyly that his language was very hard for someone as stupid as herself, which made him laugh and disarmed him. When night bombing forced the party to adjourn to an underground night club renowned for its black-market booze, they went with the crowd and began to dance.

The Russian's name was Romain Gari de Kacew.

3

'Lesley's Frog'

In the Free French capital, life was intense, worldly, amorous.
Marriages, divorces, births, affairs and explosive separations which
apparently enraged 'le grand Charles'.
    Jean Pierre-Bloch, head of Free French counter-intelligence

L ESLEY WOULD HAVE met stiff competition for her Franco-Slav
aviator, and she was surely equal to it. London's women loved
airmen, adored the Free French, and especially revered the Polish for
their fanatical courage in the air ever since the Battle of Britain.

De Kacew had fought a good war, Lesley heard. After France's chaotic collapse in June 1940 he had been among the first of the tiny band
of 'esperadoes' who escaped by improbable detours and death-defying
means to Britain, Hitler's island enemy, which was still holding
out against the German blitzkrieg, but only just. When France had
announced its surrender, Romain had been an instructor with the
French flying school; they escaped to Morocco, but the colony allied
itself with France's defeat. At the existential moment, he escaped
again – *towards* battle, *away* from defeat – to Casablanca, where Romain
(using his excellent Polish) smuggled himself and two other deserters
among Polish troops on board a British ship bound for Glasgow.

In London he signed up with the embryonic force of Free French
servicemen committed to liberate German-occupied France, led by
the unknown, intransigent General Charles de Gaulle. They were a
motley bunch of misfits: too young, too old, not even French – de
Gaulle was said to have complained that they were all Jews and social-
ists. Romain was shipped with a handful of Free French airmen to the
only French outposts that had responded to de Gaulle's quixotic appeal
to fight on, in equatorial Africa. He spent the next two years on a

meandering odyssey, hardly seeing action, posted from one remote station in central Africa to another. Reaching Damascus, after an epic journey via Khartoum, he nearly died of typhoid. After months of convalescence and a stint of bombing enemy ships in the Mediterranean, in late 1942 he was among 2,000 troops transported on a two-month voyage from Suez to Scotland via the Cape of Good Hope. Crammed with eight others in a two-berth cabin, he sat silently writing the early chapters of his first novel in a notebook.

In England the Free French airmen of the Lorraine Group were retrained to fly Boston bombers and at last, throughout the autumn of 1943, were unleashed on a relentless rota of low-flying raids to disable strategic sites across the Channel. Romain was a navigator, sitting in the transparent nose-cone and releasing bombs on split-second timing. The bombers 'hedge-hopped' in formation to avoid accidentally killing their own countrymen, but rooftop flying took a terrible toll of aircraft and lives. On 25 January 1944, his plane was hit by flak; shards of Plexiglas nailed the pilot's eyelids to his eyes, blinding him, and Romain fainted when his stomach was perforated by shrapnel. The rear gunner piloted them back on the emergency controls, helped by the blind pilot and the semi-conscious navigator, who were rushed to hospital. This near-fatal adventure earned Romain the Croix de Guerre.

Somehow he had finished his novel, possessed by it, writing through the night and shaking awake his protesting Nissen-hut comrade to read him the latest episode, finally snatching brief sleep before dawn bombing raids. He signed it off 'On operations with the Lorraine Squadron of the Free French Air Force, England, Autumn, 1943'. Then in London he had found his way into the smoky fug of Le Petit Club Français in St James's, where French literary exiles met up to argue and intrigue. Romain tracked down his hero Joseph Kessel, an older Franco-Slav writer-adventurer who knew his early short stories and recommended the novel to influential others. After six months' silence, Romain heard that an English publisher would translate his book and publish it in December.

At thirty, Romain was emerging from the most intense and formative few years he would ever experience. He had survived a winter of high-risk raids that had decimated his flying fraternity. With his first novel's acceptance he had been born as a writer. After convalescing and retraining, in May he was posted to administrative work at the Free

French headquarters in Carlton Gardens. He was floating unattached in this 'boiling' capital full of chance meetings and intrigues. And there, at one of those babbling drinks parties given to entertain the exiled Free French, he met Lesley.

Or did he? Interviewed in *Vogue* in the 1960s, Lesley gave Polly Devlin another account of their first meeting, at odds with the one she described in *Mind's Eye* and her memoir of Romain. She said she was asked to read the typescript of *Forest of Anger*, reluctantly agreed to add it to her pile of manuscripts by 'promising' new writers, and was struck by its originality. She invited the author to *Vogue*'s studios to be photographed for 'Spotlight', and that was how they met. This version is simple, direct and businesslike enough to be convincing. On the other hand it was also a neat sign-off to her interview for *Vogue*'s Golden Jubilee issue, making the magazine responsible for her first meeting with the man who became her new husband, and marrying Romain the reason why she quit as *Vogue*'s features editor. I have gone with her official version, which is romantic but chronologically confusing. Both originated with Lesley. The choice is yours.

When he arrived for their next rendezvous Lesley opened the door to him wearing red sequinned harem trousers and a white silk blouse embroidered with pearls; the baggy wool trousers, she assured him, were a practical measure for keeping warm. The furniture, in similar mode, was mostly in the bedroom: an enormous, rather battered eighteenth-century gold bed, and an Italian baroque table with a scratched marble top. The house's other compelling wartime luxury was a bath with a working supply of hot water, which Romain monopolized, plotting paragraphs in his head.

Both were adventurers on a cusp, ready for change. Like a stray cat Romain found the shortest route to Lesley's hearth and soon moved in, basking in her outlandish domesticity. In a snapshot they sit sunning themselves among rugs and plants dragged outside to the roof terrace, the sash window raised behind them; Lesley is shaded by an absurd little fringed parasol, Romain slouching in a windcheater and slacks. In another snap a relaxed Lesley, wrapped in a crocheted shawl, smiles out past the camera; one hand framing her face is pushed into her curly hair, her elbow on the breakfast table.

She had left Anne Scott-James in possession of the flat at Swan Court and despite the acute housing crisis had like a hunting dog scented out another small but perfectly formed lair. She must have laid siege to its owner, Olivier Wormser, later governor of the Bank of France, before capturing her trophy (or part of it; the upstairs apartment might have been all she could afford). Number 32 St Leonard's Terrace is a delectable eighteenth-century corner cottage in Chelsea village, with its front door, Janus-like, at the side on to Smith Street. It stands westernmost in a block of Georgian brick houses of different heights, all blessed with tall windows, delicate fanlights and perfect proportions. The front looks over small paved gardens, flushed with magnolia and wisteria, to the green expanse of Burton's Court across the road and the bell-towered Royal Hospital beyond. King's Road is a minute's walk to the north and once again she was close to her beloved river.

As ever, the frame in which she set herself was all-important and St Leonard's Terrace gave her scope for self-expression. An inveterate collector of people as well as things, she instantly knew that Romain too was a collector's item, falling into her most prized 'exotic' category. His dark-blue battledress enhanced his strange looks: the startling blue eyes at odds with his matt olive skin and dead-straight blue-black hair flopping untidily from a central parting, the long mournful crooked face that would suddenly light up with malicious glee; his small ineffectual hands that seemed hardly to belong to him until he took hold of a pen and started to write.

For his part, Lesley must have been almost as piquant as he appeared to her. Her blonde curls and pink-and-white colouring were classically English, but reserve was not part of her repertoire. She was in her prime: experienced, passionate, her romantic impulses countered by a subversive sense of the ridiculous. Her personal life in the five rackety wartime years until she met him had been picaresque to the point of risk, yet she combined an impressive social itinerary with a home such as he had hardly experienced. He was invalided out of flying service, away from his comrades, adrift in a foreign country. To the airman billeted for seven years in Nissen huts and worse, Lesley offered a *foyer*, a flagrantly seductive one at that, although Romain seemed unaware of its finer points.

It was hardly a bourgeois household. She might serve up gull's eggs on pretty mismatched plates for breakfast, or bring home the comedienne Beatrice Lillie for a spaghetti supper in the kitchen. Lesley tended to deny her practical side, but she was a deft manager as well as a connoisseur of good things, and a natural entertainer who could turn a plate of sandwiches into a party. The house was a popular port of call for swarms of visitors who clattered over its bare floorboards, intrigued to meet 'Lesley's Frog'. Her friend Edna (later the painter Eden Box) often stayed with her handsome lover, Canadian airman Marston Fleming, and would soon leave her banker husband to marry him. Lesley acquired a ginger cat called Mortimer: she always liked to have animals around her and Romain enjoyed his antics. They were both passionate advocates for animals in general and regarded their pets as distinct individuals on a par with their human friends, forging another bond between them.

As exactly as Lesley remembered what she wore to her second meeting with Romain, she was vague about when they met. She said it was after Romain had started work at the Free French headquarters in Kensington in mid-May, and before the Allied landings in Normandy in early June. But if their meeting is dated by the night bombardments, it couldn't have taken place until *after* the Normandy landings. The first VI flying bombs, Hitler's secret weapon that Churchill had warned about (and dismissed with 'Britain can take it'), were unleashed on London a week after D-Day on 6 June, in reprisal for the Western Front's advance to the Normandy beaches. The chronology in Romain's memoir, *Promise at Dawn*, was (deliberately) even more misleading and he did not mention his meeting with Lesley.

June, at any rate, was a time of high tension, following the months when vast numbers of Allied troops, tanks and aeroplanes massed in southern England in utmost secrecy before the D-Day landings. After the invasion was launched, the nation hung on the news; people queued outside newsreel cinemas to watch footage from the French beaches.

Although this massive show of force by the United States decisively shifted the balance between the Allies, the midwar zeitgeist was still powerfully Russian. For two years, daily news stories had stoked solidarity with the besieged soldiers and civilians who clung with superhuman courage to their ruined cities for month after month, sustaining huge losses until finally, against hideous odds, claiming the defining victory at Stalingrad. Soon after D-Day, dispatches from the East reported an immense new counter-initiative by Russian troops, sweeping the Germans westwards along a front that stretched for hundreds of miles. They were beginning the advance on Berlin.

A week after the Normandy invasion the Germans counter-attacked by sending their new pilotless flying bombs over England. The random explosions of up to a hundred V1s daily over London was unnerving. There would be a tearing sound that cut out, then rose to a roar as it crashed, cutting a deadly swathe of destruction with glass splinters from the blast. Close to St Leonard's Terrace, a round brass plaque is set into the pavement in Turk's Road, 'In memory of almost 100 American GIs and WACs killed at Sloane Court by a German V-1 in 1944.' That hideous explosion could have been the bomb that blew in the windows while Lesley and Romain sat eating breakfast in bed. By then Lesley usually ignored the air-raid sirens and stayed where she was rather than going to the air-raid shelter.

They spoke English together, on Romain's insistence: he wanted to learn the language and picked it up quickly. He enjoyed listening to Lesley's confident, well-modulated sentences and fastened on her turns of phrase. She drew up a whimsical reading list to amuse and instruct him. The onomatopoeic names in Dickens and Beatrix Potter tickled his fancy, and he adored the often spiteful characters and alarming adventures of Squirrel Nutkin, Mr Tod and the like. His favourite was Mrs Tiggy-Winkle (maybe for her surreal ability to change identities and metamorphose from washerwoman into hedgehog and back): Lesley said he later came to read it to calm himself down in times of stress. She recited poems by Blake, Richard Lovelace and Byron to him, and entertained him with Harriette Wilson's outrageous memoirs.

She played Scheherazade to Romain's Shahryar, spinning stories to entice and keep him from straying from home and herself. He was surprisingly ignorant of Russian history, its traditions and legends, and was eager to hear more, so that, far from her picture of her young self listening to the Traveller, Lesley became the storyteller. 'Tell me something. Anything,' he would urge her and then listen, enthralled by the tales from a far country that she had adopted for her own.

He had an obsession with names. Indeed, Lieutenant Romain Gari de Kacew, as he was introduced to her, was not his real name; but then many Free French personnel had adopted a pseudonym in order to protect their families in occupied France from reprisals. Kacew was his real patronymic, he told her. He had chosen a warrior's name: 'Gari' in Russian means 'burn'. Most people called him 'Gary', which Lesley disliked, objecting that it made him sound like a bandleader, but the name stuck. She was far more charmed by the Russian nicknames he gave her, by his way of calling her upstairs with urgent cries of 'Laskov!' or 'Lesloukian!' after her fondness for Armenian rugs. Lovers' nicknames are hardly unusual – but how many other couples spend hours thinking up surnames for themselves, as she remembered she and Romain did?

Who was he, really? Quite soon she ran into discrepancies in his past. The pieces often didn't fit together. She longed to know more, yet far from deterring her, his very elusiveness attracted her, as it had with Komisarjevsky and Pascal. She came to realize that direct questions often received contradictory answers and she gleaned more from unguarded asides when he was not on the defensive. He spoke fluent Russian and could quote Pushkin's *Eugene Onegin* at length in that smoky bass voice, so un-French in timbre. Yet when Lesley introduced him to her good friend Feliks Topolski, the Polish war artist, they broke into Polish – Topolski was tickled when Romain 'addressed me in a rough Warsaw schoolboy's tongue (of the very school which used to fight it out with mine – they tough, we superior)'. Another time when she complained of the cold, Romain snorted and told her she should try Poland in January, where as a small boy he had been sent outside to play in the snow, dressed in short trousers and a little fur coat; 'they' were furriers, he added dismissively.

She could see that for Romain the Run-Away Game was existential. In purely physical terms his first years had been a transition in several stages, a long stopping journey with his mother, Mina, from somewhere unspecified in the East (actually Vilnius in Lithuania) via Warsaw to Nice by the time he was fourteen. He was spectacularly undomesticated, having been brought up from early adolescence in a modest hotel run by his possessive, demanding mother, whose toil and deprivation had paid for his education and training as an air force cadet. From childhood she had instilled in him her fanatical belief in France, haven of democracy and freedom, where she would see her only son reach pinnacles of success as a diplomat and literary genius; it was her voice, he would insist, that he heard urging him to resist France's defeat in June 1940. In 1941 a letter had reached him in central Africa telling him of Mina's death, which allowed her to escape the ignoble deportation of French Jews to death camps by the people whose civilization she had believed in as a child believes in a fairy tale. Romain never mentioned her death to his wartime comrades, but his near-fatal illness in Damascus must have been partly the delayed aftershock of grief.

More important to Lesley than who he was, was what he was: a writer. So adept at spotting talent, she was impressed by his first novel and his ferocious dedication to his work. Just 170 pages long in translation, the episodic narrative combined surreal fantasy with a poetic naturalism quite unlike most wartime documentary fiction. It followed the struggles of a band of mostly Polish partisans trying to keep themselves and resistance alive in the frozen Lithuanian forests surrounding the German-occupied city of Vilnius, during long months when the balance of the war depended on the Russians' epic defence of Stalingrad. Cresset Press had asked Romain to find a more stirring title and soften his bleak ending, which he must have been working on when he met Lesley.

It was a first novel by an unknown author, set in central Europe, larded with Polish, Yiddish and German quotations, and about to be published in translation: unpromising ingredients for a commercial venture. But its Resistance theme and despairing humanism were unusually timely; it had already attracted attention and a chapter was to be published in the influential French exiles' journal, *La France Libre*.

The prospects for *Forest of Anger*, as it was now called, were looking good – almost unnaturally good. Convincing evidence has been unearthed by David Bellos, the author of a monumental forthcoming biography of Gary, of a wartime London seething with spies and secret agents. André Labarthe, founder of *La France Libre*, was in Soviet pay, as was his colleague, Moura Budberg, the former mistress of H.G. Wells and Gorky, who was paid by MI5 while working as a double agent directly for the Kremlin. Counter-propaganda was needed to promote the Soviet war effort since the Americans had stolen the victor's laurels on the Western Front. This prophetic novel, written with heartfelt sincerity by a Free French war hero, could have been ordered for them.

In the unlikely event that Lesley suspected Romain's novel was being used to further the Soviet cause, as a dedicated Russophile she would surely be the last person to care. She was passionately intent on ensuring that *Forest of Anger* and its author won attention and acclaim, by whatever means. She doesn't mention correcting the English translation, as she sometimes did with his later fiction (probably she had no need to; the translation is excellent). But with an eye to publicity she had him photographed by Lee Miller, who took a rare portrait of Romain smiling, and by the celebrated *Vogue* photographer Horst, who caught a grave demeanour. He studied the photograph dispassionately and amused Lesley by remarking on the 'incredible beauty' of his face. Neither Romain nor his novel found their way into Lesley's 'Spotlight', probably because there were too many items for the December issue and something had to be cut.

Forest of Anger came out in time for Christmas sales. Was Lesley surprised by the jacket notes about the author? The blurb announced: 'Lieut. Gary has both Russian and French blood in his veins: he took his university degree in Warsaw and, in fact, served in Poland in 1939.' Not a word of this was true. Romain was anxious to promote himself in the best light for his book's success and reluctant to omit any potentially helpful element. Instinctively he identified with the Polish airmen who took off alongside the Free French at Hartford Bridge, in Spitfires proudly bearing the Polish colours and the slogan 'Wilno 1940', where the Free Polish air force had been born. At the same time he was honour-bound to follow his mother's ambitions for him as a Frenchman. Then again he was swayed by the overwhelming pro-Soviet spirit of the time. Finally, above all, he wanted to please Lesley, who absolutely insisted that he had to be Russian. Landlocked in London, she had met in Romain a man who seemed to embody Russia for her. Why else would his first language be Russian, and his novel about Resistance be framed by the epic struggle in the East (one of his suggested titles was *The Outskirts of Stalingrad*)?

Evidently it was Lesley who clinched Romain's decision to *become* Russian at this formative time in his life. It was as if he was trying out nationalities and identities like so many suits of clothes, to see which fitted him best. He was finding it equally difficult to adapt to civilian dress after nearly eight years protected by his leather flying jacket and uniform. She took him to have a suit made by a Savile Row tailor where they spent ages choosing the material from bolts of flannel and tweed, then had to concede that the svelte fitted English cut was hopelessly wrong for his build.

He surprised her again when they decided to get married early in

1945, a decision which was probably down to Lesley. She came home one evening to find him sitting with his head in his hands in what she called his disaster pose. In a tone of deep despair he warned her that there was something he must explain about himself. With an effort, embarrassed and defiant, he confessed that he was Jewish. In his reluctance to reveal his Jewish ancestry she glimpsed how heavy a burden it was for him.

Lesley was not in the least deterred by the prospect of being a 'goy wife', as he put it when he cheered up, but for her part he *had* to be Russian. The one did not negate the other in her reckoning and a Slav husband was the destiny she had written for herself. That defining obsession of Lesley's must have been strangely familiar to Romain, for it mirrored in reverse his mother's fixation with France. Lesley's 'elective affinity' to Russia, forever defined by Komisarjevsky's influence, was like a force of nature, obvious and unavoidable. It ran through her journalism at the time, proof that feelings can be facts and, as such, impossible to ignore.

For both Lesley and his mother, Romain personified their 'landscape of the heart', although their dreams pulled in opposite directions, as Lesley came to see. Brought up by Mina to revere his adopted homeland and ready to die in its defence, Romain longed above all to be truly French, only to meet Lesley's conviction that he held the reins of her Russian *troika*. Yet the bureaucratic result was that marriage to her chosen Slav had made her a citizen of France. All these conflicting forces were meanwhile overridden by the exigencies of their shared wartime loyalties. Romain and Lesley trod water, waiting for the cresting wave that would move them on.

Conversely, what did Romain know about Lesley? Extrovert and sociable as she appeared, she too fostered secrets. We are left with a one-sided equation, partly because their divorce in 1962 was so acrimonious that Romain wrote her out of his life afterwards. This was cruel but consistent, neither the first nor the last time that he severed links with his past when he moved on to a new life.

Romain's war record and his promise as a writer made him an excellent foil for her. Escorted by her dashing Franco-Slav airman, she sidestepped the need for 'breeding' in the exacting social strata where she continued to mingle for *Vogue*. In grander circles she deftly deployed the brittle, stylized manner that fascinated Romain in the London party world still surviving in the 1940s. At the same time, the war had blown holes in the old niceties; glamour was as at least as important as ancestry and after seven years at *Vogue* Lesley was an expert in the field. In all this she had much to teach him.

Lesley's friend and ally Topolski described in his tortured English the match between her, 'a supreme *précieuse*', and 'this lovely sensitive brute' as 'a harmony of extremes': 'he entered her subtleties smoothly – under his man-of-action uniform a budding *littérateur*'. Theirs was a meeting of two opportunists, *agents provocateurs* who tacitly recognized one another.

Evidence for this is encoded in Romain's novel *Lady L.*, which he wrote in English many years later in Los Angeles. Lesley was extremely attached to this novel, the account of a Pygmalion-like transformation of a lovely guttersnipe into a scion of society elegance, trained to infiltrate circles of money and power by her anarchist lover. Passionately romantic yet calculating, Annette becomes a double agent to save herself and her own, duping the man she loves as well as the aristocracy among whom he has planted her. The confident insouciance that Annette/Lady L. learns to use as her cover is as intrinsic to her personality as her charm, wit and ruthlessness. As the original book jacket (which Lesley designed) suggests, 'a certain form of detached sophistication can be more anarchistic and subversive in its nature than the bombs of the conventional enemies of society'. Of course the thread of impersonation and disguise, which runs through his work, could also be said to describe Romain himself, especially in the French text, which appeared several years later, after he and Lesley had separated. But Lady L's character in the original English version is all Lesley, and the novel's light, spare tone has the precision of true psychological insight.

Soon after they met Lesley took Romain to meet her mother, who became genuinely fond of him, as he did of her. Lesley had found the flat in Richmond for Martha after war was declared and kept a room there for herself, furnished with all the treasures she was reluctant to risk in bomb-prone central London. Romain and his mother had left everything behind in Eastern Europe; he was astounded by evidence of Lesley's past, gazing at childhood mementoes that she had kept, and her mother before her, as extraordinary examples of continuity. She watched him wander round her room, opening a parasol made of

Russian playing cards, leafing through her art books, picking up gros-point cushions showing scenes from her travels, studying the pictures on the walls. There were icons, of course, and lots of portraits, etchings and Victorian photographs, which had mostly been transformed by Lesley: carefully painted over the heads of the originals, the faces of her cats, dogs and birds gazed out at him. Lesley's memoir of Romain recalls her astonishment when he reproduced the room and all its contents in *Lady L.* fifteen years later.

The war had taught Romain that home was a notebook and something to write with. Pushed back into his essential identity, he found it in the creative intelligence with which he viewed the world and transformed his experience into the stuff of fiction. Less obviously, Lesley's inner landscapes were at least as developed as Romain's, although hers were often expressed in her physical circumstances and surroundings. She acquired grand manners with which she held the world at bay and, with her already vivid persona, gave the impression of somebody squarely planted in reality. Yet her theatrical decor and exotic clothes were so many ways of indulging the rich vein of escapism that would also emerge in her writing.

Romain never used the familiar 'tu' or 'toi' to his wife. His 'vous' put her at a distance which she sometimes regretted. It formalized their arrangement, defining its permanence, distinguishing her from other women. She liked her men to be masterful, and Romain, outrageously spoilt by his mother, was used to having everything done for him at home. Notwithstanding the insistent deadlines of her own working life, she flattered his self-importance in a mocking, subversive way, tiptoeing around him teasingly as he wrote.

Her buoyant temperament made her impervious to his descents into wordless depression, which could last for days and affected more impressionable spirits. Sometimes his moods related to his mother: he would rant on about Mina's impossible love that threatened to suffocate him, then be smitten with guilt at his disloyalty. 'Quit the wailing wall,' Lesley would tell him briskly, or 'Can we drop the curtain now?' There was plenty for her to deal with on her own account; she had many friends and her freelance work was about to peak. '*Oh, Lesley est un numéro*, she does what she likes,' he shrugged, baffled.

Her robust health irritated Romain, who suffered from various ailments and injuries which he regarded with a mixture of hypochondria and detached fatalism. He had been badly buffeted internally when his plane was hit in January and he had a hiatus hernia. An infected jaw, on top of the typhoid that had nearly killed him in North Africa in 1942, had left his face frozen on one side, giving him a lopsided smile. Also his nose had never been set properly after a flying accident in 1940, and the crooked septum left him with sinusitis and migraines. In 1944 he had his nose reset in a military hospital, which reduced the worst effects. He bore this stoically, telling Lesley he always knew he would come through – like Sartre, he believed he was preordained to success. Yet she was shocked when he told her once he detested himself so much that he didn't mind suffering: partly a residue, perhaps, of the grief and guilt that burdened him after his mother's death.

Romain had to submit a request to the Air Ministry for permission to marry Lesley. His authorization was duly received in spring 1945. Caught in the cold crosswinds of convention and reality, they both felt a lowering of the spirits, possibly realizing that this was a match between two unmarriageable parties. Romain developed a violent head cold, which Lesley shrewdly diagnosed as a psychosomatic attempt to postpone the event, and he retired to bed. Tramping up and downstairs carrying trays of invalid food, she began to get annoyed. If he was no better by Tuesday, the groom croaked, he wouldn't be able to go through with the ceremony. 'Oh darling, do make an effort. It won't be the same without you,' Lesley replied, then burst into peals of laughter at her own sally.

Neither of them seems to have enjoyed the wedding at Chelsea Register Office on 4 April. Lesley put it down to the banal event, in bleak contrast to her dreams of exchanging crowns in a Russian Orthodox ceremony. There is also a whiff of reluctance on Romain's part, an echo of Byron's disastrous marriage to Arabella. Both bride and groom were the sole offspring of deceased parents; neither family nor friends were present, only their witnesses, Romain's former commanding officer Henri de Rancourt and his English wife Rosemary, who had often offered open house to the Lorraine airmen at Hartford Bridge. Afterwards they lunched in Prunier's, one of the few restaurants in London where fish was still on the menu.

Curiously, they were photographed separately on the day. In the portrait of Lesley she is seated and looking away from the camera, beautiful, rather thin, not happy but very determined. Typically she would capture this expression exactly in her words about a picture of someone else: Laurence Hope, one of the elusive women writers and travellers who were her role models. It was, she wrote, 'the face of a woman who knew what she wanted, sought for it, fought for it, but who knew, too, how to yield: the face of a passionate woman.'

The couple did at least leave a subversive sting in the marriage certificate. Of the seven salient details required of them, on Romain's part his own name (Romain Gary de Kacew) and his father's name, nationality and occupation (Leon Gary de Kacew, French diplomat, deceased) were invented. Admittedly the *nom de guerre* was standard practice, though there was less need for that precaution since France's liberation. Lesley, who hadn't admitted her age to Romain, shaved off three years (she would do so again in her entry to *Who's Who*). She possibly also omitted one marriage, if her later interviews are accurate, although according to the records Robert Alan Wimberley Bicknell, 'from whom she obtained a divorce' (as her marriage certificate to Gary states), was her first husband.

The documents that Romain produced at the register office gave his birthplace as Wilno, Lithuania. Lesley noticed this, but she said she never asked him to explain it. On one level she knew, as she wrote decades later, that he had come from 'a deprived quarter of Eastern Europe' where as a poor Jewish boy, possibly illegitimate, he would have been mocked and bullied by his Polish and Christian classmates. She wrote that he was so vague about his father's identity and his birthplace that she concluded he knew neither where he had been born nor who had fathered him, though she was surprised that his mother had never taken him into her confidence. He often compared his features with those of Ivan Mosjoukine, trailing the notion that the Russian star of the silent screen was his father. He allowed Lesley to believe that he came from Russia; Kursk was mentioned and Mina was probably born there. That was the answer she preferred and chose to accept.

Lesley's acceptance of the lacunae in his past, her understanding for his need for secrecy, allowed him psychological *lebensraum*. They struggled with each other's mythologies; for the time being he accepted her mysteries as she did his, much as Don Quixote and Sancho Panza, at the end of their wanderings, agree to accept one another's claims to have had magical experiences, even if they are sceptical about them.

If he ever confided to her the true facts of his past, she never admitted it. After his death in 1980 she willingly spoke to his biographers, yet never corrected the fictional account of events, which they followed, in his autobiographical novel *Promise at Dawn*. Not until the 1990s, after the Soviet Union's collapse, did researchers in post-Soviet Vilnius confirm that Romain had been born of Jewish parents, in his father's house, in the Lithuanian capital, and that Leib Kacew, who gave Romain his name, was his biological father. These facts were eventually revealed to French readers in the fifth French biography of Romain, published in 2004.

Even so, heroic research failed to establish where Romain lived in early childhood, during the inconceivable turmoil that fragmented and transformed central Europe during and after the First World War. Vilnius changed hands no less than eight times before Romain was ten years old: in 1914 it was part of the Russian empire; by 1923 it had been absorbed as an enclave of Poland. His father was apparently drafted into the Russian army. My own theory is that Mina and Romain escaped from the German-occupied city to Svencyany, her family's home town, surrounded by forests on the borders of Lithuania and Poland, landscapes that repeatedly recurred in his writings. When the war was over they returned to Vilnius, rejoining Romain's father after his release from the army. But Leib soon took up with another woman with whom he had a second family, and the failure of her marriage finally decided Mina to make a new life for herself and Romain in France.

Lesley was never greatly interested in exhuming the early history of the man who had shared her life. She preferred the mixture of myth and reality that Romain created with her and presented to the world. 'Leave him to his legend,' she said.

4

The Columnist

It is impossible to overestimate the importance of the cinema to
my generation.

Anne Scott-James

MEETING ROMAIN COINCIDED with a burst of activity for
Lesley. After seven years she had outgrown *Vogue* and quit the
staff in late 1944, although she continued writing for the magazine
intermittently down the years; her last contribution was for her own
centenary. On 30 December she began a regular column on cinema
and film for *The Leader*, a relaunched weekly journal edited by Charles
Fenby. The former racing paper was radically revamped for a readership starved of intelligent news and feature coverage in the national
dailies, whose pages had been drastically reduced by paper shortages.
Writers, too, needed new outlets; George Bernard Shaw, Rebecca
West, Antonia White, Bertrand Russell, Tom Driberg and A.L. Rowse
were among the contributors.

Cinema was *the* mass medium of the 1940s and most weeks Lesley's
column ran to a couple of thousand words over two close-printed
pages. The essay form suited her; she neither intellectualized nor over-
popularized, but pursued her personal bents. Her best-known piece,
'Red Tape and Blue Pencil: the Autocracy of the Film Censorship',
has been consulted so often at the British Library that the pages are
falling out of the bound copy. Published at the war's end, it was an
energetic attack on the complacency and excessive secrecy with which
the British Board of Film Censors, a non-governmental organization
appointed by the film industry itself, operated.

She countered the 1936 statement by Lord Tyrrell, president of
the Board – that 'to-day's cinema needs continued repression of

controversy in order to stave off disaster' – with a devastating example of the Censors' pre-war contribution to appeasement by cutting scenes of Nazi persecution of Jews in the Soviet film *Professor Mamlock*, so as not to offend Hitler. Lesley described her attempts to get the Board to define its policy, always stonewalled by 'the Voice' on the phone, and listed the more ludicrous categories of what could not be shown or said according to the British Censor and the Hays Code in America. This art form with great progressive potential in the post-war world, she concluded forcefully, should not depend on the dictates of an unelected and secretive junta.

Lesley wrote more often about British cinema than about Hollywood, tackling such subjects as Dickens's perennial appeal to film-makers, the attraction of horror movies, or costume designers' desperate shortage of raw materials. She cited the British film industry's strong showing in reportage and the need for government support in order to compete in the international market. She made an admirable case for toning down Technicolor, as in Olivier's production of *Henry V*, where the pastel-pink and blue costumes still jar today.

Her preoccupation with everything Russian still prevailed, even in the example she used to illustrate her piece on censorship. Although plenty was going on in French cinema for her to write about, her features displayed an obsessive Russian bias, whether in the context of the politics behind films, children on film or children's cinema. Her survey of Russian cinema in February 1945 (probably largely derived from the Russian Cinema in Charing Cross Road) was knowledgeable, informative and stoutly prejudiced in its favour.

As at *Vogue*, her profiles followed a trail of contacts. She made copy out of her friend Eric Ambler, who lived in Kensington with his 'elegant dark' wife Louise, an American fashion illustrator. Ambler had started out in advertising, then turned to fiction after calculating that spy thrillers would pay best. Seven years and six acclaimed novels later, he could claim a dollar a word for serials in the US and turned to writing film scripts. After his daytime war work in the Directorate of Army Kinematography, he moved on to nightclubs, the noisier the better, where she atmospherically evoked his table crowded by talkative Americans: William Wyler, Garson Kanin, John Huston of *Maltese Falcon* fame (all at once?).

At supper with the Amblers Lesley met the director Billy Wilder, whose first Hollywood film *Double Indemnity*, co-written with Raymond Chandler, was a sensational hit. She wrote about him, too: 'The façade is Austrian baroque, but the structure is, I fancy, Pittsburg steel.' She was intrigued by the working partnership between the ebullient, fast-talking Wilder and the academic ex-lawyer Charles Brackett. Another subject was the producer Anatole de Grunwald, whom she must have met during filming of *Major Barbara*: 'His Russian parentage (he was born in Leningrad) gives him that volatile and excessive quality peculiar to that nation.' She added approvingly that he was 'a first class flirt' who conversed like a Wimbledon champion with expert rallies and returns.

As at *Vogue*, Lesley's interviewees were more often the backroom men and women who wove fantasy out of wooden backdrops, greasepaint and sub-standard tulle than the stars themselves. She did vividly evoke a supper at St Leonard's Terrace with the comedienne Beatrice Lillie, who treated them to a new monologue, 'Maud Agreed' ('One not heard here yet'). Lillie made excellent copy, with her hopelessly incompetent timekeeping (missed three consecutive transatlantic liners because she couldn't get up in time for the boat train). Lesley left an indelible image of her proudly modelling her new platinum mink coat; the next second she flung it on the floor, declaring that it looked even better as a rug.

By then Romain was going back and forth to France on his own affairs, but whenever he was in London Lesley introduced him to her friends on the fringes of film – the youthful polymath Peter Ustinov was one such – along with artists and writers. The best thing in Romain's novel *The Colours of the Day* (1953) is a portrait of a mini-mogul, a fraudulent fantasist whose uncertain identity is dissolving in the dream world of film-making. This was years before Romain ever went to Hollywood, so his mysterious behind-the-screen insider's knowledge probably came from their hectic months in London when Lesley was immersed in the cinema.

In August 1945 she stepped up her output with a second weekly column, for the *Daily Mail* every Monday. Her contact there was the books editor, none other than Peter Quennell, who was good at working his way into comfortable literary niches; this was not the only timely introduction she would owe him. Her first 'Private View' appeared on 6 August 1945 and was advertised as a 'new kind of column for women *(men will want to read it, too)*'. She introduced herself as 'a starch-heavy, Spam-weary, coupon-craving creature like almost every other English-woman of today', who after so many wartime directives and duties was surprised if her voice was still her own.

Her subjects reflected post-war preoccupations. After much talk of what sort of woman servicemen want to come home to, what, she demanded, about the sort of man servicewomen want to come home to? On 20 August, the first week of peace after Japan's surrender, she called for the speedy formation of a new world order, and urged that, on a national scale, forces hospitals be turned over to civilian management without delay.

She warned about the effects of the new deadly insecticide from the US, DDT, which could wipe out wild species. This was softened by a surreal vision she had spotted on the Berkshire downs, of nine minute Shetland ponies practising a complete circus routine all by themselves in a field. The team worked professionally during the panto season, she was delighted to report, and regularly ran through their act, pairing off behind the leader, who was known as 'The Master'.

The village she was visiting was Aldworth, where her friend Anne Scott-James had bought a cottage. The following week Lesley wrote about Anne's then husband, the journalist and war reporter Macdonald Hastings, whose 'London Letter' broadcasts had a wide following abroad. She impudently described him as a 'lanky, jumpy, schoolboy creature' in his mid-thirties who was the first journalist to be dropped into the war zone by parachute. Whenever possible, he would head down to the Berkshire cottage to hunt or shoot with 'an emotional spaniel called Ruins'. Lesley added that he liked to hold forth, was a first-rate talker but no conversationalist, and was either rushing around or fast asleep; his wife was 'the only beautiful and able journalist I know'.

A few years later Anne got her own back in her novel *In the Mink*, which leaves a flavour of the 'Amy' (Lesley) and 'Jean-Pierre' (Romain) roadshow:

> towards the end of the war, Amy startled us all by getting married. But having shocked us by this heresy, she relieved us by marrying the only man alive who could have coped successfully with so personal a person . . . . I adored him at sight, but he lived in a state of *Cherry Orchard* gloom.
>
> He never saw a gleam of hope in any quarter. He was constantly ter-

rifying us with descriptions of his stomach condition, which (he said) must kill him within a year. And even as he spoke, he passed his plate up for a third helping of lobster, which he sandwiched in between bortsch soup and a large Welsh rarebit. And the day he sold his first novel on good terms to America he made our flesh creep with stories of the poverty he and Amy would have to face in France, where unemployment, he said, would soar, prices would rocket, and he and she would go starving and naked. 'We shall eat *rats*,' he said, his head sunk in his hands, 'as they did in the siege of Paris, and we shall drink from the sewers.' At this point Amy fainted and had to be brought round with a good swig of wine.

. . . As a husband, Jean-Pierre was both commanding and demanding. His gloom could only be kept within bounds if he had anything he wanted within minutes of thinking of it, so Amy was kept pretty busy staving off his suicide. She referred to him as 'Japanese overlord' and to herself as 'poor little faded paper fan'. My own name for him was the Happy Little Bunny, which used to bring a wan smile to his world-weary face.

Lesley, dashing off two columns a week, reverted to her obsessions. In September, she began with a complaint about a new exhibition at the Whitechapel Gallery, in which every painting tiresomely carried a message, and led into reviewing a new book on Russian painting. She attacked a propaganda-filled picture of Gorky (unable to resist adding that she had once met him) standing in the Collective Bakery, as bad art, preferring Kustodiev's 'atmospheric genre painting of fat, greedy, oily priests sitting round the samovar, in the stuffy, ikon-lit depths of an old provincial inn'. How many *Daily Mail* readers would be interested in genre paintings of 'oily priests sitting round the samovar' is not recorded.

On a more mainstream note, she complained about the quarantine laws, a perpetual grievance of hers, on behalf of a soldier home from overseas whose mascot dog was impounded. And against knee-jerk complaints about the record-breaking divorce figures, she argued feelingly from experience, after her divorce from Robert Bicknell in 1941, that slow, costly legal procedures made it extremely hard for couples to take divorce lightly.

The Foreign Secretary had appointed a committee to look into employing female diplomats. What about their husbands, she asked?

Listing all the usual feminine requirements of tact, discretion, and domestic accomplishments, she added that in case the male spouse might fall for another woman and give away secrets of national security, there must be no gossip about work to him at home, where his priority should be his hard-working wife's comfort.

She aired strong views on food: Britain had plenty of excellent raw materials, but its preparation was a disgrace. Although Lesley did not credit Constance Spry, whose wartime cookery book she had illustrated, she was a convert to Spry's pioneering campaign to improve English cooking. In one of her postscripts (headed 'Hashish Corner') Lesley announced that she was going to send a parcel to friends in America, packed with wartime rations she had come to loathe: 'Spam, dried egg, powdered milk, dehydrated vegetables, desiccated soups, *Forever Amber* . . .'

A new reprint of Dostoievsky's *Crime and Punishment* reminded her of her friend Rodney Ackland's forthcoming dramatization for Robert Helpmann. While working on it, Ackland would wander round to borrow books from Lesley's Russophile collection and would then act out his latest scene with blood-curdling realism, staggering drunkenly and fingering the meat cleaver.

By October, she was beginning to get a rough response from readers. She urged those who wrote her 'pogrom-minded letters on the subject of Hampstead refugees' to send in more, because she enjoyed burning them. Her column must have been commissioned partly on the strength of her contacts, but Lesley's views on who was who differed from those of the *Daily Mail*. Apparently she was urged to write up her social diary, which she did for a few weeks in lacklustre fashion.

Then her report on a lunchtime interview with Helena Rubinstein appeared on 11 November. The reigning queen of cosmetics had been born in Krakow, so fell into Lesley's starred Slav category, and better still, had just visited Russia. Together they mourned the loss of icons to war damage and discussed their common passion for junk. The grandly wrinkled Rubinstein declared herself uninterested in conventional beauty or facelifts. Lesley enthused over the fortunes she had made by her business acumen and 'masculine force', and finally dwelt ecstatically on Rubinstein's armoury of jewels: on her wrists alone she wore six strands of 'pink and grey pearls and cabuchon emeralds'.

'Thieves don't like my stuff,' Rubinstein remarked carelessly. 'It's too much recognizable.'

Lesley's breathless admiration for the tough Jewish businesswoman and her outsize sparklers was apparently a column too far for the *Mail*'s commissioning editor. A blazing row must have ensued, for the following week the paper appeared without Lesley's column or any comment on its absence. She might have used disagreement over her piece as an excuse to leave, for something else was always on the horizon. This time it was Romain's career.

Romain had not wasted his year working at Carlton Gardens. Lesley quickly learnt that no matter what diversions were dangled before him, the will to write ran through him like steel thread, fame being the great incentive. In late 1944, *Forest of Anger* was accepted for publication in France, ironically titled *Education européenne*. Romain's novel had been overtaken by historical events, however. By then Vilnius, and Poland as a whole, had been occupied by Red Army tanks, but far from being liberated as he had hopefully forecast in his English epilogue, Polish partisans had been rounded up by Soviet police and shot or deported. Poland had been part of the trade-off agreed by Churchill and Roosevelt with Stalin as the price for Allied victory. Romain was appalled; but between late 1944 and March 1945, he rewrote his novel, removing the Polish emphasis and 'Europeanizing' it to fit harsh political reality. The revised novel suited the communist-heavy French Left very well. For Romain, intent on protecting his unchanging moral theme of despairing humanism, the core of his book remained the same.

In 1959 the novel would be republished in the United States and in the UK after Romain had again rewritten it, this time adapting it to the height of the Cold War. It was the first of many examples in which Romain manipulated his fiction according to language, place and historical circumstances. He would do likewise with the myths he projected of himself.

When the book came out in June 1945, Romain sent a copy to Albert Camus, who worked for the prestigious publishing house Gallimard. Camus recognized the moral vision in the novel and his generous reply made Romain weep with joy. *Education européenne* hit a sensitive nerve in France at the war's end, when the nation urgently needed a healing image in its recovery from the bitter years of occupation. The reviews were almost unanimous: 'This is a literary event.' . . . 'Not a novel of the Resistance but *the* novel of the Resistance.' . . . Romain had already had the satisfaction of seeing *Army of Shadows*, the Resistance novel by his hero Joseph Kessel, advertised on the back of his own English edition. Now he had the exquisite pleasure of receiving Kessel's unstinting praise: 'In the last ten years, ever since we first heard the names of Malraux and Saint-Exupéry, there has not been a novel in French fed by a talent as deep, new, and brilliant as this one.'

Romain was staggered by the collective response, which was propelling his novel towards the autumn's prestigious literary prizes: the Prix des Critiques and the Prix Goncourt. Meanwhile he was about to be demobbed and urgently needed paid work to supplement his writing. He wrote to André Malraux, de Gaulle's new minister of information in the provisional government and another writer-hero for Romain, setting out his achievements: the book, his war record, his knowledge of languages. His wife was ill and couldn't move from England (in fact Lesley must have been about to start her *Daily Mail* column); could Malraux help him with 'un job à Londres'? A plan to appoint Romain as cultural adviser to the French ambassador in London was set in motion, but was vetoed by Gaston Palewski, close adviser to General de Gaulle, on the grounds that Gary was too young and inexperienced. (Palewski, Nancy Mitford's beloved 'Colonel', was an inveterate womanizer, prompting the wholly unsubstantiated suspicion that he might resent the presence on his turf of a potent younger man with a fine war record and literary promise.)

Romain had to find another way of joining the closed ranks of the Quai d'Orsay. He had not gone unnoticed by the new regime in France, as one of only five of the Free French Air Force Squadron's original 113 volunteers to have survived the war. He was promoted to captain in March 1945. That summer he was presented with the Cross of the Liberation and received the Legion of Honour from General de Gaulle under the Arc de Triomphe. Romain was intensely proud of his decorations, mourned his dead comrades and kept in touch all his life with his fellow Companions of the Liberation. The distinction had been created by de Gaulle to reward their wartime loyalty, which for Romain was permanent and unconditional.

Under de Gaulle's provisional post-war regime, the French diplomatic service was to be part purged of its collaborationists and opened up to allow applications from Free Frenchmen who had helped to liberate their country. Romain was invited to apply and on 25 October was appointed to the external department of the Ministry of Foreign Affairs. His knowledge of Slav languages seems to have cancelled out the disadvantage of his French naturalization (even after the war the diplomatic corps was uncomfortable with Jews; Romain was urged to keep his assumed name rather than his Jewish patronymic).

Meanwhile the judges' panels for the literary prizes were boiling up to a decision. Hearing that he was tipped for both, Romain hoped for the more celebrated Goncourt, which promised a bigger allowance of precious paper, boosting sales for the winner. The awards were swayed by political considerations in the fractious post-war climate. The previous Goncourt winner had been a Russian communist, and in the continuing power struggles between Gaullists and communists there was opposition to a successive prizewinner from a similar background. By that time, too, public opinion had swung away from the Soviet Union, whose armies now occupied Eastern Europe. Romain came to regret his compulsively fanciful biographical notes, which stated that he had been born in Kursk to a Russian father and a French mother. On 7 November he was consoled by the Prix des Critiques, which brought him 100,000 francs and nationwide recognition.

In the space of a month he had acquired a career with excellent prospects at the Quai d'Orsay and become a fêted literary figure. What was more, he was following a well-established select tradition of writer-diplomats in France, from Stendhal onwards. Romain Kacew, denied an officer's stripes in 1939 because he was a too-recent immigrant, had proved his French citizenship with his war record and now joined the elite who would represent a liberated France abroad. Moreover, his first book was among France's foremost post-war bestsellers, highly praised by the writers he most revered. It was exactly as his mother had predicted. As his friend René Agid reflected later, plenty of Jewish mothers boast of a glorious future for their sons; Romain was exceptional in possessing not only the talent but also the ambition and force of will to achieve it.

★

Little more than a year earlier, when Lesley first met Romain, he had been rootless and unknown with no definite prospects. In the autumn of 1945, her husband – she enjoyed referring to him in this way – was a much-decorated war hero who had landed a highly acceptable career: two, in fact. New horizons beckoned, which for Lesley were infinitely desirable. Most women who by their own efforts had risen as high or as fast as she had in the space of a few years, starting from nothing, would have mourned their lost careers. Yet far from clinging to her journalistic successes and scandals, she was chafing to leave Fleet Street and London. Like Becky Sharp, she far preferred the prospective gains of wedlock to the hard-earned wages of toil. Providence would surely intervene and bring to Romain a posting to a remote oriental country, preferably one with a different alphabet. She would live in the grand manner as a diplomat's wife, no longer obliged to scribble for a living.

Apart from saying goodbye to her mother, the most painful aspect of leaving was moving out of St Leonard's Terrace. They left poor Mortimer in the garden; he had met with a traffic accident and was buried with due honours. In her luggage Lesley packed his portrait, commissioned by Romain, with the ginger cat's furry face, limbs and tail meticulously painted over a Victorian photograph of a small boy in petticoats. She still had it fifty years later in Garavan.

Tearfully they locked up the house and set off for Paris. The Run-Away game had started in earnest, though they had no idea where Romain's first posting would be.

5

En Poste

And indeed the most coldly calculating people do not have half
the success in life that comes to those rightly blended personalities
who are capable of feeling a really deep attachment to such persons
and conditions as will advance their own interests.

Robert Musil, *The Man Without Qualities*

I N AN IDIOSYNCRATIC piece for *Vogue* written at the end of the
war, Lesley mused on cities and the era that best represented them:
Pushkin's St Petersburg, Regency London and so on. Paris was the
exception that proved her rule. 'I wonder,' she reflected with more
prescience than she realized. 'Does Paris reflect, or absorb? Either way,
its flexibility is unique. It belongs to all time.'

The post-war reality was altogether more sombre than she had
imagined. National jubilation after the 1944 liberation had evaporated
to reveal the French people deeply divided by the war. Lesley, who
had wholeheartedly embraced the Free French cause, was dismayed to
encounter a dubious aspect of that famous flexibility in the 'terrible
discretion' among people about their experience under occupation. In
general, those who had suffered tended not to speak about it, while
those who were suspect spent hours justifying themselves.

Baron Élie de Rothschild, released from prison camp, returned to
the Rothschild town house in Paris, which had been the official billet
of a Luftwaffe general. Rothschild remarked to the old family butler,
Félix, that the house must have been very quiet under General
Hanesse's occupation.

'On the contrary, Monsieur Élie. There were receptions every evening.'
'But . . . who came?'
'The same people, Monsieur Élie. The same as before the war.'

Later, Lesley would come to know Élie de Rothschild well in Paris. For the time being, away from her throng of friends and acquaintances, she had to get used to an unaccustomed isolation with Romain. The splendid Hôtel Bristol in the rue Saint-Honoré where they were billeted was cold and dark; in December, electricity supplies were limited to morning or afternoon and were fitful at night. Hot water was so scarce that at bedtime they left the hot tap turned on and if the splutter of gushing water woke them they would leap up for a bath, whatever the hour. On the other hand, after strict rationing in London, they were astounded to find plenty of cream, eggs and other unheard-of luxuries.

Paris had not been kind to Romain when he was a law student there in the 1930s, burdened by his immigrant status as a Jew from Eastern Europe, poor, hungry and trying to write. Although avid to return to his adopted country after the war, he was still a foreigner in the city, where he had to adapt to a new civilian role. He met up with Camus, and with Sartre and de Beauvoir in the cafés of Saint-Germain-des-Près, but he was an outsider amid the post-war literary ferment ('Qu'est-ce que ça veut dire "existentiel, existentialisme"?' he wrote to Raymond Aron). Lesley was indignant at his reception at the Quai d'Orsay, where the notoriously Vichyist *ancien régime* was not unduly cordial towards a naturalized Frenchman. His modest appointment as embassy secretary, second grade, was followed by an anxious pause as he waited for his first posting.

Romain had few friends in Paris aside from René and Sylvia Agid, who were quick to welcome Lesley and enjoyed her company. René, a hard-working doctor, had become a close friend of Romain's when they were at school together at the *lycée* in Nice, where his father was proprietor of the magnificent Hermitage Hôtel. René and his Swedish wife Sylvia had made a foursome with Romain and Sylvia's friend Christel Söderlund, Romain's first serious girlfriend. Christel had left Romain and returned to her husband and small son in Sweden, but Sylvia, an Olympic athlete and talented designer, had stayed to marry René and bring up their two sons in France. Cosmopolitan, clever and as spiky as Lesley in conversation, Sylvia was one of few long-standing allies who could tease and criticize Romain freely yet fondly.

Other than the Agids, Lesley's chief memory of that time was of wandering with Romain through cold, unlit streets, forever getting lost (she marvelled at his wartime role as a precision-bombing navigator) in search of one artist's studio after another. They would perch for hours on packing cases in attics, freezing or stifling by turns, while each painter dragged out every single canvas for their inspection. Lesley interpreted this as Romain's romantic archetype of Paris, where artists starved for their vocation in Montmartre garrets.

Having to consider a dependent wife was as alien to Romain as being one was to Lesley. Dismayed by this unpromising start to their life abroad, for the first of many times during their fifteen-year marriage she took evasive action. She returned to London where she still had her weekly film column for *The Leader* to write, her mother to see, friends to catch up with and packing to do. Packing was a serious business for Lesley, who routinely travelled with a large trunk (a Turkish marriage trunk, it was claimed), containing such essentials as a toile de Jouy quilt, rug and/or drapery, a silver teapot, candlesticks, books and an icon or two to contrive a decor even in a train sleeping car.

She was in England when Romain telephoned to tell her he had been posted to Sofia, Bulgaria. The call came through on 14 December, so she had been with him in France for only a month before escaping home again.

An Eastern European posting was to be expected, given his background and language qualifications, which he had possibly embellished in his application. His low-grade status on the bottom rung of the administrative diplomatic ladder was disappointing; but Lesley was delighted by the prospect of Bulgaria, a corner of the Balkans virtually unknown to European visitors and well on the way to Russia, close to her desired horizons.

Urging Lesley to join him as soon as possible, Romain left on a long and tortuous journey by plane, boat and train via Algiers, Benghazi, Cairo, Ankara and Istanbul. On arriving in Sofia he quickly immersed himself in the rapidly shifting arena of Balkan politics. Bulgaria was exceptional in Eastern Europe in having regarded Russia as its traditional ally since the 1870s, when tsarist troops had fought beside Bulgarian patriots for independence against Ottoman rule. During the war King Boris had been tempted by Hitler's offer of Macedonia to side with the Reich, but Soviet troops had routed the Nazis in 1944 and were now embedded in Bulgaria, leaving British and American members of the tripartite Allied Control Commission powerless to prevent communist encroachment.

Although he was only a junior ranking member of the French legation in Sofia, Romain's cosmopolitan background, quick wits and sensitive antennae for character and atmosphere made him a natural candidate for diplomacy. A Slav polyglot, he picked up Bulgarian quickly; he could speak Russian to the Soviet occupiers and, thanks largely to Lesley, English to the British and Americans. He also found the unselfconscious beauty of Bulgarian women very much to his taste.

Thrilled though Lesley was with Romain's posting, she was strangely slow to set off to follow him. She recalled that on hearing he was leaving Paris, she hurried there herself and stayed with the Agids while waiting for her instructions to join her husband in Bulgaria. Her journalism, however, tells a different story. She must have spent Christmas with her mother in London, and her columns appeared regularly in *The Leader* until mid-January, when a footnote said she was having a few weeks away – an odd way to sign off before leaving the country altogether. But then her pages returned in mid-March to report on a 'busman's holiday spent cinema-going in France and Switzerland', although she wrote as much about Switzerland's 'almost exasperatingly smug' atmosphere, as about the movies there. Her last article, on religion in film, appeared on 20 April.

Lesley and Romain could conceivably have gone to Geneva together before he left, to visit François Bondy, another good friend from his schooldays in Nice. If she went on her own later, which seems more likely, her detour seems like a declaration of independence in view of its timing. It was not essential for her writing, since she had to work the visit into her film column. Did she go to visit Bondy, possibly to consult him and complain about Romain's wayward behaviour so soon after their marriage? Unlike most of Romain's friends, Bondy continued to speak fondly of Lesley after their divorce and insisted on crediting her influence on Romain when he began writing in English.

She also made time to judge the textile impresario Zika Ascher's competition for young designers, sitting on a panel of experts alongside Anne Scott-James (by then editor of *Harper's Bazaar*), Audrey Withers from *Vogue*, and the artists Graham Sutherland and Henry Moore. Meanwhile she besieged Romain with letters appealing for advice about what household essentials she should bring out with her, virtually everything being in short supply. Romain, who had no concept of domestic arrangements beyond unpacking his clothes in the gloomy apartment that the Legation had found for them, left her none the wiser.

Lesley's journey was as roundabout as Romain's and she dallied on the way, drawing it out even further. René and Sylvia saw her off with all her trunks and baskets on the packed train from the Gare de Lyon to Marseilles where she arrived, exhausted, only to find that the Romanian boat on which she had booked a berth would not embark for days. The hotels were full of American soldiers and she had nowhere to stay. Seeing her burst into tears, the porter struggling with her baggage told her he would take her to a place in the Canebière, run by a friend of his. This turned out to be a *maison de passe*, run by a well-built madam in curlers who was delighted to put up Lesley, a Free French serviceman's wife, and sat on the bed beside her chatting for hours. Lesley stayed there until the boat embarked on its three-week meandering voyage around the coast of Greece and the Levant.

On board she flagrantly enjoyed the attentions of a Turkoman jewel merchant, an ardent admirer who introduced her to his friends at every port and took her round the markets whose aromatic heaps of Mediterranean plenty left her giddy with pleasure. Was it Abdul, or a friend of his, who first told her the story of Aimée Dubucq de Rivery, the convent girl from Martinique who was kidnapped by Corsairs, sold to the imperial harem and said to have become Kadine, then mother of the sultan? Aimée would eventually reappear as one of Lesley's quartet of heroines in *The Wilder Shores of Love*.

The voyagers arrived at Istanbul by the Marmara at twilight, romantically 'sidling round under the point of the harbour with the silhouette of the Blue Mosque'.

Having finally reached the Orient that had beckoned to her all her life, Lesley was in no hurry to leave, despite surprised messages from Romain asking why she was taking so long. All her senses were sated. She charmed her way into the Topkapi palace, years before it was invaded by tourists, and was overwhelmed by her first encounter with oriental architecture. Its new language of beauty was a defining revelation to Lesley. She responded powerfully to the dynamic aesthetic in the Islamic arts: the arabesques of abstract pattern endlessly repeated in mosaics and inlays, harmonizing with the sensuous textures of embroidered textiles and carpets as fine as painted miniatures. Here was the real start of her fascination with the Islamic East that came to rival her obsession with Russia. The aftershock of that mesmeric pull on her imagination became the driving force behind her first book. *The Wilder Shores of Love* is saturated with the allure of the Orient's visual and cultural forms, as well as its eroticism, that Lesley felt, in love, in Istanbul.

She prowled through the kitchens, mosques, libraries and state rooms, the fabulously ornate pavilions and kiosks, the harem, the sultan's quarters and, above all, Sultan Murad's room, to her 'the most beautiful room in the world'. She marvelled at the gilded canopied beds and marble fountains. Together with the Kremlin, the Topkapi palace was for her the apotheosis of voluptuous beauty, artistry and infamous cruelty that had held her in thrall since childhood. Lesley's orientalism was of a very particular cast; it was so to speak site specific. She was possessed by the history of power, seduction, secrecy and intrigue that haunted the hidden rooms and gardens of the seraglio. She revisited it again and again in print. In *Wilder Shores* the elusive French sultana, Aimée Dubucq de Rivery, is less a subject than an excuse for Lesley to dwell on the exquisite surroundings in which she was imprisoned as the sultan's favourite. *The Sabres of Paradise, Pavilions of the Heart*, magazine articles, her cookbooks, and especially her portraits of Pierre Loti, all returned to the counterpoint of its rigorous purity, extravagant splendours and blood-soaked history.

In the streets of Istanbul, Lesley recklessly indulged herself in the food markets and pastry shops. Her cookbooks linger over memories of crossing the Bosporus for romantic breakfasts on the Asiatic side, although the circumstances vary. In *Round the World in Eighty Dishes* her trysts were held in a rococo kiosk in the grounds of a summer villa, where to the sound of lapping wavelets they munched through exotic feasts rounded off by fruit, pastries and tea from the samovar – she added that it took her all day to recover. In *From Wilder Shores* she was taken inland by horse-drawn carriage to a yellow house and garden next to one of the Turkish graveyards that she found so expressive. There she met her lover over Caravan Tea brewing (again) in the samovar, fruit and a dish of rich clotted cream made from buffalo milk, served with wild honey.

At last she tore herself away to complete her journey in the local overnight train, devoured by insects, arriving at Sofia the following morning. Romain seemed in unusually good spirits, which were soon explained when she heard that he had plunged into an affair with Nedi Trianova, the daughter of a Bulgarian diplomat. His superiors disapproved, since Nedi was widely suspected of being a spy for the Bulgarian secret service. Lesley, still under the spell of Abdul and Istanbul, confounded the gossips with her laissez-faire response. Instead of berating Romain she befriended his beautiful mistress, who in return was unfailingly helpful in finding supplies of all the household necessities that Romain had failed to tell Lesley to bring with her.

Both Romain and Lesley had just emerged from a long and arduous war. Both enjoyed rapacious appetites for what they desired and neither was used to deferring to anybody else. Like many a traveller before and since, their escape from home or barracks to oriental zones and warmer climates unleashed a surge of unbridled indulgence. Travelling separately, each joyfully slipped the leash and seized whatever opportunity presented itself. Then when they came together again, they had to find a way of living with it.

Lesley was intensely feminine in character and relied on a courtesan's charms to get her own way. She wanted Romain and she wanted the life he offered. She had achieved the improbable feat of marrying him, but what she could not do was force him to be faithful. Her ecstatic affair in Istanbul was probably partly a response in kind to earlier adventures of his. The fact that she so quickly accepted his liaison with Nedi implies that such things were not new to her, even so early in their lives together.

The age difference between them was an inescapable fault line in the marriage. Lesley was ten years older than Romain and her character had been 'formed' since childhood, as she herself conceded; she was biddable only when she chose to be. There was no question of their starting a family. Lesley was already forty when they met, and was emphatically unmaternal where children were concerned. It would be wrong to put a mother-son gloss on the relationship between Lesley and Romain, but that 'almost maternal' possessiveness that he described in *Lady L.* was one of the ties that bound him to her.

What Romain wanted from Lesley was less obvious. He had written to a friend, cynically, that he had got married, 'as one does'; but he was often cynical in letters to his friends. He had told Lesley early on of his great love, Ilona, the beautiful grey-eyed Hungarian girl who had lodged at the Hôtel Mermonts, before returning to her parents. She was delicate in health, always dressed exquisitely, and wore the finest silk stockings, he told Lesley, who was annoyed to hear this in wartime when austerity forced her to make do with wrinkled cotton. He had lost touch with Ilona during the war. If ever he found her, he said, she must come to live with them, to which Lesley, in the early transports of romance, had cheerfully agreed.

He had also made it clear that his sexual preference was for young women, explaining that his fantasies were about really young girls. Lesley refused to be shocked. After all she was a connoisseur of talented rotters, having already survived a tough apprenticeship with Komisarjevsky, and recovered enough to seduce his son, not to mention her interlude with 'the strange Hungarian', Pascal. She preferred marriage to Romain despite his vagaries to life without him – which is not at all to say that she did not object to the vagaries. His betrayals were extremely painful for someone as proud and wilful as herself. At the same time he depended on her, too, and the key to this lay in the pattern they set for themselves in Bulgaria.

In Sofia they lived at first on the wide straight Ulitza Christo Botev, dominated by the massive bulk of Mount Vitosha looming to the south. Sofia was still tiny, having been promoted to Bulgaria's capital city only seventy years earlier after national independence. Children played in the main streets where cars were almost unknown, and cavalry troops and carts drawn by oxen or buffalo clattered over the cobbles. A few blocks away church, mosque and synagogue stood only yards from one another, proof of Ottoman tolerance on spiritual matters during centuries of Turkish rule.

Both Lesley and Romain were drawn to the country, to its mingling of East and West and the open-heartedness they met in its people. Uniquely in Eastern Europe, Bulgaria had escaped the wartime frenzy of anti-Semitism; most of its sizeable Jewish population had survived after mass demonstrations in their support, and gipsies, too, now returned as a large minority. But Romain was appalled to observe the deteriorating political situation, which he later invoked as vividly as Lesley described their surroundings. King Boris had died and his young son Simeon ruled with a coalition government, but it was dominated by the Communist Party. By 1945 the real head of state was the Bulgarian returned from Moscow whom Romain described as 'the legendary George Dimitrov, hero of the Reichstag fire trial, who Hitler hadn't dared to execute'. Dimitrov, head of Comintern, the Communist International between the wars, was by then mortally ill and so pale that he had to rouge his face before he appeared in public.

At the Union Club in the city centre, Romain met the last Bulgarian liberals, lingering between unpalatable options of flight to the West, prison or death. He befriended their courageous Francophile leader, Nicolas Petkov, who was convinced that America would protect them from being swallowed by the USSR. Romain tried to warn them not to expect such help; to his despair he would soon be proved right.

During this contradictory time, at once depressing and exhilarating, Lesley flung herself into transforming their gloomy apartment, turning lace curtains dyed with cherry juice into tablecloths and damask tablecloths into curtains, hanging icons and curiosities. Ottoman-Balkan interiors, with their low divans set round the walls and richly patterned kilims, became a basic vocabulary in her decor for the rest of her life. In her travel writing she avoided the obviously picturesque folk elements so distinctive to Bulgaria, but she would have hunted out fragments of the embroidered textiles used in the wonderfully variegated peasant costumes. Bedbugs made their presence felt, migrating from the crowded flat below; after the initial horror wore off Lesley claimed that she 'quite enjoyed picking them out of my lacey bedjacket before going to sleep'. When they entertained, Nedi's mother came to the rescue with tablecloths and cutlery.

Lesley became almost as fond of Nedi as was Romain, despite their well-founded suspicion that she was passing information to Bulgarian intelligence; she had to earn enough to keep herself, both parents, her sister and a cat called College Boy, all living with her in a two-room flat. Nedi became a household fixture, their one precaution being to avoid talking about anything confidential in her company. Eventually she fell in love with another French diplomat and sometimes they made up a foursome, although these arrangements were complicated by a jealous wife. Once the quartet stole a brief holiday together on the shores of the Black Sea. After Romain was posted elsewhere Lesley kept in touch with Nedi and she came to visit them in France.

They acquired a Macedonian cook-maid, Raiina, who padded

about the kitchen barefoot and was an erratic worker. One or several children could usually be found loitering near the fridge, and her husband regularly delivered their voracious baby to be fed, so guests would be ushered in by Raiina with Borislav clamped to one breast. She soon learnt to disarm Lesley with dramatic stories of gypsy rituals, performing bears, Raiina's wild Bashi-Bazouk uncle and so on, exchanged in an unholy mix of languages that left Romain and Nedi helpless with laughter. Friends persuaded Lesley to install a Polish housekeeper to restore order, but she soon became bored and reinstated Raiina, relishing the barely controlled chaos.

Eager as she was to move from their sinister flat, Lesley was aghast to hear that a major political purge would soon leave better places available. When their transfer came through, Raiina arranged for a pair of gipsy removal men to deal with the furniture. Watching the barefoot Tziganes dextrously pile everything into a van was entertaining enough until Lesley realized they were going to leave it all in the van overnight, with the result that she and Romain had nowhere to sleep. She had to bribe one of them to set up the bed in the new flat, which he did with much ribald prodding of mattresses and bouncing on bedsprings.

In Sofia they learnt the business of diplomatic entertaining. When he chose Romain could be hugely charming and a brilliant conversationalist; but he was impatient with small talk, as a non-drinker never learnt to pour alcohol in proportion to its strength and, when sunk in 'Slav gloom', could be silent for days on end. Lesley, on the other hand, enjoyed the niceties of diplomatic protocol and Becky Sharp like again, observed them meticulously ('Don't forget, always curtsey to the papal nuncio'). She was an iconoclast who embraced tradition while rejecting convention. She *liked* standing on ceremony, however mockingly; it reassured her of her status as a French diplomat's wife *en poste*, and her flair for socializing was unfazed by formal receptions. Lesley's piquant conversation, Carmen-Miranda table settings of fruit and foliage and taste for ethnic cooking all raised their entertaining several notches above conventional table talk, floral sprays and bland diplomatic cuisine.

Lesley civilized Romain, smoothing over his disregard for formalities. She made a frame, at once bohemian and worldly, which displayed them together, whatever their separate exploits. Her rococo Russo-Turkish scene-setting and the domestic dramas of Raiina and

Nedi added to the overall effect. It was zany, camp, definitely not *comme il faut*: a vivid extension of herself. It was misinterpreted by the French: Lesley was deeply offended when one of Romain's biographers described her crowded, glittering decor as kitsch. Lesley's style was harmonious in its excess, *her* taste, never bad taste. Her husband tended to shrug off their fanciful home surroundings as one of his wife's eccentricities. Yet for Romain, the hermit crab, it was oddly soothing for being so clearly Lesley's personality that was on show, not his. Her flamboyant confidence hid his uncertainty; it was part of the glue that held them together for so long.

Her gift for self-presentation in its various forms was advantageous for his career, as they were both aware. Less obviously, it added depth and colour to the persona of the cosmopolitan war hero-writer-diplomat that he was building for himself. In time he came to resent his debt to Lesley and like his hero Malraux, who never mentioned his first wife's central role in (and funding for) his Far Eastern adventures, Romain erased his ex-wife from his memoirs. Hardly a mention of Lesley or their fifteen-year marriage can be found in *La Nuit sera calme* or in his later docufiction. In a way he did her a favour, for his silence allowed her to preserve the secrecy about herself that she preferred. His discretion left her the option to reveal herself only when she wanted, and then only as much as she found useful.

There was another postscript. Decades later, friends were sceptical when Lesley told them that Romain had visited her in Menton not long before his death, and had urged her, 'Make me another home like this.' Why should she lie? He meant what he said literally: he wanted her to create a home for him to live in. He sought somebody else's shell, expressing another personality, for his fragmented self.

Paradoxically in view of Cold War politics, the only receptions where everybody relaxed in the inevitable diplomatic round were at the Russian embassy. Vodka flowed freely and army officers served enormous wash-bowls of caviar with blinis – once Romain ate so many that he made himself ill and had to be taken home. The frostiest Western diplomats melted when the Russians spontaneously burst into song, or joined hands to dance an energetic *horo* and even, once, a Slav version of the 'Sir Roger de Coverley', joyfully led by Lesley.

Fraternizing with the Soviets was frowned on by their fellow diplomats, especially the Americans, and especially given the couple's close connections with Nedi. Lesley took a different view. Where others avoided Red Army officers as carriers of the Communist virus, she engaged with friendly Slavs from eternal Russia. She continued to practise her halting Russian with them, which was useful when she came to apply for the special permits needed to travel outside Sofia. She left agonizing about politics to others, apart from helping individuals as best she could. Her penchant for doomed heroism was satisfied by the leaders of the 1876 rising against the Turks that began in Koprivshtitsa's Street of the First Shot. The Bulgarian patriots were even more inept at organization than the Russian Decembrists and accordingly met hideous fates ('Dashed his own brains out against a wall,' Lesley claimed approvingly of one). She was the first to admit that she saw the place through a prism of the past. It was part of the paradox of Lesley that an opportunist living so energetically in the present could so ardently inhabit the nineteenth century.

She and Romain bore Sofia's extremes of heat and cold stoically, huddling indoors in sheepskin coats and fur shakos when snow was deep and fuel was short. In high summer they escaped the dusty streets for the Black Sea where the legations and military missions had requisitioned villas fringing the coast, long before the empty beaches were developed for tourism. On one visit Romain and Lesley found Euxinograd, the neo-French chateau built by Ferdinand of Bulgaria, and Queen Marie of Romania's tiny summer palace at Balcic. Euxinograd was 'Arcadia and Ruritania in one'; the royal gardens, dropping down the hill to the water, were still tended and bathers could reach up to pick warm, ripe grapes from vines overhanging the sea.

Marie's three-room summer pavilion inspired Lesley's monograph about Romania's dashing English queen, granddaughter of Queen Victoria and the reforming tsar, Alexander II. Patriotic, heroic, with a high if sometimes misplaced sense of destiny, Marie adored dressing up in order to live the part, whether in peasant costume, nurse's uniform or 'basic Balkan Royal'. Lesley was brilliant at choosing subjects with whom she could identify: 'She was undoubtedly narcissistic – delighted with herself – but not self-satisfied. There is a great difference.' 'She always loved to express herself through rooms and houses. She had many.'

Wandering through the abandoned rooms at Balcic, Lesley paused in the octagonal bedroom, which since the war had been commandeered by politicians and military supremos for nights and weekends of pleasure. She mused wistfully that by the time we come to create and savour such a gloriously romantic 'frame for loving', we have lost the passionate spontaneity that inspired it. Twenty years later the fancy was echoed in *Journey into the Mind's Eye*, when the teenaged Lesley, on holiday in Corsica with the beloved Traveller, ardently wishes them altogether elsewhere, together on the Trans-Siberian. He will have none of it: '*Pussinka dousha*, don't you know yet, that Gallantry Bower is wherever we are together . . . it's here and now, whenever we kiss.'

More self-identification: while Lesley was always mindful of setting and occasion, Romain was hopeless about such things, oblivious of romantic context, never remembering birthdays and anniversaries. But in Sofia he gave her one unforgettable birthday present. At midnight she heard the strains of music outside and opened the windows to find a gipsy band, singing the wild songs she loved to the wailing strains of the *gaida*. Thrilled, she told Romain so. '*Des foutaises*,' was his laconic reply. Her special present for him was an old edition of Pushkin printed in the traditional Russian typography that he prized.

She inveigled him into some sightseeing: they marvelled at the fine eleventh-century frescoes in the tiny church at Boyana, drove out in the diplomatic car to Rila Monastery and to the Festival of Roses in the valley where an overpowering attar of roses was made. Romain, however, was increasingly absorbed by legation affairs when not engrossed in writing his third novel. Sometimes work took him to Belgrade, leaving Lesley lonely and prey to homesickness. Once, hearing from England that her mother was ill, she hurried home as quickly as the trains could carry her across Europe, carrying a batch of Raiina's biscuits as comfort food for Martha.

They were always short of money. Romain was as chronically vague about it as she was, so she accepted whatever freelance journalism came her way, always clearing commissions first with the legation, as expected of diplomats' wives with outside interests. She struggled to learn Bulgarian. She befriended Atanass, a gipsy boy begging at the Alexander Nevsky cathedral, whose mother helped a seamstress to cut out *chalvàri*, the baggy Turkish trousers they wore, and invited Lesley to a 'wedding' that turned out to be a circumcision. In old age Lesley recounted how she had wangled permits from the Soviets and Nedi helped her with timetables for the few trains still running. Bundled up in a floor-length sheepskin *shouba*, issued to diplomats' wives against the cold winters, Lesley would disappear for days on end to explore the countryside. These accounts varied, though: did she go often, or just once, by car, with other diplomats' wives who were terrified by 'the mad boy whose feet were back to front' coming into her bedroom to stoke the stove? A photograph records her visit to Vratsa. She kept a journal, which became the basis for her first travel pieces, but they include no mention of travelling solo in Bulgaria.

Romain's superiors noted his ability to mix with Bulgarian artists and intellectuals outside diplomatic circles. They were also impressed by his acute analysis of Communist consolidation in Bulgaria as part of the broad strategy of the Comintern. His work obliged him to observe and report on political events in Sofia, while leaving him powerless to intervene on behalf of the liberal opposition with which he sympathized. Nine-year-old King Simeon was dethroned and exiled in September 1946 and widespread purges that year picked off nationalists in their thousands. Romain was plunged into depression by the persecutions that ensued, culminating with Petkov's show trial in August 1947; he was haunted by visions of the 'black tongue' of the hanged man.

He had more cause for despondency with his writing. His second novel, *Tulipe*, was ready for Calmann Lévy in March 1946 and was published the following year, to puzzled notices and disastrous sales. After the poignant humanism of *Education européenne*, this was a dark, disorganized farce, savage and cynical, reflecting Romain's profound disgust with humanity after the Holocaust and the post-war betrayal of Eastern Europe. *Tulipe* sold fewer than 200 copies; at first he blamed his publishers, so when Gallimard offered him a sizeable advance for his next book he wasted little time in accepting it. He would stay with Gallimard for the rest of his life.

Romain's first diplomatic assignment put him through a crash course in Realpolitik and the experience seared into his development as a writer. The fierce cynicism in his thinking, already evident in *Tulipe*, was reinforced. His ensuing works show a violent swing between humanist idealism and the furious, grotesque humour of the 'disenchanted' novels, a dichotomy that appeared equally in his volcanic mood swings from day to day.

★

As so often throughout his life, Romain's name was a matter for confusion. Although officially he had reverted to Romain Kacew when he left the military, his use of a *nom de guerre* as well as a pen name meant that he was generally known as Romain Gary. The Quai d'Orsay made it clear that they preferred it to Kacew. Lesley, of course, preferred his original name to Gary, which she found banal. This was symbolic of her efforts to reclaim what she saw as his essential Slav self, against Romain's own attempts to lose his Eastern background in favour of his adopted French nationality. In France it would become a source of latent friction between them. But in Bulgaria, bordering on the Orient, where again Russia was dominant and he felt culturally at ease, husband and wife were content with the roles they had made for themselves and each other.

Despite the threatening political situation, physical discomforts and their initial adventures, they remembered Romain's first posting more fondly than anywhere except his last, in Los Angeles. During those eighteen months Lesley believed she saw Romain in his proper context, when he was closest in reality to the way she wanted him to be; while for Romain, Lesley was at her most fulfilled and forgiving. The novel he wrote while they were living in Bulgaria, *Le Grand Vestiaire*, was dedicated to Lesley, the only one of his books in which he offered her this tribute.

In Bulgaria all their sympathies were with this small country of 7 million people, independent for a few decades after as many centuries of foreign rule and now falling under the iron grip of communism. Romain's Slav upbringing worked in his favour there, both personally and professionally. For Lesley, so attuned to the spirit of place, it was no coincidence that she was happiest there. In the mysterious human desire for elsewhere, the need for fantasy and the urge to travel are offshoots from the primal instinct for escape. Like other travellers before and since, she was consumed by nostalgia for places she had never visited. In her migrations *en poste* with Romain, Bulgaria was as close as she would come to her inner landscape; in its voluptuous folds of countryside she felt most at home. It was as if her instincts identified with this little-known, proudly Ruritanian country, and the way the face it hid from the outside world was countered by such a vigorous sense of national identity within. The Byzantine icons and frescoes, the blowsy flower designs, Islamic patterns and rich soft red in its decorative arts, the spicy Balkan food, the plangent village voices singing their Balkan laments in discordant close harmony, all marked her for life. Afterwards Lesley invoked her time there with exclamation marks, lovingly, like Pierre Loti: 'Bulgaria!'

In November 1947, Jean Chauvel, secretary-general at the Quai d'Orsay, nominated Romain as *consul adjoint* at the Moscow embassy. Lesley was ecstatic, but Romain was relieved when the appointment was cancelled days later when it was realized that the Soviet authorities deemed his fiction politically incorrect. Instead, in December he was summoned to Paris, where he was delegated to the Foreign Affairs department there dealing with central Europe, starting in February 1948. Even though the Communist stranglehold on Bulgaria was by now intolerably tragic, the appointment came like a prison sentence to them both.

The diplomatic corps came to the station to see them off. Snow was falling heavily. Lesley had already burst into tears when Raiina, having escaped from her new position with another madame, rushed round to the legation with a photograph of herself and a cake she had baked for the journey. Now she wept again in earnest and Romain, always susceptible to emotion, began to cry in sympathy. As the train carried them inexorably westward on their three-day journey, Lesley sank into memories like an exile, consumed by transports of grief.

In France, the land of liberty, their lives were far more confined by poverty and convention than in communist Bulgaria. The Quai d'Orsay's central administration, where Romain was working, was riddled with protocol, underfunded and offered no living allowance for staff based in Paris, where subsistence costs were highest. Unlike the elite echelons from which most staff were recruited, Romain had no family fortune or connections to fall back on.

Although they stayed in Paris for two full years, longer than Bulgaria, he and Lesley lived like gipsies, decamping every few weeks to another hotel or borrowed apartment. At first they stayed in cheap hotels, eating frugally in bistros when not reduced to long supperless evenings in their room. In the Pas-de-Calais, which Lesley called the

Pas-de-Confort, Romain reworked his third novel, according to legend sitting in the bathroom astride the bidet.

For a few weeks they rented Marguerite Duras's flat in the Quartier Latin where they lay sleepless above a throbbing nightclub. On the Right Bank they squeezed into a comfortless pied-à-terre in a larger apartment belonging to the Marquis de Saint-Pierre on the rue du Faubourg St-Honoré. A few weeks later Lesley was packing and unpacking again; they moved seven times in all, leaving her with a lasting dislike for the inhospitable city. Without a space to make her own she felt cramped and deprived of half her personality. The boulevards and grandes places of the French capital left her cold; Nancy Mitford teased her that Parisians would be offended by her unflattering comparisons of their fair city with Sofia. She wandered round the Marais, Paris's ancient Jewish quarter, and whiled away afternoons in a little cinema showing Yiddish films as the nearest she could get to exoticism. Romain, doing his best to assimilate, was bemused.

Try as he would, Romain's foreignness became more noticeable in France. His looks, his accent, his volatile temperament gave him away, and he was still finding his way around the capital. Even his heroic war record and evident patriotism, so valuable in France's representatives abroad, appeared naive and excessive to his compatriots at home. Conversely, he always appeared more French when he was away from his adopted country, especially later in the United States where he played up to the hand-kissing Gallic stereotype and was regarded as quintessentially French.

Among the few people who made them feel at ease were René and Sylvia Agid. From Bulgaria, Romain and Lesley brought precious edible presents: for seven-year-old Yves Agid, the first banana he had ever seen; for his parents, a kilo of caviar. They celebrated by devouring half of it together that evening.

Lesley, restless in Paris, was inching her way back into print. *Vogue* accepted features on esoteric subjects, one of them a piece about animal portraits, which only she could have suggested. Anne Scott-James commissioned for *Harper's Bazaar* a profile about a pseudonymous painter whose naive pictures of lions and leopards lolling peacefully beside prams or tea parties had become a *succès fou*. 'Eden Box' was none other than Lesley's best friend Edna, now Eden Fleming, who often put her up at 7 Montpelier Terrace in Knightsbridge. Lesley's affectionate profile concealed Eden's true identity, although a photograph of her in one of her lacy peignoirs gave the lie to her discretion. Max Hastings commissioned her to write the text for a picture story about a dance photographer in *Strand* magazine and she interviewed Nancy Mitford, an ardent francophile, happily settled in her apartment in the rue Monsieur.

The beautiful career that had seemed assured in 1945 obstinately continued to elude Romain. His fiction was a barometer of the times. *Le Grand Vestiaire* (*The Company of Men*), whose first draft he had written in Sofia, was set in Paris and dealt with the highly charged theme of collaboration. The fatherless boy in a hostile world, his seedy black-marketeer protector, the symbolic wardrobe, hung with clothes, in the French title all spoke of the uncertainties of post-war France, faced with moral and monetary bankruptcy. Lesley appreciated the raw honesty and energy of the novel, as well as its dedication to her, but it was not well received by French readers.

At the Quai d'Orsay, Romain was embroiled in the political development of central Europe, in an era of momentous post-war realignments. He had watched with horror as the Iron Curtain fell across the continent, cutting him off from his cultural roots. Now he was in the department dealing with the future of Germany, divided between the occupying powers. Preparing documents for discussion, he maintained that having fought three wars with Germany since 1870, France had to rethink its defensive attitude: 'Fear of Germany is a defeat in itself,' as he said later to his colleague Jacques Vimont. He argued for an economic and political integration that would reunite Germany into the community of Europe, a viewpoint that put him far ahead of his time.

In late 1949 his request to be posted to Athens was accepted, then swiftly withdrawn, no reason being given. Shortly afterwards he was informed that he had been posted to Berne with a small promotion, starting in February 1950. It was not what either he or Lesley wanted, but it was work.

★

Some time in 1949, Romain and Lesley travelled south to Nice during his holiday leave. They paid a visit to his mother's grave in the cemetery at Caucade, and went on to see his aunt Bella, and his cousin Dinah and her children. Romain also met up with Sacha Kardo Sissoeff, a friend and rival from the *lycée*, who offered to show them a ruined watchtower and some outhouses that were for sale in a village outside Nice. Lesley never liked Sacha, she found him devious; later she had more reason to dislike him because he was party to Romain's other life away from her, with other women. The twelfth-century fortified village of Roquebrune was inconvenient to reach, first by bus from Nice, then a daunting climb up a track from the coast road. Sacha led them to an entrance in a dark corner stinking of urine and cats, leading off the uneven cobbled rue de la Fontaine. They pushed through the ancient door and a tangle of jasmine to find the crumbling tower. Beside it, on a different level, was a jumble of stables for mules, rabbit hutches and hencoops in a separate lot which could be thrown in with the tower for almost nothing. The buildings defied all structural coherence. But the dazzling Mediterranean light, and the hawk's-eye panorama stretching on both sides over the blue sea and rocky coast, were so bewitchingly romantic, the project so stunningly impractical, that they decided on the spot to buy.

For Lesley the near-impossible was infinitely more seductive than convenience. She quickly saw how to fashion something out of the dank heaps of stones, turn the tower's middle room into their bedroom and the one above into Romain's workroom. The low dark stables, then reached from the tower via teetering planks of wood, could become a bathroom and kitchen, linked by a staircase to the bedroom. The rubble would be used to flatten out the surrounding ground and turn it into a green handkerchief of terrace in the lee of the little pink church next door.

In one sense buying the eyrie at Roquebrune was almost a question of survival, for they urgently needed a permanent perch that would provide them with continuity in between Romain's postings.

For him it was a homecoming. Nice was the one place he *had* talked about to Lesley: the longed-for destination for Mina and himself after the grim transitory years in cold, anti-Semitic Warsaw. When he reached the Bay of Angels, his past had dropped away and his future stretched ahead like the blue horizon. There he had thrown himself into becoming French at school, made his first friends, learnt about sex, fallen in love and become a man. He had adored the Mediterranean at first sight, swimming out into La Grande Bleue to shake off his adolescent torments; he would name a triptych of novels after his Brother Ocean. The sun suited his olive skin, the warmth relaxed him, and the refuge at Roquebrune would allow him to write undisturbed.

Lesley, too, had memories of the Côte d'Azur, although hers were harder to trace. In *Mind's Eye* she nostalgically relates how the Traveller drives her with his aunt Eudoxia and his two sons along the Riviera as a postscript to their enchanted summer holiday in Corsica. As autumn approaches they settle close to the border, sometimes crossing over to Ventimiglia and San Remo for the day. She and the Traveller climb high into the hills above Garavan to the Russian graveyard and make love there. On the coast she floats in the warm shallows, looking up at the villas scattered among citrus trees and palms below the high crags and the blue-domed, Russian chapel. The sight is lovely, yet not the landscape she craves. When had Lesley been there before, and in whose company? Did she visit the Côte d'Azur with Komisarjevsky? Or was she remembering the years at Roquebrune with Romain?

For now, like Romain she had no permanent home and only the room in her mother's flat in west London to store her belongings. Since she left England, her creative energies had been underused; the ruined tower was a challenge by any standards and it would keep her busy during Romain's more mundane postings. Equally important for her, the dramatic location, tucked among the medieval alleys of Roquebrune on one side, embracing sky and sea with the other, satis-fied her craving for the exotic. She and Romain would be in France, for his sake; yet in the Rapunzel tower, clinging to the rocky Ligurian peaks, she could imagine herself anywhere.

In Berne they were at least comfortable, unlike Paris. They lived in part of a large house in Kirchenfeld, the diplomatic zone. Lesley's oriental rugs stamped her presence on the imposing reception area, where a grand staircase led up to galleries at the sides, while Romain made a writing den for himself in a room leading off it. The bathroom was next door and he spent much of his writing time in one or the other, draped in a towelling toga.

The French embassy was built on a hill to impress the population with the French ambassador's pre-eminent status. Below it was the consulate, more attractively housed in a villa, but nothing could be done about the heavy hand of protocol that oppressed their daily existence. Romain sat morosely in his basement office; Lesley baulked at the bourgeois Swiss; and when the dread föhn wind blew, even the natives lost their temper. She at least appreciated the museums and galleries in which Romain was never remotely interested.

Romain's new position proved to be grindingly boring, except for the presence of the ambassador, Henri Hoppenot, an exceptionally gifted diplomat and writer who, like his wife Hélène, had wide cultural interests and many friends in the arts. In fact Romain, who was still listed in the diplomats' directory twice, under Kacew and Gary, owed his Berne appointment to the ambassador. On a visit to the Quai d'Orsay, Hoppenot heard that the French ambassador to Greece had rejected Romain's posting in Athens on the grounds that he wanted 'neither a Jew, nor a Bulgarian, nor a member of the *cadre latéral*' at Athens. The Quai protested against this flagrant prejudice but failed to change the ambassador's mind. Hoppenot, who had been interested in Romain's novels, told the head of personnel that he would accept Romain at the embassy in Berne. 'It's a lottery,' he confided to his wife, 'but it'll be a change for me to have a talented writer as my colleague.'

Hoppenot became a protector and adviser *in loco parentis* to Romain, who greatly respected his moral authority. Hélène Hoppenot, a gifted pianist and photographer, published some fine books of photographs of their travels and, with her husband, translated Conrad into French. She also diligently kept a journal, in which she noted her first impression of Romain – 'A handsome boy with a matt complexion, very blue eyes and long black eyelashes, well mannered' – and, brilliantly, of Lesley: 'his English wife has the slightly magical charm of nonsense rhymes.'

Their dinner table was a civilized oasis in the usual stiff diplomatic round, not only because the French embassy's chef had a fine Balkan touch with pastry. Hoppenot was a friend and contemporary of the musicians Darius Milhaud and Paul Claudel, and as patrons he and Hélène had befriended many distinguished artists who mingled with their diplomatic guests. Soon after *les Romain Gary* arrived in Berne, the Hoppenots had attended a showing of Jean Cocteau's film *L'Orphée*, mainly on Cocteau's insistence. Lesley, hearing this, asked:

'Does he still wear the sleeves of his shirts and jackets too short?' Yes, now she mentioned it. 'It's to show how delicate his wrists are . . . Yes, yes, I assure you, it's well known.'

Lesley found a kindred spirit in humane, sophisticated Hélène Hoppenot. She joined the ambassadress in her formal presentations of newly arrived diplomats' wives to the other embassies: a remnant of centuries-old 'Spanish protocol' which had survived in Berne, according to Lesley, whose smattering of Russian and Bulgarian was helpful with Slav speakers. Formally hatted and gloved, they had to present their calling cards and introduce the new wives to each embassy, nibbling the national delicacies proffered and making stilted conversation for exactly fifteen minutes. Mme Hoppenot appreciated Lesley's cultured intelligence, though she did not always welcome the younger woman's tendency to confide in her at moments of crisis.

Lesley had to do her share of catering for France. Romain was reliably unhelpful both before the event, when he would heedlessly help himself to fruit from Lesley's still-life table decorations, ruining her beautiful centrepiece before the guests arrived, and afterwards, when the hired staff often deserted, leaving her with the washing up. They acquired a Lithuanian maid who enthralled Lesley with memories of terrifying invaders who surged through the villages during the First World War. How Romain reacted to these reminders of his birthplace is not recorded. In a typical vignette she described him in bed, fretting about his digestion while dictating recipes from a Russian cookbook for the following day's meals.

Their ménage had shifted into a new phase, pitilessly invoked in a passage in Romain's new novel in progress, whose working title was *La Baie des anges* (published in 1952 as *Les Couleurs du jour* and translated into English as *The Colours of the Day*). In it, Willie Bauché, locked into an unrequited marriage to a beautiful Hollywood star, vengefully muses on the ageing of women.

> She still had five or six years of youth, then six or seven years of beauty, after which her face would be only intelligent . . . He studied particularly the little spot just under the chin which always creases first, like heavy cream; age takes women by the throat and all that goes to make the tenderness of a neck disappears, making way for reality . . . The eyes, naturally, never grow old, but that only makes their situation more difficult.

Lesley was nearly fifty; Romain was not yet forty and compulsively active sexually. When desprived of sex he felt ill, like an addict without a fix. His now-blatant affairs with younger, firmer flesh would have crushed most women. Lesley complained bitterly about what she called his tic below the belt but refused to let it destroy her own sense of worth. Their friends felt the fallout from 'two enormous egotists rowing all over Europe'.

Nonetheless, she was protective of his talent and prepared to intervene on his behalf. When his protracted attempts at playwriting were rejected repeatedly by the actor Louis Jouvet, leaving him badly demoralized, Lesley wrote to Claude Gallimard asking him to put in a good word for Romain. Nothing came of it.

The household found him ever more grandiose, Japanese Overlord in his kimono or towelling toga snapping his fingers for cups of tea, while Lesley mockingly shuffled about him making obeisances as his Paper Fan. There were still days when she could tease him out of histrionic scenes, or shift the black depression that descended for days on end, but the tiger's tail was becoming harder to tweak. He had a way of fastening on misfortune until everyone around him, even Hadji the little stray dog they had adopted in Paris and brought with them, was reduced to despair; then he would brighten visibly, having achieved his purpose. In *Journey into the Mind's Eye* the Traveller's perverse enjoyment of minor disasters like missed trains, and outright disappointment when things went according to plan, was a trait borrowed directly from Romain.

Lesley was lonely in Berne. When Hadji died, her paroxysms of grief astonished Romain; and Hélène Hoppenot, to whom she poured out her feelings, was taken aback by Lesley's lack of control. She could almost be mourning the death of a son. When she cried that Romain didn't know what it meant to love an animal, Mme Hoppenot sensed that Lesley meant 'to love' at all.

Money was another area of conflict. There was never enough, and even if there was, neither of them believed it. Romain was so disorganized that when he came home from the office in Sofia, Lesley found his wages spilling out of his coat pocket. After earning her living for two decades she found it as hard to be dependent on him as he found it difficult to share his salary with her. Now the ruins at Roquebrune were a new financial drain.

By mid-1950 Romain was alarmed by rumours that Hoppenot might soon be posted to Moscow, and Romain with him. On a trip to Lausanne and Geneva with Hélène Hoppenot, Lesley told her with evident irritation that the prospect was making Romain ill, and he had told the ambassador that the atmosphere in the Russian capital would leave him incapable of working there. Lesley, of course, would have liked nothing better. In the event, like so many other passing dramas, Hoppenot's appointment fell through and none of them went to Russia. Hélène, recording Romain's joy on hearing the news, reflected: 'Strange man, this Gary, both child and wholly adult, never content with what he has.'

Lesley often escaped from Berne to supervise and even physically help with building work on the crumbling tower. She stayed in Nice with Romain's friends Suzanne and Roger Agid (René's brother, who followed their father into the hotel business), climbing the rough path from the road every day. The village had been half deserted since the war and the handful of families who lived there spoke a baffling dialect of partly Saracen origin. The only telephone was in the post office, few houses had electricity, and the logistics of getting supplies up the hill were daunting. But slowly the work progressed. The workmen, stopping for their midday saucisson sec and vin rouge, gave Lesley recipes for pan bagna and pain perdu, which made their way into her cookbook years later.

Lesley and Romain fiercely coveted their eagle's nest on the Ligurian coast. Once it was made barely habitable, he seized as much leave as he was allowed and sometimes overran it. Primitive as it was, they coexisted better there. Lesley took over the tiny kitchen, whose stove was the only source of heat in the house, and worked her way through the recipes of Edouard de Pomiane. Romain, in his Red Army overcoat, climbed the ladder-staircase to his room at the top of the tower, whose windows were still unglazed from its earlier use as a storeroom for tomatoes and herbs left to dry in the wind and sun. With a cartoonist's precision Lesley describes him scribbling in his unformed, childish script like a man possessed, his head swaying and his hair standing on end. Sometimes he disappeared to prowl the steep dark alleys at night, living in his imagination.

In the afternoons Romain descended the old stone steps to the beach at Cap Martin. Lesley, high above, would settle down in the shade with a glass of wine to write, or to embellish their cave-like dwelling in her inimitable fashion – the curé, on his annual round to bless the houses of the village, found himself face to face with a painting of the Baby Jesus transfigured into a little dog in a pink dress. Soon friends were applying to stay. After guests left a mess in the house and unpaid bills at the village store, Lesley was annoyed enough to threaten to ban outsiders from using it.

The *longueurs* of Berne encouraged other travels. Lesley visited Vienna briefly where the embassy secretary was a friend. A keen opera-goer, she extolled Wagner to Romain, whose reply came scribbled on a postcard to 'Darling Lesley' that he would have none of her Wagner. 'Je crâche sur sa tombe.'

In February 1951 she sent in her uncommissioned piece on Queen Marie of Romania, 'The Fading Garden and the Forgotten Rose', to her old friend Peter Quennell, now editor of the *Cornhill* magazine. Like its publisher John Murray, the quarterly journal was famous for its travel writing. Quennell, however, had left for Greece on a British Council lecture tour about Byron and was about to leave the *Cornhill*, as John (Jock) Murray, its new editor, explained in his reply. Murray had read her 'splendid piece of travel nostalgia' and would be glad to publish it. Better still, he liked both her other suggestions: extracts from her Balkan journal worked up from Bulgaria; and a piece about the medieval Jewish settlement at Djerba in Tunisia, where she was about to spend three weeks with the new Secretary-General Jacques Vimont (a colleague and friend of Romain's from Berne) and his wife.

Murray added that he would be pleased to meet Lesley when she came to London in April. So began a highly productive working relationship and friendship, conducted mainly through correspondence, which launched Lesley's literary career. She wrote to him again from Tunisia on 1 March, unable to resist her address there: 'Salammbo'. They haggled briefly about money; Jock Murray pointed out that the *Cornhill* could not match the fees paid by newspapers and named ten guineas for first serial rights, which Lesley, reluctantly back in Berne, accepted on account of the journal's prestigious reputation.

That spring she also went to Paris and to London, where she called in at *Vogue*. Jock received proofs of 'The Fading Garden' and also her manuscript of 'Fragments of a Balkan Journal', which he accepted but wanted to cut. She wheedled with him to allow her 7,000 words, and mischievously urged him to cut the other essays instead.

Lesley's travels in the Levant had redirected her eager appetite for research. Staying with the Vimonts in Tunisia, she had been fired by conversations with Algerian-born General Georges Catroux. The only army general who had joined de Gaulle's Free French in 1940, he had then served variously as French governor-general of Algeria, minister for French North Africa and French ambassador to Moscow. 'Talking Sahara' with Lesley, Catroux had told her about Isabelle Eberhardt, Geneva-born Slav mystic who fell in love with North Africa, lived to transvestite excess in the desert and improbably drowned there in a flash flood at the age of twenty-seven. Eberhardt had married an Arab, was an outcast among the French colony and had travelled south with the French legions commanded by General Lyautey, to report on their campaigns in southern Algeria, where Catroux's older brother had met her. This freakish voluptuary had never been 'discovered' or translated into English; Lesley was impressed by Eberhardt's desert writings although they had been bowdlerized by an unscrupulous editor. In Berne, lacking other excitement, Lesley and Romain had taken up spiritualism and became terrifically excited by a 'blind' horoscope she had commissioned of Eberhardt, which they considered so astonishingly accurate that she wanted it included in the profile she sent to Jock Murray.

In July 1951, Romain had nearly finished the draft of his new novel. Gallimard sent a secretary with an exotic Egyptian name from Paris to type it out. Lesley dreaded the prospect of Romain's 'working evenings' when the typewriter would fall silent and she would have to summon all her English restraint to avoid scenes. She increasingly found reasons to escape: to Roquebrune in August, to London in late September. In October she returned to Algeria and Tunisia with an Irish photographer, but Lesley preferred the sort of trip that involved staying in beautiful houses and her visit was less successful after she left the Vimonts'. Hélène Hoppenot, also on a working trip photographing Tunisia for a book, met her on the island of Djerba. Hélène was feeling ill after a boat trip and cried off supper, but Lesley 'tenaciously' arrived for breakfast. She was full of complaints about her ungentlemanly travelling companion, and the accident-prone travels that she described to Hélène were not what appeared in her memoirs. She seemed to have no planned itinerary and was actually missing Berne (which she found unbearable when there).

If chaos and disorder were sometimes cultivated in the Gary household, there was no need to exaggerate the confusion in her absence. Telegrams from Romain addressed to Lesley chez Vimont in Tunis, and her agitated letters to him at Berne, missed their targets. She was furious to discover in a North African newspaper that Henri Hoppenot had been appointed France's permanent representative on the Security Council at the United Nations in New York, and that Romain had subsequently agreed to join him in the New Year, without consulting her. Meanwhile Romain was detached to join the press and information service covering a United Nations session in Paris. He left Lesley to clear and pack the apartment in Geneva, booked himself into the elegant Hôtel Lutetia round the corner from Gallimard and with considerable nerve, given that his last two books had been outright commercial flops, asked his publishers for a loan on the rights of his next one, since the Quai d'Orsay would only pay out expenses months in arrears.

When Lesley finally joined Romain in Paris, they were invited to the important Christmas leaving party for the Hoppenots in Berne, but as they hadn't booked train reservations in advance they were unable to travel. 'Neither of them has an iota of practical sense,' lamented Mme Hoppenot. Lesley had to return to Berne after Christmas to 'pay, pack and follow' her husband to New York, as usual with no idea where they would live.

Even so, she left with good news in her pocket. In almost the last letter that Jock Murray addressed to her in Berne, he wrote: 'As you know, I have always hoped that you would find the time and inclination some day to write a book.'

6

New York

Character plus opportunity equals fortune.
  Lesley Blanch, *The Wilder Shores of Love*

LEAVING LESLEY BEHIND to tackle the removals, in January 1952 Romain crossed the Atlantic by liner with other members of the eight-man French delegation to the United Nations, to be led by the permanent delegate on the Security Council, Henri Hoppenot. This time the Quai d'Orsay had found Romain a position that suited his talents brilliantly, as press attaché responsible for putting across French foreign policy to the American media and the public at large.

The United Nations Organization had been born three years earlier in December 1948, when its delegates moved into the purpose-built house of glass overlooking the East river. The hopes that rose with its proud announcement of a universal declaration of the rights of man had swiftly been dashed by the spread of the Cold War across the globe. As the European powers began to shed their Far Eastern domin-ions, the United States moved in to defend the 'Free World' against the spread of communism in Korea and Vietnam, the resulting tensions and dissensions being faithfully reflected by the UN's delegates.

France's reduced status as a great power after its wartime defeat made Romain's task more daunting, and his country was isolated by its outdated colonial policy. Messy end-of-empire struggles were already at their height in French Indochina and were boiling up in North Africa, where violent nationalist movements were emerging in Tunisia, Morocco and Algeria. At the UN, Romain had to court sup-port for the French vote among the hundreds of journalists prowling the corridors of the new UN building on East 42nd Street. And it fell to him to speak for France to the people of America, accepting scores

The house in Grove Park Gardens, Chiswick where Lesley Blanch was born in 1904

Burlington Court, beside Chiswick station. Lesley was brought up in flat no. 8 (top floor, far left) from the age of two

Lesley's eighteenth-century house by the Thames at Richmond, nostalgically evoked in *Journey into the Mind's Eye*

Left: Feodor Komisarjevsky in 1935

Below: The Merchant of Venice, set designed by Lesley Blanch with Feodor Komisarjevsky for the opening production at the new Shakespeare Theatre, Stratford, in 1932

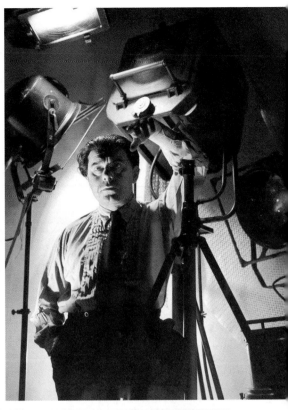

Above left: The Polish-born ballet dancer Marie Rambert, who travelled to Russia with Lesley in 1934

Above right: Gabriel Pascal, Transylvanian director of *Major Barbara*

Vadim Komisarjevsky, son of Feodor

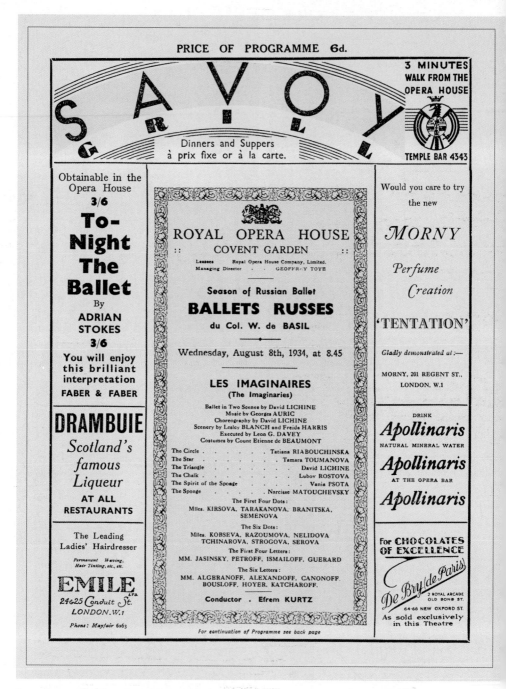

ROYAL OPERA HOUSE
:: COVENT GARDEN ::

Lessees   Royal Opera House Company, Limited.
Managing Director   -   -   GEOFFREY TOYE

Season of Russian Ballet

BALLETS RUSSES

du Col. W. de BASIL

Wednesday, August 8th, 1934, at 8.45

LES IMAGINAIRES
(The Imaginaries)

Ballet in Two Scenes by David LICHINE
Music by Georges AURIC
Choreography by David LICHINE
Scenery by Lesley BLANCH and Freida HARRIS
Executed by Leon G. DAVEY
Costumes by Count Etienne de BEAUMONT

The Circle . . . . Tatiana RIABOUCHINSKA
The Star . . . . Tamara TOUMANOVA
The Triangle . . . . David LICHINE
The Chalk . . . . Lubov ROSTOVA
The Spirit of the Sponge . . . . . Vania PSOTA
The Sponge . . . . . Narcisse MATOUCHEVSKY

The First Four Dots :
Mlles. KIRSOVA, TARAKANOVA, BRANITSKA,
SEMENOVA

The Six Dots :
Mlles. KOBSEVA, RAZOUMOVA, NELIDOVA
TCHINAROVA, STROGOVA, SEROVA

The First Four Letters :
MM. JASINSKY, PETROFF, ISMAILOFF, GUERARD

The Six Letters :
MM. ALGERANOFF, ALEXANDOFF, CANONOFF,
BOUSLOFF, HOYER, KATCHAROFF.

Conductor . Efrem KURTZ

For continuation of Programme see back page

Programme for *Les Imaginaires*, Lichine's 'blackboard' ballet performed by the Ballets
Russes at Covent Garden, crediting Lesley Blanch with Frieda Harris for set design

'Should Women Wear Trousers?' Anne Scott-James proves they should in *Picture Post*, November 1941

Audrey Withers (second left) and Anne Scott-James judging a talent competition for young designers with Graham Sutherland (half hidden), Henry Moore and Lesley (off camera), in April 1946

Lesley at home in a crochet shawl, photographed by Norman Parkinson, 1944

Lieutenant Romain Gari de Kacew, Lorraine Squadron, Free French air force. Lesley, impressed by his forthcoming first novel, asked Lee Miller to photograph the author. *Forest of Anger* was accepted for publication in 1944, so the handwritten date is a mystery

Lesley Blanch and Romain Gary
at St Leonard's Terrace, Chelsea

Lesley Blanch *à l'orientale*,
cocooned in robes on a nest of
kelims

Romain Gary in pensive mode

Above: Hélène Hoppenot, friend and adviser to Lesley *en poste*

Left: Ambassador Hoppenot with the Papal Nuncio in protocol-ridden Berne, Switzerland

Below: Roquebrune village on the Côte d'Azur where Romain and Lesley bought their ruined tower

of invitations to address schools and universities, meetings and associations of every persuasion.

The press attaché's role combined a demanding mixture of diplomacy and public relations. Romain had to respond on the spot to questions, assertions and accusations, all the while closely following the elected French government's swerves and reverses in foreign policy. His ham-actor tendencies, inherited from his mother, which entertained and irritated his friends, now found a remarkably productive outlet. He had a genius for improvisation, aided by his facility with languages and exceptional fluency, and took pride in his ability to speak compellingly on causes that were anathema to him. He was unfazed by journalists' directness and enjoyed sparring with them; with the American public he relied on charm and eloquence to deflect aggression. Soon he was speaking almost perfect English with a Slav timbre, deepening his French accent when seguing into seductive mode.

In early January, while Romain prepared to leave Paris, Lesley returned to Berne, intending to pack up their furniture and belongings, and leave within the week. Instead she succumbed to flu and retired to bed. This was not wholly inconvenient, since it allowed her to complete her long essay on Isabelle Eberhardt for the *Cornhill*, which she must have realized was significant to her development as a writer. Distracted by her work, she was more dilatory than usual about supervising the packing process and the paperwork that went with it.

From Berne she travelled to Paris, to fit in some last-minute fact-checking and picture research at the Bibliothèque Nationale. Then she went on to London, where she called on Jock Murray at 50 Albemarle Street with her corrections and two photographs of Eberhardt: Lesley had strong views on illustration and did her own research. After making her farewells to her mother and friends, she embarked for America by sea.

Arriving a month after Romain, Lesley found her mutable husband already transformed into a citizen of the New World. His speech was full of Americanisms and to suit his new image-conscious persona he had developed a native New Yorker's fixation with health and fitness, watching his diet and jogging in Central Park. Lesley was at the extreme opposite end of the spectrum in her reaction to America, which was to sharpen her English accent and become ever more attached to everything European.

Her first priority after she arrived was house-hunting. Romain, brought up in a *pension*, was comfortable in hotels whose impersonal service he found convenient, and was quite prepared to live that way indefinitely. He was unmoved by Lesley's distress on discovering that the furniture sent from Berne had been so badly packed that her treasured eighteenth-century gilt dining chairs arrived in shreds, all uninsured because the person she had charged with insuring it, hadn't. The stuff was all hers, he told her, nothing to do with him, and he would be more than happy to start afresh with modern furniture in a brand-new apartment.

Lesley had no intention of submerging her own preferences in his. Instead she tramped the streets until she found a place that pleased *her*. The ninth-floor apartment had an enormous living room with views of the Manhattan skyline, but there was only one other room and minimal storage space for clothes, hardly enough to accommodate a duo of such violently individual personalities in comfort. Romain complained that the TV set in the bedroom, where Lesley was mesmerized by live daily broadcasts of the House Un-American Committee's communist witch-hunts, would give off X-rays and make him impotent. But Lesley liked the location by the East river on the Upper East Side – New York's Chelsea – in a Hungarian quarter, which to her way of thinking qualified as exotic. The French Embassy was a few blocks west, overlooking Central Park, and Romain could walk south all the way to the United Nations building beside the river, thinking about his next novel.

At first Lesley was dismayed by New York, which left her pining for North Africa and London. She was affronted by breakfasts drenched in maple syrup that had to be eaten in diners, giant fruit tasting of nothing, the myth of labour-saving living, armoured brassieres sold in 'corsetoriums' and funeral homes everywhere. The city's fabled pace of living was as much a myth as its labour-saving devices, she declared: New York should really be called Sleepy Hollow, so slow were its mail and delivery services, supermarket check-out counters and even the famous American drawl.

Her dissatisfaction masked deepening problems. Romain was sloughing off the skin of his old life and his wife seemed to be part of it. For the first time there was talk of divorce. Friends were enlisted to sympathize with their separate accounts of intensifying pain and farce. Lesley confided to Hélène Hoppenot that she loved Romain, but he was unbearable, dropped his clothes on the floor and expected her to do everything: why must he behave like *un vrai moujik* at home? His behaviour towards her had changed, she protested. Hélène refrained from telling Lesley that she too had changed in her attitude to Romain, no longer hiding her irritation with him in front of strangers.

That summer, husband and wife both travelled across America, but separately. Romain set off for a solo grand tour by Greyhound coach and local buses, which he later described almost without drawing breath over a dozen pages in *La Nuit sera calme*. His travels took him via Memphis, New Orleans, Los Angeles and Oregon, ending with a hasty return to New York as his money ran out, in a frenzy of anxiety about his health.

Setting off after him, in sharp contrast to Romain's bohemian weeks on the road, Lesley trumped him with a retaliatory tour across America driven by wealthy friends in a Cadillac (he could rarely get the better of his wife). These friends were possibly the American writer and editor Fleur Cowles and her husband Mike, heir to the Cowles Media Company, or even the man who became Fleur's third husband, timber magnate Tom Montague Meyer, whose name she added to her own to become Fleur Cowles Meyer. Lesley was impressed by the great landscapes of the Sierras and Arizona, and enjoyed Hollywood, where she was lent a house with a pool in Beverly Hills and was gratified to find all her old friends from her Brogue days there before her, living in luxury. She met up with Romain who, absurdly, was passing through Los Angeles at the same time; they agreed at least on their mutual culture shock, before departing on their separate ways. In San Francisco she was shaken out of sleep one night by a minor earthquake, then fell in love with Chinatown, before returning to New York.

The aftershock was doubly effective for Lesley. The time she spent away was enough to make the apartment feel like home when she returned, despite the city's melting humid heat. The trip had resigned her to being in America. She was like a cat that could settle in a new place only if its basket was close at hand; now that she had her apartment, she could work, play and enjoy herself. She admitted, though, that Romain found the basket an irritant. He dreamt of living on an empty yacht, afloat and free.

The other effect of the trip was to jolt her into work. Directly after returning from her trip she started on a book, knowing that if she did not get down to it immediately she never would. She submitted a proposal to the New York publishers Harcourt Brace and Knopf and, gratified by their interest, sent her handwritten outline to Jock Murray, hoping that he too would like it. Jock replied perceptively that 'It is only proper that the irritations of life in New York and the inconvenience of earthquakes should have stirred the creative impulse and that you should have been stirred to get down to a plan.' He agreed to her synopsis of several monographs, linked by an overall theme of nineteenth-century women who had lived and loved in Arabia. The episodic arrangement seemed sensible for her first book, given her interrupted way of life. The heroines she wanted to portray were not travellers in the mould of Isabella Bird or Lady Hester Stanhope. They were romantics, who instinctively sought escape from the 'whirring wheels of industrialization' in Europe, in exchange for adventure and fulfilment in the East (a state of mind that nicely mirrored Lesley's rebellion against modern living in twentieth-century America). The subjects then chosen were Isabelle Eberhardt, Jane Digby El Mezrab, Isabel Burton, Aurélie Piccard Tedjani and possibly Mme de la Tour d'Auvergne. To her naive query about how soon he could publish, he asked for her earliest finishing date. She was so encouraged by his response that by late September 1952 she had already finished 25,000 words on Lady Ellenborough (Jane Digby) and had started on Isabel Burton. Lesley was living in New York, but in her imagination she was living in nineteenth-century Syria with her errant heroines. The libraries offered excellent research facilities and she made the most of the cooler weeks before the diplomatic season resumed.

That autumn, Romain's fourth novel *Les Couleurs du jour* was published in France. He had published nothing since *Le Grand Vestiaire* in 1948 and had invested months of time and effort in revising his new book. Despite his and Gallimard's high hopes, it vanished almost without trace in France, though *The Colours of the Day* was better received in translation in America and Britain the following year.

The Colours of the Day is an uneven work, sometimes overlooked in the Gary canon, dominated by its high-flown love affair between a heroic Free French veteran, Rainier, engaged in the never-ending struggle for liberty and humanity, and Ann, a beautiful Hollywood star. Ann's husband Willie Bauché, the dark opposite who loses Ann to Rainier, is a far more interesting creation. Rainier and Bauché effectively represent their Janus-faced creator: the idealist man of Resistance and the compulsive liar, image-maker and fantasist, competing for the idealized love object. It was the first time that Romain's divided personality and duel with reality had been so clearly expressed. That theme and dialectic would continue to haunt his fiction until his death, and beyond.

Still the longed-for acclaim that had met his first novel eluded him. Again he was plunged into despair, as well as frustration at having to put aside the kernel of his new novel-in-progress after the UN Assembly reopened for business that winter. There at least he could shine: his charismatic, adrenaline-fuelled performances for TV and radio were the envy of more conventional diplomatic colleagues and made him something of a star.

Romain's promotion and new public role brought a heavier workload to Lesley too. She was subjected to hectic bouts of entertaining, often at short notice, catering for eight at lunch and up to sixteen for supper from a kitchen which she complained was hardly bigger than her travelling trunk. Then there were incessant outside invitations to be attended in décolleté and long gloves as diplomat's consort (some scribbled notes on trimmings to her cocktail suits and a sketched evening gown are crossed out on the back of a later letter to Murray). Nonetheless she was beginning to enjoy herself as well: lunching in Runyonesque restaurants with S.J. Perelman, attending a service at a Harlem chapel called The Holy Ghost Filling Station. She was looking forward to seeing the copy of the *Cornhill* containing her Eberhardt article, always delighted to read her own work. She also found the time to write for *Life*, a prestigious commission that she was keen to carry off successfully.

For their Christmas card that year she drew Romain and herself as baseball players – he wielded the bat, she caught the ball – against the New York skyline with a Nativity star glittering above the Empire State Building, captioned 'Joyeux Noël from the Manhattan Dodgers 1952'. By this time she was among the intimate friends invited to the Hoppenots' Christmas Eve present-giving ceremony with the family and household staff.

★

Lesley's dream commission for *Life* was a profile of Georges Simenon. During two weekends at his house outside New York that autumn, Maigret's creator spoke to her so freely that Lesley doubted whether she could use the most explosive material. Simenon's wife not only allowed him complete freedom to indulge his compulsive sexual predation, but would check into another room at the hotel where he took his conquests and wait for him to join her afterwards. Then there was his curious relationship with the cook . . . Lesley was still writing up the piece in late January 1953 when a friend called to say she had just read the article in the *New Yorker*, assigned to someone else. Stupefied, she discovered through her agent that the *New Yorker* must have heard about the *Life* commission and cut in with its own profile, about which Simenon and his wife had said nothing to Lesley.

'Seared' by this experience, Lesley retreated to freelancing for the less cut-throat *Reporter* and returned to her book. By late March she had already sold the American rights to Simon & Schuster and had been thrilled by leaked readers' comments about the work in progress. She told Jock that she had finished Isabel Burton and intended to add some final details to the Lady Ellenborough section. Her last subject or subjects had still not been finalized: she had dropped another candidate, Emily Sharef of Kazan, for lack of material and was now reconsidering Aurélie Piccard Tedjani. She planned to give Murray the complete manuscript in August after adding some final research from the Ashmolean and British Libraries.

Meanwhile, apart from the couple's UN duties, which included dining at the Rothschilds' penthouse in Park Avenue where genuine Tiepolos hung on the walls, there were glamorous evenings at El Morocco with the glitterati: Erich Remarque; Paulette Goddard and Anita Loos, both of whom became friends. Diamonds were de rigueur, Lesley noticed, but everyone else's were real, unlike hers which came from Macy's.

Jock Murray was impressed by her progress despite the distractions: 'Your control must be like iron,' he commented. Indeed, Lesley and Romain were both ruthless about their writing. He got up early to put in an hour or two before his working day began and seized writing time during lunch hours when he could, although he never worked late at night, needing his eight hours' sleep. Lesley had the advantage of days free for research and writing; at night she sometimes stayed up to scribble into the small hours, clad in her dressing-gown and listening to Lizst on the radio. Their real ruthlessness came at each other's expense. Romain had no scruples about interrupting his wife while she was writing, even on a trifling excuse. Lesley made allowances for *his* creative time, which they agreed had sacred status, but she showed little interest in his UN job apart from the attendant socializing. If she ever attended a session of the General Assembly she never mentioned it, unlike the politically aware Hélène Hoppenot.

To Jock Murray Lesley related her conquests; to Mme Hoppenot she confided her problems. Romain, seething with frustrated ambitions for wealth or fame or both, was unsettled and talking about moving again, to the Far East or the Pacific. Later that summer he was due to return to Paris for an operation to remove his gall bladder, and she was upset that he wanted to go alone. Now that she was too old to have children, he could think of nothing else. Lesley went so far as to tell him she was prepared to adopt, but fortunately this was not what he wanted.

Nonetheless, despite their ailing marriage Lesley's ability to exploit her circumstances in her best interests quickly asserted itself. 'Character plus opportunity equals fortune', the saying that she used to describe Aimée Dubucq de Rivery, her final choice for her fourth subject in *The Wilder Shores of Love*, could have been invented for herself. Her early misgivings about New York faded as she made contact with old acquaintances from London, among them the ballet set (the Ballets Russes had fled to the United States in wartime, where many of its dancers stayed on) whose circles overlapped with New York's Russian colony. Grand-Duchess Marie and Princess Natasha Paley, the last of the Romanovs, attracted a little court of émigrés, among whom Lesley cultivated the old Countess Tolstoy and Alice Astor, then Princess Obolensky. She befriended Count Hilarion Voronzov and hung on his tumbling rush of anecdotes about his influential ancestors in Tiflis and the Caucasus.

A connoisseur of eccentricity, Lesley grew fond of the emotional Carson McCullers, who lived with her mother 'up the Hudson', padded the streets in gold-mesh bedroom slippers and despaired of ever meeting a 'normal' man. (McCullers wrote a generous puff about *Wilder Shores* for Lesley's publishers.) Through her, Lesley met Truman Capote and Tennessee Williams. 'Giddy boys' took her to the Puerto Rican dance halls where they watched male dancers competing like fighting cocks. Ali Khan, encountered in grander circles, was intrigued to hear about Lesley's sorties; one evening soon afterwards she saw him at a scruffy dance hall, leading in a beauty on each arm.

Their cramped accommodation relieved Romain and Lesley of the obligation to have guests to stay, but he was called on to entertain and sometimes escort a stream of visitors passing through New York. Neither of them ever forgot a weekend they spent in Washington with André Malraux and his wife Madeleine. Malraux's non-stop flow of monologue in his weird swooping voice mesmerized the entire lounge car throughout the long train ride from New York, continued unbroken in the taxi to their hotel and all through dinner, and hardly faltered the following day on their visit to the art galleries, which had been specially closed to other visitors. Romain, who hugely admired Malraux but never visited museums if he could help it, had to lie down before lunch in order to recover from the double assault on his energy. Lesley, wisely steering away from intellectual topics, found that cats were an excellent mainstay (Malraux was another cat lover), and he was sympathetic and interested concerning her quest for illustrations for her book.

In late summer 1953, Lesley visited London to deliver her manuscript. Only then was a contract drawn up and agreed with John Murray. 'The Simon & Schuster title, of which she appears to approve, is THE WILDER SHORES OF LOVE,' Jock Murray's memo of 14 August commented. Before writing her book she had stressed her intention to avoid anything akin to E.M. Hull's notorious bodice-ripper *The Sheikh*, Rudolph Valentino (equally notorious as the sheikh in the movie) or the early-nineteenth-century 'false-orientalism' of Byron and Delacroix. However, when she came to the presentation of *The Wilder Shores of Love* she was unable to resist the allure of stereotypical oriental images to seduce her readers. She had designed a jacket and the publishers were going to use 'rather a doubtful endpaper' of a nude reclining across the double-page spread. Lesley was charming but steely with her English publisher, insisting on a final clause in her contract which stipulated that she held translation, film, TV, dramatic, American and all serial rights, although Murrays could act as her agent in the sale of translation rights, in which case they would get an agent's 10 per cent commission.

Her other priority in London was to see her mother and pour an avalanche of complaints about Romain over her extensive round of friends. She returned to New York after a long absence to find the flat empty and neglected. She was loyal about the excellent reviews that met the London publication of Romain's *The Colours of the Day*, but she admitted months later that she had come back to emotional turmoil.

Then there was a panic over the proofs of *The Wilder Shores of Love*, whose arrival in February threatened to coincide with the fortnight's leave that Romain had planned in Guatemala and Mexico. Lesley, determined to go too, barely managed to correct the proofs in time despite Romain's sudden urge to invite guests to lunches and suppers at home, for which she had to cater. The day before they left (a week late), Charles Boyer and the French theatre company all trooped in and stayed until teatime. Once she would have fainted at the matinée idol's glance, now all she could think about was what to pack and her proof corrections.

They flew to Guatemala, travelling on by small plane and broken-down bus at an exhausting pace and spending no two nights in the same bed. Lesley admitted to feeling middle-aged for the first time. Romain was overwhelmed by Mexico and for once was seized by an insatiable urge to see *everything*: every Aztec or Mayan ruin, baroque church, market and dusty street. In searingly hot Yucatán, bundled up in jeans, socks, gloves, sunglasses and hat against iguanas and the savage sun, Lesley clambered after him over the ruined temples, pleading for a rest, while he ploughed on. Nonetheless, like him she was fascinated by the sinister splendours of Mexico and its ferocious beauty. She took detailed notes, which she later combined with notes from two later visits and made into a fragmented impressionistic journal like her Balkan diary.

Later that spring Hélène found her again in despair about Romain. Their biggest crises seemed to be cyclical, boiling up in late spring around his birthday, so often a cause for his despondency. He wept, he cried that he couldn't go on: 'It's his Russian soul exhaling,' as Mme Hoppenot put it, but at this stage Lesley would have none of Romain's Russian soul. He wanted to join the Service de Valeur (Service des Oeuvres), which would allow him to indulge his passion for the cinema and go to the Cannes Film Festival with Martine Carol. The trouble was that Romain's mood swings were so violent, his impetuous greed so arbitrary, it was hard to know when to take him seriously. Lesley didn't ask so much of him, she told Hélène; when they married they had promised each other their freedom and she had freely given it. But was it enough for her to say 'I adore him', her friend wondered, to oblige him to honour the contract?

Lesley was also concerned about her mother, who lived alone and had been ill. She thought of returning to England that autumn, but quailed at the prospect of a short visit inevitably followed by a painful leavetaking. In the event she did not make the trip.

Romain's frustration at his constipated career intensified after June, when the head of state, Pierre Mendès-France, appointed a new government. Mendès-France and Romain had been Free French air force comrades during the war, and although they had not warmed to each other Romain hoped that newly appointed Gaullist ministers might help his cause. Instead he returned from his annual summer leave in Roquebrune in desperation, bitterly watching colleagues overtake him in the directory of diplomatic ranks.

The Wilder Shores of Love was published on 1 September 1954 and was an instant sensational success. It was the British Book Society choice for that month and the US Book of the Month Club's recommendation. It topped the best-seller lists: by 10 September British sales had reached 22,000 and Simon & Schuster were reprinting in the US. Features and extracts were splashed over newspaper and magazine spreads: US *Vogue* featured it; *Mademoiselle* took an extract.

The book was a gift for reviewers. Even Freya Stark was gently complimentary. Her husband Stewart Perowne announced on the BBC Arabic Service that 'It should be read by everyone who is interested in the interplay of East and West, and more particularly in the relations between Arabs and Europeans.' The *Sunday Express* found it 'a dazzling experiment in biography'; *The Economist* called it 'spicy' and 'rococo' while adding that the author tended to add gossip and scandal for effect 'with a parenthetic "if the story be true"'.

Elizabeth Bowen in the *Tatler* picked up the unsettling message that emancipation is not every woman's dream. Lesley's subjects 'definitely reacted against progress: the East drew them, the East they sought . . . In each case, the dominating daydream became reality.' She found

Isabelle Eberhardt the most compelling and concluded that the book was saved from vulgarity by Lesley's 'lightness, kindness and irony of style, and her respect for the human passions'.

Time Magazine in the US concluded that male readers might well be fascinated but would 'find it hard to swallow the idea that [Lesley's subjects] were in search of "feminine passivity." By comparison, the Four Horsemen of the Apocalypse seem like little old softies.'

Her old friend Peter Quennell in the *Mail* found Jane Digby 'something of a bore' but agreed that the 'brilliant sketch' of Eberhardt was 'undoubtedly the best'. The *TLS* too was intrigued by Lesley's portrait of this 'violent, strident, uncomfortable creature', a 'clever and shrewd' conclusion to 'a sophisticated, witty though often flashy book'. The exception was the *Astrologer's Quarterly*, whose chief interest was in the horoscope Lesley had commissioned for Isabelle Eberhardt. The reviewer found the map 'a striking piece of work, though one could not expect Mrs Hone [the astrologer], or anyone else, to do justice to this native's truly deplorable disposition and habits'.

Wilder Shores brought Lesley cult status on both sides of the Atlantic and transformed her creative life as well as her circumstances, establishing the territory that would characterize her writing thereafter. The trajectory which had carried her through her early years as an artist-illustrator, via journalism and travel writing, now launched her into a new medium that suited her perfectly. In her books she could explore and reinvent the exotic landscapes and past eras that had possessed her imagination since childhood, and inhabit the lives of the historical figures with whom she passionately empathized.

Her elegant, racy recitative of the four runaways' adventures was irresistible to a generation of female readers deprived by years of post-war retrenchment. *Wilder Shores* opened up far horizons, bestowing on the Middle East and the Islamic world an aura of fascination, and planting in her younger readers a seed of curiosity that often bloomed years later. The intensely visual cast of her imagination could have been sparked long before her recent travels, by the nineteenth-century orientalist landscapes and genre paintings that hung in the galleries of her childhood. Her heightened verbal descriptions, dwelling on detail, summoned up the splendour and squalor of North Africa in visceral intensity. 'The uneven cobbled alleys were slimy with filth; rats fattened on the refuse; entrails glowed red on the butchers' stalls, beside the bouquets of carnations or jasmine with which the Arabs love to surround themselves. Sometimes, behind a tattered calico curtain, a blue-tiled courtyard could be glimpsed, with a fig tree, or a fountain'.

Wilder Shores hardly needed high-octane marketing to give it mass appeal. It was 'historical', yet the text vibrated with the energy and éclat of fiction. If the publicity focused on the 'romance' of her subjects in the loose contemporary usage (regardless of the reality of the sultan's seraglio and Eberhardt's surreal desert drowning), the telling was Romantic in the nineteenth-century sense: picturesque, original, free and imaginative in style.

A distinctive voice had emerged, powerful enough to soar into headier flights, yet knowing exactly when to puncture them: witty, psychologically astute and utterly without sentiment. 'So loving a nature,' Lesley Blanch remarks crisply of Isabel and Richard Burton, 'must have been an especial pleasure for him to torment.' The text sparkles with aperçus about her female adventurers, their impulse to travel and their commitment to loving. Each comment offers perceptive insight into character and motivation, and each could apply with equal accuracy to Lesley herself.

Much of the book's success was due to Lesley's choice of subject matter, which was both original and influential. She uncovered a rich seam of inspiration for other writers, starting a rush to mine the lives of women travellers. Digby, Burton and Eberhardt all later became subjects of exhaustive research and scholarship, giving rise to reservations about the factual accuracy in Lesley's *profeels*, as she referred to them. Nearly twenty-five years before *Orientalism*, Edward Said's seminal study, Lesley could not avoid the pitfalls awaiting a Western sensibility plunged into exoticism and 'The Other', and her emphasis on the 'civilizing' influence of her heroines (Lady Jane Digby, Aimée Dubucq) over their Eastern surroundings lacks contemporary political correctness. All the same, Lesley had no truck with imperialism as such and her psychological acumen and recondite knowledge give her portraits a clarity and edge unmatched by subsequent renderings.

The most elusive of her protagonists, Aimée Dubucq, instantly attracted the greatest attention; her story was serialized in French *Elle* and British and American *Harper's Bazaar*. The absence of pictorial proof (or any other sort) of Aimée in the harem didn't deter Lesley from dwelling on her physical appearance in voluptuous detail. Apart from the upturned nose which Lesley observed in the sole existing portrait of the sixteen-year-old girl, there is a hint of the author's fancied younger self in outlandish travesty, hennaed and bejewelled, shimmering behind the figure of the *giaour*. The erotic vision of the twenty-one-year-old fair-skinned, golden-haired beauty, groomed in the school of love as an odalisque for the Sultan's pleasure, beckoned seductively to Hollywood. Aimée was irresistible, the lascivious West's classic erotic symbol of the East, surrounded by all the props: pirates, white slaves, eunuchs wielding 'slashing hippopotamus-hide whips', steaming heaps of decapitated heads, the harem (though one whose occupants wielded hidden power), jewels, opium and debauchery. MGM and Warner Brothers competed for the story and MGM eventually bought rights for *The Blonde Sultan*, to star Elizabeth Taylor (who was renowned for her dark hair). Lesley's friend Gavin Lambert wrote a screenplay.

Yet in contrast to the other three heroines in *Wilder Shores*, later researches on Aimée Dubucq, fainting white slave and later calculating French Sultana, only boomerang back to Lesley Blanch. Historians have added little except the occasional aside, this one by Philip Mansel:

> There is no hard evidence for the story that [Sultan Mahmud II's] mother Nakshidil, Valide Sultan [Queen Mother] from 1808 until her death in 1817, was a cousin of the Empress Josephine and influenced her son to Westernize. As Valide she could have established contact with the outside world. Such rumours, like later stories about Ataturk's mother, reveal Western unwillingness to attribute successful modernization to a Turk.

The genie of the seraglio, whose adventures seduced publishers, agents, Hollywood moguls and thousands of readers, dematerialized and faded away. The script was put aside, the movie never made (possibly for lack of historical evidence), and the Scheherazade who had conjured her up moved quietly on.

Even so, the legend refuses to die. Lambert insisted that he had found Nakshidil's tomb in Istanbul, and a source referring to Father Chrysostome, the priest who had listened to her last confession and given her absolution. Her story reappears in the historical thriller *Turkish Gambit* by the Russian writer Boris Akunin: 'In Turkey she is known by the name of Nashedil-Sultan. She gave birth to Prince

Mehmed . . . His mother taught him French and gave him a taste for French literature and French free-thinking. Ever since then Turkey has looked to the West.'

Romain, opening a copy of *Wilder Shores* after it was published, read Lesley's dedication to him and burst into tears. Not long afterwards, at a dinner given by the Hoppenots for the sculptor Alexander Calder (who had invited himself and his wife over to adjust the mobile that his hosts owned), Romain was overwhelmed by admiration for Calder, touched by his unassuming innocence and dishevelled clothes. He launched into praise for the extraordinary talents of the French embassy personnel in Berne and New York: the ambassador a writer and poet, his wife a distinguished photographer, he himself a novelist, his wife a biographer, and so on. His hosts, wondering what had triggered his outburst, concluded that he was doing his best to hide his chagrin at his wife's success.

Later *Elle* magazine persuaded him to write a piece about the experience, which they headed 'Lesley is a sorceress' with the subtitle 'Does a successful wife undermine a man's self-confidence?' He later made light of his reaction in an article for *Actualité littéraire*, amusingly describing being pursued into the bathroom in their flat by a journalist wanting to quiz him about being 'Monsieur Blanch'. But that was after *The Roots of Heaven* had finally brought him the coveted Prix Goncourt and he could afford to be ironic.

Meanwhile it was all the wrong way round, surely. Romain was forty and in his prime, yet his verbal cartwheels and charismatic performances in the glare of the US media were ignored by his taskmasters at the Quai d'Orsay, and his early literary promise had all but faded out. He anxiously examined his face each day for fresh wrinkles; fretting against the ravages of ageing, he exercised violently and insisted on a diet of red meat and salads. When Hélène Hoppenot agreed that growing old was dreadful, but added that one got used to it, he was aghast: what she had just said was the worst thing of all. Almost certainly pure envy prompted him to subject Lesley to a new round of catering night after night for supper party guests he had invited. Yet, relegated to second place in her marriage to a Don Juan years younger than herself, his well-rounded wife excelled in the kitchen and entertained their guests with aplomb, while her first try at authorhood had taken her straight past him into the best-seller lists. Suddenly she was an international celebrity. Twisting the knife still further, she was already deep into her next project, an edited version of the Regency courtesan Harriette Wilson's memoirs for Simon & Schuster in the US (about which Murray was cautious).

At the mercy of his own capricious temperament, Romain was always dissatisfied with his lot. For her part Lesley's narcissism was a formidable defence against his contagious fits of depression; though not impenetrable, it armed her enough to maintain a punishing schedule and (when they were not persecuting each other) often to enjoy herself. Nonetheless the marriage was hard to sustain in their small flat while he languished in a state of cosmic desperation.

Romain and Lesley had a way of drawing everyone around them into their turbulent affairs, even the Olympian Hoppenots, whose circles of acquaintance read like an international *Who's Who* of the arts and diplomacy. Romain's travails at the hands of Quai d'Orsay bureaucracy continued. Ambassador Hoppenot sent a fusillade of memoranda to Raymond Bousquet, head of personnel at the Quai d'Orsay, reviewing Romain's outstanding work at the UN and pointing out that his promotion was two years overdue. It was deplorable, he protested, that younger Vichyist staff, placed 'by mistake' in the *cadre complémentaire*, should be promoted before a professional diplomat with Romain's wartime honours and the highest recommendations. Finally, after Hoppenot had doggedly sent copies of his report on Romain to every relevant head of department, the minister of foreign affairs and the French ambassador in Washington, his efforts succeeded. At the last moment, shortly before Romain's UN term came to an end, he was offered a London posting, working on the Treaty of Brussels.

Lesley, basking in her newfound celebrity, saw no good reason to leave and had no wish to return to London. She was negotiating with MGM for the film rights (she got the fee she held out for and immediately invested it), answering fan mail, broadcasting radio interviews and being fêted everywhere. She wrote vaguely to Jock Murray just before her husband quit New York that where he would live was uncertain; he would be better off in a hotel, which was more or less how he treated his home, expecting a leg of lamb to be sizzling in the oven for him day and night. She would not be lonely without him in New York and had plenty of business to attend to.

Scatty as she claimed to be about 'buisness' [sic], Lesley revealed admirable acumen in choosing her advisers. Her friend and confidante Anita Loos told her not to show her hand in the matter of film options before the book was published. Then she took on Robert Lantz (a fellow contributor on *The Leader* ten years earlier) to negotiate the agreement with MGM on the Aimée story, despite an existing arrangement with her agent Marie Rodell. Rodell's fury was redoubled when she discovered that Lesley had also forgotten to inform her that John Murray was signed to deal with translation rights and they had been negotiating against each other. Lesley blandly admitted that she was completely in the wrong and suggested that the 'chic' solution would be for John Murray to arrange to pay the commission on each sale to Ms Rodell.

Lesley's associates were inveigled into dealing with all manner of unexpected tasks for her. She had already stayed overnight with Jock and Diana Murray on visits to London; now her publisher found himself sorting out her income tax. She had decided to claim French nationality for tax reasons, though still a British citizen and not resident in the USA. Murray and her accountants, delightfully named Lionel Lemon and Co., were requested to negotiate her royalties and tax matters between them. Osyth Leeston, her editor at John Murray, was also enlisted to look after Lesley's mother, redirecting payments from Lesley's advances to Martha, sending her proofs and finished copies, and checking on her health.

That autumn *Wilder Shores* made Lesley a celebrity. New York loves a winner and she purred with pleasure, savouring her success. Romain was taken aback when Arab-speaking journalists at the UN, delighted to meet Mme Gary unmasked as the famous Lesley Blanch, fell on the book as a delicious diversion and eagerly discussed an Arabic translation. Among the guests at a gala dinner in her honour were Judy Garland, Anita Loos, Alistair Cooke, Mainbocher and either Rodgers or Hammerstein (she wasn't sure which). Lord Beaverbrook, Lesley's neighbour at dinner another evening, had told her she must return to England where anything she asked for would be hers. She was invited to Osbert Sitwell's birthday party. Noël Coward wanted to play the part of Richard Burton! The Eartha Kitt song 'Monotonous' could almost have been written for Lesley: 'And, furthermore, Ike likes me – Monotonous . . .'

★

Chaotic to the last, Romain phoned Mme Hoppenot at 9 a.m. on the day his boat was due to sail and asked to see her in five minutes' time. Rushing in, he explained breathlessly to the startled ambassadress that as he owned no luggage (Lesley had always done his packing before), he had bought some trunks that were too big to go through the front door of the flat and had had to be packed outside in the communal corridor. The stress of his departure had kept him awake for two nights, and he had nowhere to stay in London. Tears welled in his eyes; he must leave her for his boat embarked in two hours and he still had to say goodbye to her husband. Hurrying off to M. Hoppenot's rooms, he fell into the ambassador's arms, weeping.

Romain reached London in a state of exhaustion and was immediately plunged into crisis. His arrival at the embassy just preceded an ambassadorial changeover and at the last minute the ambassador designate, Jean Chauvel, refused point blank to accept him. Raymond Bousquet at the Quai d'Orsay hurriedly wired Henri Hoppenot in New York, telling him to prevent Romain from leaving, 'due to an unforeseen obstacle', but by then Romain was already halfway across the Atlantic.

In London, finding himself in a humiliating position of professional limbo, Romain sent a panic-stricken telegram to Hoppenot, begging him to keep his position open in New York, but he had been so frankly thrilled to leave that this was no longer an option. He flung off to spend Christmas and the New Year in Roquebrune, incommunicado except by the post office telephone, while Bousquet strove to find a solution.

Was it was another case of Vichyist–Gaullist antipathy? Or of professional envy (Chauvel too fancied himself a writer)? It seems that Chauvel believed he recognized himself as the character in a short story by Romain. Romain swore that he had written the first draft in Sofia in 1948 long before he had met Chauvel or known anything about him (forgetting that Lesley and he had left Bulgaria in December 1947). But the ambassador would not recant.

The Hoppenots, reading Romain's letter of self-justification, couldn't help smiling at the unhappy timing and sequence of events. He concluded with a flourish of admiration for Madame Hoppenot (M. Hoppenot rolled his eyes at this breach of convention) and added that he was suffering from a cold and was feeling mildly paranoid, 'due no doubt to my Jewish blood or perhaps to my grandfather who was only a cobbler in Lithuania' – which was a really likely prelude, he continued ironically, for a future ambassador of France.

The Hoppenots had a way of inviting confidence, and Romain's frank admission of his origins was not the only occasion when he and Lesley let down their guard with the ambassador or his wife. The previous October, Hélène and Lesley had taken a trip together to Lancaster, in the Amish region. On the way home, while they were discussing family matters and the presence or absence of maternal love, Lesley let slip that she had felt no maternal love whatsoever after she had given birth to her daughter. Then she bit her lip with embarrassment at the accidental revelation. Hélène couldn't help asking whether she was still alive. Lesley, blushing and mortified, replied that she had not brought up the child and had no idea what had happened to her; it was something from her past that she was unwilling to talk about and had never mentioned to anyone. Hélène, shocked, hoped that she had kept her disapproval well hidden. I found no other record of this traumatic event in Lesley's life. It is inconceivable that Mme Hoppenot would have invented this revelation or, equally, that Romain ever heard about it.

After returning to London from Roquebrune, he turned down offers of posts in Addis Ababa and Belgrade, and succumbed to a breakdown serious enough for his admission to the King Edward VII Hospital for Officers, 1 Beaumont House, W1. He wrote to René and Sylvia Agid that he had reached the end of his nervous energy and was incapable of making any decisions.

Long afterwards, in his memoir *La Nuit sera calme* (1974), he attributed his crack-up to the stress of his continual performances defending France's voltes-face in policy in front of microphones and TV cameras during sessions of the General Assembly. Although Romain had embraced French citizenship, at heart he was an internationalist. The United Nations Organization had embodied his greatest hopes for humanity, and seeing UN ideals corroded daily by venery and national interests affected him like a personal attack. Eventually he evacuated his disillusion into a scathing satire, *L'homme à la colombe (The Man with the Dove)*, published pseudonymously in 1958.

What he did not mention as contributory factors to his breakdown were the humiliating obstructions to his career, plus his wife's meteoric rise to fame as a writer in contrast to his own continuing lack of success. Lesley herself was certain that her achievement in the face of his failure badly eroded his morale.

The hospital urged his wife to rush to his bedside, as he was threatening to throw himself out of the window. Lesley impassively told them not to worry until he had actually climbed on to the window sill. (She said afterwards that she had been told by his psychoanalyst on no account to be oversympathetic.) After his discharge he took a flat at the South Kensington end of the Brompton Road, still unable to make the smallest decision. His refusal of a covetable job offer in Tehran was the last straw for Lesley, who had already vaguely suggested a book on Persia or Afghanistan to Murray; Ali Khan, no less, had promised her all the contacts she would need. Jock sympathized, 'very sad' that Romain had refused Persia.

While convalescing, Romain stayed one weekend with Anne and Macdonald Hastings in Anne's cottage at Aldworth, Berkshire. She was pleased to see him, though dismayed by his impenetrable silence during their long walk together over the downs. After the weekend she and Mac had to return to London, but she offered Romain the keys and invited him to stay on. Rose Cottage was cosy, the weather was fine, the sweeping downs superb for walking, and she employed a first-class cook. So it was that Romain made his first serious inroads into writing *The Roots of Heaven*, the novel about African elephants that would finally win him the French literary honours he craved, in rural Berkshire.

In New York Lesley had been frankly relieved by Romain's departure. A week later when she joined Hélène, her granddaughter Anne, her close friend Renée de Becker and the staff at the ritual present-giving ceremony round the Christmas tree, Mme Hoppenot observed that Lesley was unusually composed for 'une personne si tumultueuse'. In February Lesley confided that Romain had heard from friends that she was 'fort gaie' in his absence and was bombarding her with almost illegible tracts of theatrical despair. Lesley resisted; at last she had time to get on with her own work without distraction. For *The Game of Hearts*, her edited version of Harriette Wilson's memoirs, Simon & Schuster in New York had persuaded her against her better judgement to intersperse Harriette's racy narrative with inserts by Harriette's contemporary and arch-rival, Julia Johnstone. Poor Jock Murray was sent the inserts separately; the cutting and pasting was too time-consuming a process for her to repeat it. Pleased with her long and idiosyncratic introduction, she was hopeful that he would publish. Then she tackled *Round the World in Eighty Dishes*, her cookbook for young readers, to be published by Simon & Schuster. By March she had finished the text; the need for clear explanations and meticulous accuracy in the recipes left her thoroughly disaffected with children and saucepans. Typically equally of Jock's caution and Lesley's powers of persuasion, he had turned down these projects when she first suggested them but ended up publishing both. Meanwhile the phenomenal success of *Wilder Shores* continued to astound them. By March Swedish, German, French and Dutch translation rights had been sold, and Japanese, Israeli and Norwegian translations were being considered.

After finishing her book projects and attending to some journalism, plus more press and radio interviews, she had to catch up with all the day-to-day turmoil of winding up their years in New York, packing and leaving. She eventually arrived in London in late April or May 1955, where she stayed with Eden and Marston Fleming at 7 Montpelier Terrace, near Harrods. She and Romain were both emotionally exhausted and relieved to be apart. The marriage, it seemed, was definitively over.

Romain was certainly behaving oddly. Soon after his arrival in England he had delivered Lesley's weighty manuscript of Harriette Wilson's memoirs to Jock and Diana Murray and dined with them at home. He had a streaming cold, and they lent him a sweater and three handkerchiefs. The following May he wrote to Jock from King Edward VII Hospital, claiming that he was being treated for ulcerous colitis. The handkerchiefs had been enormously helpful because whenever he had a serious problem, he could distract himself by worrying about them instead (he eventually returned them after having them monogrammed as a gesture of thanks). He went on to urge Jock not to publish Lesley's edited Harriette Wilson book in Britain: 'specialising in scandal' was demeaning to her and would damage her reputation in Britain. A few days later he retracted, praised her magnificent writing and editing and apologized profusely for meddling in her affairs.

Ambassador Chauvel grudgingly authorized Romain to stay in London until August at the latest. He left early for his annual leave in Roquebrune, where he always felt better. At the end of it his future was still unsettled and his leave was extended until the end of September. For once he had the luxury of weeks, months even, to sink into his writing, in solitude, in the place he loved best. When not scribbling obsessively in the medieval tower, he ran down to the sea to swim and sun himself into a stupor.

In this healing atmosphere he at last began to relax and think about reassembling his fractured existence. Romain had been the party agitating for divorce, but now he contacted Lesley and suggested she join him there. As impossible as they had found life together, there were still ties that kept him bound to his wife. By late June she too was installed in Roquebrune, happy and distracted, looking after Romain, cooking for them both, chivvying workmen and despairing of her writing.

Nonetheless, Lesley was determined not to lose her newfound creative momentum. Their erratic marriage made her all the more ambitious to capitalize on the success of *Wilder Shores*, which had proved unquestionably that she was a writer. In July she visited London to push on negotiations for her projects with John Murray. Two contracts were agreed, with Mme Arnaud, her French agent, for her cookbook and more importantly, a new biographical project for Murray on Shamyl, the fabled nineteenth-century Caucasian warrior prophet, provisionally titled *Sultans and Warriors*. The cheap portrait of Shamyl that had caught her imagination as a little girl had stayed with her and his presence had haunted her prodigious readings of Russian histories and memoirs. In New York her imagination had been unexpectedly sparked by Count Hilarion Voronzov, who was descended from Shamyl's great enemy Count Michael Voronzov, viceroy of southern Russia and commander-in-chief of Russia's Armies of the South. Now the imam was her quarry and she was about to follow him across Europe.

She travelled on to Venice, which was insufferably hot, returned to Roquebrune, then went on to Athens. From there she embarked on her main object, a research trip to Istanbul in pursuit of a descendant of Shamyl's, but he had left for Smyrna and eluded her. Shivering in the biting north wind, she was lent a chic Burberry by an emerald merchant in the souk. She cultivated a Turkish historian, and an archivist in the seraglio whose only common language was Bulgarian, fell in love all over again with Istanbul and Broussa, and visited Konyia and Izmir. Baulked in her research on Shamyl, she was distracted again by the glittering history of the sultan's palace and became enthused about Pierre Loti, the nineteenth-century French writer who had evoked the city so brilliantly. But if she wanted to write about him she would have to be quick about it, because 'Sachie' Sitwell, whom she had met and gone about with in Istanbul with his wife Georgia, had shown unmistakable signs of interest in Loti.

She returned to Roquebrune in September, leaving untouched the bank transfer that Murrays had laboriously arranged for her in Istanbul. Besides embarking on the Loti piece, she persuaded Romain to help her rework the unsatisfactory translation of *Wilder Shores* which had been commissioned by the French publisher Plon. But he was soon distracted and went off to visit René and Sylvia Agid at the extraordinary mansion in Savigny-sur-Orge that they had bought after the death of René's father. He left behind his best suit on his way to London and asked them to send it on him – he could not dine out without it – then returned to Roquebrune until 7 November. He was still without a new appointment, having turned down four offers. In October Lesley wired M. Hoppenot, who was temporarily posted to Saigon, to ask on Romain's behalf whether he stood a chance of being posted there as press attaché, assuming it was still free. M. Hoppenot diplomatically replied that he would naturally welcome Romain but the work was hard and the climate unbearable; he agreed with his wife that steadier nerves than Romain's were needed for the diplomatic crisis there.

At last, on 16 November 1955, Romain heard that the foreign minister, Maurice Couve de Murville, had agreed to his promotion and he was appointed as consul general for France to Los Angeles, starting on 15 January 1956. In December, the ministry having reviewed his career and attached his wartime Resistance record, his promotion came through, together with the award of several months' back pay. For the time being, his agonizing displacement was over and he had a future.

While Romain came and went, Lesley stayed on and on at Roquebrune, wearing her burnous over layers of summer clothes as autumn, then winter, set in. She felt protected by the ancient thick whitewashed walls in the jumble of little rooms connected by crooked staircases, and distracted herself by painting bright naive patterns on the undersized doors where visitors banged their heads on the lintels. She supervised more building work: a new bathroom was laboriously installed, and a Turkish room, 'sort of Russian-Turkish faux Gothique Arabe', which pleased her enormously and amazed everyone who saw it. Her finances were the only brake on her fantasies, which had been inflamed by her visit to the seraglio and by the influence of Loti, who had created his own quarters *à la Turque* at his home in Rochefort.

She had plenty of work to attend to. Romain had helped her less than she hoped on the French translation of *Wilder Shores* and Plon was uncooperative about her corrections, so she put it aside. That autumn, her cookbook *Round the World in Eighty Dishes* was published in New York by Harper Brothers and she began the process of adapting it for British readers after Murray received a severe reader's report: 'It cannot be designed simply for those living in London and yoghourt, avocados, pineapples, aubergines, peppers etc are difficult to obtain out of London and also very dear.' She had originally written the book for children, after the young son of friends of hers on Long Island had disappeared to the kitchen and produced an excellent omelette for them all. Now she was turning it into a kind of illustrated notebook, which was due in early 1956. Murray liked her treatment and encouraged her to continue with her pen-and-ink drawings to accompany the text.

Despite being hampered by a lack of reference books she reworked her Loti piece for the *Cornhill*, as Jock Murray had tactfully requested; she was desperately anxious to see it in print before Sitwell cut in. She had inherited from her mother a love for Loti's 'travel novels', in which he evoked with melancholy ecstasy his ports of call as an ensign in the French navy, 'placing a *moi* in every landscape', as Lesley neatly put it, always adding a tragic romantic entanglement. She looked indulgently on his eccentricities and recognized in him a kindred spirit for whom exoticism expanded from background material to his whole subject. She empathized too with his escapist wanderlust, his way of turning the spirit of place into an act of possession, his ecstatic nostalgia. Istanbul was his greatest passion and for Lesley he was the supreme interpreter of the Constantinople of his day. 'Loti in Loti-land' gave her the excuse to revisit the city and, true to her subject, to perform that same sleight of summoning up its sinister beauty with him framed in it. Eventually she would write a full biography; meanwhile her essay for the *Cornhill* stamped her claim on him, capturing the essence of Loti and his Elysium.

7

Los Angeles I
Lady L.

Here, if anywhere else in America, I seem to hear the coming
footsteps of the muse.

William Butler Yeats, visiting Los Angeles

A MONTH AFTER Romain took up his new post in Los Angeles
on 3 February 1956, Lesley had yet to arrive. More dramas had
erupted between them in January, leaving her in Roquebrune doubtful whether she would join him in America at all. Had word reached
her from Paris about Romain's fresh scandal?

The news of his promotion had surely gone to his head, for on a
visit to London before Christmas he had arranged to have lunch with
Elizabeth Jane Howard. They had met earlier that year over supper,
when she was involved with his friend Arthur Koestler; since then the
couple had separated. Wasting no time, Romain told her matter-of-
factly that he had fallen in love with her when they were first introduced. He was about to be posted to Los Angeles and proposed that
she should join him there as his official mistress. While there was no
question of a divorce from Lesley, the Quai d'Orsay would accommodate a regular arrangement and would foot the bill for shipping her
furniture. He believed they would be very happy together, and while
she was considering it why didn't they have lunch.

Elizabeth Jane Howard was committed to the credo of romantic
love, but was nonetheless dumbfounded by Romain's proposition;
she hardly knew the man and here he was talking about furniture
removals. She sensibly suggested that they spend a trial week together
in Paris first, to which he agreed. In terms of physical attraction, she
said, 'I realized fairly early on in the week that it wasn't going to work';
his Byronic tendencies did not appeal. Afterwards he seemed relieved

when she let him know that she wasn't going to join him in America. His relief would have been redoubled if Lesley had got wind of the affair from one of the friends he introduced to Ms Howard in Paris (to see if they approved, she suspected).

It seems Lesley *had* been told about this exploit, unless there were others, since she admitted to being extremely upset by private upheavals in the New Year; while Romain's new post was in any case briefly thrown into doubt by one of France's recurring post-election political crises. She had planned to visit London but changed her mind and stayed on in France, reluctant to leave her Arabian Nights refuge in Roquebrune and her new companion, a talkative little cat who draped himself round her neck while she cooked and slept beside her with his head on the pillow. Murray was delighted with her drawings for *Round the World in Eighty Dishes*, pasted up in order and dispatched in time to meet his February deadline. That month, snowed in, frozen up and running out of coal, she revised the American text and sent that off too. Then she lingered beneath the almond blossom to check translations and proofs of the Loti essay, which had been sent out to her, rescheduled to appear in the *Cornhill*'s spring issue. James Lees-Milne, who was also seeing out the winter in his house in Roquebrune, sat with her in full evening fig during the intervals of *Rigoletto* at the Opera House in Monte Carlo, sternly proof-correcting her grammar and punctuation.

When she finally arrived in Los Angeles in March, Romain was already entrenched at the consulate and delighted with his new posting. Lesley made up for her absence by forcefully asserting her occupation of the Consul-General's ground-floor living quarters, directly below the administrative offices on the first floor of the consulate. She was critical of the modest Spanish-colonial style of the house and its location at the 'wrong end' of Hollywood. The former bohemian now saw her *raison d'être* in terms of maintaining her husband's status, especially in Los Angeles, city of the self-made, where appearances were all. Of course they were to her, too.

Outpost Drive is tucked behind and above Hollywood Boulevard; just past the back garden of the former consulate, the road curves away into the steep green Hollywood hills. A round tower at the join of the L-shaped building of number 1919 holds a curved staircase and a central hall, leading into a sunken dining room with a painted ceiling in the left wing, and to the right a spacious reception room with a tiled floor and french windows opening on to the garden. Behind that were separate quarters for Romain and Lesley, each with their own bedroom and bathroom, plus accommodation for live-in household help.

The household underwent savage upheavals as carpenters and decorators worked their way through the rooms, before Lesley unpacked and arranged her baroque cargo of furniture and chattels, asserting her dominion over the premises. Orange swags and canopies framed the reception rooms along with high-density paintings, icons, orientalia, books, cushions and curiosities. She battled with the maid and fostered the garden, helped and hindered by two gardeners, one Mexican and one Japanese, who struggled for supremacy on alternate weeks.

After making herself at home and acquiring three kittens, Lesley lost no time in picking up old acquaintances and making new ones. Whenever she could, she worked out of doors among her books, on oriental rugs strewn over the back lawn. The cats chased after hummingbirds and butterflies, scattering her notes, while keening strains of Bulgarian folk harmonies rose from the record player to the ears of startled consulate staff and visitors.

Romain's new post was equivalent to ambassadorial rank, but administrative rather than political. Apart from routine consulate bureaucracy (births, deaths, marriages, visas, green cards, stamping of passports, etc.) and business matters, which were dealt with by a staff of seven working on the first floor, there were demands on his time from a constant round of press conferences, receptions, openings, hospitality to visiting dignitaries, and so forth.

The consulate staff quickly learnt that Romain was 'not cut from the same cloth as most diplomats' and was bored by the more tedious dealings with his French constituents. His beautiful secretary Odette Benedictis, who first met the new Consul-General in the kitchen, wearing nothing but a pair of boxer shorts and munching a raw carrot, was enlisted as his discreet ally and mistress-in-reserve. On the other hand Jean Ortoli, the joint-consul and a career diplomat, disapproved of Romain and refused to deputize for him in his absence. After persistently badgering the Quai d'Orsay, Romain managed to acquire a second joint-consul, Yvonne-Louise Pétrement, to shoulder the brunt of the administrative load and cover for him during his sometimes lengthy leaves of absence.

The consulate's territory was enormous, encompassing diverse French communities scattered over Arizona, New Mexico and southern California. Lesley was especially intrigued to hear of 2,000 Basque shepherds up in the Sierras, whom she longed to lure to the consulate to enliven the annual Bastille Day celebrations, but they never had time to leave their flocks.

Despite the continual interruptions of his professional life, Romain made it clear to his staff that he was a writer first. Nothing could deflect his relentless inner demon. Every morning he wrote in his office from seven until ten, when the consulate opened for business, and during quiet spells he disappeared to do more writing.

Lesley arranged the Consul-General's formal lunches and dinners, and sometimes stood in for Romain as escort to French diplomats and VIPs passing through Los Angeles and hoping to be shown round Hollywood. She also had a hand in hosting the grand receptions and cocktail parties, which were generally organized by the consulate staff. The ambience created by the new Consul-General and his wife was decidedly un-French. Instead of Gallic formality and Louis Quinze furniture, visitors met Romain's unpredictable brilliance and Lesley's crisp English manners, framed by a decor akin to a Turkish harem. Their singular presentation was welcomed in Los Angeles where fantasy was endemic and every conceivable style flourished. Mexican Aztec, Victorian Gothic, Russo-Turkish bordello, Streamline Moderne were all equally incomers to the desert city, even the garden plants and trees which so quickly reverted to jungle wilderness.

Like so many other artists and writers before and since, Romain and Lesley flourished in the liberating atmosphere of the sprawling metropolis, peopled by émigrés and birds of passage like themselves. Romain would become impatient to leave before long, as he always did; but Lesley came to love their niche there, and when their time was up she felt like an exile from paradise. Beyond its hospitable climate and easy living, she found it hard to explain the attractions of Los Angeles. Its vitality and the intoxicating sense of freedom it seemed to offer were infectious. The very lack of a historic past made its uncentred suburbs a haven for every cult and stylistic extreme; while the film industry sucked in creative talent from all over the world, along with countless drifters and dreamers. The city depended for its living on glamour and unfettered fantasy. 'The theme of illusion and reality is very common in Europe,' Lesley's friend Gavin Lambert wrote in his novel *The Slide Area*. 'In America, illusion and reality are still often the same thing. The dream is the achievement, the achievement is the dream.'

The Consul-General and his wife had the advantage of being part of the Hollywood circuit as soon as they arrived. Part of Romain's job was to publicize French films and French stars, and to take state dignitaries round the studios. A newsreel clip still exists of a studio round he made as escort to Ava Gardner and sundry awed visitors.

Among the British, French and other foreign expats living there, Lesley found plenty of friends and acquaintances from her years as a journalist in London. She and Romain befriended their neighbours, James Mason and his wife Pamela, who ran a complicated ménage and held a lot of 'rackety parties'; Lesley became godmother to their son Morgan. She caught up with Peter Ustinov, now a successful film-maker, whose skills as a raconteur made Romain sulk; with Anita Loos, down from New York on script-writing business; and with Laurence Olivier and Vivien Leigh.

Cecil Beaton was there, forging towards his apotheosis just as Lesley had predicted years earlier, as costume designer for the lavish period musicals that the studios saw as their new moneyspinners. His designs for Minnelli's *Gigi* (1958), following Anita Loos's hit stage adaptation, were considered a triumph. Lesley remembered his delighted boast that the costume department had 'a whole room full of buttons', and his groans at the prospect of another party where the hostess would be rigged out in a tiara. She watched, fascinated, as couturier-trained cutters and stylists fitted exquisitely crafted costumes on mannequins moulded to the perfectly formed, surprisingly tiny bodies of the stars.

Lesley soon made a new friend in the top drawer of Hollywood's elite. When she arrived in Hollywood, her friend Fleur Cowles Meyer from New York wrote a note introducing her to the director George Cukor: 'Apart from the chic + elegance and imagination they bring diplomatically to Hollywood, Leslie Blanche [sic] brings her own magic self. You have probably read her remarkable book "The Wilder Shores of Love". I envy Los Angeles for having her – I shall miss seeing her myself.'

Lesley followed this with a playing card on which she scribbled that it would have to do as her visiting card until she unpacked. Cukor, charmed by the gesture, promptly responded with an invitation and they were soon on intimate terms. He became an important mainstay for Lesley, who came to see him as her protector and mentor after she separated from Romain.

Cukor was by then a veteran Hollywood director, best known for his polished social comedies (*The Philadelphia Story*) and screen adaptations of literary classics (*David Copperfield*, *Little Women*) which became touchstones of their era. Civilized, cultured, with a reputation for his adroit management of Hollywood's divas, Dietrich and Garbo included, he was also brilliant at nurturing new talent: Katharine Hepburn, one of his discoveries, made eight pictures with him, including two of her best-known films with Spencer Tracy. After she had got to know Cukor, Lesley would write perceptively that he 'has not, or has passed, *ambition* in the destructive sense. This makes him perfectly free. And being perfectly sure of who he is, what he is, he does not envy – is not eaten up by competition.'

The director lived on Cordell Drive in the Hollywood Hills in a mansion surrounded by terraced gardens punctuated by statuary, with a beautiful pool, where he did much of the early work on his movie projects and held superbly staged Sunday soirées and parties. Single and discreetly at ease with his homosexuality, he relied on a circle of friends and loyal courtiers for companionship. 'Friends are of enormous importance to me,' he once said, 'but every relationship must be handled according to its own logic.'

Lesley, addicted to the mystique of scene-setting, adored the ambience created by this master stylist in the split-level suite of rooms leading to his oval dining room with suede-lined walls where guests dined in intimate luxury. She was soon complaining to Cukor that his friends would have to boycott his parties because they put everyone else's efforts to shame. Several of her friends were habitués at Cordell Drive: Christopher Isherwood and Don Bachardy, the writer Gavin Lambert, and Cukor's old friend and associate George Hoyningen-Huene, the St Petersburg-born photographer of stratospheric arrogance and flair. Huene's boldly stylized, surreal compositions in the 1920s and 1930s had changed the course of fashion photography and hugely influenced his colleagues and successors, including Lesley's friend Horst.

Cukor, who returned often to themes of disguise and masquerade, found much to intrigue him in the writings of both Romain and Lesley. The director's approach to the past, vividly revealed in his films, was another storyteller's trait he shared with Lesley: not 'reconstructed' but 'as if it were the present ... *still there*'. Her emphatically visual imagination and her knowledge of set design made her more than an entertaining guest to Cukor, and led eventually to her working with him.

Lesley also enjoyed returning his hospitality, staging her own dinners at the consulate. *Les Romain Gary* kept a fine table and the company was varied and animated. Among their regular guests was Alan Jay Lerner, reigning king of lyrics, whose 1956 smash hit with Frederick Loewe, *My Fair Lady*, broke all records for Broadway musicals; he remembered Lesley's knack for inviting rising talent along with alpha players, notably Paul Newman (wearing a flat cap) and Joanne Woodward, iconoclastic young anglophiles who spent their winter honeymoon in England in 1958. Among the guests mingling at the consulate they could always expect to meet writers, whose company they enjoyed.

Introducing Isabel Burton in *Wilder Shores*, Lesley excused herself for writing so much about Richard Burton: 'it must be remembered that her whole life and being was bound up in his.' If Romain wasn't Lesley's *all*, in the sense of body, heart and soul as Richard Burton was to Isabel (though perhaps he was, at that), her life was nevertheless hitched to his. Romain's choice of postings dictated where in the world she would live, her status as a diplomat's wife depended on his, and the demands of that role invaded her daytime and evening hours. In New York she had managed to exploit her available time and the city's research facilities to spectacular effect in *Wilder Shores*; and having delivered two lighter books to Murray the previous winter she was longing to immerse herself in her ambitious new Caucasian history. Now, in Los Angeles, the balance was shifting and Romain was galloping ahead.

He had started the year before with his professional, literary and personal affairs all in a state of more or less catastrophic failure, yet within months his fortunes had been dramatically reversed. In 1956 the year arrived when the outlandish ambitions imprinted on him by his mother, so many worlds away in Vilnius, came to fruition at last. If Romain now seems to claim more than his share of attention, it is because Lesley's trail so often converges with or is hidden behind his frenetic, insistent trajectory towards success – even though they were apart for half of their first year in Los Angeles, sometimes at opposite ends of the globe.

When Lesley joined him at the consulate, Romain was working hard to finish his new novel, *Les Racines du ciel* (*The Roots of Heaven*). In April he sent the typescript to to his publishers who replied enthusiastically, while warning him he should condense it, cut out repetition and watch his grammar. Romain, in a fever for them to publish in September, was too impatient to make radical revisions. Lesley said she never understood why Gallimard failed to insist on far more stringent editing.

Given the amount of time Romain spent elsewhere or was otherwise employed in 1956, his joint-consul's irritation is understandable. From mid-June to 1 August he, and presumably Lesley, spent his summer leave at Roquebrune. Two months later he was off again to accompany his precious revises in the diplomatic bag to Paris, where he stayed for ten days to check the first pulls of his novel off the press. No sooner had he returned to Los Angeles than he was sent to La Paz, Bolivia, to fill in for three months as temporary chargé d'affaires. He travelled alone, arriving on 8 November.

Had Lesley been staying at the consulate when his *ordre de mission* came through, she might have gone with him to Bolivia. But as she implied to Jock the following April, referring to her seven months' absence from Los Angeles, she had already left Los Angeles in September, almost two months earlier. Most likely she went on from Roquebrune to London, where she camped with Eden and Marston Fleming, delving for material on Shamyl and his Murid warriors who defied the Russian imperial armies for so long in the remote Caucasian mountains.

She had come upon Russia's campaigns in the Caucasus through her avid reading of the memoirs and fiction by the great Russian writers, so many of them posted as officers to serve in the Armies of the South: Gogol, Lermontov, Pushkin, Griboyedov, Tolstoy, Herzen and more. In New York she had hung on Hilarion Voronzov's memories of his grandmother Elizabeth, the last Vicereine of the Caucasus from his boyhood in Odessa before the revolution. A formidable power behind the throne, the princess had been arrested and imprisoned by the Bolsheviks and according to legend had complained that she had not been shot ahead of the other prisoners, as her age and rank demanded. She had been released and died in Germany. In a tiny rooftop apartment Lesley had also met the aged Tamara Grigorievna, niece of the Georgian Princess Anna who had been kidnapped by Chechen bandits in a dramatic episode of Caucasian history. This would become a focal point in Lesley's narrative.

Stirred as she was by these personal contacts, her chosen project was almost perversely difficult. Central Asia in the nineteenth century was an area virtually off the map for British explorers, who were regarded by Russia as envoys of a hostile power, since the Victorian empire competed directly against imperial Russian ambitions to conquer the territories bordering Afghanistan and India. As a result the Caucasus was comparatively unknown to British historians. Her first-hand sources for research were historical and military archives in Moscow, St Petersburg and Tiflis, where documents were written in Russian, Turkish or Arabic, not to mention Caucasian dialects, all of which would have to be translated. Even if the Soviet authorities allowed her access, the prospect of months of work in Russia and Georgia was daunting in every respect: language, permissions, comfort and expense.

At the London Library she had a stroke of luck. J.F. Baddeley, author of *The Russian Conquest of the Caucasus* (1908) and *The Rugged Flanks of Caucasus* (1940), had left to the library his special collection of books, his notes and his annotated index. In this portion of the Baddeley Bequest, Lesley unexpectedly found her Caucasian guide and mentor.

Baddeley was a Russophile journalist who had lived for many years in St Petersburg as the London correspondent for the *Standard*. Sociable and well connected, he first visited Russia in 1879 with the Russian ambassador who was a friend of the family, and became a fluent Russian speaker. After his first journey to the Caucasus for the *Standard* to cover an official visit by Tsar Alexander III, he returned several times on longer visits, making expeditions to Siberia, Mongolia and China. He was an intrepid traveller and an entertaining writer who could state from first-hand experience that while the mountaineers of Daghestan 'were not in my time addicted to brigandage . . . The Tchetchens were . . . The only rational principle on which a stranger travelling in their country – few ever did – could act, was that of trusting entirely to his guides for the time being.' He also delighted in the detail that Lesley found irresistible – such as his illustrated description of the Lesghynka, a sideways dance of 'imperceptibly minute, incredibly swift' steps. (Lesley sometimes used it as a nickname.)

Although he was no military or geographical specialist, Baddeley had a gift for evoking landscape and was a diligent scholar with a clear grasp of history. His books were invaluable sources in their own right and his index referred her to new areas of research as well as fresh revelations in works she knew. Especially valuable to Lesley was an atmospheric collection of ninety-seven mounted plate photographs of the fierce Caucasian peaks towering above the snow line, hung about with clouds or bisected by glaciers, and of the remote settlements and feral people who clung to a harsh existence in their folds and valleys.

These discoveries enabled Lesley to push on with her work, time-travelling in her imagination in the London Library's familiar stacks and reading room. The 'cherished project' of pursuing her research in Russia was no longer essential, as she acknowledged in *The Sabres of Paradise*. Her search for material about Shamyl took her twice to Turkey, in the first and last of her five years of work on the book, but never to Russia or to Soviet Chechnya and Georgia, as she was apt to imply later.

Meanwhile she could stay on conveniently in London, filling a growing pile of notebooks. She could perch with the Flemings in Knightsbridge, or with her mother in west London, and regale her friends with gossip about her exploits in Hollywood, waving regally from a chauffeur-driven limousine with a Tricolore pennant flying on the bonnet as she sallied forth with Romain to a première.

In mid-December she was deep in research when her French agent Odette Arnaud, who also now acted for Romain, telephoned her. *The Roots of Heaven* was shortlisted for the Prix Goncourt and strongly tipped to win. She must hurry to Paris to join her husband for the awards.

Romain had been in La Paz a week earlier when excited local journalists rushed to the consulate to congratulate him on winning the Nobel Prize. Hungry as he was for fame and success, this honour seemed excessive even to Romain, who delayed celebrating until the official telegram from France arrived. Not the Nobel, but the Prix Goncourt, was his at last. As soon as the Quai d'Orsay's permission for (unpaid) leave came through, Romain flew to Paris. When his plane touched down at Orly airport on the 14th, Lesley was waiting to plant a wifely lipstick kiss on his cheek in front of a crowd of photographers.

They were booked into the Hôtel du Pont-Royal, a few steps from his publishing house. Lesley had arrived on the night train from London in a hurry with hardly any cash and somehow Romain never had any; embarrassingly, she had to borrow from the hotel concierge.

In his absence since the award had been announced a thirst for information about the author had built up in the press, and he was plunged into a turmoil of interviews and publishers' meetings. He had never been part of Paris's literary elite, so journalists were gratified to find 'the mysterious Goncourt 1956' as exotic as his Latin American posting and the central African setting of his novel had promised. He arrived in a lightweight summer suit, a tall, bronzed, blue-eyed diplomat-traveller with 'shiny eyebrows' and a 'petite moustache de guitariste', who crunched an apple for breakfast and disarmed them with 'charme slave'.

Whereas his first novel had been hailed as a book that spoke for its wartime epoch, *The Roots of Heaven* made Romain a star. His role at the UN had given him practice in dealing with the media; he cultivated publicity and made sure that he gave good copy, all of which added to his image. He was photographed with Lesley feeding the elephants at the zoo (she was assiduous with photographers, as their friend Sylvia Agid showed in a witty cartoon sequence). His accounts of himself varied in the telling, he never denied any of them, and the variations multiplied when writers made mistakes or looked up one another's stories in the cuttings files.

From then on the Romain Gary mythology developed its own momentum, clustering around the writer like a swarm of flies that couldn't be swatted away. Romain was born (this time) in Wilno, Russia . . . His father was a Russian commercial attaché . . . His mother had given him the name Romain Gary, to make him sound French . . . He had fought in the Spanish Civil War . . . His wife was a best-selling American novelist . . . He had been in a plane flying over Africa that killed an elephant as it crash-landed; he blacked out and came to as a man ran towards him shouting, 'Hunting elephants! Aren't you ashamed?'

This last anecdote (which none of his air force comrades could verify) was purportedly the inspiration for his novel. Set in French central and west Africa, where Romain had been posted in 1941, it follows the lone crusade by Morel, former French Resistance fighter and concentration-camp survivor, to save the African elephant and other fauna from being hunted to extinction. In the death camp, to keep his hopes alive, Morel had summoned the image of great herds of elephant roaming the wilderness as precious symbols of liberty. Twined with the environmental theme, which put *The Roots of Heaven* ahead of its time, was the strand that ran through all Romain's work: the human quest for improvement, symbolized by the Islamic image of a tree of life. 'Our needs – for justice, for freedom and dignity – are roots of heaven that are deeply embedded in our hearts, but of heaven itself men know nothing but the gripping roots.'

Romain's novel is a great slab of fiction: uneven, exasperating, yet exhilarating in its vigour and vitality. *The Roots of Heaven* explored questions about the human soul and the nature of good and evil in the manner of the nineteenth-century Russian writers. The novel's strength lay in its narrative force and in the author's imaginative sweep, written in vigorous spoken storyteller's language, defying the consciously literary style of the psychological novel then dominant in French fiction. Even before the Goncourt winner was announced the rumours ensured that, as René Chabbert in *Dimanche Matin* put it, 'This season, as everyone knows, the fashionable book [à la mode] is by Romain Gary and is entitled *The Roots of Heaven*.'

The award was exceptionally controversial. Morel's story was told by a series of observers and written as it were from the inside out, revealing Romain's uncanny ability to inhabit each character in turn, but also making it repetitive. Many, if not most, reviewers complained of its length; the most virulent attacks targeted Romain's use of the French language. His persistent enemy Kléber Haedens complained that *The Roots of Heaven* read like a poor translation and he had rarely seen a book containing so many errors in French; it hammered the same simple ideas and themes relentlessly and would be improved by being cut by three-quarters. Carmen Tessier in *France-Soir* infamously implied that Gallimard's editors had helped Romain with the writing, which was furiously denied by Camus and caused a major literary rift.

For the defence, *Le Canard enchaîné* disarmingly concluded, 'We don't care if M. Gary writes badly, because we like elephants. This M. Gary is in his way a charming elephant. And an elephant with tusks.' More significantly, Romain had powerful supporters outside narrow literary coteries. Embedded in *The Roots of Heaven* is a Gaullist message; Romain was a sensitive conductor of the zeitgeist, and his writing reflected the beginnings of a shift in public opinion towards de Gaulle, who had exiled himself from the political forum since his resignation ten years earlier and was quietly writing his memoirs at his family home in Colombey-Les-Deux-Eglises. In declaring his loyalty, Romain placed himself in the political mainstream, which arguably helped to win him the Goncourt. But he thereby alienated the influential intellectual Left, which was already hostile to his diplomatic status as a spokesman for government foreign policy.

So the image took shape of Romain Gary, war hero, adventurer, diplomat, Gaullist, all elements conforming to a right-wing political stereotype. The elements were accurate in themselves, but missed the mark in describing the Left-inclined, libertarian, Eurocentric instincts of the self-described 'minoritaire'. The growing gap between image and reality affected the way his books were received and would cause him increasing anxiety and unease.

To crown his triumph, Romain gave a gala reception and dinner. It was held in a magnificent town house in the Boulevard St Germain, lent for the evening by his friend and fellow Gaullist Jean de Lipkowski, whose noble Polish Catholic ancestors had had French nationality conferred on them by Louis XIV. Romain, once barred entrance to the Warsaw *lycée* by poverty, must have savoured the *ancien régime* Franco-Polish setting, the panelled rooms hung with chandeliers and tapestries. Among the glittering Parisian throng were the foreign minister, Christian Pineau, the British ambassador Sir Gladwin Jebb, the Duchess de la Rochefoucauld, leading literary figures and members of the Goncourt jury.

Romain's personal guests were René and Sylvia Agid, his proxy family; Sigurd Norberg and his wife; and René Bauden, his wartime comrade who had landed their damaged Boston bomber when Romain and the pilot were injured in 1944. Sylvia left an affectionately barbed account of the event in a letter to their old friend Christel Söderlund in Sweden. Romain, she said, had behaved like a capricious diva; while Lesley darted through the crowds, trailing an immensely long red stole from her friend Pierre Balmain over her tailored grey suit (she had no time to have a dress made), charming *le tout Paris* and ignoring the late arrival of the canapés. Sylvia held her own among the '*grosses légumes*' who, she concluded, were less important than they thought. Lesley barred her and René from slipping away early, so they were still there at midnight to hear Henri Hoppenot speak in Romain's honour, quoting another diplomat-writer, Saint-John Perse. They also heard Romain's emotional reply, thanking his mentor for giving him time to write, and the airman Bauden for saving his life. Then he couldn't resist launching into an attack on the critics who had trounced his book: 'C'est bête!' said Sylvia.

Hoppenot, hearing of Romain's request to be posted to Los Angeles in 1955, had sighed at the prospect of his colleague behaving like a fox in a hencoop among the Hollywood starlets. His friends gossiped that success would turn his head. All their predictions were justified: Romain, swiftly adapting to his circumstances, *was* inflated by the new twist in his fortunes. Yet his artless pleasure in his newfound fame could be disarming. For the first time in his life he could afford to make grand gestures. In restaurants he picked up the bill for lunches that swelled to a dozen guests.

In January, after the celebrations, he sailed back to the United States on the *Queen Mary*, embarking while on board on a passionate affair with a young fashion model, Romy Van Looye. Although she was going to live and work in New York, he rented a second apartment specifically for her visits to Los Angeles until a serious car accident forced her to break with him in 1958.

Romain's compulsive womanizing has been exhaustively itemized elsewhere, although it would be pointless to attempt a complete tally. 'He was so lecherous you can't imagine,' said an English woman friend who was devoted to both him and Lesley. Outside diplomacy and his writing, his amorous exploits were almost his sole diversion. In Los Angeles his affairs were usually confined to afternoons in his rented studio apartment in Laurel Lane, which Lesley and her intimates knew about and gave an unprintable nickname. Soon his reputation earned him the sobriquet of *consul sexuel* in the Hollywood gossip columns. Yet despite his Don Juan reputation, in his writing he derided masculine values of force and virility in contrast to 'feminine' emotional values, and the further he strayed from romantic fidelity, the more he extolled its virtues.

He remarked that Lesley was very 'dix-huitième siècle' about his behaviour. She had no option, other than leaving him. In her memoir she frankly admitted that 'the sexual impulse was his motivating force'.

Sex both stimulated and soothed him; by her account, to him it was an addiction like smoking or hard drinking, which had to be regularly satisfied before he believed he could function as a writer.

She confided to Hélène Hoppenot in Paris that they had already broken up for good, twice, and each time he had asked her to come back: the first time in 1955, then again in Hollywood, just when Couve de Murville, the French ambassador, announced his visit to Los Angeles. Lesley wondered what Mme Hoppenot would have done in her place and tried to act accordingly.

But she was not Mme Hoppenot, and Romain was very different from Henri Hoppenot, both in his inconstancy and in his inconsistency. Although he told his lovers that he wanted to leave Lesley, he never finally made the break until his affair with Jean Seberg ruled out any other option, and even then he was reluctant to give up Lesley completely. In fact when he first confided to the Hoppenots that he had fallen in love with someone young enough to be his daughter, he added that he wished Lesley was there to advise him what to do.

Perhaps only two such escapists could have persisted with the marriage such as it had become in Los Angeles. In 1956 and 1957 they continued to find practical reasons for spending months at a time apart. This allowed Romain full priapic licence, Lesley to protest furiously to her friends about his behaviour, and her friends to comment that she could hardly expect him to behave otherwise when she was away so often and for so long.

Lesley was prepared to sacrifice a great deal to keep Romain plus the lifestyle and position that his diplomatic career offered her. There was also a tacit acceptance of each other's needs in their parallel writing lives. They had both been only children, used to psychic space and self-sufficiency. Aside from his incessant affairs, she respected Romain's need for that space and secrecy about himself. In return, his self-absorption left her imaginatively free to inhabit the wild places and tempestuous scenes that were her chosen landscapes. But the part of Lesley that longed to 'cling', as she sometimes yearned to do, had to be sternly repressed. She could not depend on him for reassurance and support.

Romain felt imprisoned by his wife's domestic framework, as his next novel would reveal. Quite often he behaved as if she were not there at all (and quite often she wasn't). Yet paradoxically their unresolved, semi-detached, abrasive arrangement in Los Angeles, like sand in the oyster, supported one of the most fruitful periods of their lives. In many respects their marriage was a duel; but in their work at least they were collaborators, and Romain's creativity especially exploded like a Roman candle into script writing, journalism and other directions.

He compulsively sought solace in sex with new partners, ever younger, even while idealizing the concept of fidelity. Lesley, childless and ten years older than her husband, found friends in the creative purlieus of Hollywood, often among the single and childless. 'Swarms of queers around her always,' as a friend of hers added. Her vivid camp persona, her *grande précieuse* presence, the exotically contrived surroundings in which she framed herself, found recognition in Hollywood's flamboyantly inventive theatrical circles. Talents such as hers and Romain's were valued commodities in an industry whose business was entertainment, where fantasy was the product.

While she was in Paris for Romain's Goncourt celebrations, Lesley took the opportunity to dig for more material in the Bibliothèque Nationale. She found rare additions to her growing library of Caucasiania at Monsieur Samuelian's Oriental bookshop in the rue Monsieur-le-Prince, and at some stage she consulted the Russian and Turkish embassies in Paris. When Romain left for Los Angeles she hurried back to London to continue where she had left off at the London Library. She also followed up trails at the Royal Geographical Society and the Foreign Office library. In February she was still in England, commuting into town on a number 73 bus, her 'reading room'. She finally left for Los Angeles in early April 1957, laden with military histories, Russian memoirs, Caucasian travelogues and bulging notebooks, having been away since the previous September.

To her surprise and relief, instead of silent gloom or explosions she was greeted by a beaming Romain, who thrust a pen into her hand and told her to use it on the English translation of *The Roots of Heaven*. He had been working on it already and had also started two new novels, all his creative juices having been stimulated by the sale of two books to Hollywood and his capture of the Goncourt in less than six months. She was delighted to find his moods so lightened by success – though his love affair with Romy Van Looye possibly helped the mellowing effect.

Lesley had not mellowed where house maintenance was concerned. She sacked the Japanese gardener and was so fierce with the maid for rashly touching up the baroque bed with cheap gilt paint and leaving outside the treasured table that Lesley had painted with scenes from her life with Romain, that she walked out. Lesley had (of course) by that time discovered Los Angeles's Russian community, from which she recruited an older woman for their household help. Katiusha added the required Slav ambience to the ménage and, though slow and an uninspired cook, could be relied on to supply borscht night and day when husband and wife were writing at fever pitch.

Lesley had introduced Romain to Robert Lantz, her New York agent and former fellow columnist for *The Leader*, who now handled film rights for husband and wife. Lantz had successfully sold *The Colours of the Day* and *The Roots of Heaven* to Twentieth Century-Fox. Darryl F. Zanuck, the head of Fox, had taken a fancy to the second, which was to be directed by John Huston. Meanwhile the film option on Lesley's Aimée Dubucq de Rivery had stalled, probably because the story of Aimée's life in the Seraglio, though steeped in atmosphere, was almost totally lacking in plot.

Now that they were both established writers at last, an irregular but distinct pattern of living began to emerge. After her absence for the first quarter of 1957, Lesley stayed in Los Angeles to look after the consulate while Romain took seven weeks' leave in Europe through the summer. Her duties included hosting the 14 July Bastille Day bash, when a crowd of 400 stormed the modest building and seized the champagne bottles, trampling over the patios and through the drawing room. When Romain returned, he and Lesley agreed to abandon socializing for writing, usually in their dressing gowns in the fiercely hot September weather. Katiusha brought their meals on trays as they sat distracted, laboriously composing in longhand. Some of Lesley's fondest memories of Los Angeles were of these times.

Romain was sometimes made to feel an outsider at the Quai d'Orsay, but in Hollywood he and Lesley were in their element. In the capital city of cinema their status was doubly underlined by his ambassadorial ranking and their publishing triumphs. Living was 'a question of style', as he wrote in *Lady L.*; and when not scribbling *en déshabille* at the consulate (as Lesley sketched them for her 1958 Christmas card), *les*

Romain Gary now presented a grand face to the world. Lesley had a wardrobe of confections in pink satin and blue tulle for gala nights, and Romain's suits and silk shirts were tailor-made.

They were invited to dine with Igor and Vera Stravinsky, with Aldous Huxley and his second wife Laura. On a sublime occasion hosted by Cole Porter she and Romain were the only guests, with Fred Astaire as the fourth; they dined ambrosially on caviar, roast pheasant and soufflé Grand Marnier. They were guests of the ageing lions of Hollywood: producers, directors and studio moguls who, like royalty, entertained only each other in a closed circuit of their own peers, following a set routine. After a first-class meal the host would flick a switch, upon which a wall and an Impressionist painting would slide away to reveal a screen on which they would watch a classic movie, or a new release that would be mercilessly dissected afterwards.

'Being French in Hollywood always imposes grandeur on people,' as Don Bachardy remarked. Romain assumed a remote gravity, imitating Ambassador Hoppenot, to make himself seem older, and a quizzical expression designed to shake people's confidence when they held forth. He and Lesley had a way of dealing with their friends separately even when they were both present. Don Bachardy, visiting the consulate with Christopher Isherwood, never saw 'the two of them ever participating in conversation; it was one or the other'.

Despite their newfound affluence and celebrity they still lived on the edge of chaos. An evening out might never take place because neither of them had remembered the address. On one occasion they got lost on the way to a conference, putting Romain in such a rage that he refused to attend at all. Another time he failed to tell Lesley that the event they were silently driving to was a funeral, and when they arrived she found herself standing out in her red coat like a beacon in a sea of black.

Romain was increasingly impatient with formal receptions which demanded his presence. Halfway through one evening he disappeared and Lesley, making an excuse to look for him, found him fast asleep curled up in a nest made of the guests' fur coats. She had to explain to the party that he was tied up with an urgent call from the embassy in Washington that would take a long time. Then she had to dash out with Mlle Pétrement to move all the coats to another room, so that the guests could take their leave. Afterwards Romain reappeared, delighted with the manoeuvre.

Lesley collected incidents like these as a connoisseur, savouring his monstrous behaviour. Recounting his worst excesses to her friends and hearing their disapproval on her behalf must have gone some way to compensate for his boorishness. What was harder for outsiders to understand was that she still loved him as much as she hated his brutal lack of consideration.

Having finished the mass of her research, she had to negotiate a worrying block in the early chapters of the Shamyl book, which was taking shape like an oriental carpet, densely packed with intricate pattern and detail. Lesley had only just come to appreciate the daunting scale of her project. She must place the man not only in his Caucasian-mountain setting in the early nineteenth century, but also in the wider geographical and historical context of Russian colonial expansion in the disputed borderlands of Persia and Turkey to the south-east, westward to Georgia, and eastward to the Caspian. For this she had to immerse herself in Persian, Turkish and Georgian as well as Russian history. Then she had to mould and compress the diverse mass of material on Sufism, regional substrata of the Cossacks, scorpion hunting and executions by cannon at the Persian court, etc., etc., into a backdrop for the dramatic sequence of Shamyl's lengthy duel with Nicholas I. The second half would be more straightforward, much of the detail for this later narrative coming from transcripts from Russia.

Meanwhile in London John Murray had kept her name in print, publishing *Round the World in Eighty Dishes* in 1956 and *The Game of Hearts* the following year. She had turned the former into a pleasing mix of recipes, anecdotes about her travels, witty drawings, practical hints and occasional plundering from more comprehensive works, notably Countess Morphy's *Recipes of All Nations*. Friends contended that the bits about dallying with Balkan brigands were sheer fantasy.

Although her cookbook had been written for young readers, it found an adult audience longing to escape the concept of food as a grim necessity and ready to be seduced by a voluptuous appeal to the senses. Lesley lacked the scholarly approach of Constance Spry or Elizabeth David, but her skittish anecdotes and sheer *joie de vivre* made tastes and aromas as evocative of place as buildings and music. She received good reviews-in-brief plus a slap on the wrist for some lapses: 'Chop suey does not exist in China. Indians do not put curry powder in rice. Persians do not make pilaf with boiled rice . . . in giving the United States only two recipes, she does them less than justice, particularly in prescribing for Baked Virginia Ham a ham already cooked.' Yet devotees would remember *Round the World in Eighty Dishes* fondly as their first taste of 'abroad', as well as a joyful revelation that cooking could be fun and a world of edible pleasures was waiting to be explored.

The Game of Hearts, Lesley's edited version of the memoirs of Regency courtesan Harriette Wilson, was published the year before *Lady L.* Their close chronological proximity is intriguing, given that in both works the protagonist was a woman who lived by her wits and beauty outside the conventional moral code and enjoyed herself into the bargain. I first read the two books at the same time and was convinced that Lesley's book had influenced *Lady L.*, though Lesley herself denied this.

Harriette Wilson had long been a favourite of hers. As a subversive outsider who lived for love and pleasure, Wilson fulfilled an exemplary feminine role for Lesley, who probably enjoyed flirting with it, as she did with Romain when he first came to live with her in St Leonard's Terrace. She was fascinated by the Regency *demi-monde* and its women practised in 'the finer shades of what might be described as pleasing', which she discussed in her long, highly coloured introduction, presenting the courtesan as an idealized companion who earned her social position through her character and conversation as well as through the skills of her *métier*.

Wilson wrote her scandalous memoirs of her amorous adventures with the Regency swells of Mayfair and Brighton after she fell on hard times, to keep her swaggering companion Colonel Rochfort in gambling money. Before publishing, she sent instalments to former lovers and patrons, offering them the chance to buy themselves out for a down payment of £200. Some, including the Duke of Wellington, refused to pay ('Publish and be damned!'). Since Wilson and her sisters, 'the Fashionable Impures', had separately or together entertained most of the masculine establishment, the book created a huge sensation. Every member of the Cabinet bought a copy.

The purpose of the memoirs was to make money by blackmail, threatening the Regency equivalent of tabloid revelation. Apart from their piquant historical interest, however, Lesley championed Wilson as an original writer whose keyhole descriptions of her intimate milieu were intensified by her self-presentation. Harriette was not only exceptional in her intelligence, independence, lightheartedness and 'brisk appetites', choosing whom to love and whom to refuse. As Lesley commented, 'she is her own Boswell': a natural comic whose freshness of character and outrageous past sizzle from her impenitent first paragraph:

> I shall not say why and how I became, at the age of fifteen, the mistress of the Earl of Craven. Whether it was love, or the severity of my father, the depravity of my own heart, or the winning arts of the noble Lord, which induced me to leave my paternal roof and place myself under his protection, does not now much signify; or if it does, I am not in the humour to gratify curiosity in this matter.

Apart from agreeing to intersperse Harriette's escapades with the confessions of her sometime friend and rival Julia Johnstone, which Lesley later regretted, she also pruned the text drastically, editing word by word rather than excising sections, which earned disapproval decades later when the book was reissued for Lesley's centenary. John Murray, having first turned it down, eventually produced *The Game of Hearts* under the Gryphon imprint. As ever Lesley used her magazine connections to advantage: *Vogue*'s features editor Penelope Gilliatt took an extract from the introduction for the September 1957 issue.

Romain, whose fiction repeatedly featured prostitutes or 'dishonoured' women, had been shocked enough by Harriette's memoirs, or by Lesley's introduction, to try to persuade Jock Murray not to publish: 'it would be specialising in scandal' and would affect her reputation. In America such things would be unimportant, but in England they mattered. His reaction probably stemmed from his intuitive understanding of Lesley's process of identification with her subjects: the narcissism which allowed her to sketch a shimmering reflection of herself in her profiles. It was the direct opposite of the motivating force of self-dislike that led Romain to occupy other people's personalities in his writing, rather than his own. 'I'm not in the least interested in myself,' he said. 'I'm a medium, if you like, for other characters.'

Romain's own mounting creative frenzy was channelled into two novels written in different languages: *Lady L.*, his first novel in English, a kind of character portrait of his wife, and *L'Homme à la colombe*, his French *roman à clef* about the United Nations. As early as 1956 he was also mulling over a sort of autobiography.

In *Lady L.* Romain returns to his obsessive theme of the impossibility of squaring an idealistic love of humanity with personal happiness, this time adding a cautionary lesson on the dangers of possessive love. His French biographers have naturally emphasized the French edition, which appeared in 1963, and it has been claimed that *Lady L.* was written as his farewell to Lesley. In fact he wrote the novel in Los Angeles when they had got back together after their separation in 1955; in this context the macabre ending acquires an entirely different significance.

Lady L. is a short, elegant Chinese puzzle of a novel, full of resonance and riddles relating to himself and Lesley. It was the first novel he wrote directly in English and the almost unnaturally assured prose suits the subject to perfection. François Bondy, Romain's most perceptive friend and critic, believed that Romain actually adopted a different authorial persona for his only English novel (as opposed to his later American fiction), and that its polished style owed a great deal to Lesley. The characters are wrapped in a tissue of assumed identities, impostures, disguises and travesty. In the French edition Romain added further complexities, including a fictitious bibliography of learned historical works about charlatans and anarchists.

Annette/Lady L. is outstanding as one of few substantial, three-dimensional female characters in his fiction (though like all the rest, she is a creature of the senses). A series of flashbacks is framed by the imposing Lady L's eightieth birthday party in her Vanbrugh mansion, surrounded by her treasures and her tediously respectable sons and their families. Shocked to hear that her beloved pavilion in the grounds, which holds the secrets of her past, is threatened with demolition, Lady L. confides in her elderly suitor, the Poet Laureate Sir Percy Rodiner, hoping he can help her to save it.

Sir Percy is horrified to hear that the blue-blooded Lady L. ('Diana') was born Annette Boudin, in early life a Paris streetwalker, who fell passionately in love with Armand, a charismatic young anarchist, and agreed to be recruited to his cause. Schooled as a young lady and planted in Switzerland, she was instructed to infiltrate the aristocracy and assist in sensational robberies to finance the revolution.

Romain's heroine has a will of steel and a calculating edge as well as a passionate nature. Annette's first conquest is the sardonic Lord

Glendale, 'Dicky', who puts at her disposal his fortune, his culture and his profoundly sceptical outlook on life. Pregnant by Armand, unable to deflect him from his idealism, she ruthlessly betrays him to the police and deceives Dicky into marrying her, to save herself and her unborn child. From then on her caustic wit and smile betray a certain cruelty. Armand, never discovering her betrayal, returns after years in prison to reclaim his lover. Since Dicky's death she has married another aristocrat, but still adores Armand and agrees to arrange a masked ball where his gang can snatch the guests' jewels (and where Romain's fascination with disguises reaches its crescendo). But the plan goes wrong and the police arrive.

Decades later, the dowager Lady L's disclosures have led the horrified Sir Percy to the pavilion. Knowing Armand would never renounce his revolutionary ideals, Annette had tricked him into hiding in her Madras strongbox as the police approached, and locked the chest for ever. So the romantic who refused to accept her fate ensured that her lover would never leave her.

At the heart of *Lady L.* are questions of identity, self-invention and assimilation. Dicky Glendale knows that 'Diana' is not as she seems and is unconcerned by this. He doesn't give a fig for conventions such as birth and nobility. He is a connoisseur of quality, and she has it: the past doesn't matter and her future is assured.

Annette's supreme achievement is to live the fiction, to pass as a born aristocrat, deceiving even her lovers. She watches Dicky, 'learning from him attitudes, mannerisms, a certain quizzical way to look at the world which were to mark her for ever'. In just such a way Romain had silently observed Lesley charming her way through London society when they first met. She had learnt the art long before she met Romain, and was his teacher. In *Lady L.* Romain deftly catches that light tone chiselled with irony, the brittle, heartless mode of Waugh, Mitford and Connolly that his wife had wielded so effectively in wartime London. Romain's ear for that 'special English sophistication of *the happy few*, with its amoral, and, in a way, terroristic sense of humour, and its superior unconcern, which could lead as well to heroism as to murder', was unique to this one work.

Apart from the ventriloquism that enabled him to capture Lesley in *Lady L.*, how much else did he owe to her? Robert Lantz, staying with them at the consulate, came upon Lesley with the cook in the kitchen, preparing for a reception, only to be interrupted by Romain, frowning over a page of manuscript: 'I have a stylistic problem.' Ignoring Lantz and sauces in a critical state, Lesley washed her hands, read the passage and was soon deep in discussion. She had a particular personal interest in *Lady L.*: its language and style are redolent of 'the thing itself' (to borrow the courtesan Harriette Wilson's self-description). Later she designed the book jacket for the English hardback and she eventually worked with George Cukor on the film project based on Romain's script, after the couple had separated.

Her provocative voice is ever present in *Lady L.*: her soft spot for royalty and clerics in their glamorous robes – 'such good theatre!' – never mind if the tumbril took them, so long as they went to their execution sumptuously dressed. Lesley enjoyed the likeness, recalling her astonishment to read in Romain's description of Lady L's pavilion an exact reproduction of her room at her mother's house that he had silently examined soon after they first met. Cushions, postcards, narguilehs, Turkish lanterns, Persian portraits, Russian icons, 'pseudo-Oriental' paintings of the seraglio or damsels ravished by desert chieftains – 'a huge, rich slice of Turkish delight' – were all recalled down to the last detail of the faces of her cats, dogs, hedgehogs and parrots in period dress gazing earnestly from their frames.

Close friends were fascinated by her reaction to the characterization. She was not in the least averse to be presented as a beautiful, ruthless impostor prepared to entomb her lover rather than lose him. On the contrary, she seemed pleased and amused, commenting only that after reading the book people would think that she had once been a whore, but that it was all the same to her.

The image of Lord Glendale, so untypical of the pink-cheeked English nobility portrayed in countless portraits, compounds the riddle. Glendale has pronounced cheekbones, the corners of his mouth are set in a permanent smile, and he regards the world's absurdities with a kind of oriental detachment through narrow inscrutable eyes.

Where have we seen that face before, and where will we see it again? He could be the Traveller's double in Lesley's *Journey into the Mind's Eye* – but that would not be published for another ten years. In this hall of mirrors, does Lesley's description of her childhood love reflect back the image of Romain's Glendale in *Lady L.*? Surely Romain, on the contrary, drew on what she told him about Komisarjevsky, the secret lover who had left his mark on her like a wound. The man who was Lesley's real mentor was the inspiration behind Romain's Dicky Glendale, as well as the elusive Traveller.

Lady L. was her essential profile in which everything was subtly understood, a homage that acknowledged the escapist's lessons Romain had tacitly learnt from her. In return he was her tutor in the looking-glass transformation of reality into fiction and allegory. A decade later, in *Journey into the Mind's Eye*, the young Lesley would be moulded and 'civilized' by the Traveller as surely as Annette had been by Glendale.

The distorting prism of fiction also allowed Romain to examine the process by which he learnt to 'pass' as an establishment figure. He repeatedly said that *Lady L.* was the book in which he put most of himself. This does not necessarily invalidate Lesley's claim to *Lady L.*, for the English version which he wrote (very quickly, in a matter of months) in Los Angeles was inescapably her portrait: that wilfully determined portrait of her on her wedding day, in fact. The French version was laboriously revised four years later by Romain in collaboration with a translator, after his great success with the 'autobiographical' *Promise at Dawn*. The extended French work effectively described the *interior* transformation he had undergone during the *exterior* events that he recounted in *Promise at Dawn*. The English version had more of Lesley in it; the French had more of Romain.

As with others who entered his orbit, Romain invaded his wife's personality and plundered and transfigured her past. Lesley didn't mind; she adored magic and mysteries, especially if they added lustre to her image. She did the same herself: consciously or not, they aided and abetted each other.

All novelists steal and transform characters from life. The exceptional factor here was the extent to which Romain's and Lesley's mythologies came to mingle with their lives and influence events. Lesley, a true narcissist, fell in love with Lady L. and in time often adopted the role of the imperious dowager that Romain had written for her – or that he had seen incipient in her – as well as rewriting her own past. So the one fed the other, and back again.

Hélène Hoppenot disliked *Lady L.* so much that she was uncharacteristically lost for words when Romain asked her if she had received a copy. Their friend George Cukor, intrigued by the novel's layers of deception and self-invention, paid $100,000 for the film option on *Lady L.* and embarked on a lengthy process of preparing it for the screen.

Romain's other novel published in 1958, *L'Homme à la colombe*, was notable for the manner in which it appeared. His scabrous fable of United Nations follies, even as fiction, could compromise him professionally, so he published it under the pseudonym of Fosco Sinibaldi. Not content with this, he asked a Bulgarian friend, Pierre Rouve, to adopt the pseudonym and the author's role. A contract was drawn up, but Rouve baulked at Romain's plan to use his photograph as Sinibaldi in the publisher's catalogue, causing the scheme to founder. But Romain resurrected it nearly twenty years later, when he persuaded his impressionable younger cousin to adopt the role of his pseudonym Emile Ajar, leading to the baroque imbroglio that scandalized literary France after his death.

The Sinibaldi novel sold few copies; Romain was disappointed. Readers apparently needed to recognize a persona behind the author's name.

Meanwhile the Lady continued to preside over 'her' consulate. The object of her possessive desire was for the time being on a long lead: often absent, pathologically unfaithful but still, officially, hers.

8

Los Angeles II
The Sabres of Paradise

With the swift movement of the troika over the smooth road the
mountains appeared to run along the horizon, their rose-coloured
crests glittering in the light of the rising sun . . . A solemn voice
seemed to say, 'It has begun.'

Leo Tolstoy, *The Cossacks*

THEIR SECOND CHRISTMAS in Los Angeles approached, bringing the ghastly prospect of powder-blue reindeer and jingling
bells over Beverly Hills. Instead, Lesley escaped with Romain across
the border to Mexico, where sugar skulls and dancing skeletons were
more to their taste, although even there they were dismayed to find the
tourist shops full of His & Hers gifts and neon-lit shrines in the streets.
Yet his location suddenly meant nothing to Romain, who was brewing a book. Lesley had hardly unpacked before he dragged an armchair
to the table with its back to the window, ordered paper, pens and ink,
and started to write, oblivious to hunger pangs. His wife, familiar with
the symptoms, resigned herself to dining out alone. Romain spent the
rest of his leave covering page after page in a creative frenzy, without
so much as a glance outside. His only distraction was to lie in the bath,
shrouded in steam and saturated in his imagination.

Writing up the episode later, Lesley couldn't resist adding an anecdote about Romain and his earplugs, although it had happened on an
earlier trip they had made to Mexico. The story was true, after all, and
it fitted her thread about *Promise at Dawn* too neatly to miss. Their
hotel room in Mexico City was suffocating if the windows were
closed, but too noisy when they were open, so they retreated to provincial Taxco. Even there the noise level was unbearable. Eventually,
in a deafening café, Romain plugged his ears with pellets of moistened

bread, delighted to have found an effective solution. After a while he began to complain of earache; his symptoms quickly got worse. Soon he was groaning with pain and convinced that he was dying of a brain tumour. Lesley had to find a taxi to drive them through the night in the greatest discomfort all the way back to Mexico City, while Romain, lying with his head in her lap, gave her instructions about his will. She then had to explain on the phone to a surprised doctor the cause of Romain's condition. The doctor managed to extricate the pellets and Romain recovered – but not, apparently, on that Christmas leave, their third trip to Mexico.

Back in Los Angeles he continued writing, showing Lesley his progress on *Promise at Dawn* every day. She was hugely impressed by the portrait of his devoted, devouring mother as it rose off the page from his impassioned scrawl. For the first time she fully comprehended the primal force of the bond between mother and son. 'In your mother's love, life makes you a promise at the dawn of life that it will never keep. You have known something that you will never know again. You will go hungry to the end of your days. Leftovers, cold titbits, that's what you will find in front of you at each new feast.' Here, too, he revealed the origins of his fierce ambition, in 'the backbreaking task' of fulfilling his mother's childlike belief in the fairy tale of his future as a famous writer and ambassador for France. Yet Lesley wondered about the motivation behind his compulsive urge to expose himself after he had hidden and mystified his past for so long.

Despite her patchy knowledge of his background, Lesley was well aware that his account was not entirely factual. His earliest memories and emotions had been harnessed and shaped; he had adapted events to create a heightened novelistic portrait of his impossibly doting mother and himself that was far more effective than the raw reality. How soon did it occur to her that this transforming treatment of *his* childhood could be applied to her own?

Romain galloped through his manuscript and in July wrote to Gaston and Claude Gallimard that it was on its way to them. Generally, after he had completed a book he was in a fever of impatience to see it in print and goaded his publishers into speeding up production. But this one was different. For the first time he was writing in the first person, showing a new version of himself to the world, revealing how far he had travelled to become a Frenchman. This book he held back and it was almost two years before it was published in France.

The pace and diversity of Romain's projects in Los Angeles often give the impression that he was leading several lives at once as, indeed, he was. Lesley was embroiled in some more than others and was fiercely partisan when his efforts were not given due credit. In March, in the middle of writing *Promise at Dawn* in French, he had to put it aside to dash off his first screenplay, an adaptation of *The Roots of Heaven* in English. She reported with glee that Darryl Zanuck was dissatisfied with Patrick Leigh Fermor's film treatment of *The Roots of Heaven* for John Huston and had asked Romain to work on it himself. Romain flew to Paris, and after nine days and nights holed up in a bedroom in the Georges V Hotel produced a working script that satisfied Zanuck. It was sent to Huston, who was already installed in a temporary village at Fort Archambault in Chad with 120 technicians and his stars. Romain had to return to Los Angeles via Washington so Leigh Fermor, who was a friend of Huston's, went out there instead and promptly rewrote the script again with the director.

When Huston had come to the consulate to discuss filming *The Roots of Heaven* over dinner, Romain and Lesley had both been convinced by the way he spoke about the project that he was the right man to film Romain's epic novel. Sceptical journalists, however, asked why Huston, a big-game hunter, should choose to film the story of one man's lonely crusade to save African elephants from huntsmen like himself. Certainly the location gave him some excellent opportunities for shooting safaris – a gruesome pile of freshly severed tusks being loaded into a truck in one scene could well have been his own trophies. Moreover, the casting did not inspire confidence. Failing William Holden to play the grey-eyed Frenchman Morel, Zanuck (whom Romain would nickname the Gorilla) had bafflingly cast Trevor Howard, who was notably unsympathetic in the part. Zanuck's protégée Juliette Greco struggled with the role of Minna, the German war victim, and everyone fell ill in the intense heat except for Errol Flynn, who avoided infection on a diet of vodka and fruit juice, but fell down some stairs instead.

The result was, as the critics concluded, 'an interesting but curiously unconvincing picture'. After the première that autumn, Lesley let slip that Romain was 'profoundly disappointed' with the film; although they both hotly denied this in print, it was true. They were angered and disillusioned by the mangling of Romain's prescient conservationist message. Nonetheless it earned him an alchemist's reputation in Hollywood as a screenwriter who could turn dross into gold and also attracted other offers, including a request by David Selznick to work on F. Scott Fitzgerald's *The Last Tycoon*, which never came off. (They were on friendly terms with Selznick and his wife Jennifer Jones, who was spoilt with every luxury; she showed Lesley her enormous bedroom with a waterfall outside that she could operate from a switch by her bed.)

Lesley was having to come to terms with a husband who was turning into an all-round media celebrity, almost before the concept existed. As Consul-General he was in constant demand for statements and performances. He was a gift to journalists: photogenic, charming and seductive of voice. He embraced the role of Gallic ambassador to Hollywood and adroitly courted publicity, borrowing from his colleague Jacques Vimont a gold-embroidered black uniform with knee breeches, plumed *bicorne* hat and sword for a ceremony commemorating Lafayette, which had an electrifying effect on American TV audiences. He even claimed that Walter Wanger had offered him the role of Caesar in the Fox production of *Cleopatra*, but Fox had preferred Rex Harrison for 'his' role. His extracurricular affairs gave the gossip columns plenty of scope for speculation.

Neither his soaring career nor shovel-loads of money and acclaim made him easier to live with. Quite the reverse: all his triumphs had turned him into 'a sort of insane Roman Emperor, domestically', according to Lesley. No matter how much he earned, a pathological insecurity left him ever more anxious about his finances. Impatient as ever, he talked of leaving Los Angeles and the Carrière within one or two months to settle in Paris. She shuddered at the thought. All the lists, inventories and packing would rest on her while Romain hurried off with his holdall. She would have to crate up her working library and leave behind the cats Norman and Titti-Mi . . . Then within hours he would change his mind and talk about staying on until the autumn. It was terribly unsettling.

She was deep in her history of the Caucasus, referring to dozens of different sources, needing above all to be able to work uninterrupted, surrounded by piles of books and notes. Her bed was strewn with maps covered with mountainous contours and unpronounceable place names, on which she plotted Shamyl's military exploits. Coping with Romain's lurches from crisis to crisis would have been enough to sink a lesser woman, aside from her duties as hostess at the consulate, with only Katiusha and hired help to call on. Journalistic commissions and business arising from her other books demanded her attention; invitations to meet the stars in Hollywood had to be resisted. She envied Rebecca West, cosseted by her wealthy husband, or Nicholas Lawford, another writer friend, protected from the world by his partner. Her one major compensation was her publisher, her constant reader, in whom she placed all her trust. Jock Murray's contribution was invaluable. All through her project, he encouraged and cherished her as an author; once she had finished her enormous draft she knew she could rely on his advice and if necessary the investment of editorial expertise, plus whatever time it took to help her rework it all over again.

Repeatedly she pushed work aside, to look after first the visiting ambassadress, then the ambassador; next the French Film Festival personnel descended en masse; then Romain dropped on her a buffet supper for twenty-two at a few hours' notice. Like her husband, Lesley was inclined to regard the duties imposed by his job as tedious interruptions to her proper work, although she enjoyed her status as the consulate's doyenne. Yet even allowing for her exaggerations, the pace was made more punishing by Romain's capricious disregard for anyone else's convenience, notably his wife's.

Despite his stellar reputation in Hollywood, and the comforts and pleasures of Los Angeles, Romain's restlessness gnawed at him. He had been away from his adopted country for longer than he had lived there and was afraid of becoming over-Americanized; perhaps he was losing the identity that he regarded as French. He also wanted to be near to France, which was in a state of deep crisis caused by the festering unrest in Algeria.

Algeria had been French since 1830 and many of its 1 million European colonists considered themselves as much Algerian as its 9 million Muslims. Since 1954, a nationalist uprising, a war in all but name, had already claimed thousands of French and Algerian lives. Any hint of French government negotiations with the rebel FLN brought accusations of betrayal from French-Algerian extremists, the *pieds noirs*.

Only after two French governments had been toppled, and a rebel 'committee of public safety' set up by French generals in Algiers had made civil war a real probability, did General de Gaulle emerge from his twelve-year retirement and return to Paris with a renewed mission to save France. After extraordinary political manoeuvrings the National Assembly granted him rights to revise the constitution, and a national referendum approved his new Fifth Republic with de Gaulle its president from January 1959.

A national crisis had been averted, although four more years of violence would ensue before Algeria reached independence. Meanwhile de Gaulle's cause needed to be interpreted to the rest of the world. That autumn, *Life* magazine commissioned Romain to explain and defend de Gaulle's return to power, as well as the French people's attachment to a man who had just awarded virtually dictatorial powers to himself.

Romain returned to Paris at the end of October 1958, under special dispensation to take time off to write his defence of France's magisterial leader. 'The Man Who Stayed Lonely to Save France', published on 8 December, was so well received that the French embassy in Washington reprinted it as a leaflet. His encomium was nonetheless far-sighted in its assessment of the general's unique position in the national consciousness. The lonely conviction that had served him in wartime now kept him aloof from party politics and enabled him to assume the voice of France.

Romain did not write as a political Gaullist: his Gaullism was historical, emotional. Lesley came to believe that he saw the general as an ideal father, symbolizing his own highest aspirations. As a diplomat, Romain too represented France, if on a small scale, and faithfully followed the general's self-identification with France and the myth he had fashioned as its leader. Romain was an ideal interpreter of this self-construction by 'the man who was France', for he recognized in de Gaulle's spiritual striving towards greatness his own credo: that only through the sublimation of life's imperfections in myth can the power of the imagination make humanity accept the lofty values that are the basis of civilization. The outmoded idealism that made de Gaulle's detractors see him as a 'living anachronism', Romain argued, was all that the Western world had left to rely on.

The essay revealed a writer at the crest of his form. At the same time *Lady L.* was published in the US and for nine weeks was listed among the twenty most-read books. Romain finished the year on a high note as both author and diplomat. Nonetheless his loyalty to de Gaulle – 'l'homme de ma vie' – continued to count against him in literary circles, while the neutral views on Algeria that he had to express as a diplomat conflicted with popular French support for Algerian independence.

During the months of crisis he had been packing and unpacking his bag, chafing for action and causing palpitations in his wife. Her commitment to her book was her only anchor. She worked solidly through 1958, using the research she had amassed in Istanbul, Paris and London, adding more from New York libraries and her Russian contacts there. Although she was turning up material in all sorts of unexpected places, there were still gaps in the narrative, which she feared could be filled only by sources in Moscow, Turkey or Tblisi in Georgia. By December that year she had reached Chapter 21, two-thirds of the way through 'The Time of the Shariat: A Study in Excess', as it was then entitled. The manuscript had swollen alarmingly; she had been commissioned to write 100,000 words, but her technique of building an overall picture from masses of detail was fatally inclusive and seemed impossible in fewer than 200,000 words.

Romain, though itching to leave Los Angeles, had agreed to stay on until the following spring, by which time she expected to finish the book. She was dejected to realize that she couldn't meet the agreed deadline of March 1959, although Jock reassured her that he would rather she missed it and stayed 'alive the other side'.

Apart from learning the guitar and playing her first tunes to the cats, all her energies were given to the book, which weighed on her more than she had ever imagined. Poisonous smogs had lifted and during a December heatwave she ate her solitary breakfast in the garden day after day, before plunging back into the Caucasus. She was probably too preoccupied to be lonely; then again who, even in Hollywood, could compare with the presence of Shamyl the magnificent, prophet warrior and leader of men?

Even pushing herself relentlessly, she had not quite finished her handwritten first draft by the end of April, meanwhile extensively rewriting the early chapters. Her revised delivery date of early June also slipped and Romain changed his mind about his hurry to leave Los Angeles. At this point she decided not to deliver the manuscript to

Jock until she had done some final checking and information gathering in France and Turkey. Instead she went first to Paris at the end of June, leaving the manuscript to be typed up and sent out, with copies for Murray, Viking US (which had not yet accepted it) and herself. The opus was so long that this had to be done in two halves.

To her frustration, she again missed seeing Shamyl's grandson (this must have been Imam Said Shamyl, the son of Shamyl's fifth son Mahommed Kâmil), who had left Munich for the Yemen twenty-four hours earlier. Pondering her next move, she made a ritual visit to Samuelian's Oriental bookshop in the rue Monsieur-le-Prince, which was a meeting place for Caucasian and Armenian exiles. (This atmospheric bookshop is still trading; the proprietor, M. Samuelian's daughter, knew Lesley well and stocks *Les Sabres du Paradis*, reissued for the author's 100th birthday.) Its crowded shelves had held many finds for her oriental library, sometimes hidden in a second or even third row of books packed behind the first. One of her favourite stories was how from the back of a shelf she had pulled out the marble-bound journal of Madame Drancy, the French governess, which so vividly described at first-hand the kidnapping of the Russian princesses and their households by Shamyl's men. At Samuelian's Lesley now had a fateful meeting with an Azerbaijani scholar called Ali-Akbar-Bek-Toptchibatchi, who was probably the most knowledgeable 'Shamylite' living in the West.

Toptchibatchi immediately plunged into a four-hour discussion with Lesley which left him impressed by the material she had gathered through Russian and Arabic transcripts. Beyond that he would guide her through manuscripts written in a Caucasian dialect impenetrable to most outsiders, which would enrich her story. Above all, he would give her letters of introduction to Shamyl's relations living in exile in Turkey, who still had relics of the great leader.

She had to attend to matters in Roquebrune for a week, before travelling in great excitement to Istanbul, at Romain's expense. She stayed at the old Park Hotel and, thanks to the addresses and letters of introduction given her by Toptchibatchi rather than the mysterious call of Fate according to her later accounts, she at last tracked some of Shamyl's descendants to an incongruous modern building in the Fatih quarter of Koska. As a boy the Imam Said Shamyl, grandson of the prophet leader, had been driven out of the Caucasus with his father and, by now a

prominent figure in the Pan-Islamic movement, was living in Koska
with his two sisters. But he had eluded Lesley in Paris and seems to have
done so again in Turkey. She never did meet him and though he is
mentioned in *The Sabres of Paradise* he is omitted from her ensuing
accounts of how she discovered Shamyl's family. At any rate it was too
much to expect the hand of fate to intervene more than once.

Best of all, she met the five surviving grandchildren of Khazi
Mahommed, Shamyl's second son, living in an old house on the shores
of the Bosporus in Besiktas, then a run-down district of Istanbul. The
door was opened by a woman with the high-set narrow eyes and long
face that Lesley instantly recognized as Shamyl's family features. This
was Zobeida Shamyl, one of the granddaughters; she was married to an
Egyptian ambassador and was only briefly visiting Turkey to attend her
sister's funeral, before flying out to join her husband in Jakarta. Mme
Shaply-Shamyl was initially suspicious of this foreigner asking questions about her great-grandfather, but Lesley's knowledge of her subject impressed her enough to invite her in and introduce her to the
family. Some of them remembered their grandfather, Khazi Mahommed.
His daughter Emiré Nafisette, their mother, had taught them the history of their family in the Caucasus that they now recounted to Lesley,
as well as the Daghestani battle chants that they sang for her. They
showed her family papers and foxed daguerrotypes: here at last was a
rare portrait of Shamyl's son Djemmal-Edin, who as a child was taken
hostage by the Russians. Lesley reproduced it in the book. She saw
Shamyl's padded saddle, and *shashkas* and *kindjals*, the slashing blades
used by the warriors.

Thrilled with these last-minute discoveries which culminated her
research, she returned briefly to Paris to consult with Toptchibatchi,
'Top' as she called him. By late July she was installed in London, where
she settled down to more than two months' solid work with Osyth
Leeston, her editor at John Murray, to add, amend, then condense
the manuscript to a manageable size; Denver Lindley at Viking in
New York had accepted it, like Jock Murray, on condition that it must
be drastically shortened. In early September, Jock reported that Lesley
was 'being splendid over the agonizing procedure of cutting'. They
had thinned the Persian section and contemporary travellers' descriptions of the Caucasus, and the work would now run to 480 printed
pages. Finally they had to make the spellings consistent; the names of

places and people were Russianized in Russian sources, different again in Arabic and French. Murray's offer to Viking that they offset the British edition was gratefully accepted.

Jock also wrote to tell Lesley's accountant, Mr Jones of Lionel Lemon, that she would like an advance that would incur as little tax as possible. Lesley's and Romain's financial circumstances became ever more chaotic as their earnings increased; now, faced with French tax demands, she had decided that it was more advantageous to be British and to pay all her taxes in Britain. Meanwhile she would stay on in London until the bulk of the work on the book was done. Once again she lodged with the Flemings, acknowledging her debt to them in her dedication, and visited her mother, who was living in reduced circumstances in west London.

She had been three months absent from Los Angeles, but still Lesley didn't hurry back to Romain. She seized a few days to be pampered by Horst and Nicholas Lawford on Long Island, before going on to New York for meetings with her editors at Viking and with her agent, who planned a campaign to sell film rights (which never materialized). Jock and Diana, who rashly followed Lesley to New York, found themselves loaded with her excess baggage, consisting of a heavy suitcase, a brass elephant and sundry parcels. To aggravate the inconvenience there was a dock strike in England, so they had to struggle on board unaided with all her impedimenta. Lesley, blithely apologetic, sketched Jock with his arms stretched down to the ground, and urged him and Diana to go to the New York Palladium on Wednesday nights for exotic dance contests. It was the last time she wrote with her old gaiety to Albemarle Street before personal disaster engulfed her.

Finally she arrived exhausted at the consulate, to be surrounded by neglect and chaos. Katiusha had had a fall and was off sick; the house and garden were in a mess; Romain was in low spirits; and the ambassador was about to arrive for a visit. The usual consulate pressures were building. The moment Lesley returned, Romain disappeared for a week's holiday, pleading nervous tension and leaving her to deal with the ambassador and his entourage of ex-ambassadors, admirals, the press and the French colony. It was decidedly inconvenient in terms of her writing, but it *was* her turn; after all, she had been away for nearly four months.

★

Although she thought she had finished the body of the book, by now she was forced to recognize how ambitious the project was. All her life Lesley had aimed high, sometimes in the past higher than her abilities to succeed. Her childhood fascination for a tinted print of Shamyl's compelling face had led, decades later, to her delving into a remote region whose culture and history were virtually unknown in the West. She had undertaken a complex work of scholarship from Russian and Arabic sources which made the highest demands on her organizational and writing skills and called for meticulous accuracy, never her strongest suit. The following six months of intensive cross-checking, correcting and finishing off, combined with high drama from Romain and the consulate's exhausting schedule, nearly broke her.

Preoccupied as she was with all the niggling problems outstanding on the book, in December 1959 Lesley was confronted by a new worry. Early that month a young French lawyer, François Moreuil, had called at the consulate with his extremely pretty young American wife and left his card with an introduction from an acquaintance of Romain's. The couple were duly invited to supper and Lesley paid politely effusive attention to Madame Moreuil, who was a Hollywood discovery, before turning to her other guests.

Mme Moreuil was Jean Seberg. She was dangerously young, a boyish Lolita who looked even less than her twenty-one years, her youth emphasized by her cropped hair and fragile features. An aura of perverse glamour clung to her, the sort bestowed by public failure on the grand scale. She had had the dubious privilege of being launched as a star by the Viennese director Otto Preminger, in two big-budget movies that had flopped spectacularly, apparently dishing her career before it had begun.

Jean had all the feminine qualities that Romain found irresistible, and the lacerating humiliation of her film debut had made her vulnerable, with the damaged innocence that he often gave to his fictional heroines. Now she was sitting next to him and hanging on his every word. Lesley wearily recognized in both parties the early symptoms of a grand infatuation. She just had to hope that it would soon subside.

9

After Supper

We are going to speak of terrible things.

Stendhal

THE TURN OF the new decade was a flashpoint for Lesley and Romain's fifteen-year marriage.

Lesley was putting the finishing touches to her Caucasian history whose late gestation after five years' work was so desperately problematic. Before she had seen it into the world she had already begun to plan an epic expedition, the fulfilment of a lifelong ambition, as the backbone for her next book. In her mid-fifties, a reputed writer, she could see a map to her future: a predictably unpredictable pattern of gathering her material in far places and then writing it up in whatever *poste* was dictated by her life as a diplomat's wife.

Romain's term in Hollywood was almost done, and yet again he was obsessed by the urge to move on. He was anxiously awaiting publication of *Promise at Dawn*, in which he would finally 'come out' with a version of his early years of poverty in Eastern Europe. At forty-five he was about to pay off the debt he owed his mother, showing the distance he had travelled to fulfil her ambitions. His autobiographical work would both enhance and reflect an odd reaction in Romain: he was moving into a kind of psychological moult, akin to his state of transition at the end of the war when he met Lesley.

Now an extremely desirable young woman had added herself to the script. Romain, who was drawn to humiliation, was gripped by Jean's story. She could have stepped out of his imagination as an archetype from his novels. At the consulate he was sometimes asked to help young women whose lives had been ruined by scavengers on Hollywood's fringes. Jean was an extreme example of the film industry's ability to pluck new faces and youthful dreams, squeeze out the freshness and grind on. Yet at twenty-one, she still retained an astonishing innocence from her small-town upbringing in Marshalltown, Ohio, and showed an obstinate determination to prove her worth as an actress.

Four years earlier, after a hugely publicized talent hunt, Otto Preminger had chosen the seventeen-year-old high-school graduate out of 18,000 candidates to play St Joan in his screen version of the Shavian drama. He said later that he had picked Jean precisely because she was completely 'unspoilt' by tuition or experience and he intended to *imprint* her performance on her. He promoted her as a star before she had shot a foot of film or, as John Gielgud (who co-starred in *Saint Joan*) tactlessly remarked, before she had learnt to act. Preminger's experiment failed; after the build-up the critics were extra-savage and the film was a box-office disaster. Defiantly Preminger cast her as Cecile, the wayward teenager in *Bonjour Tristesse*, based on Françoise Sagan's best-selling novel; that too bellyflopped in America. Then he dropped her.

Since then Jean had worked just twice in nearly two years, in England and France. Now, summoned to her first offer from Hollywood, she found herself cruelly invited to a screen test, instead of the B-movie part. On top of this, her short-lived marriage to François Moreuil, a young socialite French lawyer who had helped to distract her from Preminger's bullying direction of *Bonjour Tristesse* on the Riviera, was going badly.

Strangely, Jean's performances for Preminger had been better received in France, where she and her autocratic director attracted fascinated appraisal from the small group of film-makers who were transferring their heretical new theories from the pages of *Cahiers du Cinéma* into the ground-breaking movies of the New Wave. They hailed Preminger as an auteur who stamped his vision on every frame, and were mesmerized by the seductive young star he had created in *Bonjour Tristesse*, as the wilful child-woman who drove her father's mistress to death.

The previous summer, lacking other offers, Jean had been leased by Columbia to play the role of an unscrupulous American girl in Paris opposite Jean-Paul Belmondo's small-time crook, in a low-budget French movie. Jean-Luc Godard, the director, was nervous; it was his first full-length feature. To Jean, who disliked her part, he was a weird young man who handed her crumpled notes from his pocket each day instead of a script and could barely scrape together the change for her cab fares.

In March 1960, *A Bout de souffle* would open in Paris to sensational controversy and acclaim, turning her into an icon of youthful liberation and a muse for French cinema. Patricia Franchini changed the course of Jean's life; Paris became her new home and half of all her subsequent films would be made in Europe.

The zeitgeist was shifting, the flood tide of the 1960s with its insistence on youth was about to break and they were inescapably swept along by it. The currents would take them in different directions and leave them stranded: Lesley in the old regime, Jean in the new, and Romain uneasily straddling the two.

In Hollywood, after the fateful supper party Lesley pressed on with her work, in drooping spirits. Letters flew across the Atlantic about the epilogue . . . maps ('Top' would add essential place names to a tracing) . . . letters of permission . . . photographs of herself (nothing was right; now Cukor's friend Hoyningen-Huene promised to take some portraits). In early December, 'Top' wrote ominously to Lesley's publisher that he had found a number of errors on the list of names for the map, some of which 'are incomprehensible to me'. Lesley's book was written in English but the transcriptions were French, such as 'Tchetchnia' for Chechnya. If he had seen the manuscript earlier, he would have corrected the transliteration.

Christmas intervened; Lesley fretted about delayed or missing mail. She argued forcefully for her transcriptions to be kept and a careful note added about standardized spellings; she mostly used Russian names, taken from Russian military sources and the Baddeley archives, and could not slant the book to suit the Caucasians. She was too exhausted to deal with serializations; Jock agreed to try the *Sunday Times* or *Observer*. The *Cornhill* would take an extract and at *The Queen*, her loyal friend Jane Stockwood might consider an extract chosen by Lesley without seeing the complete text. Lesley was coming to realize that she could not hope to repeat the popular appeal of *Wilder Shores* with this blood-soaked history of tribal peoples, long ago and remote from British influence.

Production advanced slowly in a maelstrom of additions, corrections, apologies and complaints. Jock swiftly regretted his decision to go straight into page proofs. Lesley protested against Murray's jacket design. She was right to dread comments from 'the super-expert', 'Top'. Proofs were sent to him in late January. He kept author and publishers on tenterhooks for a month, then wrote in French to 'Monsieur' Osyth Leeston, claiming that the transliteration of names Lesley had used was anachronistic and misleading. He was opposed to her use of Russian sources, which in his view threw a hostile perspective on the Caucasus. Above all, he condemned what he construed as her interpretation of Shamyl as a religious leader crusading against Christian Russia. Shamyl was no rebel fanatic but a great nationalist leader, battling the Russian monster which was intent on devouring the entire world. He considered her portrait not only dangerously inaccurate but liable to cause serious repercussions in the Caucasian region. He insisted, in capital letters, on having his name removed from the work, and refused a fee.

After their initial dismay at this bombshell, Lesley and her publishers quickly rallied. The principal accusation was unsound; the book maintained throughout that Shamyl's thirty-year struggle was for autonomy and independence from the Russian empire, supported by the enforcement of the Muslim Shariat as a spiritual weapon in his campaign. M. Toptchibatchi wanted his name removed from her book: so be it. His valuable contribution to her project would be for ever erased, his name never mentioned again.

However, Toptchibatchi's reaction was salutary in showing beyond doubt that her title, *The Time of the Shariat*, was misleading and could offend Muslim sensibilities. The Shariat, the Muslim ordinance governing religious codes of behaviour, is timeless and therefore could not be used to label the specific era when Shamyl was at war with the tsars. Lesley was grateful for this revelation. She had felt herself opposed by a mysterious hidden force during the course of writing her book. Now the invisible opposition had at last been reversed by these corrective strokes of fortune: her meetings with Shamyl's family, her new title.

In March she had the fraught task of persuading her publishers to agree to change the title from *The Time of the Shariat* to *The Sabres of Paradise*. She was right to insist on the change, but Jock Murray was appalled: the jacket had already been printed, he disliked the new title which to him smacked of Hollywood, and now he had to recall and reissue all the advance publicity. In the end Murray adapted the American sleeve. Lesley's additional amendments to avoid similar mis-understandings in the text dismayed Jock and Osyth: production costs had already soared over budget and her new last-minute corrections forced them to delay publication from June to October.

In December and January Romain was working fitfully for George Cukor at MGM on the screenplay of *Lady L*. He stuck closely to the original novel. Later Cukor, dissatisfied with Romain's sometimes clichéd Paris backdrops of street women leaning against gaslit walls and accordion music wafting from cafés, would commission other writers to work on the script.

The Consul-General and his wife invited François and Jean to dine with them again (at whose behest?) before the young couple flew home to her parents in Ohio for Christmas. Jean had won her part in *Let No Man Write My Epitaph* at Columbia, but François had to return to Paris in the New Year. He called in at the consulate to say goodbye and, as he ruefully recalled later, to ask the consul-general to look after his wife.

Romain was as good as his word. He found excuses to meet Jean socially and stole time to spirit her away with him for a secret short trip to Mexico, arranging her visa (her marriage to François having given her French nationality) through the consulate. He had no expectations of a lasting affair at first and was fearful of scandal that could rise from his entanglement with a Hollywood name less than half his age. Nevertheless, Jean's youth and androgynous sex appeal represented a physical ideal for him. Her admiration for him was irresistible, and she brought out his manly protective instincts; with Lesley, his protector, it had been the other way round.

Jean has often been described as passive, but she pursued Romain as single-mindedly as Lesley had done fifteen years earlier. Before she left for Paris in late January, she too called in at the consulate and told Romain she was going to miss him. While she was reluctantly return-ing to François, her visit was a statement of intent which left the older man in no doubt that she wanted to pursue whatever had begun between them.

In February Romain took *The Time of the Shariat*, as it was still en-titled, with him to read during a trip to San Francisco. He wired his wife: 'It is an extraordinary book and will remain a classic. In admiration.' He was unstinting in his comments to friends, telling them it was an astonishing work, in places comparable to *War and Peace*. Lesley was thrilled by his praise, distraught as she was with her troublesome book which defied completion, and tormented by his fixation with Jean, which seemed to be taking a dangerous turn.

In early March, when she returned from visiting her New York publishers to be met by Toptchibatchi's devastating letter, Romain was encouraging about her development as a writer: she had left journalism far behind, he assured her. Almost her final addition to the heavily amended proofs, which were taxing Murray's patience to the limits, was a last-minute credit to her husband in the acknowledgements, 'for his enthusiasm and understanding during the years I was absorbed in Caucasian research'. Although Romain ruthlessly overrode her writing time at the consulate, given that he had paid for her trip to Istanbul the year before and had tolerated her absences for months on end while she was working on the book, it's less surprising that she wished to record her thanks to him than that this was the first time she thought of it.

Regardless of his support for Lesley as she struggled on, Romain was determined to be gone, from her and from the consulate. A few days later he left for Paris, telling her carelessly he would be going to Vichy for a month's health cure. In fact he applied to the Quai for two months' leave of absence, from 12 March to 13 May 1960. Gallimard was to publish *Promise at Dawn* in May; this time he planned to be in Paris beforehand to promote the event and, effectively, himself. *The Roots of Heaven* had made him famous, first through the Goncourt, then by association with the brouhaha surrounding Huston's film. He was newsworthy beyond the French literary pages and he intended to exploit his celebrity to promote *Promise at Dawn*. If his reputation was thereby compromised in the eyes of the literati, *tant pis*.

Of course he had other reasons for hurrying to Paris. Claude Gallimard was enlisted to book a suite in the Hôtel Lutetia where Romain installed himself with Jean in strict secrecy. Almost immediately, protecting her privacy became doubly essential and triply difficult because *A Bout de souffle* was released on 16 March to an explosion of publicity. As low as she had sunk in her home country after *Saint*

Joan, Jean now found herself in the bewildering position of being relaunched into stratospheric fame almost overnight in Europe.

There can be few more famous images of the dawning 1960s than the poster still of Jean/Patricia in T-shirt and pedal-pushers, hawking the *New York Herald Tribune* as she strolls down the Champs Elysées beside Belmondo in his gangster's hat, hands in pockets, rolling a Gauloise between his lips. More than a quarter of a million people saw the film in the first seven weeks after its release in France. Critics and audiences were jolted by the hand-held camerawork and jump-cuts which defied all film-making convention, and by Godard's carelessly amoral, louche young protagonists Michel Poiccard and Patricia Franchini. Decades later, the film writer David Thomson remembered falling in love with 'the look, simultaneously blank yet filled with understanding, in the uncanny face of Jean Seberg'.

Jean/Patricia with her boy's haircut and frock from Prisunic was worlds away from the screen diva who embodied the ideal woman. She offered the world a new image of seductive, unscrupulous youth at just the moment when it was needed. Every female student could identify with her fresh-faced *arriviste*, her ambitious young writer on the make in Paris: if not beautiful, adored by the lithe, magnetic Belmondo. 'As Mel Gussow in the *Times* put it, "she became a symbol to the young American women who dreamed about going to Paris to become Jean Seberg."'

Style journalists ever since have revisited the 'existential haircut' that branded her as the face of 1960 and 'the unwitting embodiment of the *Zeitgeist*'. 'This was a new kind of woman,' Lesley Cunliffe raved in *Vogue* more than thirty years later, 'who thumbed her nose and said "*je m'en fiche*" to the entire load of behavioural baggage which had dictated "feminine deportment". Jean Seberg in *Breathless* crystallised a new way to be: oneself. In 1959 [sic], when most women dressed and behaved like Barbie dolls, Americans found this shocking and inspiring in equal measure; Seberg was perceived as a sort of female James Dean.'

The vertiginous switchback in her fortunes had made her a new sensation in France, pursued on the one hand by paparazzi and on the other by aspiring film-makers, hoping to exploit the face of the moment. She was still married to François (to whom, in fact, she owed her sudden fame: he had introduced her to Jean-Luc Godard and had flown to Columbia Studios in Hollywood to help negotiate a cheap lease from her contract, allowing her to star in *Breathless*). She had promised to be in François's film, *Playtime*, which would start shooting in France in early June. Yet she had fallen passionately in love with Romain and with everything he stood for, and had secretly committed herself to him. Panic and confusion mounted in her until she lost control and began to smash up the apartment she shared with François. He took her to the American Hospital, where she was sedated and soon afterwards transferred to a private psychiatric clinic for complete rest. After farcical scenes when Romain, bound over by François's father (another Free French veteran) not to see Jean, secretly visited her disguised in a white doctor's coat, he persuaded René Agid to arrange her discharge to stay in his friends' mansion at Savigny. Soon afterwards she was put on a private plane fitted with beds and flown via Montreal and Chicago to her parents in Marshalltown.

Going home, Jean had to make another violent adjustment. On her eighteenth birthday Preminger had swept her off to London to film *Saint Joan*, detaching her from the sober Republican community in the Midwest where she had been born. Her forbears were hard-working Scandinavian settlers; her father, Ed Seberg, ran a pharmacy and Dorothy, her mother, had given up teaching to raise their four children at home. In her modest Lutheran upbringing, even Jean's ambition to act had been suspect as a form of showing off. The circus of Hollywood stardom had estranged her from her friends. Marshalltown had barely recovered from her much-publicized marriage to a Parisian socialite, and now she had to explain that she intended to divorce him. Her parents were profoundly shocked by this unheard-of family precedent; the stigma would scandalize the community and attach to them. Jean was adamant. Before returning to France she started divorce proceedings in the County District Court. It was inconceivable for her to admit that she was already involved with another man who was not only twice her age but married.

In Paris Romain was startled to find himself smitten. 'Je suis bouleversé! Sentimentalement . . . Une femme!' he cried to his friends. 'Oh! Cette femme m'a bouleversé . . . Je ne sais comment faire . . .'

He had effectively abdicated from the consulate, leaving his wife to mind the shop with Mlle Pétrement. In April, while he was staying with René and Sylvia at Savigny, weeping with distress for 'la pauvre petite', Lesley was making her heroic last stand as the Consul-General's representative in Los Angeles. What should have been a triumphant finale at Hollywood's most prestigious event, hosting the French table at the Oscar awards dinner (where honours went to Simone Signoret and *Black Orpheus*), became a nightmare of conflicting responsibilities. With spectacular ineptness and against all the consulate's warnings, Air France had scheduled that evening for the arrival of its inaugural polar flight direct to Los Angeles. Partway through the dinner Lesley had to leave the table, change from blue tulle to black suit and drive to the airport to meet Gaston de Monnerville, President of the Senate and de Gaulle's second in command, plus members of the French Cabinet, a hundred deputies, assorted wives and hand-picked journalists. All would be assigned to the hospitality of Mlle Pétrement and herself, standing in for Romain, during their six-day stay. The plane was hours late, so she had to return to Hollywood and repeat the whole process before finally escorting the party to their hotel and staggering back to take her place at the Oscars until everyone dispersed at 4 a.m.

Next day after a civic lunch, she supervised the sumptuous dressing of a reception room at Romanoffs with gardenia swags, paper doves and baskets of lilies and oleander, then collapsed on her bed, dog-tired, before the gala dinner that evening for 300 guests. Suddenly she heard Katiusha calling to her that the French party had all arrived at the consulate and were crowded into the drawing room. Lesley skulked in her bedroom until they had gone, but soon afterwards they surged back again, seeking first aid for Mme de Monnerville who had fallen and hurt her arm. Lesley hid again until they left, then flung on her party clothes for the reception and dinner given by Air France. On the way home she had to stop the car to be sick into a dustbin from tension and exhaustion. On and on it went, for five nightmarish days: maintaining the correct protocol; presenting guests to one another whose names she couldn't remember; escorting parties to the university, the medical school (where they watched a heart operation), the studios, San Francisco, San Diego . . . After seeing the party off at the airport she returned to the consulate to find four telegrams announcing the arrival of more visitors and burst into tears, protesting that the Consul-General and his staff had the workload of a major embassy.

While she had been out, a colony of wild bees that lived under the roof tiles had swarmed above the front door. Lesley gratefully saw the buzzing horde as her protectors: thus guarded, she spent the weekend in total solitude and on Monday had them carefully moved out of town.

That day she was devastated to hear from Romain that they must leave Los Angeles by August. Even so, she loyally extolled his success with his new version of *European Education*, purged of its earlier Russophile contents for its current Cold War readership, and compared *Promise at Dawn* favourably with Gorky's *Childhood*. Although she already suspected that her own work would not be a commercial hit, she described it poignantly as 'the book of my heart'. She had willingly learnt from it, despite all the troubles it had brought. Relieved as she was to have got through the production problems, she felt herself painfully banished from the Caucasus, her inner landscape for so long.

Worst of all, she was reluctantly forced to recognize that Romain was insisting on a separation. She was desperately upset and worried about the financial implications. How would she be able to pay for the research and writing of her books in future? The expenses would not be negligible for her next project for Murray, the one that she had decided on in New York in February, which would involve going to Russia at last.

Romain was still in Paris when *Promise at Dawn* was published in early May. In an interview for *L'Express* he said he had decided to write about himself because he had left behind the person that he once was: 'I opened myself up like a burglar opens a safe,' he confided. '. . . Now, I feel an extraordinary sense of liberation, a profound relief.' He said he had written the book in three months, then delayed publication for eighteen months more, keeping a set of proofs beside him to reread, although he changed nothing. What was he thinking of – a slip that might give him away? The conjuring trick he undertook in *Promise at Dawn* lay first in writing about the past that he had concealed for so long; then, more dangerously, in his way of leaving the reader to choose whether or not to believe it.

The publicity about the book's autobiographical status was as inconsistent as its author. The copy he wrote for an advertising insert declared: 'This book is based on my life, but it is not an autobiography. At every instant, artistic preoccupations slipped in between the event and its literary expression . . . In the end, be it by pen, paintbrush or chisel, all truths boil down to artistic truths.' Yet in June 1961 his

American publisher wrote to Romain, 'to make absolutely sure that no confusion can arise, we are now sending critics a note to the effect that *Promise at Dawn* is a true and factual account of your early life.'

For forty years after it was published, *Promise at Dawn* set the seal on his early years, narrating with disarming humour the 'essential truth' about his upbringing. As he told it, from birth the course of his existence had been marked out by his Russian mother's passionate childlike belief in France as a fairy-tale land where peace, plenty and liberty reigned. There her beloved son would be duly recognized and fêted as a literary genius, his princely metamorphosis crowned by the honour of representing his adopted country to the world as its ambassador. All her hopes and ambitions were instilled in him and even when they were apart he felt her as a presence: 'J'avais toujours un témoin en moi, je l'ai encore.' Her years of poverty and self-deprivation paid for his education and his training as an air force cadet, and all through his wandering wartime years with the Lorraine bomber squadron he was sustained by his mother's letters, urging him on. At the war's end, when his first novel had been successfully published, his battle record honoured by the Croix de Guerre and the Legion of Honour, and he had been nominated by de Gaulle as one of only 798 surviving Companions of the Liberation, he had seized the first opportunity to travel across liberated France, bearing his trophies to show his mother how her faith had been answered by his success. Only then did he discover that she had died years earlier, entrusting to a friend in Switzerland a pile of letters to be sent one by one, after her death, to her beloved son.

The friends who knew and loved Romain accepted the veracity of his mother's portrait in what was essentially fiction. François Bondy, who had lodged at the Hôtel Mermonts when he and Romain had been school classmates in Nice, wrote to his friend that he had wept to find Mina marvellously resurrected in this 'novel' that so movingly spoke the truth about her. The wider world, meanwhile, read the work as autobiography and for decades accepted its contents literally – the Russian birthplace, the unknown father, the sustaining wartime letters – which were reinforced, or further improvised, by Romain in his encounters with the media.

Whatever the relationship between the story he presented of his past and the true facts, the originality of his voice and the authenticity of its expression were undeniable. The critical consensus was that with

Promise at Dawn he had both consecrated his standing in French literature and produced a resounding popular hit. Romain had the satisfaction of proving to those critics who complained that he couldn't write
French how far he had had to travel in order to master their language,
yet that withal he could still write a masterpiece.

Apart from consolidating his literary reputation, to Lesley *Promise at
Dawn* transformed Romain's life more fundamentally. Until then he
had gone to great pains to disguise his past and shroud it in mystery.
Now he had apparently stripped away all his secrets and flaunted his
mongrel beginnings in Eastern Europe, so disdained among conventional pedigrees at the Quai d'Orsay. This, she admitted, took courage,
yet she found something almost indecent about his need to strip naked
before the indifferent world. His self-exposure was an affront to their
tacit acceptance of each other's hidden history, for so long a bond
between them. In paying off his filial dues he had also freed himself
from the obligations that bound him to Mina for so long. Lesley was in
a position to see the changes in him first and feel the effects most. He
lost no time in telling her he wanted a divorce, soon moved to Paris
and secretly threw in his lot with Jean, despite evident misgivings.
Although he made no public announcement that he had left the Quai
d'Orsay, his diplomatic career was on hold.

Yet in one respect husband and wife remained complicit throughout their separation and their worst hostilities. Lesley never let on
about his wayward attitude towards the facts about himself, even after
Romain's death when his first biographers based their accounts of his
origins on *Promise at Dawn*. She knew he had muddied the truth about
his early childhood and invented his mother's poignant wartime letters
sent to him after she died, as well as incidents like the plane crash in
Africa that killed pilot and elephant, and the duel at the Regent's
Palace Hotel. His reluctant admission to Lesley that he was Jewish was
still not conceded in his book. Her memoir never set out to deny or
correct any of his self-made past; instead she added her own layer of
legend to his.

She was surely aware, as commentators on the life and work of
Romain Gary have convincingly argued since, that this was no conventional autobiography but the deliberate fashioning of a myth.
Promise at Dawn (which he dedicated to René and Sylvia Agid, who
had known him all those years ago in Nice) takes us up to the end of

the war, by which time Roman Kacew has shed his Eastern European childhood, lost his actress mother and reinvented himself as Romain Gary, French war hero, diplomat and writer, just as she had planned. His mother's invincible ambition for her only son, their journey to the promised land, their struggles with hardships there, his Odyssean war-time wanderings have all been for a purpose. The very strength of their shared umbilical bond makes him fearless; fate *must* spare him because he will achieve the fame and success she has decreed for him. And so, with the publication of the *Forest of Anger* in 1944, he became a writer: 'we were born'.

The persona that he had shaped for himself as writer-adventurer in the mould of Kessel and Malraux was of supreme importance to Romain. Unlike Lesley, whose physical environment was crucial to her psychological well-being, his protean self depended on the frame-work of his interior habitat. To feel at ease in his skin, he needed to reinvent his image in the face of changing circumstances. Now the hermit crab could move into the shell of a new identity that he had made for himself, decorating it with whatever flourishes he chose to add in interviews and profiles. The old life would be jettisoned – wife, profession and all. The sense of liberation that he described in *L'Express* exploded over every aspect of his new existence.

But for the time being his two months' leave was over and he was obliged to return to Los Angeles until his contract expired.

Back at the consulate, Romain's tendency to see plots and conspiracies everywhere fanned a small imbroglio about Lesley's book. In Europe their friend Walter Goetz had told him that Jock Murray was unhappy with the new title to her book, *The Sabres of Paradise*, believing that Romain had persuaded her to change it. They both protested to Murray about what he hastened to assure them was unfounded hear-say. Lesley added a complaint that publication delays had lost her magazine extracts. Since these delays were almost entirely due to her own last-minute changes and additions, this must have resulted in eye-rolling at Murray's.

She was ill with anxiety over Romain's new insistence that they must separate. He was offering to buy her a place to live in Paris by way of settlement. In late May, while Romain stayed behind in Los Angeles, she flew to London, arriving 'in an exhausted and rather nervy state', to agree the revised American jacket and a new publication date: the stars were propitious for early October (Lesley took her horoscope readings very seriously). In Paris she looked at several houses, including one in Montmartre that the Agids suggested, but nothing came of them. She dreaded returning to Europe and hoped somehow to stay on in Los Angeles. By late June 1960 she was back in Hollywood, clinging to the house that had become home to her. The prospect of leaving was unbearable.

Romain was adamant: they must vacate their living quarters in three weeks. Lesley was still trying to catch up with bills and correspondence that had piled up while she finished the book, only to have to drop them again to pack up all their possessions. It was not the first time that she had prepared to depart without knowing where they would be moving to, but this time Romain's exercise machine and diving equipment would go one way, while her furniture, treasures, books and kitchen paraphernalia went another.

The Carrière had come up with no decent offer of a posting for Romain and was unlikely to do so in the immediate future, under the hostile influence of the foreign minister Couve de Murville. In any case, Romain was compromised professionally by his liaison with Jean, who was determined that they should live together (again, not the behaviour of a passive personality). However, he could not do so openly while employed by the Quai d'Orsay; the puritanical attitude to divorce of Tante Yvonne, as Madame de Gaulle was known, cast a long shadow. He was also acutely aware that his diplomatic career and status were essential to the structure of his life with Lesley. Much of his value to her, and hers to him, attached to his roving diplomatic lifestyle; without it, the role she enjoyed as the diplomat's wife would disappear, and the marriage would be cut off at the roots.

Lesley knew that too, and argued that he would bring disaster on himself if he abandoned his profession for a young woman who would never be faithful and would humiliate and leave him. It was inconceivable to her that Romain should consider renouncing his diplomatic position just as he reached ambassador status, the peak of his career, casting off his life's partner who had sustained it, for a scandalous affair with a starlet from the corn belt. She held out against divorce, begging him to consider a year apart in the desperate hope that his affair with Jean would burn out. In the meantime she refused point-blank to consider leaving 'her' consulate until she was forced to go at the end of August.

The French ambassador in Washington, Hervé Alphand, wanted Romain to stay on until the consulate's grand annual reception for Bastille Day on 14 July, which would have been his leaving party. Romain, indifferent as ever to everyone else's convenience, unable perhaps to bear farewell scenes or the hypocrisy of his position with Lesley, quit early, abruptly severing his links with Los Angeles without goodbyes to friends, colleagues or constituents. She and Mlle Pétrement were left to invent what excuses they could for him to 400 guests. Lesley still felt the pain inflicted by his callous desertion nearly forty years later.

He travelled via Washington to make his diplomatic farewells, going on to New York, where he was securing his authorial future in a three-book contract with Harper & Row and his agent 'Bobbie' Lantz. This was complicated since Romain sometimes wrote in English (*Lady L., Talent Scout*) and at other times in French (*Promise at Dawn*). To avoid 'glutting the market' he therefore planned to write half of his output in English and half in French, and have them translated and published alternately in America and France. His ability to write in two languages, neither of which was his native tongue – did he, effectively, have a native tongue? – was highly exceptional in itself; most important of all for Romain, it enlarged his psychological boundaries. Language was a tool that enabled him to multiply and divide himself authorially, allowing him to treat a book in two or more different ways, as he observed in the context of *Lady L.* Sometimes he worked with French translators, which also allowed him to adopt more pseudonyms, another obsession. 'John Markham Beach', the 'translator' of *Promise at Dawn*, was one such: the first draft in English by Gerard Hopkins was extensively revised by Romain, alias Mr Beach.

Lesley would have known from Romain's impatience to return to Paris that Jean was waiting for him. With her grandmother as chaperone she had flown from Marshalltown in early June, just before filming with Moreuil started; they soon moved into an apartment on the Left Bank with a friend of Jean and Romain's, Aki Lehman, who ran an antique shop next door.

Back in the capital, Romain was once more living on uncertainty. In some respects this suited him: places were immaterial to him, and as far as he was concerned the fact that he had left all his possessions behind in hopeless disorder was of no importance. He took a little apartment, romantically placed overlooking the Seine on the Ile Saint-Louis, where Jean secretly spent time with him. He assured the press that after five years in Hollywood he was merely on leave for two months while waiting for his next mission. He had just handed in *Talent Scout* (*Les Mangeurs d'étoiles*) to Gallimard for publication the following spring, or perhaps *Lady L.* would be published first. Now that he dictated his novels, he explained grandly, it was easier for him to move from one project to another.

Privately he was concerned about his writing output, which was seriously affected by the personal uproars surrounding him. He had dictated *Talent Scout* in four weeks, in English, and it needed to be revised and the language tidied, preferably by Lesley, on whom he relied for this purpose. Lesley, anxious to emphasize his continued reliance on her, agreed to read it.

After the humour, love, hope and grief of *Promise at Dawn* the pendulum of Romain's imagination had swung the other way into a corrosive tale of a grotesque Latin-American dictator, a native Indian who has absorbed as literal truth the Christian tenet that 'the wicked shall inherit the earth', and intends to sell his soul to the devil by every possible vice in order to inherit his share. His greatest fear is of being 'saved' by his girlfriend, a young American from Iowa with boyish short hair, delicate features and a slightly snub nose who has appointed herself his guardian angel. Her inheritance of guilt, the conscience of a white American born into wealth and privilege, makes her forever pledged to help the weak and exploited, but her idealism is laughably unrealistic. 'She was the only living thing in the world that ever scared him. She had true goodness in her – but it had taken him some time to discover this because she was so willing in bed, and he did not think that the two could go together – and her goodness always touched in him his most superstitious chord.'

Did Romain take pleasure in presenting this transparent portrait of his compliant young mistress to his wife for correction? (The later French version is more sexually explicit.) Indeed, how did Jean receive his caricature of the misguided college girl who drank, did drugs and naively believed that she could reform her depraved lover? Quite possibly these considerations did not interest him; he was preoccupied with ensuring that he had got the language right. Whatever tumultuous events were erupting in his life, for Romain his fiction always took precedence. His and Lesley's roots had become most entwined around his writing, the one area that he was most reluctant to disrupt or damage. Lesley, too, was possessive about this aspect of their relationship and darkly warned that his work would suffer without her.

Breathless had effectively transplanted Jean from America to Europe in terms of demand for her performances and she was now leased by Columbia, first to François and after that to two more French directors, in a packed schedule that would keep her working non-stop through the autumn. All three movies were low-budget productions by aspiring directors for whom Jean personified both the glamour of Hollywood and the cutting edge of the *nouvelle vague*. Twice more she was cast as a young American girl, at once victim and seductress, who acquires a sentimental education in Europe. *Saint Joan* had made her a victim but also gave her a cause. *Breathless* turned her into a subversive icon of youth. Now she was the innocent from the New World learning the ways of the old.

An image was falling into place that was at once Jean and not Jean. She had indeed been a wide-eyed young American abroad who had made an unsuitable liaison with a French playboy, before (as she now hoped) finding lasting happiness with an older, wiser man. Yet the cool blank quality she projected which so attracted French directors derived not from confidence, but partly at least from her traumatic experience with Preminger, which left her frozen and barely able to emote on screen.

Below the controlled façade her emotions were hardly kept in check. Since leaving home she had been subjected to the full blast of Hollywood's manufacturing process, which had shredded her untried personality, then dropped her before an 'official' studio image had set. The homely values of Marshalltown had no purchase in the slide areas where she was trying to balance. She had plummeted through unemployment, a failed marriage and fleeting liaisons, to be catapulted into another kind of stardom and a new relationship with a public figure, a writer whose maturity and worldly knowledge seemed to offer a haven of security. She clung to both with the desperation of a drowning woman.

★

Romain's leave came up in August. Lesley, still in Los Angeles, was outraged to hear that he intended to take Jean to Roquebrune and forbade her rival's presence in the house that she had created, so they stayed in a rented villa. Romain's writing routine continued wherever he was.

His friends were left in no doubt about his deepening involvement. Jean's happiness was contagious; she made him more relaxed, his moods lightened. She was at once breathtakingly naive in her approach to the world and sexually wanton. He told the Hoppenots he adored her and was astonished to find that he had been faithful to her for two years, which had never happened to him before. (Actually he had met Jean less than a year earlier.) But he insisted that she knew he couldn't marry her because of the twenty-four-year age difference between them.

Nonetheless 'la petite' alarmed him, he told his friends. Sylvia and René were diverted and irritated by his protestations that Jean's sexual demands were distracting him from his writing, provoking one to wonder whether (to paraphrase Thurber) he was bragging or complaining. Inevitably this information found its way back to Lesley. He was concerned, too, about Jean's self-destructive tendencies. It was hard for him to help because she didn't listen, he lamented; her impulses stemmed from her own inner voice, which overrode his.

Jean had hoped to arrange a discreet split from François but had failed to tell him about her divorce proceedings in America. The case was decided on 20 September 1960 and *Paris-Soir* recorded François's surprise on hearing that he had been divorced in the United States without his knowledge. Learning that the grounds were 'cruel and inhuman treatment', he was so outraged that he took legal action to have the proceedings declared invalid in France and countersued for a French divorce on the grounds of adultery, naming Romain, all of which delighted the gossip columns.

The announcement of Jean's American divorce stabbed Lesley like a dagger thrust just before *The Sabres of Paradise* was published, when she had hoped for her moment of triumph. Compared with the muted attention that she received for her book launch, the high-decibel publicity surrounding Jean's every movement was infuriating. Her fears that Romain would want to follow suit were confirmed when a New York journalist told her he had decided to seek a divorce; when she called Romain from Los Angeles, there was cold comfort in his assurance that he would never marry Jean.

Lesley had stayed on at the consulate until late August. Leaving parties in her honour did nothing to allay her resentment and dread at the upheavals of moving, which took five days in an obliterating heatwave. She transferred temporarily to a 'miniscule bungalene' at 611 North Crescent Drive, with her bewildered cats and extreme baggage. In late September she left the chaos behind her for a fortnight in New York, where she stayed at the Sulgrave Palace Hotel, while *The Sabres of Paradise* was launched. She appeared on the Jack Paar show, did radio interviews and was fêted by Russian princes at select receptions; her book was selected as the American Book of the Month Club's alternative choice. American press coverage was positive as far as it went, but Lesley was critical of Viking's publicity, which meant that she was disappointed by slow sales and the limited attention she received. Although she had already steeled herself to recognize that *The Sabres of Paradise* would not repeat her success with *The Wilder Shores of Love*, the proof was hard to accept.

Rebecca West's note from England must have helped to vindicate Lesley's lengthy labours to master her intractable subject matter. 'Does it strike you,' she concluded, 'that nobody, but nobody else could have written your book? It is not often I think that about a book. But all that engineering work of organizing the material and the exquisite reaction to its sensual values, only you can do the whole job.'

The Sabres of Paradise was, indeed, the perfect vehicle for Lesley to express the consuming involvement with all things Russian that had absorbed her since childhood. While her search for knowledge had led her to Shamyl's descendants and had unearthed rare contemporary eye-witness accounts, its true foundation was Russian literature. In it she distilled her voracious early reading of the nineteenth-century classics: Lermontov and Tolstoy, who both fell under the spell of the Caucasus while stationed in the Russian army there, Pushkin, Herzen, Bestoujev and many others. No wonder she considered it her apotheosis.

The extended duel between Shamyl and Nicholas I for supremacy in the mountains of Daghestan, against the broader nineteenth-century history of the troubled Caucasus, still makes relevant reading for travellers to that bitterly disputed region, charting the bloody origins of

Chechnya's death struggles with Russia that continue to this day. Aside from its historical prescience, *The Sabres of Paradise* is a spellbinding feat of storytelling, combining all the elements that most attracted Lesley. The setting is exotic, the subject spectacular and remote, the protagonists larger than life. Shamyl was the spiritual and absolute ruler of the warrior tribespeople of his mountainous domain. He stood six feet three inches tall, was fearless in guerrilla warfare, a wily negotiator with allies and enemies, and attentive to his five wives and his black-and-white cat. His religious status as a prophet, reinforced by a dramatic escape, earned him a legend for invincibility, and his fanatical followers routed a succession of Russian armies. When he finally surrendered after decades of savage fighting, he was sent into exile in Russia; but such was his heroic standing even with his enemy that Russian crowds waited at every railway station to cheer him on his way.

Like all Lesley's work, it was no conventional history. Her aim was less to record than to bring to life, and the key to her achievement was the extra-vivid visual imagination and dramatic flair that she used to animate the figures who surged up from the pages. She luxuriated in the materiality of detail: the surreal jangling of barrel organs in the tribesmen's mountain fortresses; station waiters giving the caviar a lick to make it shine before a train pulled in; Prince Potemkin's greasy, ink-spotted dressing gown lined with ermine. The tour de force is the exchange of Shamyl's son Djemmal-Edin, who had been completely Russianized after growing up as a hostage in Nicholas I's entourage, for two Georgian princesses and their household, held captive for months in Shamyl's spartan mountain eyrie. Slowly the hostages pass each other as they cross sides, guarded by facing ranks of massed Russian troops in glittering uniforms and silent lines of black-robed Caucasian horsemen.

Landscape is paramount, as always in her work. The protagonists are defined by their terrain: the cold regal magnificence of St Petersburg embodied in Nicholas I; the harsh mountain fastnesses of the Caucasus reflecting Shamyl's unconquered spirit. Sometimes there is even a circular process of identification: in a compelling digression Lesley described the heightened perception of Lermontov, a painter and writer like herself, dazzled by the textures of his spectacular surroundings that he longed to possess but could capture only by description.

There were rave reviews. Brian Aldiss wrote that 'she has something of the power of Gibbon . . . it is like a tapestry. I have read no book this year I admire more. . . . Miss Blanch's triumph,' he concluded, 'while shaking the dust off a distant war, lies in showing us that as we cannot understand our past without reference to the Russian Empire, so we cannot understand our present without reference to Tsarist Russia: for last century's Little Father has become this one's Big Brother.'

However, the book's size and esoteric subject matter assigned it for review by specialist scholars, attracting complaints about her unscholarly style. Her occasional novelistic invention of dialogue displeased the *TLS*, while Harold Nicolson wilted before 'words as thick as blackberries in October' and suspected Lesley of a schoolgirl attitude towards the '"simple, animal magnetism" of these savages'. *The Economist* was grateful to her for telling a 'splendid story' but criticized her 'overwhelming partiality and her apparently constitutional inability to keep to the point'. This was not the only review to disapprove of the book's digressive nature, although the build-up of detail was intrinsic to Lesley's historical perception.

L. Collier in the *Geographical Journal* noted that the author's passion for excess had resulted in 'a rich mixture of excessive savagery, excessive tyranny, excessive luxury, excessive debauchery and at times, almost excessive heroism. Sometimes, indeed, her statements are even more excessive than the facts', especially in the scale of the Caucasian mountains, which Lesley had never seen. He concluded, 'Its style is vivid (though occasionally florid) . . . and the figures of Schamyl [sic] and his opponents certainly come to life in its pages. The unromantic reader cannot help suspecting that they come to something even larger than life, but the facts themselves are so extraordinary that the suspicion may be unjust.'

A short penetrating review by the historian Mark Frankland posed the central paradox about Lesley's historical works. After classing *The Sabres of Paradise* as a 'splendid piece of romantic writing' which he found engrossing and thoroughly enjoyable, he regretted that the author 'has a fine historical imagination, but not the historian's purpose.' Defining his subject as 'a constant, perhaps unwinnable, battle for accuracy and explanation', he argued that history defined by its great men and exotic figures could be 'very readable and also not much more than fiction . . . books which just make use of the past to provide subject matter really do subvert the desperate purpose of serious historians.' He concluded that he would like to see 'someone like Lesley Blanch combining her good writing and imagination with some real history. They both need each other.'

'Not much more than fiction'. Romain, an astute judge of Lesley's progress as a writer, had eulogized her life of Shamyl as comparable to *War and Peace*, which was another way of saying the same thing. To Romain, however, that fictional quality was an essential ingredient in the construction of a masterpiece. His entire life was a testament – as much of Lesley's would be – to the belief that fiction, not reality, was the place to look for the truth.

Lesley always insisted that she 'couldn't invent', by which she meant that she couldn't write fiction. Not long after *The Sabres of Paradise* was published, however, she mused about the biographical process in an essay about the forgotten poet Laurence Hope, one of several short portraits of little-known subjects who preoccupied her at this time. The biographer, she contended, must combine 'detection and intuition' to produce 'a subconscious enlightenment or communication' between author and subject: an imaginative leap, in other words. A kind of magical thinking was needed to summon up the past by placing herself in it: an enviable if controversial trait, comparable perhaps to the late Polish foreign correspondent Ryszard Kapuscinski, whose poetic reportage of climactic events depended often on intuition as well as on historical analysis.

Lesley would base her claim to historical scholarship on *The Sabres of Paradise*. 'But is it history?' Frankland demurred. Judged by strictly academic criteria, perhaps not. Lesley had achieved a feat of scholarship of which she was justly proud, though she was possibly misguided in wishing to be judged by conventional standards of historical scholarship – when had she ever aspired to convention or orthodoxy? Rather, her transforming romantic artist's eye had used the scaffolding of research to create a work of literature. The scope of her book, the intensity of its description and narrative drive made it exceptional, and to sympathetic readers it bequeathes something of that quality that she mustered for herself in the making of it: the sensation of being there, of inhabiting far places and other eras as she did. As Romain recognized, *The Sabres of Paradise* was a work of art, the apotheosis of both her Slav obsession and her virtuosity as a writer.

Lesley's satisfaction in seeing her book out in the world at last was overshadowed by the annihilating prospect of dispossession. It was bad enough that she could no longer seek refuge in Russia and the Caucasus, where her mind had dwelt ever since she arrived in Los Angeles. On the greater loss she dissembled to herself: Romain had gone, but she refused to believe the separation was permanent. If it were, her life's scaffolding would collapse: husband, home, nationality, income, status. Rather than confirm her vulnerable position by moving back to France on her own, she hoped to rent somewhere more suitable in Los Angeles and stay on to write her next book. Returning from New York, she gathered her strength before leaving for Europe and more battles with Romain.

She spent most of November in France, staying in Paris and in the second-floor flat in the Agids' palace at Savigny, before visiting her mother in London. Apprehensive as she had been before leaving Los Angeles, her situation with Romain was altogether worse than she had expected, and successive shocks left her in a state of physical collapse. He was deaf to her appeals to his loyalty, he rejected her prior claim as his wife. He refused to meet her and he wanted a divorce, immediately. She called on Hélène Hoppenot in floods of tears; until now she had hoped Romain's liaison with Jean would blow over but she was forced to recognize that this young woman would never let him go. He seemed bewitched; when Lesley tried to see him, he hid in the flat where he was openly living with Jean. And he was being difficult about her allowance. 'C'est Vénus toute entière à sa proie attachée, selon elle,' recorded Mme Hoppenot, quoting *Phèdre*. She brutally advised Lesley to divorce him. Lesley would not listen. She had seen too many divorced women turning into wandering ghosts, she said, and she refused to be another. Besides, it would be for nothing: she was convinced that Jean would take all his money and leave him anyway.

Her friends were alarmed to see Lesley entrenched in a battle which she so clearly could not win. Her good friend Cukor had persuaded her to return to Hollywood with the generous offer of a job as his personal adviser on an irresistible if strangely incestuous project: Romain's *Lady L.*, based on herself. Lesley was to begin working for

Cukor in early December, but he agreed that she should start a few days later, after visiting her mother in London. Meanwhile there were rumours that Romain might win the Prix Femina for *Promise at Dawn*; if so, she was determined to assert her presence by his side as Madame Gary. Mercifully for all concerned, *Promise at Dawn* did not win the award and public confrontation was avoided.

Even so, the dramas of Romain and Lesley, Jean and François were public knowledge. The gossip columns reported that Romain had become Jean's *chevalier servant*, escorting her everywhere. At the Quai d'Orsay eyebrows were raised at his scandalous affair. Their friends were embroiled, especially René and Sylvia Agid, confidants of all three protagonists who offered refuge to each of them at different times. For years Romain and Lesley had written to justify themselves and vie for sympathy; now their letters of vilification and self-vindication competed on a daily basis.

As the year ended Lesley was back in Hollywood, holding out for financial demands that Romain regarded as ruinous. She had lost everything but conceded nothing. *She* was Madame Gary. Fate had brought her and Romain together; he was her husband and so he would remain. To her, his relationship with Jean was a ghastly temporary delusion, prolonged only by Jean's calculated wiles to keep him. She was convinced that although Jean would make him marry her, what Romain really wanted was his freedom. This view was perhaps surprisingly borne out by Sylvia, a shrewd observer who was close to all three. Sylvia suspected that Romain hankered after staying married to Lesley, whom he now saw as his mother (arguably, especially since *Promise at Dawn* had released him from Mina), while living with Jean. Of course neither woman would agree to this casting.

In December Jean finished the last of her three film commitments. By now she and Romain were openly living together in a rented apartment in the rue du Bac, though she continued to deny any plans for marriage. Nonetheless, at the same time it was becoming clear to his close friends that Jean had set herself to marry Romain; he had become her cause and, as she had already proved in her acting ordeals, where causes were concerned she was not a quitter.

Romain, invited to the Hoppenots in December, drew Hélène into a corner to confide in her. He was anxious about Jean: 'la pauvre petite' had tried to slit her wrists. 'It's a fashion among the stars, actors, actresses, to open the veins but just like the others someone arrived in time to save her,' Hélène coolly remarked in her journal, although the incident had alarmed both Jean and Romain. He longed above all for Jean to have his child, yet he had been informed by Lesley that she would not give him his freedom under any circumstances. His wife was 'the great disappointment of my life, yes, the greatest.' Why have children? Hélène probed relentlessly. To do what he had never done, to have what he had never had . . .

Romain wavered, still unable to commit himself. He was evidently frightened by Lesley. *Lady L.* was the product of his imagination, yet how closely his wife sometimes resembled the formidable creature who chose to possess her lover beyond the grave rather than lose him. Jean, on the other hand, was deeply seductive but also unbiddable, and her instability gave him concern for the future. That year she had already suffered a breakdown and had attempted suicide. He had not invented the destructive urge of the damaged innocent in *Talent Scout*. He could see when they met that Jean was a high risk, yet her fragility was part of what drew him to her.

The battle lines had been drawn. A war of attrition had started that would last for years, fought through lawyers, first for possession of Romain and then for his money, exhausting the protagonists and dividing their friends.

IO

Divorce

She well remembered a certain French saying: 'Celui qui aime bien, punit bien.'

Romain Gary, *Lady L.*

I F ROMAIN HAD pushed Lesley to the side of her own story, Cukor was reinstating her – in the filming of Romain's *Lady L.* modelled on herself. Working with Cukor on this of all projects allowed her to withdraw from the combat zone without losing face and promised excellent distraction.

By the start of 1961 she had begun work at the studio and set up in new quarters in Hollywood, a stone's throw from the consulate, at 2012 Pinehurst Road, where a Hungarian housekeeper ('Countess Goulash') kept her and the cats happily overfed. Lesley was not on the MGM studio payroll but was paid by the director personally to assist him in the preparations for *Lady L.* Alongside Cukor, she was working with George Kelly, George Hoyningen-Huene and Gene Allen, the art director, who all brought a European determination to avoid Hollywood anachronisms and to ensure that the clothes, interiors and period detail were rigorously authentic. On the MGM lot they were reproducing Paris 1900, Switzerland 1905, London 1914, and Lady L's great Venetian masked ball. Lesley researched and wrote notes on street occupations for the Paris crowds and specified Sargent, Munnings and other society artists of the day for portraits of Lady L. that would hang in her sumptuously furnished drawing room. The Cukor Collection archive in Los Angeles includes her sketches for Lady L's costumes at her eightieth birthday party.

Cukor also asked her to tighten up the script, which she found nerve-racking, to emphasize the wretched childhood background that fuels Annette's ambition to escape and eventually transform herself into Lady L. The film would open on Annette and her mother, toiling with the washerwomen on laundry barges moored by the Seine. Lesley created new scenes to emphasize Annette's love of her exhausted mother, her cold rage with her bestial father, and the mixture of artlessness and duplicity that ensnare 'Dickie' Glendale. Annette's steely character and quicksilver reactions are nicely drawn. Lady L's revelation to the shocked Sir Percy that she and Annette are the same woman, though so transformed that she can hardly believe it herself, is especially piquant given the author's identity. Lesley was now *inside* Romain's portrait of herself and reliving her own distant past as well as Lady L's.

The months went by. While Lesley rode round the studio lot on a red bicycle, making sure the crowd costumes looked authentically draggled for Paris slums, Cukor despaired of his cast and script. Ralph Richardson was an inspired choice for Lord Glendale, but MGM had foisted on the dismayed director Gina Lollobrigida for Annette/Lady L., who had to fall in love at first sight with Tony Curtis, improbably cast as Armand, the doomed anarchist lover. Both had been on full pay since January and Lollobrigida was publicly rude about the script, which had got steadily worse in the course of reworkings by four different writers. Cukor must have called in Lesley's scenes in a late attempt to pull it together, but her treatment was disregarded. Cukor's memo of 11 April 1961 to his studio boss Sol Siegel bluntly objected that he didn't understand the new script by Charles Kaufman and had no idea why the characters behaved as they did. He couldn't defend their roles to the stars and protested that the producer (Julian Blaustein, who also tinkered with the script) was undermining his authority.

By May, sets, actors, production team, costumes and art department were all ready and on hold for the director. They waited for a month. Lesley and her 'little clot' of cronies drove into the hills to escape the baking weather, dropping ice cream down each other's backs to cool down. But the bad luck that had dogged Lesley's backstage projects in the past claimed this one too. Cukor, who was also contending with a troubled Marilyn Monroe on the production of *Let's Make Love*, never arrived on set. The story was that he had had a nervous breakdown, although he later told Gavin Lambert that he 'just walked out on that one, I got a doctor's certificate to say I was sick. I don't think Metro ever quite forgave me.' The project folded after months of work and

$1 million had been spent on the sets and costumes. Lesley's cutting disappointment must have been sharpened afterwards by the tremendous success enjoyed three years later by Cecil Beaton, her old colleague and sparring partner, for the art direction of *My Fair Lady* for Cukor.

By the time Cukor's project failed Lesley had the added regret of recognizing that *The Sabres* of *Paradise* was not going to make her fortune, despite critical success and the fan letters that she had received from all over the world, including a message of flowery felicitation from Zobeida Shamyl. No interest was shown in film options and there was nothing more to keep her in Los Angeles. She reluctantly decided to fly to Paris that summer, install the cats and herself in an apartment in René and Sylvia's palatial house in the suburbs at Savigny, then visit her mother in London before spending September in Roquebrune. But the strain of the past months caused her to collapse, exhausted and desperate. She spent several weeks convalescing in a Hollywood clinic before travelling to London to look for a nurse for her mother, who at eighty-six had been discharged from hospital after she had suffered a stroke.

Notwithstanding her distress, wherever she stayed she maintained her style. Yves Agid, visiting his parents at Savigny, was received by Lesley 'like an Arab princess', enthroned among heaps of cushions and garlands, in 'un apartement de Sheikh arabe au milieu du desert' (few people who encountered Lesley at home forgot the experience). She refused to play the victim; her self-possession was always in place. Yves, who found Lesley funny, subversive, formidably intelligent and sometimes alarmingly frank, never saw her tearful or with her defences lowered. The price of her composure was her self-absorption. From now on she was her own and only concern. Her unhappiness and rage against the world emerged only in the company of intimate friends and in her letters, in which the charmed existence that she had claimed as her due for so long had vanished, while the disaster-prone incidents that she had always mined for entertainment now threatened to engulf her.

Sylvia had accused Lesley of being cold with Romain. Lesley argued in self-defence that Romain was her whole life, but he rebuffed all her loving gestures, so she had to keep her distance. As a master of style herself, she *knew* how he should be translated: brilliant linguist as he was, he needed help with the nuances. His reputation in the English-speaking world would suffer in consequence of his work being poorly rendered. Romain, she argued, had childish expectations of life and was so capricious that he never knew what he wanted. He was being led astray by a thirst for misery and self-destruction, and by a young woman who hungered for his status and a position in Paris that she could never claim on her own.

Lesley's assessment of Romain's character was sound. Yves Agid believed that she intimidated Romain; nevertheless, he said, they had something between them which he never entirely understood. As he interpreted it, '*She had accepted him*. I think she loved him very much and at the same time was intensely irritated by his behaviour, because he was so much the opposite, said nothing, played all these roles. While she was frank: when she loved someone she would say so.'

Although Lesley had always longed to 'lean' on Romain, she had been forced to recognize that she had chosen the wrong man for the job. Emotionally she had had to shift for herself, and had resigned herself, partly using her writing as her refuge, to develop the resilience to counter Romain's galvanic temperamental peaks and troughs.

Yet the changeable creature of childish impulses that Lesley described to her friends was the same man whom his young lover had chosen as the experienced, mature protector to whom she entrusted her well-being. Notwithstanding the truism that people behave differently according to the company they keep, one of the two women now battling for possession of Romain fundamentally misunderstood the nature of the beast, and after living with him for fifteen years it was unlikely to be Lesley. Jean said in an interview that she believed a man should take responsibility for his partner: 'it's his job' ('c'est son boulot'). She did lean emotionally on Romain and he did try to protect her, but she mistook his worldly status as an establishment figure for his peculiar character which, despite a capacity to show great courage in extremis, lacked conventional solidity. Even his most ardent supporters wouldn't claim that calmness and stability were among his strengths. Moreover, his conceptions of personal identity and reality were entirely his own. On these matters Romain could not reassure her.

Lesley, in turn, refused to entertain the binding power of Romain's feelings for Jean. She couldn't believe that he could be so *banal*; where was that quest for quality and finesse, the forging of achievement that he had so effectively expressed in *Lady L.*? She understood her rival's reckless determination to 'get' Romain, probably recognizing that acquisitive quality in herself; she likened Jean to the predatory temptress who sucked dry the unlucky professor in *The Blue Angel*. Yet she misread Jean's character in casting her as a conventional gold-digger. Jean was utterly unmaterialistic in that sense, but she too was a changeling, uprooted from all she held familiar, and Romain had become her anchor.

She was less than half Romain's age and her naive idealism made her seem younger still; the combination of youth, childlike innocence and wayward sexuality stoked his desire. She sat at his feet and called him 'Cher Maître', she was 'la petite'; they played up their roles in interviews with journalists, who made him her Svengali. Romain was touched by her precarious hold on the world and disarmed by her trust in him.

Yves Agid, then a medical student in Paris, saw a good deal of Romain and Jean in the first flush of their affair. He was riveted to hear his cosmopolitan honorary uncle speak openly about the 'grand séduction' between him and Jean, when such things were scarcely discussed. Slightly younger than Jean, he shared the same birthday, was a keen cinéaste and a fan of *Breathless*; he became one of her trusted *copains*, standing in as her 'walker' when Romain was busy and helping out on set during night filming. He could see that her discovery by Preminger had swept her into a dangerously privileged world of extreme personal liberty, which was violently opposed to the sober community that had raised her: 'Basically she had no refuge. She wasn't standing on a robust place.' What she craved from Romain was protection. Now a solution beckoned, 'which seemed logical, where she could have both a social life with Romain and the pleasure of creative and imaginative work in cinema – it's a logical progression.'

Jean's expectations of middle-aged manhood were based on her father, the product of a close-knit, God-fearing, deeply conservative settlers' community in the American Midwest. Romain was a nomad; part of himself was perpetually in flux to suit his circumstances, while always protecting his creative core. The boundaries to his imagination were porous and he was apt to absorb aspects of those close to him before putting them through its mills. Lesley's character was tough enough to withstand this process. Jean – who was already juggling with intrusions from her various acting roles – was vulnerable, and her insecurities made her a destabilizing force among those closest to her.

The orderly bohemian framework that Lesley had built around him was now replaced by a trail of almost continuous disruption, dictated by Jean's unpredictable itinerary. In early 1961 she and Romain left Paris together for a six-week tour of the Far East, travelling to India, Hong Kong, Cambodia, Bangkok and finally Tokyo, to which Jean had been invited by the Japanese film industry. A pattern of following his partner, an exceptional precedent for Romain, had begun. In Hollywood, Lesley's increasing agitation focused on her fears that he would go without making the necessary arrangements for paying her monthly allowance.

While Jean and Romain were away, all three films that Jean had made in 1960 were released within ten days in cinemas along the Champs Elysées; then *Breathless* was enthusiastically received in New York. This unofficial 'Jean Seberg Festival' made her hot news, accentuated by the impact that she and Romain made as a couple on their return to France. His bearlike build and mestizo colouring made an exotic foil for the slight, fair American gamine less than half his age, glowing with sensuality and trailing movie-star notoriety. She was the talismanic New World prize that he brought back to Paris. With Jean beside him, Romain's fears that his French identity had evaporated during his years abroad were soothed by her appeals to his Frenchness.

In late May they bought an apartment in the same building where they were already living. Rue du Bac, in the 7th arrondissement, is a narrow street of ancient grey stone town houses fronting hidden gardens and courtyards, in a *quartier* of old money and influence. The entrance to number 108 is through an imposing porte cochère (shades of Romain's childhood in Vilnius). The L-shaped flat was a grand succession of lofty reception rooms whose tall windows overlooked the street on one side and on the other a spacious courtyard shaded by chestnut trees.

After months of passionate absorption in each other, they had to find a strategy to return to everyday existence as a couple. Romain expected Jean to take over where Lesley had left off, running the household and their social life. Jean, too, longed to step into the role of his wife, but she had no idea how to go about it. Of course there was no question of Romain having anything to do with domestic matters.

Their Moroccan cook offered no guarantee of success for Jean's social arrangements. One evening she invited to supper, sight unseen, an English fan who had written her ardent letters. Yves was the only other guest beside Romain. The fan turned out to be a small teenager in pebble glasses with white skin and carrot-coloured hair which matched his spots. He was 'tetanised' with shyness and unable to speak a word all evening. Romain hid his head in his hands and went to sleep. Yves laughed in horror at the memory. 'She was full of generosity, of sympathy, of love for other people but that's the kind of situation she got herself into.'

Since he had quit diplomacy, Romain's solitary writing routine now spread over the whole day, with breaks for meals. When Jean, childlike, tried to sit with him while he worked, she broke his concentration. With his encouragement she studied French and mime and signed up for courses in art history at the Louvre with her friend Aki Lehman; Romain persuaded André Malraux, then Minister of Culture, to sign their diplomas.

Jean wanted to learn rather than perform. She had considered a role in a French stage adaptation of *A View from the Bridge* by Arthur Miller, but didn't go ahead with it. Columbia, roused by her European successes, offered her a part in a studio project co-starring Robert Wagner and Ernie Kovacs, but again she rejected it; in Hollywood her liaison with Romain was sure to create a scandal if news of it came out. The part that she did accept that summer was in *Congo Vivo*, a Franco-Italian semi-documentary set in the Belgian Congo. Throughout her years of film-making Jean would repeatedly agree to assignments in lesser movie productions that involved travel to uncomfortable or even dangerous locations – the Congo, Colombia, remote provincial Mexico – almost as if she would more readily risk life and health than test her limits as an actress.

In September while she was filming abroad, a snippet in *Paris-Jour* headed 'Jealousy' claimed that Romain had flown to America to see Lesley. He had allowed no one else near Jean in Paris, it continued, but he was risking scenes with his wife who had already threatened Jean with her wrath. He met Jean in Rome for her final days of filming, after which they moved on to Venice. Following his confrontation with Lesley, he and Jean decided to 'come out' as a couple, and were pictured laughing together in a gondola in a *Paris*

Match photostory to celebrate her twenty-third birthday in November.

Asked about marriage to Romain, Jean responded: 'There has never been any question of marriage, he isn't free, nor am I. I shan't be free until next January. That is, I'm free everywhere in the world except in France.' Then came her famous comments about divorce, following a question about different attitudes in Europe and America: 'I'm in favour of divorce. In general I think Americans are less sophisticated than Parisians. Here, in Paris, even if people don't get on they prefer every possible deception, to go their separate ways, and I don't like that. Americans divorce, it's more honest.' She hoped to remarry one day because she wanted to have children. Would it be to Romain? She did not know. 'All I can tell you is that he is a marvellous man, a very great friend for whom I have the greatest respect and admiration, personally and professionally.' Lesley, whom she had met in California, was 'a very fine woman, I must admit . . . but she has been separated from Romain for a very long time.'

A week later *Jours de France*, *Paris Match*'s rival, followed up with the headline 'Jean Seberg: Love has made a woman of me', above a picture of her with long hair swept up in a feminine chignon, gazing across the table at Romain. This time the interview took place in their new apartment where abstract paintings were propped against walls, armchairs waited to be unwrapped and phones to be connected. Jean, comparing curtain samples, said she had always longed to have a home of her own, but had never dreamt it would be in Paris. She felt like a grown-up at last, she said; the reason, clearly, being Romain, whose basso profundo voice could be heard through a partition dictating his next book, accompanied by a clicking typewriter.

In Venice, the legend went, 'marriage' had been mentioned for the first time. Back in Paris they learnt that 'Lesley – Mme Romain Gary' had arrived in the French capital at the same time. 'It's on her that their future now depends. And Jean knows it. But for the moment she wants nothing more than this life together in the rue du Bac. For the first time in her life she has decided on her own destiny, a woman's destiny.' And if the new apartment could be easily divided in two by a connecting door, 'it's only, she laughs, "to ward off bad luck".' Meanwhile, 'For this American and this Russian, Paris is home to their happiness.'

★

Lesley, 'that talented English writer', fought back through Sam White's Paris Diary in the London *Evening Standard*. White first referred to Jean's comment about Lesley in *Paris Match* as 'a painful lack of taste' then, the following week, questioned 'the avalanche of publicity' that had 'engulfed' Romain's 'friendship' with her.

> Miss Blanch is clearly distressed by all this.
>
> She told me: 'I see my husband regularly. He's still my husband and my friend.'
>
> It is an extraordinary situation. Rarely can a triangle have been squeezed into a more confined space. All three of them live in separate flats within two minutes' walk of each other.
>
> What is baffling, however, is why suddenly a Hollywood-style publicity machine should take charge of their affairs.

Lesley was staying in an apartment in the rue de Varenne, rented for two months from an American friend. In the daily *Paris-presse Intransigeant* her rejoinder, via Jean-François Devay's half-page column, was that she would not respond to Jean Seberg. Regally posed in a gold-encrusted kaftan, which she said was a gift from Shamyl's great-granddaughter, she explained that she was in Paris only to supervise Hachette's French edition of *The Sabres of Paradise*. Romain had translated the Russian documents she needed and in return she had just been overseeing the Hollywood adaptation of one of her husband's books.

Lesley had nothing to say about Jean, the article continued; to friends she had confided that 'she was probably very Old Wave, but found it inappropriate to discuss private matters in public.' She and Romain had been married for seventeen years; they had survived the bombardments, hard times and success together. These things were not undone in a day or a year. She remained totally confident in her husband.

Lesley's discretion, the columnist commented, was that of the diplomat's wife. Romain was only on leave from the Foreign Affairs department which still employed him. Their best friends at the Quai, Ambassador Hoppenot and Guy (Jacques) Vimont, had deplored the furore which would compromise Romain's diplomatic career if it continued.

Lesley had in effect appealed over Romain's head to the loyalty of his wartime comrades and his closest diplomatic colleagues, the few associates he truly valued. She had laid mines along the path of his return to diplomacy unless it was with her as his official consort. She also laid claim to ties linking them as writers. Without mentioning Jean, she managed to present her as a minor nuisance compared with Hitler's bombing raids. And she had publicly stated that she had no plans for divorce.

Romain phoned her, beside himself with rage, shouting that she had ruined his diplomatic career and Jean's future, and her refusal to divorce him had made it impossible for them to have a son. Lesley called Hélène, sobbing, to tell her that the journalist had misrepresented what she had told him and that Romain had reacted like a Fury. Then she wrote to him, denying that the details had come from her. She had taken the utmost care not to bother him, she protested; the press coverage arose from Jean's own declarations and their 'faux ménage'. Hélène advised her to see a lawyer and above all to decide for or against divorce. Lesley replied that in that case Romain would have to pay, adding under her breath; 'Two hundred thousand dollars.'*

'Diable!' noted Mme Hoppenot, scandalized.

Lesley was trying to fend off divorce by making the price too high for Romain to accept. He had already given up the round tower and cave-like refuge at Roquebrune that he loved, his only home in France during his years in diplomacy. All the communal furniture also went to Lesley (who had, in fairness, done the furnishing). Then he had to buy her the apartment she had stipulated in Paris and pay her monthly maintenance plus a lump sum.

Neither Lesley nor Romain was remotely realistic in their attitude to money; their perceptions of their own wealth were characterized by pathological insecurity. Lesley's claims to Romain's earnings, and his attempts to defend himself against them, egged on by their lawyers, came to obsess them both. Anne Scott-James met them one after the other for lunch on successive days and recalled that neither of them talked of anything else. '"The most extraordinary thing to me," he said, "is to find you've lived with somebody for a number of years and you've loved them and that you never knew them at all."'

Lesley's lawyers were claiming a percentage of all his earnings and he was understandably reluctant to see his royalties disappearing into

* The 2009 equivalent would be around ten times that sum.

her bank account. Although his output should have increased since he had moved into full-time writing, he would publish nothing in France between a collection of stories and the translation of *Talent Scout* in 1962, and that of *Lady L.* in 1964. His quota for publication by Gallimard in 1961 was filled in October by *Johnnie Coeur*, the play he had hurriedly finished in Los Angeles, which was poorly received in print, followed by a stage production in 1962 which was met by a chorus of raspberries, putting an end to his ambitions as a playwright. *Promise at Dawn* was a big success in the US, meanwhile, and Samuel Taylor's play *First Love*, adapted from *Promise at Dawn*, appeared on Broadway.

The war between *les Romain Gary* continued against a backdrop of exploding *plastiques* as Paris succumbed to OAS terror tactics in their opposition to Algerian independence (de Gaulle and his supporters were prime targets of the *pieds noirs*, and Romain was given a special dispensation to carry a revolver). Recriminations rippled outwards among their circles of friends and supporters. Romain had bought for Lesley her chosen apartment at 32 avenue Mozart, on the Right Bank. He hoped that a monthly income in addition would buy his divorce. Lesley, however, having accepted these arrangements, remained obstinately silent. Romain begged Vimont and Hoppenot, both greatly respected by Lesley, to intervene to bring her to reason. Next he told her that he was due for an operation and would redraft his will to disinherit her. Sweet reason seemed to descend when Lesley's friend Eden Fleming was summoned to mediate, but two weeks later he telephoned to shout at Lesley that if he recovered from his operation he would blow his brains out and leave a note blaming her for his suicide. 'In which case a divorce would hardly seems [sic] worthwhile,' his wife drily commented.

Jean's biographer tells us that as 1961 came to an end Jean knew she was expecting Romain's child; and that she later confided to Paton Price, her friend and drama coach in Los Angeles, that she deliberately fell pregnant in order to make Romain marry her. Even so, she failed to move events in the direction she had hoped.

She soon began to grasp that instead of resolving the deadlock with Lesley, she had become trapped herself. In late January 1962 she flew home to see her parents in Marshalltown, but if she had been hoping to confide in them, she quickly changed her mind. The screening of

Breathless in Des Moines had done little for her reputation locally – 'Gee, that was a funny sort of picture, wasn't it?' – which had been further dashed by an article about her in the local press based on the French coverage. What Paris had fêted as Romain's and Jean's idyllic new romance was the subject of shocked disapproval among Marshalltowners who surmised that the star they had nurtured was leading a married man astray.

Poor Jean! In Paris she had defended American values: 'Divorce is more honest.' Yet where she came from, divorce was not a preferred option. 'Jean, why don't you come back to us for a while?' the Lutheran minister urged her, voicing general concern. How could she tell her parents of a commitment to a man twice her age whose wife refused to divorce him? Unable to face their reaction, she said nothing, condemning herself to moral exile from her family.

Jean was compromised professionally by Hollywood's unforgiving moral coda which ostracized those who transgressed, as Ingrid Bergman's relationship with Roberto Rossellini had recently shown. The solution that she and Romain reached was to hide herself away in deepest secrecy, far from Paris, a plan which was wholly consistent with Romain's strategy for concealment and subterfuge. Officially she was slowly recovering from amoebic dysentery, which she had contracted in the Congo. The hiding place they chose was in northern Spain where, under Franco's dictatorship, the well-connected could find a certain scope for opacity.

By this account, her lonely pregnancy ended in Barcelona on 17 July 1962 with an induced birth by Caesarean. This presumably took place in a private nursing home, exclusive private medical treatment and confidentiality being always available to those who could afford it. Romain was away and Jean's sole companion was Eugenia Muñoz Lacasta, their Spanish cook, who kept house for them at the rue du Bac. The older woman bonded deeply with the baby and became his constant companion and surrogate mother. Although he was christened Alexandre, to her he was always Diego.

Within a month Jean had left Barcelona for Klosters, Switzerland, to rehearse a demanding part in a new movie, *In the French Style*, playing the part of an innocent abroad for the fifth and last time. They told no one about Alexandre Diego's existence. Jean dreaded the effect on her family if the news reached Marshalltown. Romain, fearing that his wife would hold them to ransom if she heard about his son before the divorce settlement had been agreed, hid their secret from all their close friends as well as from Lesley. Had she known, she would undoubtedly have told their mutual friends, the Agids and the Hoppenots. René Agid first heard of Diego's existence in a letter from Romain in January 1963, formally requesting René's permission to name him with two others as guarantors for the child's future should anything happen to his parents, and swearing René to total secrecy. Henri and Hélène Hoppenot were never told, and learnt years later from newspaper reports that Romain and Jean had a son. Nevertheless Lesley scented a bargaining advantage in his new urgency, and pressed Romain for ever more punitive terms. These enraged him so much that he refused to cooperate; so settlement remained as far away as ever.

Although Lesley agreed in principle to begin divorce proceedings in August 1962, the terms had not been drawn up. Each time Romain petitioned her for a settlement she added conditions that drove him apoplectic with fury. She saw Jean as a usurper to *her* official position of Romain's wife. He claimed to Hélène Hoppenot over lunch that Lesley had tried to stipulate that he abstain from any future return to diplomacy, so that his new partner could not replace her *en poste*. Her financial demands, coming on top of the expense of the palatial rue du Bac apartment that he had bought with Jean, made heavy inroads on their income.

He retaliated by stopping Lesley's maintenance for several months.

She took out a summons to bring Romain to court and persuaded her most illustrious friends, Cukor, Nancy Mitford and Rebecca West, to lend her money, thereby implying that he had left his wife destitute and laying the fuse to a public scandal if the case was heard.

Romain wrote to Henri Hoppenot 'a little note of despair and friendship', informing him that Lesley had not only confirmed her emphatic refusal to divorce, but was also suing him for monthly maintenance payments of 300,000 francs.

After making Lesley wait for months for her allowance, he paid her the backlog at the last minute, narrowly avoiding courtroom scenes, via Sylvia and René, who had been belatedly taken into his confidence. They were enlisted to write from Toulouse to Lesley, arguing politely in favour of divorce, to which she took great exception.

The feuds with Romain left her exhausted and fearful. She was beset by disasters, ranging from minor (an attack of flu; her home help left without giving notice) to major: no sooner had Romain paid up than he demanded a confrontation at the lawyers' offices. Then just as she started a cover story for *Show* magazine on the writer Laurence Hope (later reprinted in *Under a Lilac-Bleeding Star*) her friend Jane Stockwood had phoned in tears from London: Martha Blanch's landlord was cruelly insisting that her cat must be put down and was deaf to entreaties to spare it. Lesley begged her mother to wait until she could collect her and the cat and bring them both to Roquebrune, but her mother, in despair and no doubt knowing Lesley's frame of mind, would not hear of it. On top of everything, Lesley was being pressured to get on with her new book project and was summoned to the lawyers for yet another fight with Romain.

In April 1963 Romain told the Hoppenots that the divorce would take place in a few weeks, adding with doleful glee that he would be ruined in the process.

Still the business dragged on. For five months until August the couple were in America, preparing and shooting *Lilith*, the fine, disturbing last movie directed by Robert Rossen, in which Jean gave her most impressive performance in the title role. Lesley, grinding her teeth at the publicity that continually stalked them, must have been incandescent when Jean was invited with Romain to the White House for an intimate dinner with President John F. and Jackie Kennedy. In France they had already been lunch guests of President and Mme de Gaulle at the Elysées Palace, at which the great man had caused a stir by overriding the seating protocol and placing Jean beside him.

Not until October 2003 did the divorce go through. Romain and Jean were secretly married on the 16th in Sarrola-Carcopino, Corsica, in a ceremony arranged by the mayor, a wartime colleague of Romain's. Lesley held out for her money, while mourning the loss of Romain. The settlement that she exacted sealed off communication between them, allowing no reconciliation for years to come.

Yet long before she resigned herself to divorce she had already set in motion a process by which she would *use* her loss of Romain. By early

1961, John Murray already knew about Lesley's new project, on which they were sworn to deepest secrecy. 'The Siberian book' would take her more than seven years to bring to fruition as *Journey into the Mind's Eye*.

Knowing that Romain and Jean would marry as soon as he was free, Lesley awarded herself her epic escape at just that time, ensuring that she would be far away and beyond the reach of dreaded news reports. She would make the journey that had been in her mind for decades. Afterwards, seeing her book into print, she cauterized her grief and bade farewell to the part of herself that she held dearest of all, her great passion for Russia.

II

The Siberian Book

The human soul's need for beauty had to extend sooner or later beyond the limits of art and take aim at life itself. We thus encounter inspired creators who are pursuing lived masterpieces and who have taken to treating life and society as a plastic material.

Romain Gary, *Lady L.*

ALTHOUGH LESLEY HAD acquired French nationality when she married Romain, she never became an enthusiastic French citizen. She considered moving to London from Hollywood, but the prospect of the bureaucracy involved in the transfer put her in a panic, and in Paris she could be close enough to her mother to organize help for her.

She had chosen the top floor of 32 avenue Mozart, a solid bourgeois building in Passy, near the Bois de Boulogne, because it came with a roof terrace which offered gardening potential. Soon it was colonized by jungly vegetation and a hammock where she could sway peacefully on summer nights, gazing at the stars and dreaming of far places. Once she had exoticized the apartment (crimson-painted walls, passages hung with Indian textiles) and her innumerable possessions had been elegantly crammed in, she was back in circulation by early summer 1962.

As the scandals with Romain and Jean very publicly rumbled on, Lesley unexpectedly found a new ally in her old acquaintance Nancy Mitford. She had known Nancy 'for ever', since their circles had overlapped in London before the war. Nancy was now Paris's favourite Englishwoman, at home among the *gratin* when she chose to meet it; her bracing company and show of solidarity rescued Lesley's damaged morale and enabled her to recoup some of the status she had so bitterly relinquished as Romain's wife. She was surprised and gratified as *le tout Paris* rallied with phone calls and parties and drew her into a grand new milieu among the 'Jockey-Club set', dining in houses where a valet stood behind each guest's chair. In turn Lesley introduced Nancy to Cukor, who was visiting Europe while preparing *My Fair Lady*; he was almost the only American Nancy had ever found acceptable, she told him.

The need to 'keep up the shop front' in smart company prevented Lesley from breaking down completely. Nonetheless her old friends were alarmed by the change they saw in her. She was homesick for Hollywood, torn between the siren call of the Siberian book on one side against the emotional torments of dealing with Romain's hostility and her mother's decline on the other. She resented the petty house-hold demands of solitary living after busy consulate routines supported by staff. Jock Murray's and Osyth's sympathy and understanding were taxed to the limits in dealing with her mounting hysteria during the months before her divorce, while her collection of travel writings, *Under a Lilac-Bleeding Star*, was being processed.

All was lost; confused; wrong. She shot down an offer of work from the BBC, which had been uncooperative over her trip to Siberia. An important photograph went missing, then a library book, then several articles being considered for her collection; finally the whole typescript of the *Lilac Bleeder* (as Lesley called it) was lost in the post on the way from the typist. The French translation of *The Sabres of Paradise* was delayed because the publishers had omitted the bibliography. She decided to sack her American publisher, Viking, which had arranged to republish the original American version of her cookbook without consulting her, and move to Atheneum, which wanted to reprint it from John Murray's revised edition – provided that Murray waived the fee . . . *Show*'s sub-editors had ruined her Laurence Hope article . . . Her mother's new companion was unreliable and Lesley would have to stand in when she went on holiday, instead of trying to immerse herself in matters Siberian.

Osyth Leeston replied wearily:

> Many thanks for your letter. We are sorry to hear that the intro-duction for the Folio Society HARRIETTE has not been well edited and in consequence is giving you so much trouble . . .

The London Library were very kind and courteous over the Siberia book. I took it back to them myself after ringing up about it . . . No mention of such a thing as a large fine.

We will send proofs of LILAC STAR to you in Roqbrune [sic] and I know you will go through them as quickly as you can because we shall not have a great deal of time . . .

I am relieved to hear that you have found a copy of CUCUMBER AND CRUMPET.

We cannot waive an offset fee on ROUND THE WORLD IN EIGHTY DISHES because this would establish a precedent and for this reason some fee must always be charged . . . We have told Mr. Lantz that we will reduce the fee by almost half and make it £40. Surely the publishers must have already allowed for this in their costings . . . ?

I did not think there could be much more fuss with R. now or that this can be much more unpleasant. You must try and get some peace at Roquebrune.

I do not like to ring your mother too often in case this fusses her, though she usually likes to hear from us.

No mention in your letter of Norman and the other cat so I hope they are well.

I hope things are better, but I doubt it. Still if you can work through all that is going on you can work through anything.

Later Lesley panicked that Murray were going to miss their 1963 publication date: her book *must* appear then, giving her a public showing to defy Romain's triumph when the divorce went through. Osyth had to reassure her that she was 'shrieking before she was hit' in expecting delays and they fully intended to publish before Christmas. Lesley sent John Murray fabric swatches to show the exact shade of lilac she required for the dustjacket and the *Lilac Bleeder* appeared as intended, though not without further panics and criticism from the author about the cover.

Most of her reports from the Balkans, Uzbekistan, Mexico, Guatemala, Loti's Istanbul, Tunis, and a deeply unromantic Saharan bordello, had already appeared in the *Cornhill* and other publications, and many dated from her travels with Romain, who would have been infuriated to see himself inserted as 'mon mari' just as he married Jean at last. The title, after a Balkan phrase to describe a compulsive traveller, confirmed her mannered originality. Among her lighter journalistic pieces was an enjoyably contrarian polemic on packing, 'Always

Travel Heavy'. Her searing unhappiness was barely discernible, except in 'God Rest Ye Merry Teddy Bear', an account of a Christmas spent thousands of miles from home the previous year. She had been marooned on the way to Bokhara in Uzbekistan when her small plane made an impromptu halt; the pilot had handed her a teddy bear, and memories of others, far away and long ago, reduced her to tears. Loneliness and desolation seep between the lines.

At first glance her chosen profiles, all previously published elsewhere, seem almost perversely esoteric and unfashionable: Queen Marie of Romania, Pierre Loti, Vernon Lee and the poet Laurence Hope, author of *The Indian Love Lyrics* ('Pale hands I loved, beside the Shalimar'). But these oddly assorted individuals shared one particular characteristic with each other and with Lesley, who was obsessed with it as the theme of her 'Siberian book': an overriding affinity with a place and a people not their own. 'It never seems to have occurred to . . . those who ferret other people's lives,' she observed, introducing Laurence Hope, 'that emotions can be transported to places, houses, things – above all to countries . . . Before all else, I think she lived a love affair with a land, striving to possess it, knowing herself possessed.'

The book opens with 'Perpetuam Mobile', a fragment dropped from *The Sabres of Paradise*, salvaged and reshaped by Lesley for *Show* magazine. It tells the chilling tale of Lise Cristiani, a talented young French musician and traveller who fell fatally prey to 'the chimera of distance'. In the 1840s, after playing in Scandinavia, Lise embarked on a concert tour of Russia with her Stradivarius, her maid and her German accompanist. From St Petersburg her 3,000-mile journey in a wooden cart eastwards to Irkutsk was just the beginning. On she went, accompanying Governor-General Mouraviev on a trade mission to the northernmost port on the Bering Sea. Blizzards set in, her wealthy protector turned back, but 'the obsessed girl', her music forgotten and companions gone, followed an impatient courier on a Mongolian pony across the frozen taiga to Yakutsk, only to find herself frost-bitten, semi-conscious, alone in the endless expanses that had drawn her so far towards nothing but death. Her health shattered, Lise struggled back from her 18,000-mile odyssey to Novocherkassk in the Caucasus, where cholera claimed her. Her carved stone memorial, a cross with her Stradivarius at its foot, was inscribed 'The artist's other soul', but surely, Lesley concluded with comfortless wit, what she would have preferred was 'her mileage'.

Intentionally or not, her subject was the clearest metaphor for the hold that Russia had exerted over her for so long, not in the desire for distance but in its power over her imagination and, above all, in those Slav passions that had always led her out of her emotional depth. Central to that fixation was Romain; and now he had gone. The story would do as a fitting epitaph until her 'big book' was written.

She had already been working on the early chapters of that project in strictest secrecy. 'So quiet have we kept about this that we have not mentioned it except amongst ourselves and now I mention it to you in this letter,' Osyth wrote nervously. In 'Perpetuam Mobile' Lesley mentioned that she had already visited Irkutsk and had been shown round Governor-General Mouraviev's mansion, which housed the city's Scientific Library and regional archives. That being so, she must have made late changes to the proofs between the end of September, when Osyth wrote to enquire anxiously about her plans for the Siberian trip, and December, when *Under a Lilac-Bleeding Star* was published.

Lesley must have arranged the Trans-Siberian Railway voyage after her divorce from Romain was finalized, as a distraction to compensate for her loss and to complete her long 'Russian' trajectory with this act of possession. The great train ride was both the finale and ostensibly the focal point of her 'Siberian book', *Journey into the Mind's Eye*; yet only this last section is based on her actual trip and comes close to conventional travelogue or autobiography. She booked a first-class compartment, envisaging a romantic journey taken alone in a spirit of voluptuous regret, but the dream was derailed by two all-too-solid Russian women in pyjamas, smiling down at her from the upper bunks. Lesley, aghast, had her baggage removed and took the Moscow–Peking train the following Tuesday with Olga Maximova, her guide. This train was disappointingly diesel-driven, and Olga Maximova's information was limited to the Soviet Union's recent industrial achievements. Nevertheless Lesley, dreaming through the the shortening autumn days, with grey skies hinting snow as the train chugged eastwards, found ways to time-travel around and about the coveted historical sites and people them with decadent ghosts. Above all she summoned the exiled Decembrists, doomed friends of Pushkin revered by Lesley for their botched attempt at insurrection (vividly romanticized in her account) when Nicholas I came to the throne in 1825, and their loyal wives, who had followed them into frozen exile. Returning to the rattling progress of her own journey, she found that shifting time zones preyed strangely on the stomach, and she used her restaurant-car coupons for an all-day diet of caviar and 'insanity drops' (Armenian brandy).

They disembarked at Irkutstk, the Siberian capital where the Decembrists had been exiled. She stood on the shores of Lake Baikal, prowled through the residence of her childhood hero, Governor-General Mouraviev, and in the Historical Museum pored over early photographs of the Trans-Siberian Railway, its trains converted into armoured engines of battle during the revolution. Her chosen cultural event was an evening watching the Mongolian wrestlers; at restaurants the local youth interrogated her on the Twist and the Madison.

Then suddenly, deserting Cristiani, she had had enough. Instead of completing the final leg to Vladivostok, she decided to fly home from Irkutsk. Olga Maximova was shocked by the change to her itinerary, but to Lesley it was a change of *heart*. The fact that most of that east-ernmost stretch of track was constructed between 1905 and 1916, post-dating the Traveller's reminiscences, probably influenced her decision. She carried back with her a tiny conifer tree dug up from the taiga, which after a spell on her rooftop eyrie in Paris was eventually transplanted to Eden Fleming's garden by the Thames.

In December Osyth wrote to encourage Lesley in her progress on 'that most delicate and subtle part of the new book'. She and Jock awaited this section with intense interest: 'We look forward to seeing this very much and I think the writing of those pages about The Traveller's son will be a real challenge in skill and selection, implica-tion and unwritten comparison.' Lesley's meeting with Kamran in the Russian church in Paris comes two-thirds of the way through her nar-rative, indicating that she was already far advanced in the writing, though she might have added more detail later to the earlier sections.

But completion of *Journey into the Mind's Eye* demanded resignation and a melancholy acceptance of loss which were more than Lesley could bear. The battle with Romain was done, she had carried off the loser's consolation spoils, and her powerful survivor's instinct surged back to reassert itself. Pushing aside her publishers' blandishments and the chronic problem of her mother's care she seized every opportunity for diversion, above all in travel.

Then an unexpected chain of events took Lesley away from John Murray and the trail following the Siberian book vanishes, to reappear with another publisher.

Lesley spent Christmas with Eden and Marston Fleming in west London, visiting her sad mother, who was lonely and losing the will to care for herself. On New Year's Eve she hastily returned her contract for the *Lilac Bleeder* to Osyth with the news that she was packing for a trip to India and Nepal with the Flemings, returning in early February. Osyth wrote wistfully that she was glad to hear Lesley was making progress with the book and no doubt after Nepal she would be able to get on even faster. Osyth undertook to keep in touch with Martha and enclosed a 'partly enthusiastic' review about *Under a Lilac-Bleeding Star.*

But on the very day Lesley arrived in India, she fell and tore a ligament in her foot so badly that she was unable to walk and had to be confined to a wheelchair. Although she travelled on with the Flemings to Rajasthan, she had no option but to miss most of their itinerary and wait until the injured foot had mended enough for her to manage the journey home. Stranded on an island in Jaipur without her books and notes, she couldn't continue the Siberian project, but during days of enforced idleness an entirely new idea germinated. Unexpectedly she soon plunged into writing her first and only novel.

'That novel was a landscape – the landscape of Rajput India which I adored,' she would recall. It emerged from a tale she had heard about a party of Englishwomen who had taken refuge on the island during the Indian Mutiny and were trapped there, terrorized by the lake's crocodiles lying in wait on the shores, unable to escape or seek news on the mainland. She wrote to the squawks of green parakeets swooping overhead and leopards coughing in the forested hills. The lack of a typewriter was no problem; she always wrote in longhand anyway.

Weeks later, she was recovered enough to limp home to her crowded flat in Paris, where she locked herself away from every other demand on her time: mother, lawyers, taxes, accountants, friends all had to wait. Three months later the novel was done, at the expense of her temper, which was frayed to snapping point by the incessant demands of shopping, housework and phone calls on her working day as a woman writer living alone. Ignoring the disorder at home, she arrived at Albemarle Street, carrying not the expected Siberian book, but a short novel of perhaps 30,000 words.

That must have been the visit when Lesley worked at Albemarle Street preparing a revised master copy of *Round the World in Eighty Dishes* for Atheneum's new edition. Jane Moore, then Jane Boulenger, an editorial assistant at Murray's, was deputed to help. She was deeply impressed when Lesley shrugged off her mink-lined raincoat and slipped on the embroidered slippers that she kept at Murray's to work in, and was charmed by her fond boasts about the 'rosy-cheeked' good health of Norman the cat. They sat peacefully correcting the cook-book beside the moribund figure of Osyth, who would stagger into the office burdened by bags of manuscripts that she read all night for a literary agent, then fall fast asleep.

Lesley hurried back to Paris, escorted the cats (Norman was looking 'peaky') to Roquebrune to be cared for while she was away, then from Paris flew to Tunis for a writing commission. There she managed to injure herself again, spraining the big toe of the same foot that she had damaged in India, and was not at all reluctant to delay her departure from Leo d'Erlanger's exquisite Arab palace at Sidi Bou Said that was her favourite place to stay in the world.

After the extra days in delectable Tunis she ran out of time to return to London to deal with the depressing business of selling her mother's flat, now that she had been placed in a nursing home, before pressing on to Roquebrune to finish writing her piece and collect the cats in time to leave again for Iran on another piece of journalism.

While Jock Murray had been an exceptionally obliging publisher for many years, Lesley's contract with him was for another book entirely, and a novella of romance and revenge in Rajasthan had not been on his wish list. A letter from Osyth to Lesley at Roquebrune brought the 'sad and disappointing news that THE NINE TIGER MAN does not seem to us to succeed in its purpose (however much we try to think otherwise)' and Murrays had decided not to publish. Osyth did not include the readers' reports, apart from passing on the comment that 'One feels the author is enamoured of the situation, but cannot work it out.' 'Personally,' Osyth added, 'I wish you would consider putting this book aside for the time being while you finish the writing of the Trans-Siberian one, which we are so eager to have.'

Lesley did no such thing, but immediately set about finding another publisher for *The Nine Tiger Man*. That autumn Murrays heard through Odette Arnaud that Simon Bessie at Atheneum in America was enthusiastic and planned to publish the novel, and in due course Collins took up the British option.

Murray's had rejected Lesley's novel only to lose the Siberian book that they awaited so eagerly. The publishers who had nurtured her for twelve years, acting as her unofficial banker, accountant, librarian and book supplier, even shouldering the responsibilities for her mother's welfare, were not quickly forgiven for their lese-majesty. Osyth was now relegated to receiving recommendations for the memoirs of diplomats' wives whom Lesley was meeting on her visits to Iran. That autumn she flew out to stay with General Hassan and Hilda Arfa, who had close connections with the Shah and his family and whose own history was indeed exotic almost beyond invention.

Prince Reza Arfa, Hassan's father, had risen from humble beginnings to become the Persian Consul-General in Tiflis for the entire Caucasian region. There he met the half-Russian, half-English Ludmilla Jervis whose mother forbade the match, but Ludmilla eloped and married him in a Muslim ceremony. After Hassan's birth they lived in Russia, until Ludmilla's vengeful mother petitioned the Tsar to disallow the illegal non-Christian marriage and they had no choice but to divorce. Hassan's father later married the daughter of a Swedish professor for whom he built the fabulously ornate Villa Danishga or Daneshi in Monaco, an oriental fantasy covered with mosaics and capped with dome and minarets. It still stands today, shabby but proud, a relic of the extravagant era before the Great War.

In the 1920s Hassan, by then a dashing young cavalry officer on leave in Monte Carlo, fell in love with a prima ballerina with Diaghilev's Ballets Russes, the English-born Hilda Bewicke. Like him she spoke excellent Russian, having worked as a volunteer in a Russian hospital during the Great War. Despite Diaghilev's best attempts to dissuade her the couple married and moved to Persia, raising their family in Tehran and at Larak, their small country estate near by, where they kept a dairy farm and a menagerie of animals. The general served successive shahs under various military and civilian guises, while Hilda became part of the imperial family's retinue, was made lady-in-waiting to the Empress after the war, and assisted the charity work of Princess Ashraf, the Shah's sister.

Possibly Lesley had met the couple through another ballet link, their mutual friend Marie Rambert; alternatively they could have been introduced by Jock Murray who published the general's memoir, *Under Five Shahs*, in 1964. That autumn Lesley wrote to Osyth from the Park Hotel, Tehran, to urge Murray's to consider Hilda's memoirs and the romantic story of their home at Larak. Lesley later introduced Osyth to Hilda Arfa's friend Baronne Trenck, another English-born migrant to Persia, a singer from a family of musicians who had married four times and had written an 'undisciplined' biography.

Osyth's affectionate reply reveals how much Lesley owed Murray's staff:

Dearest Lesley,

Thank you very much for your letter about the typescript you sent us which has now arrived quite safely. It certainly looks an extraordinary story and I hope we shall be able to find something which we can use in THE CORNHILL. We will, of course, read it for book offer as well. [. . .]

I hope you will manage to look in before you leave. I am so very sorry to hear that your mother is so ill now and that you have to face this desperate decision to move her. If only we could have got her into a convent before, but you must always remember that we tried every single convent within the London area and did our very best to get her into one. Of course, she will miss having a telephone and being in direct touch with you, but the atmosphere of these places has a serenity that should surely make her happier now . . .

I have telephoned your mother since I last saw you, but I have not liked to for some time for fear of troubling her. I suppose there is nothing I can do to help?

Greetings to Mrs Fleming.

Apparently there was not.

Lesley's Christmas card for 1964 was a photograph of a figure cocooned and veiled in white under a tent canopy, surrounded by tropical vegetation: that year she had travelled to India, Tunisia and Iran. In the very process of writing *Journey into the Mind's Eye* she was already turning her back on the snowy wastes of Siberia and consigning them, with Romain, to her past. The longed-for landscapes in which she now projected herself were still Eastern but her inner compass had moved southwards, to the Islamic world where time was measured by the sound of the muezzin.

Lesley had discreetly passed her sixtieth birthday in June, although to the world she was still fifty-seven. There was much to despair of in the new era's obsession with youth, miniskirts and fright wigs being notably unfriendly to the older woman. But her wholly individual brand of exoticism put her in a class of her own, ahead of yet in tune with the 1960s fixation with everything ethnic, imported by the hippie caravans plying the southern routes from Morocco and North Africa, and from as far as Afghanistan in the east. Indeed, her own *Wilder Shores* had probably helped to plant divine discontent and the need for 'distance' in the minds of thousands of young things who were eagerly throwing in nine-to-five jobs to lose themselves, and find themselves, on the road to adventure.

Afghanistan was Lesley's new far horizon; she longed more than anything to go there, but all her plans for expeditions were baulked at the last minute. At the end of 1964 she told Hélène Hoppenot that she had reached the Afghan frontier on a commission for *Vogue*, but had been forced to return home by a desperate letter from her mother, claiming that the staff beat and starved her. Lesley said that she no longer knew when to believe her mother, who often made things up. Hélène, unfavourably impressed by her friend's ageing Hollywood star's garb of mink-lined mac and cowl hood, was disturbed by Lesley's inability to be interested in anything other than herself.

Over New Year 1965, Lesley stayed again with the Flemings, who had moved to Zoffany House, an architectural gem in a fine Georgian terrace overlooking the Thames at Strand on the Green. While there she contacted George Cukor in Hollywood, begging him to read *The Nine Tiger Man*. She felt sure it would appeal to him and was frustrated by Robert Lantz's reluctance to send him proofs, assuming that he was too busy with the launch of *My Fair Lady* (would he be coming to London for the first night?). She herself had no set of galley proofs to send to Cukor.

Her hunch was correct. Cukor moved fast: within two months Robert Lantz had accepted $50,000 for a film option.

The story that so appealed to Cukor and dismayed John Murray was a flamboyantly escapist confection of 'Low Behaviour in High Places', set in the Raj at the time of the Sepoy Mutiny in the 1850s. The gorgeously predatory Hindu Prince Rao of Jagnabad is sent to England to settle a dispute between his adopted father, a Rajput ruler, and the East India Company; there he is snubbed by the British establishment but adored by the ladies, in particular Florence, a pallid but passionate viscount's daughter, and her seductive maid Rosie. Later in India he avenges himself on the imperialists by turning a coven of twenty-three English ladies including Florence and Rosie, who are in hiding from the Mutiny, into his island seraglio. The reluctant memsahibs are forced to wait on the delicious Rosie, promoted to his favourite concubine, until Florence, replacing her, resorts to a crime of passion rather than return to her dull English husband. Rosie phlegmatically adopts a pet bamboo rat and adapts instead to a life of comfort wedded to a wealthy Arab farmer and white slave trader; hidden behind her burka, she can still enjoy illicit pleasures in the city.

For her two protagonists Lesley borrowed a technique from Romain, fashioning them from opposite facets of herself: the 'baroque angel' Rosie, a pretty chancer who relies on her wits to make her way; and Florence, the pale dreamer who 'loves too strong' and would rather possess her lover in death than lose him. The melodrama and exotic setting, high romance seasoned with farce and flagrant political incorrectness, are all Lesley; the brisk lack of sentiment is remarkably close to *Lady L.*

Cukor was seduced by the cool heartless tale, with its layers of deception and role reversals between servants and their masters and mistresses. In late February 1965 he cabled Lesley: 'Delighted Dearest Lesley feel sure we'll have beautiful exciting picture that will make us both rich + famous.'

For Lesley the ball was bouncing again, higher than ever. Lantz relayed to Cukor her wish to be involved in some creative aspect of the movie's development. The director received from her screeds of handwritten notes about the characters, which he couldn't read until they had been typed up by his secretary. Cukor took up her suggestion that Terence Rattigan be persuaded to write the script; Rattigan passed his copy of the book to Elizabeth Taylor with a 'seductive note'; another copy was to be sent to Audrey Hepburn.

In March, Cukor forwarded Lesley a review from America that deemed *Nine Tigers* a 'smasher'. With trepidation, mindful of sales figures, she was photographed for *Newsweek* and *Time and Life*. Her usually excellent health had given way to a liver condition, the French national complaint, and she took refuge in Roquebrune for a week's rest.

Cukor was happy to publicize his interest in 'Nine Tigs' to vie with Romain's literary successes and counter all the coverage of his romance with Jean, which still preyed on Lesley's thoughts. He was also impressed by her travel plans, which included Roquebrune, Afghanistan, Paris, London and Turkey: 'My brain reels . . . These do not sound like the plans of a tired lady. Will you keep me posted as to your whereabouts? I don't want to lose track of you, with all those dreamy Uzbeks or other dusky gentlemen skulking around.'

Yet again, her hopes to visit Afghanistan were dashed. Instead she returned to London to promote the book. Rebecca West called it 'exquisite'; New York journalists badgered her for interviews. Her soaring morale was clear from a skittish anecdote about a burst tap that soaked her to the skin just as she was 'mincing out' to dine one evening, followed by another flood from a burst hot-water bottle on her return, qualifying her for the name of Ondine.

In July American *Vogue* sent her to Istanbul on an enjoyable commission with her photographer friend Henry Clarke, who also had a house in Roquebrune; they returned to its airy heights afterwards to weather the heat of August.

The crises with her mother continued. Martha was so unhappy where she was that she was moved to Hazlewell Nursing Home in Putney, but she was frightened and unsettled there too, and Lesley had her transferred to a convent, hoping that the nuns would give her better care. She was assigned to a bed in a communal ward, which made her so miserable that Lesley moved her back to the nursing home again, to a different refurbished room, increasing her mother's confusion.

That autumn Lesley met Cukor at the Savoy to discuss *Nine Tigers*. Afterwards she realized that perhaps her comments about the script would be more tactfully filtered through to Rattigan via the director, rather than coming direct from her. She was buoyed up with hopes for a delicious house which had come up for sale three doors from

Eden Fleming at Strand on the Green, although the price was higher than her fee for the movie option. If only *Nine Tigers* could be made, maybe she could sell some other film rights and then settle with the cats in the familiar neighbourhood that she had loved since her childhood . . .

Abruptly euphoria gave way to exhaustion. At Christmas Lesley's legendary constitution for once failed her; she was laid low with a double bout of flu, after which jaundice set in, followed by agonizing pains which led to her admittance to the American Hospital in Paris. She had to be dosed with antibiotics and packed with ice for a week to lower her temperature before they could operate to remove her gall bladder and three enormous gallstones that had caused the onset of the crisis.

After a month in hospital she gave in to her body's insistence on rest. Only now did she recognize how much the cumulative strain of coping with the volcanic events of the past few years had drained her strength. She spent the early part of 1966 as an invalid, slowly convalescing. Jock Murray wrote to ask whether he could visit her at the avenue Mozart; when they met on 1 April she wittily claimed that the olive-sized gallstones which had been presented to her after the operation were the only gems of value Romain ever bequeathed her. Murray had just reprinted the paperback of *Wilder Shores* and Jock would have liked a book from her for John Murray's 200th anniversary in 1968. She told him she was ploughing on with the Siberian project, but he never got it, or anything else by Lesley until *From Wilder Shores: The Tables of My Travels* in 1989.

In hospital, dreading her first ever operation, Lesley had replied to a teasing note from Nancy Mitford that she was always calm in times of crisis and only resorted to raging scenes at home over piffling domestic matters.

After the loss of several of Nancy's devoted friends and correspondents one by one to death or illness during these years Lesley, another inveterate letter-writer, exerted herself to entertain her with gossip and domestic dramas. Without overstretching the comparison, they had things in common. Both were gifted, witty, resourceful women who had suffered the torments of loving a philanderer who behaved like a parody of the amorous Frenchman (possibly because neither

Romain nor Gaston Palewski was French-born). Like Lesley, Nancy was both worldly and intensely romantic; like Lesley, her displaced passion for one man had been somehow fused to embrace his adopted country.

By the early 1960s the inspiration for Nancy's phenomenally successful novels had ebbed away and she had moved on to historical biography, as well as writing for the *Sunday Times*. Her searing disappointment in her beloved Colonel Palewski's evasions was apt to emerge in savage teasing of the people who surrounded her. Lesley's well-fortified personality enabled her to forgive rudeness and even find it stimulating, making her better able than most to withstand Mitford jibes. Nancy was more important to Lesley than the other way around, but Nancy came to value her. 'She is the most difficult person on earth, never satisfied or pleased with anything,' she wrote to James Lees-Milne. 'At the same time she is full of charm and a very good friend.'

Lesley, ever resourceful in the kitchen, enjoyed devising enticing suppers to eat with Nancy, who loved food but barely knew how to boil a kettle. In summer Nancy would sometimes stay at Roquebrune, as she did in 1966, causing Lesley to fuss tremendously about getting in supplies of the correct marmalade and making her comfortable. Nancy teased her about her books – decades later Lesley mimicked her friend's drawl: '*Darling*, must you always write about people we can't *pronounce*?'

Some of Nancy's English friends were well known to Lesley: James and Alvilde Lees-Milne, much missed by her since they had given up their house at Roquebrune; Lord Berners; Edward Sackville-West; the Sitwells. In Paris Lesley befriended Jeanine Delpech, who still held a salon in the old manner. Through Nancy she met Baron Élie de Rothschild and his wife Liliane, who entertained in considerable style at the magnificent eighteenth-century Hôtel de Masseran. Élie de Rothschild was director of Château Lafite-Rothschild and a partner of de Rothschild Frères, the family bank in Paris. Liliane's flair for design was influential in the decoration of hotels and restaurants established by PLM, another Rothschild enterprise, as well as in the sumptuous refurbishment of the family house with eighteenth-century furniture, old masters and their modern art collection. Her passion for decor and her voracious reading were both interests she shared with Lesley.

The retro circles that Lesley now frequented included the Duke and Duchess of Windsor ('tiny twins with large bottles of drink', she remembered), met through Violet Trefusis, the daughter of Edward VII's mistress Mrs Keppel. Presiding like the Red Queen on the arm of a youthful 'nephew' or 'fiancé', over a luncheon table glittering with Venetian crystal and tableware bearing the monogram of Catherine the Great, Violet would rehearse her favourite charades. She insisted for instance that her true father was Edward VII, despite the fact that he hadn't met her adored mother until four years after Violet was born. Incredulous guests who challenged Violet's wilder flights were struck off and never forgiven.

Violet had been one of Nancy's conduits to Parisian society when she had first arrived in France at the war's end, but as Violet grew older and dottier Nancy cruelly enjoyed using her for target practice: 'She asked me for a title for her *mémoires* (I thought she had already written them) and was not pleased when I suggested *Here Lies Mrs Trefusis*.'

Lesley took a different line towards Violet, which intrigued Nancy. 'Lesley and Auntie Vi are still as thick as thieves,' she told Alvilde Lees-Milne. 'Lesley believes every single word she says, including that she is the 30th in succession to the throne.'

Violet was another in the line of fabulists whose capacity to impose their fantasies on the world around them captivated Lesley. It was not exactly that she *tolerated* Violet's make-believe. What scandalized other listeners as outrageous boasts and barefaced lies, Lesley saw as an admirable rejection of fetter-bound facts; in Violet's grandiose presentations Lesley saw courage. She recognized in Auntie Vi a poignant defiance of dullness and threatening reality that she had understood in Romain. With her penchant for dressing up she gladly played the courtier, obliging Violet's royal protocol. She fussed over her and made her fond offerings: a gros-point cushion, Lesley's speciality, and a little book of recipes, handwritten and illustrated, that she could still enjoy on a prescribed diet.

Violet lingered on until 1972, dwindling into a skeletal spectre at her own feasts. Recklessly generous, she had promised so much in her will to so many that Nancy (who inherited a jewel) proposed they should set up a trade union. Lesley was among the financial beneficiaries, but when the lawyers came to settle the will they found that due to Violet's muddled affairs her American account was empty; her French masseuse inherited not only Violet's palatial quarters in the rue du Cherche-Midi but also the capital intended for division between Lesley and her fellow legatees. Nancy was maliciously entertained by their attempts to hide their dismay.

Lesley's other inheritance from Violet was more lasting: a cast of mind, which would become evident after *Journey into the Mind's Eye* was published.

By summer 1966 Lesley's health was restored, although she was concerned by Cukor's silence. After the sensational success of *My Fair Lady* in 1964, the director was finding it hard to advance his next project. Rattigan produced a script for *The Nine Tiger Man* which was unusable. John Mortimer, who was introduced to Cukor by Gavin Lambert, also worked on it, with no better results. Fox was insisting on another lavish production, with a star for the male lead despite the director's own wish for a more modest picture, and a $12 million budget, which Cukor never managed to raise.

Slowly the cherished dreams of a return to Hollywood that would finance Lesley's retirement to a covetable house by the Thames faded and vanished as the tide of good fortune ebbed away. Once again she resigned herself to the gruelling task of completing the Siberian book. By January 1967 she was on the last two chapters, which she found dauntingly difficult to resolve.

However, her luck had not deserted her in the matter of her publishers. At Collins she had the great good fortune of working with Philip Ziegler, a magisterial editor before he left the company to become a fine biographer in his own right. The typescript she brought to him was close to a final draft. Always responsive to masculine authority, she trusted his judgement and gladly accepted Ziegler's suggestions for the revision that was needed. He in turn found her 'tremendous fun' to work with, always open to constructive advice about reordering passages and tidying up, though he knew she would never countenance any attempt to alter the overall tone. She was a wonderfully precise writer in some respects, he recalled, alarmingly casual in others, notably about repetition and chronology. He wanted Lesley to add more about her relationship with Romain, but she told him the subject was too painful for her to revisit. An abrupt jump in the text from her marriage to Romain to her memories of the Slav servants *en poste* was the result. 'The gap,' Ziegler said, 'indicates not so much what was there but what I would have liked to have been there.' Or was there, perhaps, another reason?

The editing process extended over the following year, and production more months again. She was in the middle of correcting the proofs when Paris erupted in the events of May 1968. Students tore up cobblestones, workers went on strike, phone and electricity supplies were cut – ideal conditions, Lesley contended later, for proofreading, marooned as she was on the top floor with the lift out of action. Hindered by petrol shortages, cancelled flights and the absence of public transport, she carried the proofs to London herself just in time to meet her deadline. She was philosophical about 'les événements' and sympathetic towards the students and strikers.

Journey into the Mind's Eye was eventually published in late autumn 1968. 'My book is not altogether autobiography, nor altogether travel or history either. You will just have to invent a new category,' she said of her most beguiling and personal work. The story of her obsession with Russia, where 'the love of my heart, the fulfilment of the senses and the kingdom of the mind all met', has become a classic on the travel bookshelves. The journey is all the more intensely evocative for being so much an interior one, begun in her nursery so long before she first set foot on Russian soil.

The Traveller, that djinn-like visitor to her parents' house, cast his spell over her childhood, filling the little girl with longing for the faraway places he described: above all for the snowy wastes of Siberia and the great Trans-Siberian Railway that in her mind's eye thundered through the house. He called her Douchinka, Pussinka moiya, Rocokoshka, Stupidichka and, when her ardent childish passion turned into something more urgently adult, teasingly seduced the seventeen-year-old English miss once she was out of her parents' reach in Paris. While she was being 'polished' in her uncomfortable Italian convent, he offhandedly introduced her to two shy, sulky Russian sons of his, born to different mothers in Russia, then treacherously played the Run-Away Game with her through the long weeks of a summer in Corsica, chaperoned by his aunt from Montenegro.

On the way home they lingered on the Riviera; bathing in the warm shallows below Garavan, where France met Italy, she looked back at the 'little pink and yellow villas' dotted between turquoise sea and high crags. Captivated though she was by the Mediterranean landscape, it wasn't hers; she dreamt of a golden-crowned ceremony when they would exchange vows. The idyll ended abruptly when her parents, alerted to their romance, summoned her home by telegram and the Traveller vanished (had there even been something special between the Traveller and her mother, long before?). Her secret, silent longing for him re-emerged in her passion for Russia, the 'giant entity' that had formed and reclaimed him.

'What I loved about her writing was the way in which she contrived to be ridiculously over-the-top romantic, yet always with a kind of dry humour that ran through it,' said Ziegler. So she described the change-ling obsession that expanded into full-blown possession: the young Lesley 'collected' Russian friends and lovers, plunged into Russia's galvanic history, devoured its literature, explored its unfashionable narrative paintings. Theatre, music, folk tales, decor were greedily absorbed; bemused admirers fed with pickled fish and kasha to the searing strains of peasant songs.

Against a shimmering mirage of images and impressions of Russia, past and present – the doomed Decembrists of 1825 as real to her as the 1930s industrial achievements that she politely admires on a visit to Soviet Moscow and Leningrad – she ranges as protagonists first herself and the Traveller, then Russia itself, as elusive love object. Like Pierre Loti, she summons up her longed-for landscape and places herself in it. All too briefly she touches on her marriage to the Russian-born Free French airman and their peripatetic diplomatic life. Finally, after the marriage to Romain is over, she takes the soli-tary epic ride on the Trans-Siberian which carries her as far as Irkutsk, where she ends her journey. Between her enchanted childhood and her arrival in Siberia, her bewitching, comic, poignant story of grand passion has been transformed into a fine book about Russia. This is Lesley Blanch's magic.

Once again her subject allowed her to put her best resources to brilliant use. In the context of Siberia's history and the great train journey, she metamorphosed the tremendous reading of her beloved Herzen and the nineteenth-century Russian lives and letters, literature and history, that had so profoundly influenced her since early child-hood. In the Tartar face and semi-diabolical character of the Traveller she gave supremely romantic form to the motivating force that had shaped her life. It is hardly reductive to trace behind the Traveller's polished Asiatic skull, aesthetic authority and wisdom the profile of Komisarjevsky (who like Romain also appeared as himself), and in the extravagant emotions and enjoyment of misfortune, Romain's histrionic excesses. After Lesley has lost the Traveller, her marriage to Romain, the Russian writer and war hero, falls into place as another appointment with her Slav destiny. Only after losing him does she complete her passage through life with the journey on the Trans-Siberian, at once her real farewell to Russia and the context for her fictional denouement. How she must have savoured the symmetry and poetic justice in returning the compliment of secretly morphing Romain into fiction, as he had done with her in *Lady L.* She even divided him up to appear twice: once in her composite portrait of the Traveller and later again, briefly, as himself.

All Lesley's books are *sui generis*; but *Mind's Eye* reveals the writer's voice at its most individual and distinctive, at once borrowing freely from the works she loved, yet at the same time truly original. Exceptionally, her voice manages to convey that elusive quality of charm that so rarely translates from life to the page. Lesley herself now floats to the forefront, now flits behind the giant literary and historical figures who haunt her narrative, so many shades who had kept her company for so long. By a singular sleight of hand she, the narrator, becomes both love object and unrequited lover, beguiling her audience with glimpses of her transgressive loves only to whisk veils over them: first the precocious schoolgirl joyfully abetting her seduction by the gratifyingly experienced Traveller; then the voluptuous woman seeking her lost past in the arms of his sly, ardent son Kamran; finally the solitary traveller at the end of her journey, in Siberia at last, mourning the love of her heart in the long-desired landscape, journeying once more into her mind's eye.

Not all of those who knew Lesley were amused by the book's claim to autobiographical status. Her friend the playwright, novelist and screenwriter Rodney Ackland, prodding it suspiciously in the *Spectator*, came closest to challenging Lesley's self-portrait *à la russe* and his critique is penetrating enough to deserve quoting at length. 'A rather odd book, rather disconcerting,' he began.

Like a trendy film, it continually poses questions about truth and illusion, dream and reality, fairy-tale and fact; and, as in listening to Ravel's La Valse one seems to perceive the dancers only in desultory and tantalizing glimpses . . . so does Lesley Blanch's self-projected protagonist, Pussinka, appear to us as, entranced, enraptured, she moves with her Svengali-like partner through the paces of an erratic but voluptuous pas de deux. Or is it, after all, a pas seul? . . . Difficult to make out . . . or to be certain of anything connected with this character she calls The Traveller – her teacher, mentor, lover, more-than-father-figure, Tartar dream prince – now man, now phantom – or phantom of a phantom? Symbol? Archetype? Impossible to tell.

Ackland rehearses the story of Lesley and the Traveller, through her marriage to Romain, to the denouement in Irkutsk when, in a secret meeting with a Serbian contact, she hears of a last wartime sighting of the beloved, delirious from battle injuries and insisting he must return to England to someone he once loved. 'Now it will be seen,' he continues, 'that this is a big, romantic, tear-jerking, slightly off-beat love story with a certain "epic" grandeur in the broadness of its sweep.' Whereas autobiography by its nature lacks form, he detects here the work of a skilful novelist producing a tightly constructed novel. In forcing 'every incident, memory, dialogue and character into the right shape to fit' into the Slav pattern of her life, Lesley barely sketches in her supporting cast. As for herself as the protagonist, if Chekhov's three sisters had gone on and on about going to Moscow as Lesley did about Siberia, they would have 'remained as unknown in the history of the theatre as they were beyond the confines of their tedious provincial town'.

'Impossible to believe,' Ackland concluded testily,

that Mrs Blanch, whose interests, as is known from her books, fantastically heterogeneous and always accompanied by an encyclopaedic knowledge, range from India at the time of the Mutiny, pioneer women travellers in the Middle East, London during the Regency, and chocolate-penis festivals in the Balkans, impossible to believe that she could ever have taken seriously as a portrait this obsessed, one-track-minded, Pussinka-Stupiditchka of *Journey into the Mind's Eye*.

Some of her friends agreed with with Ackland's objections to the autobiographical label ('Absolute baloney!'), others again laughed it off half admiringly as the flight of an imagination unable or unwilling to distinguish between truth and fantasy. Her editor was certain that the Traveller was a real person in Lesley's mind and, equally, that he was a composite: 'It's a dream world, isn't it,' Ziegler said fondly, adding with amusement that 'nobody in their senses would imagine that it's factual'. The remarkable thing was that over the years that was exactly what came to pass: evidently proving that most of us are unable to resist an enticing story, especially one that so eloquently illuminates the elusive relationship between landscape and the heart.

In due course Lesley hardly had to polish her revised version of events, which was pasted over her past following the same technique in life that she had applied in the writing of *Mind's Eye*. Decades later when the book appeared in French translation for the first time to celebrate her hundredth birthday, it was billed as partly fiction on the cover. Yet not one of the flock of respectful interviewers (including two of Romain's biographers) who descended on her at Garavan queried her story or asked which bits were 'true'; the legend was far too seductive to question. When Sickle Moon reissued the book in the UK in 2001, Lesley herself was very annoyed that through an oversight it appeared without the subtitle 'Fragments of an autobiography'.

What was Lesley's intention with her ambivalent creation? Why did she so insist that it was the truth? Countless authors write novels based on themselves, Nancy Mitford for one, but she never claimed that the blissfully funny family portraits immortalized in her novels were anything other than fiction. Lesley's book had a different trajectory and she was too intelligent not to know what she was about. Like Romain's *Promise at Dawn* (which, as we have seen, she read shortly before she conceived the idea for the Siberian book), her *Journey* left the reader stranded midway between history and make-believe, wanting and willing it to be 'true'. Compare and contrast with Romain's sleight of hand as analysed by Ralph Schoolcraft: 'Using the means of fiction, he has invented himself in the real world, giving himself a past that serves to explain his present.' Lesley applied the same technique in *Journey into the Mind's Eye*. She too invented an enchanted childhood which foretold the shape of her adult life. She too created a legend which, once it was released into the world, developed a life of its own, circulating in the minds of her readers.

Although Lesley's tour de force was similar to Romain's, her creative impulse sprang from different roots. Romain's arose from the compulsion to multiply himself and escape from the 'I' that he found so constricting. Lesley, on the contrary, always circled back to herself and her formidable solipsism insisted on rewriting her life to impose the 'Russian' fate she had decreed for herself. Partly, too, facts per se left something lacking: reality needed to be enhanced as another form of artistic expression, like dressing up à l'orientale or rearranging an interior. So the childhood home that she described in *Mind's Eye* acquired a nanny, cook and governess, implying a more substantial background that was better suited, to be sure, to the society Lesley was keeping in Paris at the time when she was writing her book. But though convenient, that aspect of conscious self-betterment was not the pulse that powered her writing. Wasn't it rather that her imagination had never truly accepted her shabby beginnings in a top-floor flat and long ago, like Fitzgerald's Jay Gatsby, she had forged a platonic conception of herself which to her was more authentic than the real thing? Her historic transformation had begun with her move to the house in Richmond and had been sealed by her marriage to Romain. Her journey into her mind's eye bestowed on Lesley the rightful status of comfort and privilege that *should* have been hers in the first place. The damage inflicted by divorce was healed by the 'incorruptible dream' of the Traveller's tale, to which she would remain faithful always.

Rather like Dr Johnson's morbid fear of death, Lesley had an intense and un-English aversion to failure (yet her failures were heroic, proof of her courage) and she painted over the experiences to obliterate them. Thus her first marriage, her attempts to break into theatre design and, indeed, all the disastrous aspects of her marriage to Romain are shaded out or banished altogether. It was not her way to resort to petty rehearsals of events to vindicate her side of things, or to use fiction as a visible form of revenge.

Yet revenge it was, deliberate or not, and how exquisitely achieved. The whole of her existence with Romain, all their fifteen chaotic, creative, tormenting years together, had been boiled down to barely thirteen pages in her 'autobiography' – and eleven of those devoted to the Russian cooks and bottlewashers (such *characters*) they employed *en poste*! In the twinkling of her pen she had found and lost the supreme love of her life before she had even reached adulthood, decades before she met Romain. Her ex-husband had been cut off at the knees (or worse) and relegated from the apotheosis of her Russian myth to a faint echo. His smoky Russian voice, his Slav temperament, his mystifications were all *reminders of somebody else*; her marriage to the 'Russian writer' was a mere chapter, a footnote even, in the destiny that had already been predetermined by the passion that had shaped her life. Romain had not even been able to grant her lifelong wish to travel on the Trans-Siberian! That achievement, too, would be hers alone.

What was more, her revenge was both public and hidden: the stiletto had been driven home in full view of the world, yet so neatly that nobody detected it. Only one (male) reviewer of the newly translated *Voyage au coeur de l'esprit*, thirty-five years later, interpreted her 'confession' as an ultimate belated act of vengeance on Romain by his spurned wife.

Deftly she shored up her construction. Romain had shown how a myth is authenticated when it appears in print and how rarely it is challenged. Like him she created her picaresque heroine then conjured her off the page and into reality. Taking a leaf also from Auntie Vi's book, Lesley adopted in life the imperious presence of Lady L. and with steely charm shot down early signs of scepticism in her visitors. One couldn't question the existence or identity of the Traveller, for instance, without being made to feel unforgivably rude in delving for vulgar facts.

Lesley became increasingly grand, a personage photographed for the newspaper colour supplements in flowing kaftans at home among her massed possessions: grouped with Nancy Mitford and Mary McCarthy as one of 'three successful writers living in Paris', or with Merle Oberon and the Countess of Kenmare in 'People at Home Abroad', photographed by her friend Henry Clarke. The Royal Society of Literature elected her a member (she had never heard of that august institution before, but was flattered nonetheless). Beatrix Miller, the London editor of *Vogue*, encouraged her to air her idiosyncrasies, for instance in a big feature on scent whose entire first page is a panegyric on 'noble' pronounced noses (like her own), as against the 'typical American non-nose' (like poor Jean's), which was atrophying under attack from deodorants and air conditioning. Again for *Vogue*, she revisited Bulgaria with loving affection.

★

In September 1968 the newspapers carried reports of Romain's and Jean's separation and impending divorce due to 'geographic differences'. Jean's work would keep her in the United States for the indefinite future. 'In spite of my love for Jean and America, I do not wish to become an exile,' Romain announced, adding that their intention to divorce was in order 'to preserve the happy memories of the past'.

The statement was diplomatic about the reasons for their separation. Throughout that summer Jean was filming the musical *Paint Your Wagon* with co-stars Lee Marvin and Clint Eastwood. A year later she confessed to a sympathetic journalist that she had fallen for someone else and 'because I'm a bad liar I had to tell Romain about it'. A less sympathetic Hollywood columnist picked up this titbit. 'Who's the man?' the *LA Times*'s Joyce Haber asked, adding: 'I'll give you a hint. It isn't Lee Marvin.'

Over the next two years Jean seemed to fulfil Lesley's darkest predictions about her successor. In 1970 her divorce from Romain was announced in a swirl of headlines, bracketed with their remarriage soon afterwards because Jean was pregnant. But gossip column scuttlebutt hinted that the father of the unnamed (though partly identifiable) 'Miss A's' baby was a leader of the militant Black Panther Party (Jean had been an active supporter of the Black Panthers in Los Angeles). In August *Newsweek*, which had a circulation of 6 million, ran a news item naming Jean in relation to the rumour. Romain immediately instructed lawyers to prepare a lawsuit for slander. Soon afterwards the baby, Nina Hart Gary, was born prematurely and died two days later. Romain claimed in an emotional accusation headed 'The Big Knife' in *France-Soir* that Jean's shock at the calumny in *Newsweek* had caused her to miscarry and he later took the journal to court for damages. The funeral was held in Marshalltown, where Jean had the tiny coffin opened before the ceremony, seeking 'witness to the lie'. That autumn, returning to Paris, she suffered a serious breakdown and stayed in hospital for several weeks.

Although they never lived as a couple again, Jean stayed on in the adjoining half of the L-shaped apartment in the rue du Bac to be near Diego, who remained with his father. Their names were still linked in the media. Romain continued to be watchful of Jean's reputation; indeed he directly contributed to it with his 'documentary' novel

White Dog, recounting the disintegration of their marriage, which was published in their *annus horribilis*, 1970. In 1971 he directed the second of two disastrous films starring Jean; their friends were appalled but Jean, virtually his only supporter, wrote gratefully to him that she knew he had done it to give her a reason for living after her breakdown.

The news of Romain's split from Jean made no difference to the estrangement between him and his first wife. Romain was excised from Lesley's life. Her friends had to declare their loyalty, either to herself or to her ex-husband; she would not permit both. Anne Scott-James was one friend who was convinced she lost touch with Lesley because she also remained on good terms with Romain. Lesley denied this, pointing out that she had no way of knowing which of her friends, if any, still saw him.

Her mother's death at Hazlewell Nursing Home on 10 January 1968 left Lesley feeling amputated. She fussed over Nancy, Violet and the cats; she had many friends who loved and valued her; but the wider world turned around her own. The disarming, inflexible carapace of Darling Self was in place, hardening over the years. No interview or profile, however skilful, managed to pierce it.

However, Lesley had no intention of relegating herself to the past and in any case her victory was only half complete. So fiercely had she coveted her life with Romain as the diplomat's wife *en poste* that he claimed she had tried to find binding legal means to prevent Jean, the usurper, from inheriting it. Now that she had got *Journey into the Mind's Eye* out into print and made her loving farewells to Russia, she turned her agile mind towards finding an honorary place among the cherished circles of envoys abroad. Having lost the passport of privilege bestowed on her by marriage, she had already embarked on cultivating it for herself. Resolutely she realigned her mental compass towards the South and the East. Soon she would be an inside visitor among the real-life courts and harems of the supreme despotic rulers of the Orient.

12

The Peacock Throne

In my teens, I began to read European literature and soon discovered that the Persia in which I lived was very much like the nineteenth-century Russia described by its great authors. Not only our way of life and the settings, but also the characters were the same: Aliosha, Prince Myshkin, Masha, Natasha, Nina . . . down to Gogol's petty bureaucrats and Chekhov's country folk.

Shusha Guppy, *The Blindfold Horse*

IN 1969, LESLEY reached Afghanistan at last, on a commission for the *Sunday Times*. The theme came from Eve Arnold, the colour magazine's distinguished senior photographer, who had been haunted by a speech by President Bourguiba to the women of Tunisia: 'Come out from behind the veil. Come into the twentieth century', and wanted to explore those millions of hidden lives photographically. It was the heyday of the colour magazines, when art directors and photographers drove the editorial, and Arnold had broad scope to develop photojournalism stories of her choice. With Michael Rand, the art director, she planned 'Behind the Veil' as a series of ground-breaking visual essays supported by strong text. They arrived at Lesley for their writer, on the basis of *The Wilder Shores of Love*. 'She was a romantic, I a realist,' as Arnold saw it. 'The idea was that we would complement each other and bring forth provocative essays.'

Michael Rand's deputy Meriel McCooey went to Paris to woo Lesley. Standing in her crowded hall, McCooey became uneasily aware of many pairs of eyes trained on her – Lesley's portraits of her departed pets, stiffly posed in their Lord Fauntleroy suits and crinolines. Lesley was immediately drawn to the project but unwilling to travel with another woman; she tried to insist on Henry Clarke as her photographer until it was explained that Arnold's role was non-negotiable. The next step was to invite her to meet the *Sunday Times* team in London. Lunch was arranged at the Wig and Pen Club, Eve Arnold having gone to the trouble of finding an eating place which would prepare Lesley's favourite steak and kidney pudding. But when the chef arrived to serve the pudding with a flourish, the guest of honour dismayed them all by accepting only a spoonful. Arnold felt obliged to add an enormous tip afterwards to mollify the chef.

Despite this unpropitious start, the project went ahead. They decided, poetically and geographically, that their target areas would be 'the mountains of Afghanistan, the deserts of Arabia and the waters of the Nile'. Their first stop was Afghanistan, where they stayed for what Arnold remembered as 'three of the happiest months' of her working existence and inflamed Lesley's imagination for the rest of her life.

They were lucky in the timing of their trip. The following year the Soviet armies invaded Afghanistan; before long the opium trade, introduced by the CIA, would spread its stranglehold over the countryside, but in 1969 'the wild and lovely kingdom' was still one of the last untamed frontiers and their trip was one long adventure. It began with an invitation to the king's birthday gala, proffered through a royal niece known to Lesley; the climax to the celebrations was a game of buzkashi, polo played Afghan-style with a headless goat carcass (in Tamerlane's day it had been played with the head of an enemy) and lead-tipped, braided whips.

Every day brought fresh excitement, exotic new assaults on the senses; the fierce landscapes, the handsome people, the 'splendour and savagery' of the rugged life there gripped them both. 'Violent rhythms, violent emotions – these are the country's heart-beat,' Lesley concluded, after they came across a ragged band of unveiled women, singing defiantly as they marched between armed guards, who turned out to be convicts serving sentences for murder.

In their manner of travelling, as in other things, the two women were polar opposites. Eve's workmanlike freight consisted mainly of her photographic equipment; while Lesley was so laden with baggage that she needed help to find her gold slippers and other essentials among the clutter, which became heavier daily with new acquisitions from the bazaars. 'As the French say, in any combination of two people there is the one who offers the cheek and the other who kisses the

Book jacket design by
Lesley Blanch for
Romain Gary's novel
Lady L.

Portrait of the author on the
jacket sleeve of *Lady L.*

Drawing of Lesley by Don Bachardy, 1959   George Cukor in the mid 1950s

The former French Consulate on Outpost Drive, Los Angeles

Hollywood ghosts: these reference stills taken in June 1961 show completed sets for *Lady L*. which Lesley helped to design for Cukor at MGM. *Above:* the great drawing room, dominated by portraits of Lady L., scene of her eightieth birthday party and flashbacks to her masked ball. *Below:* laundry barge on the Seine in Paris where Lady L's mother slaved to death

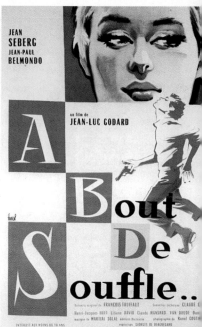

Above left: Jean Seberg in Jean-Luc Godard's *A Bout de souffle*, filmed in summer 1959

Above right: Poster for *A Bout de souffle*, 1960

Jean Seberg and Romain Gary in Venice, November 1961

Buzkashi game in Kabul, Afghanistan, held to celebrate the King's birthday in 1969. Lesley was present, reporting for the *Sunday Times*. Photograph by Eve Arnold

Imam Shamyl of Daghestan   Farah, Shahbanou of Iran, crowned in 1967

Paul Pavlowitch as Emile Ajar in *Les Nouvelles Littéraires* no. 2562, 9–16 December 1976

LES LIVRES D'ENFANTS
un dossier réalisé par Marc Soriano pages 15 à 22

DIRECTEUR : PHILIPPE TESSON

hebdomadaire
de l'actualité culturelle
semaine du 9 décembre
au 16 décembre 1976
54e année
prix 4 F.
N° 2562

les **nouvelles**
littéraires

AJAR PARLE

Emile Ajar, alias Paul Pavlowitch, longtemps traqué et Goncourt malgré lui en 1975 avec La vie devant soi, vient de publier le récit de cette aventure qui l'expulsa de l'anonymat auquel il rêvait. Mais Pseudo est beaucoup plus qu'une autobiographie et Emile Ajar n'a rien consenti à la notoriété... Nous l'avons rencontré dans sa ferme du Lot, dans le même état de légitime défense... P. 3 et 4

Left: Romain Gary in 1979, the year before his death

OPPOSITE PAGE
Above: Pierre Loti at home beside the tombstone of his Turkish love
Below: Lesley 'at home', Petra, 1965

Madame Blanch Gary aged 101 in 2005

cheek,' Arnold concluded. 'I wound up as the kisser: I was in charge of money, travel arrangements, etc. But Lesley was such good value, with her sparkling ideas and her charm, that I took on the responsibility without qualms.'

Before they left Afghanistan, she was determined to photograph a tribal wedding in the Hindu Kush, traditionally held in autumn when the nomadic Kuchis brought their huge flocks down from the mountains. The question was how to find them. One day, spotting the Atan – male – dancers whirling down the road to the wedding, the visitors followed them into the encampment. Eve grabbed her camera, leapt from the car and ran to photograph a group of dancing women, narrowly escaping being torn apart by their savage guard dogs. After the tumult subsided, she and Lesley were welcomed as honoured guests first to the bridal tent, where the bride sat in her finery with eyes closed, and then outside where the men sat feasting and firing off festive rounds from their rifles.

The two women were exotic visitors, rare Westerners who enjoyed special status as independent women outside the bounds of Muslim convention. Once they were inside the forbidden quarters, the women were happy to talk openly; equally, the travellers were admitted to the society of men who, starved of female company, were gratifyingly appreciative of their presence. Afghan men were stunningly handsome, as Eve Arnold's gallery of portraits showed, making this a hugely morale-boosting interlude for Lesley. Was it then that she had one of the sexual encounters that she later regaled with Rabelaisian gusto to Yves Agid, who was taken aback by her bawdy frankness?

The travellers returned home for Christmas, Arnold to do battle with the *Sunday Times* accounts department, which announced that their entire budget for the three stories had already been used up. Incensed, she sent in their expenses, claiming that their chief extravagance had been bottles of Coca-Cola, which she and Lesley had used for brushing their teeth to avoid the hazards of contaminated water. In the New Year they set off again, visiting all seven states along the Trucial coast in the Gulf, still British protectorates at that time, where 90 per cent of women went veiled. Their final destination was Egypt where the veil had been lifted in 1929.

Their subject was exceptionally tricky to cover, especially for Arnold whose cameras were forbidden in the harem. In order to gain access the two visitors depended heavily on their contacts among the elite ruling families, towards whom Lesley was excessively respectful. Sheikh Zaid, the ruler of Abu Dhabi, whom they met surrounded by his four wives and umpteen children in the harem, was delighted by Lesley's blonde hair and presented her and Eve Arnold with a platinum watch each. 'Lesley loved it all,' recalled Arnold drily. 'Her article wound up with words like "allúring" and "turquoise waters" and phrases like "iridescent ambience of femininity". From time to time we found it expedient to work separately.'

In Egypt they found a divided country; its sophisticated urbanites a world away from the illiterate farmers along the Nile. Given that the feminist movement had been linked with the nation's struggle for independence and the veil lifted decades earlier, they concentrated on women's achievements since their emancipation. In Cairo, Lesley stayed with Amroussi and Zobeida Shaply-Shamyl, granddaughter of the Caucasian prophet, with whom she had kept in touch since *The Sabres of Paradise* was published. Although Mme Shaply-Shamyl's exotic ancestry made her a collector's item, she was wildly unmanageable. A passionate devotee of Circassian history, she had written a feverishly plotted novel that she hoped Lesley would bring to heel and bless with an introduction. Lesley quailed at this suggestion and also at Mme Shamyl's attempts to marry her off to her brother, a diplomat in Turkey, who had a *yali*, a summer pavilion, on the Bosporus and two good-looking sons. Staying in Cairo with this 'extremely tenacious, exhausting, intellectual' individual proved less than ideal, since neither Zobeida nor her diplomat husband, a devout Sufi who spent most of his time praying, was remotely interested in worldly comforts. Before long, Lesley moved on to join Eve Arnold in Upper Egypt, where they seized time to visit the antiquities at Luxor and picnic in a felucca on the Nile by starlight.

The results of their expeditions were published in three long instalments in November 1970. That Lesley's essays were outshone by Arnold's magnificent pictures was in the nature of photojournalism, but in truth Lesley was more comfortable writing about the past than the present and it showed in her stiff, declamatory style. Documenting women's emancipation was never where her interest lay, and she wielded facts and figures about birth control and education politely but unenthusiastically. Her writing was far more effective when building atmosphere, above all in Afghanistan, where it began to sparkle with the spontaneous energy of her better work.

She was unfashionably sympathetic to the veil, expanding on what it stood for in the Islamic world: for 'tradition, protection, equality, seclusion' on the one hand, and for 'intrigue' and 'coquetry' on the other. She argued in its favour as a lifestyle, as well as a mystique lost to the progressive feminist West. Perhaps Muslim women did not envy their Western counterparts, she suggested. Perhaps they were less attracted by 'the necessity of *doing* rather than *being*.'

She had a valid point in warning that women seeking independence could find themselves exchanging one kind of servitude for another; however, her refusal to challenge the orthodoxy of the veil meant that she never looked for contrary evidence. In the Trucial States, where virtually the entire female sex covered their faces and married women wore their beak-like mask everywhere except in bed, she quoted with apparent approval Sir Richard Burton's comment that 'Women all the world over are what men make them', merely adding that Muslim women seemed to 'glow' with an 'inner content'.

Dispatched to reveal the lives of her sisters in Islam just as the debate about women's liberation was boiling up in the West (Germaine Greer's *The Female Eunuch* was published in 1970), Lesley politely declined to focus on the frustrations and tragedies of a shadowy population that was sequestered without rights or responsibilities. Her rose-tinted orientalism did her few favours beside the clear gaze of Eve Arnold's camera lens – or even compared with Jane Digby el Mezrab's response to the way Bedouin women lived, more than a century earlier: 'I walked with the Sheikh to our dinner and paid a visit to his wives. What an environment those women have. In what darkness they live.' Jane Digby was conscious of the special privileges she enjoyed as Medjuel el Mezrab's wealthy Feringhi wife in contrast to the harsh, stunting conditions suffered by most tribeswomen. Lesley, from an equally privileged outsider's position, refused to look.

Nevertheless her approach was consistent in that she had always believed in femininity rather than feminism, even while living as a liberated woman. Despite her driving will, her credo was in the traditional concept of women wielding power through intrigue and coquetry within the household, behind the throne; that had been *her* ideal way.

There were fundamental contradictions in her thinking, as in most of us. The physical confinement endured by most Muslim wives would have been insufferable to her, a free spirit who fiercely guarded her freedom to think, work and travel as she chose throughout her marriage to Romain. Nor could she ever have tolerated Jean as a permanent addition to her own ménage with her husband. Yet now she unquestioningly defended the benevolence of Islamic patriarchy and even argued in favour of polygamy, maintaining that the loss of man's protection would be a stiff price for women to pay for their liberty.

She had fallen in love with the Muslim way of life, replacing the impassioned nostalgia for Russia that had been her obsessive theme all through the years with Romain. The Islamic house turned inwards towards its courtyard, the hidden harem and the veil, all echoed the love of secrecy that was becoming essential to her. Barefaced reality was not where Lesley lived, nor was it where her men had lived. The masks and shadows cultivated by Romain and the other incorrigible mythmakers who had passed through her life were so many latticed windows and closed doors to the past, whose mysteries were what drew her to them most.

In Paris her friends were thinning. Nancy had moved out to Versailles in the late 1960s; almost immediately she developed the agonizing condition that resisted diagnosis and left her bedridden and tormented for nearly three years until her death in 1973. Violet, too, was fading and died the year before Nancy.

Lesley found less and less to keep her in the city. Every summer she escaped to Roquebrune; then she had friends to visit in Persia and Tunis, while Gavin Lambert, her friend and confidant from Los Angeles, was an habitué of Tangiers. All aggravated her perpetual itch to move somewhere in the Middle East – Morocco perhaps, or even Afghanistan. Instead she found a pretty and surprisingly functional little pink house just above the railway station at Garavan, the last stop on the French Riviera before the trains crossed into Italy. She sold the flat in the avenue Mozart, partially let the eyrie at Roquebrune (the tower where Romain had done his writing could be let separately), and spent most of 1972 reorganizing her living arrangements there and at Garavan.

Nine, Chemin de Vallaya was perched above a lane climbing steeply past villas and citrus groves into the rocky heights brooding over Menton. Inside the gate, cypress trees stood darkly beside the steep steps to the front door leading through thickets of bay, orange, mimosa and palm trees. Through a small entrance hall, the dining and living areas flowed into one another in a single open space. On the far side was an alcove for her study. Doors led off into her bedroom, bathroom and kitchen, and below was a spare bedroom and separate accommodation for staff, at such time as she found any. A rampant creeper was lured to drape over the balcony, adding privacy and giving her an extra reading room. A local decorator came and went; Lesley painted and tiled and arranged, and by late summer she had it more or less as she liked. The little station a few metres below ('trains almost under the bed'), then just a sandy halt without platforms, could almost have been her personal stop on the line snaking along the coast: so convenient, she said, for lunching in Nice, or dining at the palace or at the casino in Monaco.

She was pleased with her new nest. That winter she enjoyed its comforts, the quiet lane, the oranges and the soft sunny climate, and hardly missed Paris except for a few close friends and movie-going. Sacheverell and Georgia Sitwell visited and bestowed their approval, along with other friends.

Soon after she transferred to Garavan, her article 'My Day . . . and what of it?' appeared in *Vogue*. A definitive expression of Lesley's contrarian charm, it deserves to be read in full. She claimed that her day usually began and ended with a crisis, which her friends assured her was part of daily life, but she was quite unfitted for it, being unable to add up, read timetables or otherwise 'cope'. Nor indeed could she decide where to live, or even where to sleep – one night she might drag her sleeping bag into the garden, or in Paris lie in her hammock under the stars.

For someone so clearly averse to routine, each day was to vary according to where she found herself. 'I seem to have lived many different lives, in many different countries: for many years I have been, as it were, scattered between two, and sometimes three, households, while fidgeting to be off elsewhere – to some radiant unreal horizon, even more complicated though, from afar, it seems desirable.'

She had noticed (polishing her traveller's image) that whenever she was away, covering remote terrain, nothing seemed to go wrong, whereas at home in the Midi she was interrupted by constant alarms. 'Drains, for example, should not have to be considered part of one's day in the twentieth century . . . '

Her ideal day would be to 'slop about in an old padded Persian caftan cooking sustaining meals for darling self and darling cats as the whim takes us' (Lesley's oriental wardrobe was now intrinsic to her image). She would work for hours, leaving the phone to ring and letters unopened, distracting herself with garden chores or by embarking with her paintbrush on an elaborate wall frieze. There would be more writing later, listening to music, ignoring the clock – a habit acquired in America along with sorties to all-night shops and cinemas, a welcome diversion from her exhausting social round. Her self-sufficiency, so prized by Lesley, was ever her armour.

The next year she was splashed across a spread in the magazine, lolling à l'arabe on a divan in her new room with its Moorish arches. The photographer was Henry Clarke again, and the excuse was Lesley's collection of gros-point cushions, embroidered freehand. Magic carpets, she called them, taking her back to places (and pets) she had loved: an Afghan teahouse, the Kremlin's onion domes, Norman the cat in exotic dressing gown with his medicines. As she stitched they came back to her: 'Ah! Needlework, thy name is Nostalgia!'

That winter she fell ill again with a liver complaint, which affected her skin and was treated by an Italian doctor with injections and a strict diet. Her little cat Titti-Mi had died and now Norman was ailing; she lost him in June, the same month as Nancy Mitford. Lesley hated partings and was inconsolable for months, only emerging from mourning in October with a six-week visit to Iran.

Persia, as she preferred to call it, had become a significant new stopping off point on Lesley's map ever since her first visit in 1964. Needless to say she had excellent contacts in Tehran: Hassan and Hilda Arfa, devoted to the Pahlavis, were received at the imperial court. General Arfa, former Persian ambassador to Turkey and Pakistan, had retired from the diplomatic corps but still moved in those circles. She also cultivated her acquaintance with Sir Denis Wright, the British ambassador, an Iranophile who enjoyed sharing his enthusiasm with her. Possibly it was on this later trip, when she was feeling low and needing to be energized by new challenges, that the idea began to gell in her mind for an ambitious biographical project, for once set in the present, not the past.

Meanwhile she was right to be worried about her new book for Weidenfeld & Nicolson. She had undertaken it as a commercial venture to help defray her moving expenses. But after her commissioning editor Tony Godwin left, she had no special friend or ally to rely on there, and most of the picture research (which she usually undertook herself) was to be done in-house. The art editor promptly went on maternity leave and Lesley's worst fears were confirmed when *Pavilions of the Heart: The Four Walls of Love* appeared in 1974 sprinkled with errors – one of the illustrations was printed upside down – and containing an errata slip. Worse, what should have been designed as an elegant coffee-table book scattered with well-chosen pictures, appeared as solid chapters of text with a sixty-page insert of jumbled illustrations in the middle. Lesley was beyond fury; she felt her work had been violated. She did not present a copy of *Pavilions of the Heart* to the London Library and rarely included it in her list of published works.

Yet her theme was perfectly tailored to her fixation with the material detail of the past. It enabled her to frame her favourite historical figures in their 'settings for lovings', and so inhabit the places and possessions they held dearest. Location was always a – sometimes *the* – protagonist for Lesley. She included several rehashings of earlier treatments: of the seraglio at Istanbul *again*, although this time focusing on Sultan Murad III's room; Queen Marie of Romania's miniature palace at Balcic; and Blagodatsk, the fearsome first prison for the Decembrists in Siberia, which allowed Lesley to summon up the scene where Princess Maria Wolkonsky rejoined her husband in exile, ecstatically kneeling to kiss his chains. Of the new material, her chapters on the desert retreat of Aurélie Piccard, who had nearly qualified for *Wilder Shores*, and George Sand's country house at Nohant in the Berry, best illustrate Lesley's peculiarly acute sensibility to *genius loci*.

Piccard's early life in provincial northern France in 1849 had taken an exotic turn during the Franco-Prussian War of 1870–1 when she was relocated with the government-in-exile to Bordeaux; there the Postal Director, her employer, entrusted her with the fiddly duty of extracting messages from tiny cylinders flown out of besieged Paris on the legs of carrier pigeons. This attracted the interest of an Algerian prince, Si Ahmed Tedjani, who proposed marriage; she accepted and decamped to southern Algeria with him, taking her family with her. In the desert outside his tribal *zaouia*, where he was the spiritual and secular ruler, she built Kourdane, a flashily furnished domed villa that claimed her heart more completely than Si Ahmed or, after he died, his feckless brother Si Bachir, who became her second husband. The Princesse des Sables devoted herself to French interests during the First World War, but failed to adapt to her homeland afterwards, and struggled back to Kourdane to die. The French decorated her with honours and arranged her funeral with pomp and circumstance; yet to the Arabs she was their saint or *maraboute*, worthy of burial beside Si Ahmed, reclaimed by 'the desert she had loved more than any man'.

Some of Lesley's characters resisted the required romantic atmosphere – by all accounts Piccard was cool towards both her husbands and became domineering and acquisitive in later life – and her sharp focus on descriptive detail tended to blur over dates and other precise historical points. 'It was for love of her [Safieh Baffo, Italian concubine], I like to think, and for the purposes of this book maintain, that he built the perfect room known as Sultan Murad's Bed-chamber,' she declared, apparently with no stronger evidence that the Sultan's favourite was Italian than Lesley had found for Aimée Dubucq's Westernizing influence over her son, Mahmud II. But the room is described with consummate precision.

Her evocation of George Sand's house at Nohant reveals Lesley at her idiosyncratic best. Despite the notoriety that trailed after Sand in Paris for her love affairs and her cross-dressing (mainly to gain access to cheap men-only seats at the opera), Lesley held that 'that marvellous life force, at once vigorous and calming, which drew so many men of genius to her side', stemmed from her grounding in the countryside where she had been raised. Her manor house of honey-coloured stone in the Berry offered an ambience combining the traditional country landowner's comforts with the stimulating company of artists and intellectuals. Lesley argued against Sand's critics that the eight years Chopin spent with Nohant's generous and thoughtful chatelaine, there and elsewhere, probably prolonged his life, which was already threatened by tuberculosis. Little Chop-Chop, as Sand nicknamed him, was installed in a room soundproofed with padded doors so that he could compose at his piano day or night. Delacroix stayed across the courtyard for weeks or months at a time; Turgenev and Pauline Viardot were house guests; politicians, actors, writers came and went. In the evenings all joined Sand and her children over the salon table, entertaining the company with their new drawings, a play for the puppet theatre or a reading of their latest chapter. Promptly at midnight their hostess withdrew to continue her own work-in-progress, in order to maintain this enviable regime.

Lesley speculated frankly about the sexual character of her subjects. In *Wilder Shores* she had been fascinated by the contrast between Isabelle Eberhardt's promiscuous taste for Arab lovers and her entirely sexless presence. For all George Sand's notoriety in her amours, Lesley saw not a sensualist but a woman who was always in search of satisfaction, whose dominant trait was maternal. Every lover was gathered into the bosom of her family life. Lesley was intrigued by Balzac's description of Sand as a comradely fellow artist, not in the least flirtatious.

Sand's domestic style was very different from her own, yet it allowed Lesley to analyse her ménage with Romain which had lasted for so long. Even carefree bohemian 'creative artists', she contended, need certain 'bourgeois stabilities' to protect them from the pressures of daily existence and often produce their best work from the refuge of a well-run household that offers comfort and security. Chopin, a cherished cuckoo in Sand's nest at Nohant, exemplified her thesis, despite Sand's picnics which annoyed the composer, and her republican politics which appalled him.

And it was true that after Roquebrune, Romain never found his Nohant.

Romain was approaching sixty and living alone for almost the first time in his life. After the long, nightmarish wrench of separation from Jean, he never remarried. 'My first wife was too old and my second wife was too young,' he would shrug, as if he had had no say in the matter (which was possibly how he regarded his marriages). He had a sort of extended family around him (Jean Seberg and Dennis Berry, her third husband, lived in an apartment across the courtyard, close to Diego who was still cared for by Eugenia in the separate mezzanine flat); staff to look after him; his publishing house a few minutes' walk away. But the imposing apartment was alarmingly empty and bleak. He rotated between the rue du Bac, his villa in Majorca in summer, and a small impersonal flat in Geneva, where he went to consult his lawyers and financial advisers.

He was becoming a Left Bank 'character', a regular sight in the *quartier*, kitted out in theatrical outfits: during one phase he was encased in black leather and blackened his beard and sideburns. His histrionic melancholy had a mesmerizing effect on young women, who bewitched him in turn with the vain hope that his next affair might be the fugitive lasting love. Yet his desire always far outstripped satisfaction and the fidelity that he wrote about with such longing eluded him.

Did Lesley keep up with his writing? Perhaps she avoided it. Rather as she had done in *Journey into the Mind's Eye*, Romain was circling round his past at this time, trying to exorcize it. In *White Dog* (1970) he had novelized himself and Jean using the medium of demotic French and American. *Europa*, its successor two years later, came (for Romain) unusually close to a *roman à clef*, disguised by the almost unnaturally contrasting formal French prose that befitted his cultured diplomat protagonist. Danthès, world-weary French ambassador to Rome (a position Romain coveted), is losing contact with reality, descending through erotic horror into madness as he endures the death of love.

Danthès's passion for the chimera of Europe that lured him into diplomacy is reflected in his love for two sirens who led him to perdition. The first, Malwina von Leyden, was an entrancing sophisticate twelve years older whom the young Danthès was forced to renounce for his career; Edwina, his second great love, is a girl twenty-five years his junior, who suffers from mental blackouts. (*'My first wife was too old and my second wife too young.'*) Malwina, the older woman with a scarlet past, is unmistakably modelled on Lesley, borrowing his first wife's deliberately unfashionable elegance worn as naturally 'as if she had cultivated her own ghost', as well as her Scheherazade's gift for summoning up the past as if it were more real to her than the present, adding a lustrous shine to duller, greyer events. This subtle description of a rare storyteller's art rooted in the geography of place and time, is overlaid by the bewitching courtesan's savage transformation twenty years later into a malevolent cripple. Edwina, blighted and degraded by madness, is equally emblematic of Romain's second wife Jean, whose personal and political rebellion after they separated had culminated eventually in psychotic breakdown.

Two years later his 'memoir', *La Nuit sera calme*, was published as a series of interviews with his old friend François Bondy, who revealed after Romain's death that it was 'a kind of autobiographical novel . . . a joke, a trick, a hoax if you will. The manuscript of the book was quite complete when he gave it to me and suggested only that I insert some questions and remarks of my own in order to fill it out.' Nonetheless this fictive account has been mined ever since by biographers and commentators, including myself. Romain revisited his marginal adolescence in the Midi, then picked up from *Promise at Dawn* after he became a diplomat and writer, dwelling on his years in the United States and Hollywood. After his spiteful portrait of Malwina in *Europa*, he erased Lesley completely from his own story. A throwaway remark that Romain had learnt English from his first (unnamed) wife was almost his only acknowledgement to her existence, in response to Bondy's prompting.

Romain met Hélène Hoppenot for lunch, bringing a signed copy for her and Henri. She read it with mounting disbelief: 'Divided between laughter and indignation as I read the book which Romain brought us "The Night will be Calm" (fine title). Such a profligate [*dévergondé*] imagination is dangerous for he makes his readers believe in facts which he presents as if they are part of his experience.' Henri Hoppenot was more amused than annoyed: 'It's all pure fiction . . . Everything transformed,' he concluded. 'Falsified too,' added the outraged diarist, who was justifiably proud of her daily journal of public and private events kept over several decades, whose factual accuracy made it a precious historical record.

Hélène asked after Lesley. Romain told her eagerly that he personally bore her no ill will; but mutual friends who had met Lesley on the Riviera said she had turned her head and spat when his name was spoken.

Had her absence from *The Night Will be Calm* added to his offence, or her presence in *Europa*? Then again, was Romain responding in kind to her amputation of *his* role in *her* life, in *Mind's Eye*?

Still there was no rapprochement.

Lesley was juggling deals with three different hardback publishers, aside from separate paperback arrangements – Pan was bringing out a new edition of *Wilder Shores* – and her finances were in a muddle. Enraged to discover that British tax was being deducted from royalties on her John Murray books although she paid tax in France, she engaged a Monte Carlo solicitor who wrote a savage letter accusing Murray's accounts department of failing to claim a refund. It soon emerged that she had never filled in the tax form they had sent her, so no tax exemption certificate had been awarded. With sinking heart she realized that not only was it her own fault but the solicitor's bill would probably be greater than the refund owed to her. Shortly afterwards she became a client of the literary agency A.D. Peters, which took over her business affairs related to writing.

Personal correspondence could arouse her wrath too. Following a note from Osyth Leeston telling her that an old acquaintance from Australia was trying to contact her in Paris, Lesley flew into a rage. How dare these slight acquaintances claim friendship after being out of touch for forty years? Short of an offer to inherit a fortune, she could see no reason to reply. Naturally it would be quite different if the correspondent was a suitably elevated *Arabisant*, like Sir Laurence Grafftey-Smith (Murray published his memoir *Bright Levant* in 1970 and he became a pen-friend of hers) . . . Osyth, much amused, passed the letter on to Jock, adding that Lesley had nothing to fear since her address had not been sent to the letter-writer. Lesley's patience began to run thin even with Mme Shaply-Shamyl after a hail of requests for help on her frenzied history of the Caucasus.

If her ability to behave outrageously was unimpaired, so was her capacity to cast a spell when she chose. Although by now she looked her age, and had grown undeniably plump, Lesley could still dazzle with 'this unbelievable charm, and interest in very interesting things, bringing things into one's knowledge that one hadn't known about'. As once she had followed the slightest lead and cultivated every remote acquaintance that spoke to her of Russia, now she quested after their oriental equivalent. The dazzling beam of her energy and enthusiasm on recondite Persian and Islamic byways sparked the interest of scholars and specialists who were flattered by her attention into sharing their knowledge. Her flair for collecting people was unerring – how had she got acquainted with the king of Afghanistan's niece before her working trip with Eve Arnold? Where once she longed to run off with the raggle-taggle gipsies, now sheikhs and generals fell helpless before her determined advance. Whether it was a question of furthering her knowledge or her interests, it was remarkable how often the two coincided.

Lesley especially prized her friendship with Gerald de Gaury, the much travelled, strikingly handsome and impressively connected former soldier, diplomat and Middle Eastern specialist. In the First World War, recovering from the first of four injuries separately sustained at Gallipoli and on the Western front, he taught himself to read Arabic. After the war he was posted to Iraq and Kuwait, where he was British Political Agent, and in the Second World War led possibly the last successful cavalry campaign against a German sympathizer who had staged a coup in Baghdad. He was special emissary to King Ibn Saud and one of the first visitors to Riyadh, the Wahhabi capital.

De Gaury's books and photographs revealed an artist's sensibilities and a self-confessed 'fondness for the esoteric' that matched Lesley's own. He recalled that during a visit to Isfahan he hoped to meet the famous miniaturist Massawar and his cat, which he had heard 'sits tranquilly beside him while he works and patiently lets him pull out a hair of its whiskers for use in making finer strokes.' But 'his two apprentices, who were wrestling instead of working on borders, which is their task', told de Gaury that like Massawar 'the cat too was out'. He wrote perceptively of past travellers and the differing temperament and motivation that lured them to the desert. He was fluent in Arabic, had travelled in Persia, Turkey, Yemen and the Balkans, and Lesley loved 'talking Arab' with him as she had done with General Catroux in Algeria.

At home her social life was seasonal. Shoals of summer visitors to the Riviera would drop in or stay with her in Roquebrune or Garavan, then vanish in winter, when she settled down to write.

Roquebrune acquired its own season as a coterie of migrants flew in from New York, London and Paris to open up their houses for the summer months. The steep stone-paved streets would ratchet up to a round of junketings: 'We were all cutting capers, very giddy and gay up there.' Lesley was quite at home in moneyed company and in great demand. Secure in her own originality, spurning Pucci and Gucci, she was famous for her Arabian Nights outfits ('I used to say, I cannot dress if I don't go to Aleppo, there's nothing I want to wear unless I can get it in Aleppo'). She would emerge from her cave-like dwelling draped in oriental robes topped by 'a turban with a great brooch stuck in. You'd walk through the village to somebody's house for a dinner party and the village would all go, oooh! Dis donc!'

It was somehow typical of Lesley that Henry Clarke, US *Vogue*'s chief photographer since the 1950s, successor to Horst and Cecil

Beaton, lived in an exquisitely furnished house virtually next door to her in Roquebrune. Clarke and his partner Raymond Poteau, an antique dealer, became close friends and Lesley increasingly relied on them for company and shopping outings in their car after they came to live in the Aumonerie full-time. Jean van den Bosch, Belgian ambassador to London, and his wife Hélène, and Lady Iliffe, second wife of Lord Iliffe, the provincial newspaper magnate, also had houses in Roquebrune. Through Henry Clarke, Lesley got to know Pat Creed, widow of the couturier Charles Creed, who still did work for British *Vogue*. Pat in turn introduced Lesley to Alfredo Bourret, a former artist for French *Vogue*, and his friend Lex Aitken, who would call on her at Menton.

After 1973 Lesley, too, stayed there seasonally. The village kept up some of its old Ligurian customs, such as the annual procession, feast and ball in August to celebrate its escape from the plague centuries earlier under the protection of the Virgin. But the baker, who once sang Italian arias as he slapped the dough, left; shops closed and buses were rare. She led an odd existence, switching from feast to famine and back again, fostering her knack for magicking meals from nothing to feed unexpected guests. Once Katharine Hepburn, last met as Cukor's neighbour in Beverly Hills, escaped from filming *The Madwoman of Chaillot* on location on the Riviera and climbed the steep hill to call on Lesley unannounced. She lost her way and wandered through the streets chanting to herself, 'Je cherche un portail bleu avec une tête d'ange . . .' In the 1970s, Osbert and Anne Lancaster stayed in the village with friends who brought them to tea with Lesley. Anne remembered that though Lesley 'was delighted to renew an old acquaintance with Osbert, she was cool to me'.

Despite her new refuge at Garavan, Lesley was always fidgeting to go away. 'France you see to me is a country which has such beautiful variations of country and such charm but I don't really want it. Better in Italy. I'm much better when I get over to Tunis.' In the 1970s she lost her link with the lovely 'Arab palace' at Sidi Bou Said where she had stayed with such pleasure, after her friend Leo d'Erlanger died and his family sold up. In January 1975 she tried Morocco, visiting Gavin Lambert in his house up in the hills behind Tangier, which reminded her of California. His book of interviews with Cukor, which had just been published, made them both nostalgic for the director and

Hollywood. They travelled together to Fez, where she loved the ancient medina enclosed in its massive walls and gateways. From there she took the early-morning bus to Marrakesh, where David Herbert had arranged dinner parties for her; though Lesley preferred to picture herself sitting under a palm tree, intent on the life of Pierre Loti that now preoccupied her.

Soon Loti had to be put aside for a more pressing special request. This was not the sort of undertaking that could be lightly refused, even if she had wanted to. It was a commission from the ruling house of Pahlavi in Tehran for Lesley to write the biography of Her Imperial Majesty Farah, Shahbanou of Iran.

The idea for a life of the Shahbanou probably came from Lesley. She had already been introduced to the royal couple by Hassan and Hilda Arfa, her friends and hosts at Larak; Sir Denis Wright, a fan of the empress, had presented to her a copy of Lesley's *The Sabres of Paradise*. Like everyone else Lesley was charmed by Farah Diba, the Shah's third wife, who had replaced the beautiful Soraya, divorced by him for failing to give him an heir. Farah had quickly produced a son, followed by three more children, and was widely popular as a civilizing influence at court as well as a softening foil to the stern, autocratic Shah. Intelligent and hard-working, especially in education and welfare initiatives, she was also a patron of the arts.

Lesley's natural sympathy for rebels and revolutionaries had never hindered her intense interest in royalty, the more flamboyant the better. The Turquoise Kingdom's Peacock Throne bordered on the fantastic, making her subject all the more compelling. In the last quarter of the twentieth century, here was an oriental despot who was trying to create a great civilization to match the pre-Islamic dynasties of ancient Persia two millennia earlier. In the mid-1970s the Shah seemed unshakeable on the throne of Iran, afloat in petrodollars and the pivot of Middle Eastern power politics, courted by America and Britain. Lesley lingeringly recited the traditional Persian titles by which His Imperial Majesty the Shahanshah was known, Light of the Aryans, King of Kings, and Allah's Shadow on Earth . . . yet the Pahlavi dynasty (including the surname) dated only from 1926 when his father Reza Shah, a former army officer, had seized the throne from the Qajar monarchy. After the Allies forced Reza Shah to abdicate during the war because of his support for Hitler, Mohammed Reza made it his life's work to continue his father's programme for a Western-style modernized society through ambitious land reform, industrial development and sweeping social change.

A contract was drawn up between Lesley, Collins and the Iranian embassy to publish the book. She occasionally took Philip Ziegler, again her editor, to the Iranian embassy in London to discuss progress with 'the sort of Lord Chamberlain figure' (probably Asoudah Alam, former prime minister and adviser to the Shah, who died in 1978) on his visits to London. At one stage, Ziegler became nettled as they argued a financial point. 'I said, "Last time we talked about this, you said such and such." "I may have said this, but have you got anything in writing?" he said. And I used this line I'd always longed to use: "Sir, I thought I was speaking to a gentleman." And he sort of quivered, the blow struck home tremendously.'

The biographical exercise was far from straightforward and Lesley navigated numerous rocks on her way. On the Iranian side it was a useful public relations initiative, introducing to the world the sympathetic, approachable Empress who had been crowned with the Shah at their joint coronation and had been designated by him as regent to the Crown Prince if he died – setting a double new precedent for the Persian monarchy, and a modern example for Persian women. For her part, Lesley somehow had to gratify imperial wishes at the same time as satisfying Western readers' obsessional interest in the Shah's fabulous wealth and his powerful secret police network, Savak, whose outrages against human rights were targeted by the international media.

Her own social environment was among the elite monarchist circles of Hilda and Hassan Arfa and their friends: did they deny or defend Savak's fearsome hidden network of 60,000 agents, who were said to control another 3 million informers prepared to denounce their fellow citizens, often for money or self-interest? Lesley did ask the Shahbanou about Savak's use of torture and was informed that the press had greatly exaggerated it. She avoided head-on conflict in her writing, stating that her sources had been limited to her own interviews and research and the Shah's autobiography.

The project gave her extraordinary inside access to the imperial family, allowing her to observe the 'scenes from a life' that she would fashion into an official portrait of the Empress, as well as much more that could never be mentioned. She relished boasting to her friends that the 'grace-full' Shahbanou had invited her as a personal guest, enclosing a first-class ticket to Tehran. And she was mingling again with high-ranking diplomats – a point scored over Romain, which still mattered. After 1974 the new British ambassador was the gifted Arabist Sir Anthony Parsons, a formidably bright, approachable figure who, with his wife, made Lesley welcome at the British embassy when she visited, as did James George and his wife at the Canadian embassy.

Aside from the perks and the prestige, the project was no sinecure for someone who had passed her seventieth birthday in 1974. She spent three years darting back and forth to Tehran via Paris (Air Iran had no flights to the South of France), often in torrid heat, and sometimes elsewhere, for instance when the Empress opened the World of Islam Festival in London in 1976. Her fortnight with the royal entourage on holiday at Kish, their private seaside retreat, after the fiftieth anniversary celebrations of the Pahlavi dynasty in March 1975, must have been especially trying. Swarms of overindulged royal children played pop music at top volume and buzzed about on motorbikes when not kicking up sand on the beach – all anathema to an elderly biographer who disliked children, shunned the sun and whose fractured arm was in plaster after a fall. She watched with distaste as the Shah and his retinue were served Bloody Marys, defying the Islamic alcohol ban, and as a phalanx of bodyguards swam out to surround him in the warm sea, human bait protecting him with their bodies from shark attacks. She drily dubbed the pyramidal palace complex with its sharp-angled balconies and blue-tiled roofs Style Kish, and mourned Kish's legendary past as Sindbad the Sailor's island. Not the least of her worries was having to use a tape recorder; the Shahbanou, watching her technophobic interviewer jab the buttons in hopeless confusion, took the machine from her and recorded the conversation herself. She told Lesley she had advised the Shah to do likewise.

The Shahbanou emerged from the interviews as helpful, direct, devoid of vanity and touchingly eager to be a 'good Queen'. She disliked the security measures that kept her isolated from ordinary Iranian life and sometimes spontaneously rearranged her itinerary to see things as they really were. Lesley was especially impressed by her commitment to save Iran's incomparable architectural heritage, in particular its old houses, largely from the juggernaut of the Shah's great plans to drag his country out of its feudal past. The Shahbanou was credited with creating museums to house the Persian heritage of carpets and of Qajar paintings. She was sometimes less successful at imposing good taste on the various imperial palaces whose decor Lesley reviewed critically, flinching at anachronisms like a box of Kleenex next to a solid-gold samovar in the dining room at the new palace of Niavaran.

She dutifully followed Farah Diba's early progress, visiting the French convent in Tehran where she had gone to school; she interviewed her mentor Soeur Claire, her school and student friends, her mother and her aunt. Farah was studying architecture in Paris when she was 'discovered' by Princess Shahnaz, the Shah's daughter, who told him she had found the young woman who would be his next wife. Lesley even interrogated the celebrated Parisian hairdressers Carita Soeurs, Rosie and Maria, who had arranged the bride's hair for the royal wedding in 1959 (and had done Lesley's own hair in the past). Despite her footslogging, the results were anodyne.

In noisy, dusty, polluted Tehran she pined in vain for the bazaar and the remains of the old city whose inhabitants sat munching watermelon under the trees while urchins splashed in runnels beside the pavements. Her research awaited her in modern office blocks and government buildings; there to sit through newsreels and sift cuttings about the working Empress's literacy campaigns and countless worthy projects. In retrospect the royal couple's well-intentioned labour laws, their land reforms to redistribute farmland among small farmers and cooperatives, the creation of the Literacy Corps and Health Corps, and so forth, make poignant reading. Their hard-working days and sleepless nights, drawing up fresh schemes to improve the lives of their subjects, appear as so much royal running on the spot; their initiatives were always imposed from above on a sullen people, never democratizing the process or gaining their loyalty.

Lesley's inevitably hagiographic profile pointed up fundamental malaises, especially the extent of the Shah and the Shahbanou's isolation from their subjects. They were hermetically sealed first within the inner circle of the Pahlavi princes and princesses, the Shah's many brothers and sisters, who enjoyed inconceivable wealth and privilege. Rumours were rife of nepotism and corruption; writing about Iran in *Vogue*, Lesley reported 'impertinent' gossip that the plumbing fixtures in the Princess Shams's new palace were made of solid gold. In their palaces, the imperial family were screened behind bullet-proof glass, closed-circuit television and armed guards who frisked every visitor (including the weary biographer); outside the palaces, the Shah and Shahbanou were whisked everywhere by helicopter to avoid attacks from terrorists. A closed outer circle of flattery and a stifling formality surrounded them at the Court, for which Lesley had to equip herself with a wardrobe of full-length evening and cocktail frocks, gloves and hats and joust with 'the elliptical courtier's approach'. 'The Imperial Court radiated a hard, meretricious glitter,' wrote Sir Anthony Parsons; 'the main function of its elaborate ritual and rigid protocol seemed to be to shield the monarch from direct contact with his people.'

Although Persian culture was generally considered to embrace both East and West, Lesley maintained that its people wanted their head of state to express 'an oriental language of luxury', which the Shah had undertaken to fulfil; but having inherited no royal traditions, he had to invent the ceremonies and trappings of his monarchy. These monumental displays attracted Lesley just as she had been drawn by special effects for cinema and stage, only more so. She revisited the coronation of the Shah and Empress in 1967 as pure theatre, revelling in the magnificence of the brand-new state coach ordered from Vienna, and the 'lovely, very feminine crown' made by Pierre Arpels for the Shahbanou – the ultimate costume jewellery, set with real stones. She lingered on its 1,469 diamonds, 72 emeralds and rubies, 105 huge teardrop pearls and its centrepiece, 'a fluted, hexagon emerald about the size of a smallish tangerine'.

She dwelt too on the fantastic extravagance of the 2,500th anniversary celebrations of the Persian Empire, presided over by the Shah at Persepolis in 1971. Kings, queens and heads of state were housed in sumptuous tents attended by their maids and hairdressers, while teams of chefs from Maxim's in Paris laboured to produce lavish banquets of quails' eggs stuffed with caviar and peacocks stuffed with foie gras, all flown out to this latter-day Field of the Cloth of Gold set on the arid Asian plain. The Shahbanou had had a miserable time of it, fighting off flu and dreading a terrorist attack.

Some of these state occasions were hardly more than special effects. Lesley would have heard from British embassy staff about the curious affair of the state ceremonies for the fiftieth anniversary of Pahlavi rule in 1976. Television viewers afterwards watched the Shah and the Empress apparently being driven in the horse-drawn state coach for miles, past cheering subjects, to the marble mausoleum of Reza Shah. Yet Anthony Parsons and his wife, who were guests, heard the Shah's helicopter land, then almost immediately saw the royal couple walk to the mausoleum and climb the steps to take part in the ceremonies. Later, driving back to Tehran, Parsons was startled to see four horses' heads poking out of a security van, followed by the state coach, wrapped in plastic, being carried past on a tank transporter. The triumphant drive through rapturous crowds, covering no more than a few yards, had been faked by the cameras for news reports. Needless to say, this aspect of the proceedings did not feature in Lesley's account.

In 1977 she returned twice to Iran, the first time to conduct a last interview with the Shahbanou and leave the manuscript with her. That summer she was summoned again for six exhausting final weeks in Tehran, cutting and amending the text until her royal taskmasters approved it. She spent a few days recovering in quiet, orderly Switzerland, lounging for hours on the decks of lake steamers on their daily round. (She might have been staying with James Mason, a Swiss domicile and still a good friend after their years as neighbours in Hollywood.) Then there was domestic catching up to do, especially on the garden. More editing followed in London, where she stayed with Pat Creed. She had triumphantly manoeuvred the embassy into agreeing in her contract that her editor should accompany her to Iran to help with the final stages of the book; but alas, when the time came for Ziegler's visit, mounting civil unrest prevented it. Then the launch party at the Iranian Embassy in London, scheduled for May 1978, was cancelled at the last minute.

Even the most experienced diplomats failed to predict the counter-revolution that overtook the country so swiftly and completely that year. The influence of his Western friends on the Shah made him widely unpopular. Mullahs and students united against what they saw as cultural and economic colonization by the US, while merchants rebelled against inflation and assaults on their traditional way of life. Mass demonstrations were met with violence by an army untrained to deal with civil unrest, aggravating the resentment of the crowds . . . General strikes paralysed the country's daily existence . . . The armed forces' loyalty wavered . . . The American Embassy was besieged and its staff taken hostage, revealing widespread hostility to the US, which abruptly cut its secret channels of advice and support to the Shah.

Within months the apparently impregnable dynasty was swept aside and in January 1979 the imperial family flew into ignominious and permanent exile. The Shah soon succumbed to cancer and his family trailed from one country to another, seeking refuge.

Days after the Shah's departure, the exiled Ayatollah Khomeini returned in triumph to Tehran, where he was hailed as the nation's prophet leader. The sixty-year rule of Reza and Mohammed Shah was wiped from Iran: streets were renamed, royal palaces closed, Reza Shah's mausoleum razed and the imperial portraits that hung in every house destroyed, as Iran sank into a counter-revolutionary theocracy.

Lesley's links with Iran were abruptly severed by the revolution. She was philosophical about the political and religious ferment that followed, regarding it as an inevitable historical process. At the same time she was appalled by the West's cynical desertion of the Shah, which she later described as 'one of the most ignoble episodes of modern history'. Her book sank almost without trace (except for advance extracts printed in *Cosmopolitan* UK). Although the Iranians had paid a percentage in advance, Collins was apparently left with several thousand copies in the warehouse and Lesley lost out on royalties. At the end of the year she sent copies to one or two friends sympathetic to the Pahlavis' personal tragedy, Pat Creed among them, for historic interest. She was better able to resign herself to another abandoned project since this one had been commissioned and was therefore not really hers. She hoped it read as well as it could, while aware that it was not her best work. For Ziegler it was the least satisfactory of the books he edited with her, since it gave her no liberty for invention: 'She really had to more or less stick to the facts . . . . Details got in the way of the perfect story, the image that was true even though not accurate.'

Loyal to her subjects, Lesley returned to the biography of Pierre Loti who had already begun to absorb her attention before her Persian interlude. She made working trips to Paris to see her typist and to delve into research at the Bibliothèque Nationale. Occasionally she stayed in luxury with the Rothschilds, savouring their chef's exquisite meals, or more informally with Susan Train, the capable, amusing American expat who manned American *Vogue*'s Paris bureau and became its chief in 1985.

Train had met Lesley in 1965 when they both accompanied Henry Clarke on a *Vogue* fashion shoot in Syria and Jordan, starting in Damascus and going on to Palmyra, Aleppo and Petra. Lesley seemed quite at home in these surroundings and Train was impressed by her knowledge of the region's history and romantic tales of its European residents (Jane Digby, the Burtons): 'She'd read so much and seemed to know everything.' They stopped in a village whose quaint houses had caught the eye of Henry Clarke. After attending to the models and helping to set up the shoot, Train looked around for Lesley who was nowhere to be seen. Eventually she found her 'in a room, smoking a narguileh with the village elders. She was perfectly happy there, sitting on the cushions, smoking a hookah.'

They enjoyed each other's company and had much to offer the other. Although Train's job on *Vogue* kept her travelling a great deal, she found time to help with shopping commissions and when Lesley was staying in Paris they enjoyed 'flâner-ing' and film-going in their spare time. Sometimes she visited Menton and took Lesley for outings. In short, she became an essential anchor person and support for the older woman in her later years. In London Lesley came to rely on another younger friend and helper, Georgia de Chamberet, the daughter of family friends and a god-child.

For years Lesley had been nagging Murray to find a paperback publisher for *The Sabres of Paradise*, always the work in which she took most pride, but most houses were deterred by its length, while she refused to cut the text. In 1978 a paperback edition was published by Naim Attallah under his Quartet Books imprint, to Lesley's lasting satisfaction. Later, when de Chamberet worked as an editor at Quartet, she reprinted *Round the World in Eighty Dishes* in paperback, and was working on a revised edition of *Under a Lilac-Bleeding Star* when she left the company. *Wilder Shores*, meanwhile, continued to be more often in print than out of it, published under various paperback imprints.

13

The Life and Death of Emile Ajar

Mon 'je' ne me suffit pas.

Romain Gary

I N 1977 LESLEY came upon a package in a graveyard of bills and circulars lying ignored in a corner by the front door. It contained a copy of Romain's new novel *Clair de femme*, and a note from him inviting her to meet him and his son when she was next in Paris.

Was this was his first overture? She did meet Diego more than once, although their friendship did not survive the trauma of his parents' deaths in 1979 and 1980.

Romain developed an occasional habit of phoning Lesley: oddly, usually from a call box. Vestiges of their old familiarity returned as she listened to his conspiratorial voice divulging a fresh crop of scandals and secrets. A *scandaliste* herself, she was well qualified to receive them, becoming one of a handful of confidants who were party to the bizarre and finally nightmarish adventure of Emile Ajar.

It began as Romain approached his sixtieth year in 1974, a prospect he dreaded. Once again he had fallen into a state of crisis and flux, leaving him profoundly out of sorts with himself. In the past his evolution and resolution had emerged through his writing.

Although he had long since returned to France, Romain remained an outsider in French literary circles. He was a storyteller, a *picaro*, a rogue, whose creative impulse stemmed from the reactions of an exceptionally agile and responsive mind to the sweep of events around him. His approach and style were unfashionable in the experimental era of structuralism and the *nouvel roman*, and his literary reputation suffered further from his consistently misconstrued Gaullism. He was disturbed by his dwindling book sales and the way in which French critics often reviewed him as a cliché, beginning with a biographical paragraph about the Free French war hero–diplomat–author and ending with a sentence dismissing his new novel.

He protested that his books were being received in the context of a false concept of 'Romain Gary'. Like the diplomat Danthès in his novel *Europa*, Romain felt imprisoned behind an alien public image of himself, his 'je', which was stifling him as surely as the Man in the Iron Mask. He wanted *to start from somewhere else.*

In 1974, the year of Romain's sixtieth birthday, three books by him were published within months of each other under three different names. *The Night Will be Calm*, his quasi-fictional memoir, naturally appeared under his own name. His next work, *Les Têtes de Stéphanie* (translated as *Direct Flight to Allah*) was a fast-paced thriller which was published under the alias of Shatan Bogat. This Bogat was purportedly a former arms trader and shipping magnate, but despite the intriguing curriculum vitae his deft exercise in pulp fiction sold poorly, and six weeks later Gallimard revealed that Romain was behind the fictitious author.

His third book published that year was not dictated to his secretary, Martine Carré, in the usual way, but was written secretly by hand in a black notebook. Romain gave it to her to type in strictest confidence and afterwards locked the handwritten original in a safe. The first his publishers heard about it was when Pierre Michaud, a businessman from Brazil, delivered a manuscript to Robert Gallimard on behalf of an unknown young writer friend by the name of Emile Ajar, along with an impudent letter which intrigued the publisher. A panel of readers submitted reports; one of them, Raymond Queneau, a master of *jeux d'esprit* and the celebrated author of *Zazie dans le métro*, shrewdly suspected a hoax by an established author and persuaded them not to accept. Romain immediately sent Michaud with his typescript to Gallimard's sister company, Mercure de France.

Mme Simone Gallimard and her editorial director Michel Cournot were delighted to have stumbled on that rare literary find, an unsolicited novel by an unknown writer showing genuine talent. It was a droll, poignant fable of the loneliness endured by a solitary social misfit living in Paris with only his eponymous python

Gros-Câlin ('Cuddles') for company. The theme and storyline were unexceptional compared with the novel's weirdly accomplished stylistic effect. The maladroit contorted language was peculiarly expressive, the anecdotes digressing and recoiling on themselves like Gros-Câlin himself.

When the novel was published in September 1974, Mercure de France could only repeat the information supplied by 'Ajar's' lawyer, his mediary. The name was a pseudonym; the author had been born in Oran in 1940, had been encouraged to write by Camus, had studied medicine and was currently living in Rio. The novel attracted attention – less for its quirky originality, as the publishers hoped, than concerning the mysterious author's identity: the press worked up a head of speculation about it. Sales were middling.

In *Gros-Câlin*, the python's owner describes the high point of magical optimism in its life-cycle, the moult, which 'represents in their nature the moving moment where they seem to be about to start a new life, with a guarantee of authenticity . . . the hope of becoming a completely different sort of animal . . . evolved'. Each time the promise of renewal is doomed to disappointment: 'they always find themselves the same.' Romain, on the contrary, had sloughed off his old skin and was exulting in his own creation of a brand-new one. As he wrote later in his epitaph, he felt as if he had been reborn and allowed to start all over again.

During the next six years he embarked on a phase of frenzied creativity, alternating new novels by 'Ajar' with others by 'Romain Gary', as well as rewriting older works for reissue. Even as he started on the next Ajar, 'Gary's' new novel was being prepared for publication by Gallimard.

Romain's knack for timing was matched by his talent for picking controversial subjects. He had wielded 'terrorist humour' against the Shoah in a grotesque farce, *The Dance of Genghis Cohn*. In the apparently documentary *White Dog*, set in Los Angeles and Paris, he had exposed black racism and misogyny as well as rewriting the end of his marriage to Jean Seberg. Now he tackled the great masculine taboo, impotence in the older man. *Your Ticket is No Longer Valid* (published in France in June 1975) is an outstanding example of how Romain used his late fiction not only to examine his own predicament in the context of a pressing broader theme, but also to project an image of himself, the author, to the world. He complained bitterly of being typecast by his reading public as the war-hero-diplomat, yet the theme and his apprehensive, ageing protagonist could not have been better calculated to reinforce 'Romain Gary's' failing status and reputation. Indeed Romain's sexual anxiety was genuine; he talked about it openly with his men friends and even on TV when publicizing the book, putting further distance between over-the-hill Gary and promising-newcomer Ajar.

Since his cousin Dinah had succumbed to dementia, Romain had befriended her youngest son, Paul Pavlowitch, who lived in southern France with his partner Annie. Paul was something of a drifter who had not yet found a vocation in life. A voracious reader and autodidact, he was in awe of his famous cousin whose writing seemed to come to him as naturally as life itself. In the summer of 1971, Romain invited them to Majorca together with Diego and Jean, who was still living in the adjoining apartment at rue du Bac. They had all got on so famously that they spontaneously decided to buy three cottages in the Causse, to be restored by Pavlowitch, with the idea that they could occupy them as a little tribe, separately or together. Paul and Annie had already moved there. Romain also persuaded Paul, with helpers, to redecorate his apartment in Paris. He was becoming absorbed into Romain's orbit, part of the family.

Ajar's second novel made its way to Mercure de France. Michel Cournot, again its first reader, disliked its manipulative theme, personified by this 'heartbreaking kid and his agonizing granny': an Arab foundling raised by his ailing Jewish foster-mother, a concentration-camp survivor, in an attic on the mean streets of Paris's immigrant quarter, Belleville. 'It's not a book,' Cournot complained to his wife, 'it's soliciting.' She told him to reconsider: Ajar's novel gave an authentic voice to the dispossessed and would pierce the hearts of thousands of readers. Everyone else at Mercure de France agreed with her and production went ahead.

Ajar was first a pseudonym, then a rumour; now the shadow began to materialize. His publishers received two telephone calls from their mystery author: the first to tell them he had written a new novel, and wanted a contract; the second to ask for their response to the typescript.

Paul Pavlowitch couldn't remember exactly when Romain first asked him to adopt the persona of his alter ego. At first it seemed to him no more than an outrageous practical joke; then again he and his mother owed a great deal to his cousin, who was now calling in the debt. It was Paul's voice that Mercure de France heard as Ajar, speaking according to the script Romain had written for him.

The dream of 'total fiction' that Romain had envisaged in his virtually unreadable polemic about the nature and future of fiction, *Pour Sganarelle* (1965), had almost taken shape. The last step was to 'give life to this picaro, who was both character and author, just as I had described him'. Paul shouldered 'Ajar's' murky personal history (Algerian, failed medical student, wanted in France for a botched abortion) and agreed to a rendezvous with his publisher in Switzerland. Cournot, meeting the skinny young man with intense dark eyes in a dusty Geneva flat, never doubted the authenticity of this feral, gipsyish presence which signified 'all the pages of Ajar' to him. A further meeting with Mme Gallimard, this time in Copenhagen, in a little wooden house that Pavlowitch had rented with Annie, also passed off successfully.

Finally, to placate the press which was avid for Ajar, Romain's master plan was for Paul/Emile to give a single interview to *Le Monde*, before vanishing into the shadows again. But during the interview Pavlowitch replaced Romain's scenario with improvised half-truths based on his own Eastern European origins and upbringing in Nice, finding it easier to avoid slips in a story that was closer to what he knew.

Romain, though outwardly delighted with the ruse, was inwardly dismayed and furious. Ajar was no longer his creation and had already slipped out of his reach. 'From then on, the mythological character I was so keen on ceased to exist and became Paul Pavlowitch . . . I knew that Emile Ajar was doomed.'

La Vie devant soi appeared in 1975 and quickly became the book of the moment, like Lesley's *Wilder Shores* twenty years earlier. Ajar was a phenomenon, a 'super-Queneau' who seemed to have sprung from nowhere, free of literary influence. He attracted thousands of new readers who rejected arid intellectual exercises and certainly anything by the ageing, overexposed Romain Gary. Critics raved or reviled it; they were never indifferent. 'A baroque and deeply moving master-piece', '. . . a new genre' of 'magico-poetic realism . . . a work of art . . .'

What an irony for Romain to savour! Some of the very reviewers who had sneered at his faulty grammar and incorrect French in *The Roots of Heaven* were now in ecstasies over the poetically mangled street argot of Momo, his Arab urchin, and Michel Cousin, the lonely misfit in *Gros-Câlin*. A new term, 'Ajarism', described the aphorisms supplied in such rich profusion by their author's supple imagination.

As his reputation grew, rumours about Ajar's identity were rife. Two weeks before the big literary prizes were announced, a journalist from Cahors who knew Annie traced Paul through clues left in his inter-view. They reached a curious agreement: the journal would respect Ajar's anonymity but would photograph Paul semi-recognizably in Paris.

As the odds on Ajar's book winning the Goncourt shortened, Romain's legal advisers warned him so severely about the risks of scan-dal, and even a prison sentence for fraud if he accepted the prize, that a last-minute letter was sent to the organizers to refuse it. But it was too late. The president of the judges' panel replied that they had voted for a book, not the author, and M. Ajar was still the laureate. So Romain acquired his unique and dubious position in the award's long history, as the only recipient to have won it twice, an honour specifically for-bidden by the Goncourt's statutes.

Forty years earlier a young Jew from Eastern Europe by the name of Roman Kacew had tried and failed to establish himself as a writer in Paris. Several lifetimes and pseudonyms later, writing in the idiom of an Algerian *métèque*, an outsider, one of Paris's new *Misérables*, he had created a voice so distinctive that it had conquered the closed elite world of *Parisianism*, as Romain called it. An unknown young writer had broken through the barriers of the literary establishment and car-ried off the accolade. Above all, Romain had 'materialized' the impos-sible mirage that had obsessed him for so long: he had created a 'total novel' encompassing both character and author. Yet at the moment of transformation, the new identity that freed his creative imagination had been blighted, stolen by Pavlowitch. He had been dispossessed of his mythological existence; someone else was living it in his place.

Romain was a lonely exception to the almost universal paradox of the pseudonymous author who wants to be unmasked. His first and final imperative was that he would take the secret of Emile Ajar to his grave, to which the corollary was that he would do whatever it took to defend it.

Long ago he had concluded that the demands of literature made it impossible for a great writer to be honest. Good fiction was true to itself, he argued, yet inevitably dishonest in terms of 'reality'. Where Ajar was concerned he had no moral compass, and no one to provide him with one since his friend Robert Gallimard, initially taken into his confidence, had left him on his own after warning of the ethical issues raised by Ajar. Romain immediately embarked on a fiendish new stratagem which would 'authenticate' Ajar as a separate entity from Romain Gary and allow the fiction to fertilize reality itself. His cousin had embedded himself in Emile Ajar's existence. Very well: he too would be welded into the master plan.

In the Causse, Paul and Annie greeted the radio news that Ajar had won the Goncourt with cheers and laughter. But soon another journalist unmasked Pavlowitch as Emile Ajar and revealed the family link between him and Romain Gary. Hurrying to Paris to consult Romain, he was chased by photographers and his picture was published in all the newspapers. Romain, finding swarms of journalists outside his front door, phoned Annie in a panic, threatening to use his revolver on himself, convinced that Ajar had been traced back to him. She firmly told him to calm down: the hacks weren't interested in *him*, but in his now-famous cousin, Pavlowitch-Ajar. Retrieving his sang-froid, Romain confided to the hovering reporters that his cousin was hypersensitive and slightly unhinged; he had used the pseudonym for fear that his creative urge and peace of mind would be destroyed by public exposure.

Mobbed by the media, Paul and Annie escaped briefly to London, Romain to his flat in Geneva. When they reassembled in Paris Romain informed them that he was working on a new book and Paul was in it. Paul, still Romain's greatest admirer, eagerly agreed to type the draft that Romain had scribbled at demented speed in ten days. What he read was a pseudo-confession, a shapeless paranoid rant written in a psychiatric clinic in Copenhagen, purportedly by himself. The narrator, Ajar-Pavlowitch, was certifiably insane. Romain appeared in it too, savagely parodied but clearly recognizable: 'I have an uncle who I call Tonton Macoute, because during the war he was an airman and he massacred civilians from a great height . . .'

Romain later claimed that the Paul-Emile character was entirely imaginary, created to 'fix' Pavlowitch as the author of the Ajar books by making Romain the main target. His cousin, meanwhile, pinned inside Romain's novel, found himself witnessing the cruel exposure of his own petty confessions while his personality was dismantled, picked over and infected with Romain's worst faults. *Pseudo* is a sadistic tour de force, as vicious to Romain-Tonton (a pompous cynic who writes only for profit) as to Paul-Emile (unstable, drugged, haunted by wild fears and fantasies). Romain, who had first-hand dealings with insanity in those close to him and was himself now heavily dependent on tranquillizers and sleeping pills, reproduced the disjointed thought processes exactly from his own private terrors. The tone fitted his fragile, fractured 'Paul Pavlowitch' like a second skin.

Pseudo was a manic comedy of terrors in which every other sentence had double or triple layers, like a piece of music composed entirely in harmonics, those ghostly notes teased out of string or reed instruments in barely audible counterpoint to the dominant theme. Ajar's history is all there – the journalists' pursuit of the man behind the pseudonym, the publisher's visit to Copenhagen, the lawyers' disapproval, the Goncourt – but subtly rearranged to shift the identity of his characters, hiding Ajar's genesis. Ajar is not Romain but Pavlowitch, who cracked up after his pseudonym was pierced when he won the Goncourt. Meanwhile Paul-Emile is inhabited by other ghosts, retreating like voices in an echo chamber: 'I had two characters battling inside me: the one that I wasn't and the one that I didn't want to be . . . Each day I set myself to invent characters that I wasn't, so as to become less and less myself.'

Trapped in the fetid reaches of Romain's imagination, burning with rage and frustration, Paul plunged into drink and amphetamines. Romain watched his disintegration with beady interest, noting the useful descriptive detail. He ransacked Paul's family history to bulk out the text, then tightened the garotte with a malignant fantasy, igno-miniously issuing from Paul-Emile, that Tonton Macoute had had an affair with his mother decades ago and might even be his father.

All this time Romain was plotting the book's future in advance like a chess game. The defamatory content would be a problem for Mercure de France, especially since it concerned one of its sister com-pany's leading writers – himself. He wrote to warn Mme Gallimard that Pavlowitch-Ajar had told him, Romain, that he was writing a book about them both. Romain had replied that he refused to read it and guaranteed not to take legal action, provided it respected the privacy of Jean and Diego.

During the last weeks while Romain revised the text and turned it into literature, the murderous hostility between the cousins began to subside. By the end of January 1976 the book was finished. Paul invited Michel Cournot over to read the typescript. He devoured it on the spot; he said it hit him like a meteorite from outer space. Romain, behind the scenes, was urgently anxious to see it in print, but Ajar's publishers, believing *Pseudo*'s virulent content could damage sales of the Goncourt winner, judged it too soon to publish.

When it appeared in late 1976 the effect of *Pseudo* was just as Romain intended. It distanced him from Ajar-Pavlowitch, who was assumed to have hastily 'vomited' this unsavoury work to avenge him-self on his ageing cousin and rival. To nobody's surprise but his own, it did not sell well. It had achieved its purpose, even so. Now that Ajar's anonymity had (apparently) been pierced and his identity con-firmed, the press lost interest and moved on.

After the demonic gestation of *Pseudo*, Pavlowitch went home to his family in the Causse and Romain reverted to his Gary oeuvre; his next book for Gallimard, *Clair de femme*, was published in 1977. Yet Ajar would let neither of them go. The phantom author had become a profitable business of rights, contracts and royalties. With book club sales *La Vie devant soi* sold a million copies in France. It was translated into twenty-two languages, excluding English. Paul-Emile was wined and dined, signed documents and agreed a lucrative film option: *Madame Rosa* (also the English title of the book), released in November 1977, was a hit in France and America, winning an Oscar for Best Foreign Film.

By now both longed more than anything to shake off each other and Ajar, the gremlin who crouched on their shoulders. Romain convened meetings with his lawyer to try to control the way the story of Ajar would eventually be broken; he wanted Pavlowitch to wait until five years after his death to make the revelation. He was terrified that his cousin would crack. The paranoid fears and anxieties, self-hatred and escalating drug-dependence that he had given Paul-Emile in *Pseudo* were his own bequest. The ventriloquist's dummy had seized his master by the throat and was throttling him.

The final sentence in *Pseudo*, which dismayed Ajar's publishers, had read: This is my last book. But Romain had one more Ajar brewing. In spring 1978 he immersed himself once more, and Pavlowitch signed Ajar's contract for a new novel.

By late August Ajar's last novel was completed.

L'Angoisse du roi Salomon (*King Solomon*) was a poignant meditation on old age, its protagonist another variant on Ajar's trademark naive savant whose words dipped into deeper meaning through their misuse. Once again the literary acrobat performed his high-wire act, hovering audaciously between slapstick, droll wordplay, sentiment and anguish. Mercure de France, relieved and delighted to see their author's return to winning form, published in early 1979. Ajar's fans found their faith restored by his tolerance towards human frailty, and the fragile hope embedded in his ending.

Soon after *King Solomon* was finished a final bitter argument blew up between Paul and Romain, causing an irreparable rift. Following the book's publication, a frosty joint meeting with Romain's lawyer hammered out a concordat between them. If Paul revoked their arrangement and revealed Ajar's true identity, his payments would cease immediately. After their meeting, Romain wrote his *Life and Death of Emile Ajar* which he intended for posthumous publication.

Once death had been the feared enemy of his ambition. Now it was part of his strategy.

Pavlowitch knew Ajar's fourth novel was the last. He had developed no alternative career, and although he was still receiving his share of Ajar's earnings, his literary proxy had become crucial to his self-esteem. Seizing the advantage of *King Solomon*'s success, he asked

Simone Gallimard for a part-time job at the Mercure de France offices as a literary consultant. She agreed to his dangerous request, mainly to deter Ajar from straying to another publisher. Paul-Emile's regular close contact with Ajar's publishers left Romain ever more fearful of deliberate or accidental betrayal.

During his last years Romain continued to write obsessively, ceaselessly, switching from Ajar to Gary, from English to French and back again. Now he steeled himself to wind up the works of Romain Gary. He approached the task with extraordinary dedication, methodically ticking off translations, a stage adaptation and the revision of an earlier novel, *Les Couleurs du jour*, which he retitled *Les Clowns lyriques* and was cynically amused when reviewers assumed it was a new work.

He was determined to leave a memorial fitting to his better self with 'Gary's' last novel. *Les Cerfs-volants* (*The Kites*) is set in France and in Poland, his twin loyalties, and for his material he transformed research that he had gathered about the wartime Resistance in occupied France, from the time that tested his own humanity and turned him into a Frenchman. He had been commissioned to write about the Companions of the Order of the Liberation some years earlier, but he was in the middle of writing *Pseudo* at the time and the authorial conflict between the two projects was too great to straddle. Later, having accepted the task, he couldn't see how to shape the individual stories into a satisfactory narrative and officially resigned from it in 1977. Now his final work of fiction would make use of some of the Resistance material he had researched for the project.

Apart from Romain's perpetual adjustments to the shifting scaffolding of lies that he had built around Emile Ajar, he was exhausted by his dealings with Jean. The instability that he had detected when they first met had grown worse over the years, compounded by alcohol and drug abuse. During a serious breakdown in 1976 she was prescribed lithium, whose disastrous metabolic effect left her swollen into obesity, the cruellest insult to someone whose identity and self-esteem depended on her looks. Her marriage to Dennis Berry had definitively ended in late 1977, after she chose to remain in Paris when he moved to Los Angeles. Since then her life had gone inexorably downhill in a disintegration that those who loved her could hardly bear to watch.

Romain increasingly bore the brunt of her care. He took her with him and Diego to William Styron's country retreat in Connecticut during the summer of 1978 when he was writing *King Solomon*; she was thin again after a drastic cure, but her stay there failed to halt her decline. Her state of mind fluctuated violently; she checked herself in and out of clinics. Romain was anxious to protect Diego from her erratic behaviour and the marginal drifters who had replaced her friends; he was also desperate to defend his concentration from being torn away from his final work of fiction. In February 1979 Jean was committed to a grim state asylum, apparently permanently.

To the amazement of everyone close to Jean, she recovered enough for doctors to pronounce her fit to leave a month later. Back at her apartment she reverted to her restless ways and drifted into a fitful affair with an Algerian restaurateur, then with his nineteen-year-old nephew Ahmed Hasni, who made wild conflicting claims about himself. Soon he moved in with her.

Astonishingly, that spring Jean landed a part in a bona fide movie among friends. The producer was Georges de Beauregard, who had produced *A Bout de souffle* and two more of her French films; Raoul Coutard, Godard's former cameraman would direct. In early August she even went ahead with her first few days of filming in Guyana. On her return to Paris she tried to avoid Hasni, unsuccessfully. Within a few days she was with him again.

On 30 August, Hasni informed the police that Jean Seberg was missing. On the evening of Saturday 8 September, her body was found, wedged on the floor behind the front seats of her white Renault, covered with a blanket. The corpse had been lying there for more than a week. Suicide was indicated by a half-empty bottle of mineral water, empty containers of barbiturates and a farewell note to Diego. The police at first assumed that in the small hours of 30 August she had taken the water and pills to the car and driven it round the corner to rue du Général Appert, where she had swallowed the overdose. But blood tests revealed a potentially lethal alcohol level in Jean's body, so high that it would have rendered her incapable of driving. Then the glasses that she always wore to drive were found in the apartment. Could someone have driven her round the corner, parked the car and left her to die? The questions mounted, hindering a confident verdict of suicide.

Le Figaro reported that according to Hasni, Jean had been upset after seeing *Clair de lune*, based on Romain's novel, at the cinema the evening before she died. Romain responded with a press conference, at which he claimed that her suicide had been caused not by his film but indirectly by the FBI, whose undercover campaign to blacken Jean's name with rumours about her unborn child's paternity in 1970 had in effect destroyed her. He declared the calumny had caused her miscarriage, psychosis and later annual suicide attempts. He produced copies of FBI documents which detailed Jean's support for the Black Panthers and stated she must be 'neutralized'.

Their friends, already horrified by Jean's death, were dismayed by his intervention. Some thought he had lost his senses; Lesley concluded he had become addicted to publicity. Romain, distraught, tried to defend himself: 'I've fulfilled my duty,' he protested to René Agid, and to Paul Pavlowitch, 'The image of Jean is still intact.'

Even as his fears of the worst that might happen to Jean turned into horror, Romain summoned his imaginative concentration to complete his final novel. The prodigious effort he must have put into applying his mind to work during the months before and after her death is well concealed. Character, language and metaphor are all of a piece in *Les Cerfs-volants*, a wartime fable as deftly constructed and light in touch as its title, its narrator the last of Romain's adolescents forced to make lonely choices that will define him as a man.

After correcting the text early in 1980, Romain sent a copy to the Chancellor of the Order of the Liberation. He received in response the accolade of an order for a special edition for the Companions, the only association with which he had ever identified. While Romain had not been able to write the intended historical record of the Resistance, his comrades gracefully accepted the integrity of his fiction. The same message, simple to grasp but hard to accept, had threaded through his writing ever since his *Education européenne* and was repeated here for the last time: 'The Nazis were *human*. And what was human about them was their inhumanity.' Men and women must first accept both the best and the worst in themselves; then only by their faith in the chimera of civilization and progress can they inch towards it in reality. His final book, dedicated 'A la Mémoire', to memory, was symbolically published on the eve of the fortieth anniversary of de Gaulle's famous first appeal to the French to fight on

The novel was well received. 'You have got to be mad to write another book on the last war, the Occupation and the Resistance!' began one review, but 'Here is a brave lesson in happiness, a superb defiance of bitterness.' 'Story of war and grand passion, perpetuation of a certain idea of France, the hand of the fabulist, fable-writer, fabulous Gary is back on full form, light as a kite,' *La Presse Nouvelle* concluded.

After that he had finished 'defecating' fiction, at least on the page. 'Finished with that shit,' he wrote to Pavlowitch.

Now that he was no longer working his anxiety and melancholia, aggravated by the tranquillizers and antidepressants he was taking, gave great concern to his friends. Apart from the tormenting presence of his dybbuk Ajar, he worried obsessively about his tax and financial problems, about his health, about Diego's well-being. A lifetime of skirmishing with the enemies of his baroque alternative reality had exhausted his resilience.

Suicide often featured in Romain's fiction and he had frequently been tempted to take his own life; Lesley was not the only one who had been taxed by his cries of wolf. Once René Agid had dashed to Paris after a desperate SOS from Romain, only to find when he arrived and burst in that Romain was lying in the bath smoking a cigar. Conversely, the prospect of ageing had always filled him with horror. René's son Yves believed that Romain was in revolt against the prospect of a pathetic death at the end of lingering old age. He didn't want to die like everyone else; he wanted to approach death 'with panache', like a character in his fiction.

Romain twice visited Nice, where he had first seen the Mediterranean and begun life as a Frenchman, meeting up with old friends. René advised him to declare the truth about Ajar as the only way to shift the burden of deceit that oppressed him so heavily. Yet Romain held back: Pavlowitch had become addicted to his role and proved himself a *picaro* equal to Romain inventing Ajar's narrative.

While he was in Nice, Romain called to see Lesley at Garavan. Her little pink villa perched between bay and rocky peaks made him nostalgic: he wanted her to find him somewhere to live, high up, overlooking the sea. He had already asked Ida d'Agostin to look for a house for him in Roquebrune. Lesley was dismayed to see how ill and aged

he looked. She said afterwards that she had set herself to find somewhere for him, implying that it might be for them both, but she must
have known it was no more than a dream.

Diego was Romain's great concern and consolation. Eugenia,
Diego's nanny, had died in 1976 and Romain was preoccupied by the
need for a maternal influence. In spring 1979, months before Jean died,
Leila Chellabi, a Moroccan-born actress and singer, had moved in with
Romain and Diego at the rue du Bac, but her presence could not
replace those they had lost. Diego had passed his baccalaureate the previous year and in July, after his seventeenth birthday, Romain took the
step of legally emancipating him. Father and son holidayed together in
Greece. Still Romain's anxieties tormented him. Friends were shocked
by his deterioration since Jean's death, the burden of grief made heavier
by its disturbingly inconclusive nature. A detailed autopsy raised more
questions than it answered; the inquest was reopened at Romain's
request but again failed to resolve the doubts.

That autumn he spoke of suicide so often that in retrospect the
question had shifted from 'if' to 'when'. 'I'm going to kill myself.
Tomorrow, in a week or in a month,' he told Annie Pavlowitch in
November.

The note that he wrote before he lay down and shot himself in his
bedroom, in the late afternoon of 3 December 1980, began: 'Nothing
to do with Jean Seberg. Lovers of broken hearts are requested to look
elsewhere . . .'

At his funeral Romain was honoured by the Companions of the
Liberation, the only fraternity he had ever treasured, in the chapel of
the church of Saint-Louis at the Hôtel des Invalides. A special dispensation had to be arranged because he had committed suicide and no
mass was celebrated because he was a Jew. The coffin, draped with a
French flag and bearing his decorations on a velvet cushion, was carried to the sound of drumbeats by eleven uniformed airman, to the
courtyard where the mourners gathered. Among them were Jean
d'Ormesson, Maurice Druon, Claude Roy, his fellow writers; his
publishers Robert and Claude Gallimard; Claude Bourdet and other
Companions from the Liberation. The Secretary of State for Foreign
Affairs was there to represent the government. There was much weeping, especially among the women.

To replace the funeral mass Diego insisted on one concession to his father's unconventional past: the plangent voice of the Polish singer Anna Prucnal, delivering a slightly risqué Polish love song. The address was given by General Simon, Grand Chancellor of the Order of Liberation.

Lesley, wearing a fur shako, was there to mourn him, and accompanied his intimate family and friends to the cremation at Père Lachaise Cemetery afterwards. René Agid, who had been with Romain only three days before he shot himself, trying once more to find a way out of his anxieties, was missing, too devastated to attend.

Those closest to Romain struggled to accept his suicide. Just before Christmas, Diego told a journalist with heroic dignity: 'My father considered that he had nothing more to arrange, or to say or to do. His oeuvre was complete, he had no novel in progress. He had brought me to my bac which I passed last year. He judged that I had become a man. Then, he left.'

Perhaps by pulling the trigger Romain had drawn together all his conflicting identities in a single last defining act. The man who Yves Agid knew was always acting out one scene or another, prey to fantasies and fears, stricken by hypochondria and black melancholy; a fragile barque, yet one made of steel: 'This was also the man who went to war, who committed himself to de Gaulle, who knew very well what he was doing, and perhaps his suicide, too, is an image of that.'

Lesley was shocked and profoundly saddened by Romain's death, if not greatly surprised. She knew well his phobia about growing old, which was stronger than his fear of dying. In time she came to respect the way he put an end to his anxieties at the moment and in the manner he chose.

The following spring she heard from Diego that he proposed to fulfil his father's wish for his ashes to be scattered over the sea near Roquebrune. On 15 March Diego arrived at Garavan, carrying the urn and accompanied by Leila Chellabi. Turbulence followed Romain to the very end: it was raining, with choppy seas. Lesley was unwell with a bad cold, so only Leila Chellabi embarked with the ashes in the small boat that had been hired for the purpose. As it left the quay and steered out into the slapping waves, Diego looked away. Lesley, the survivor, stood beside the son she had never had, and through the mist that blurs all things but memory watched as the mortal remains of Romain's unquiet spirit were cast out to sea, to be cast over the seething surface of his Brother Ocean.

However, like a Shakespearean character who though mortally wounded persists in declaiming his speech, the man refused to die. Romain would not have been surprised, François Bondy's tribute suggested, by the 'fictional publicity' about him that went on proliferating after his death. 'Who knows what a full bibliography of his writings would look like?' Bondy wrote presciently, pointing to the 'weakness for literary hoaxes' that had led Romain to ask his old school friend to turn his 'autobiographical novel', *The Night Will be Calm*, into an extended interview by adding questions and comments.

On 3 July, Bondy was one of the guests on Bernard Pivot's book programme *Apostrophes*, devoted to Paul Pavlowitch's sensational revelation of the Ajar affair in his book *L'Homme que l'on croyait*, which had been hurriedly published without advance publicity by Fayard, revealing Romain's 'literary hoax' of the century. It was a riveting case of live news breaking and crackled with drama. Pavlowitch admitted that he had written the book because he had not been strong enough to remain silent and that Romain probably regarded the part he, Pavlowitch, had played as one of theft. Michel Tournier was awestruck by the power of Romain's creative urge which had poured forth so many works by both Ajar and Gary in his last years, and concluded that 'hoax' was a wholly inadequate term to describe an episode that encompassed both Romain's phenomenally successful rebirth as a new author and his suicide.

Bondy insisted that Romain had revealed yet another persona as the author of *Lady L.*, the one truly English novel he had written, thanks to his wife Lesley Blanch.

Pavlowitch had now broken his side of the agreement not to reveal the identity of Ajar. Diego, guarding his father's legacy, objected that the revelation was unauthorized and sensation-seeking; his lawyers revoked the contract, and Pavlowitch forfeited his entitlement to a share of Ajar's earnings.

Days later, Gallimard published Romain's thirty-page testament, *Vie et Mort d'Emile Ajar*. It ended, 'Je me suis bien amusé. Au revoir et merci.' ('I've enjoyed myself very much. Goodbye and thank you.')

Suddenly Romain's critics (who had not held back from hostile, even overtly anti-Semitic comments about him after his death) were compelled to swallow the discomfiting news that Ajar's gloriously inventive novels had been written by his apparently clapped-out Gaullist cousin, whose later works of fiction they had trashed with almost ritual pleasure. Once again the literary columns exploded with speculation, outrage and glee. Jacqueline Piatier, shocked, recalled the outright written denial that he was Ajar which Romain had given her for publication in *Le Monde*. Ajar was a money-spinner, so who got the profits? *Libération* demanded. The whole exercise was born out of 'Yiddish Angst', Jean-Marie Rouart concluded in *Le Quotidien de Paris*. Simone Gallimard issued a statement announcing that she had known nothing about the hoax, but Ajar's admirers had nothing to regret; his work was sufficient to itself, whoever had written it.

'Two souls dwelled, Faust-like, in his breast,' reflected Bondy, 'and he put an end to one before finally putting an end to the other.'

Although Lesley had watched the Mediterranean receive Romain's ashes, his spirit did not rest quietly in his watery grave. On the contrary, he came to haunt her more after his death than while he was alive. Biographers, journalists, television researchers and PhD students made their way to Garavan to quiz her about her late ex-husband, trying to understand and explain the conflicted protean individual to whom she had been married for fifteen years. All of his books in French were reissued and migrated in bulk to the bookshop shelves, fulfilling his ambition as they never had in his lifetime. (Volume was the mark of success, never mind the quality, he had told Lesley when she urged him to spend longer on polishing his fiction.)

Perhaps the greatest of many paradoxes about Romain Gary concerns the posthumous growth in moral stature of his work. In 1976, at a low point in his shady imbroglio with Pavlowitch-Ajar, he had attended the funeral of his hero André Malraux, France's first minister of culture, honoured in death. As Romain joined the Companions of the Liberation in the memorial ceremony at the great courtyard of the Louvre, did he muse on the contrast between the pomp and glory awarded to the French statesman, and the devilish nest of lies about himself that was about to be released in *Pseudo*? The imbalance between the two men's status then was indeed profound. Yet by a strange trick, posterity has dramatically reversed the perspective. Malraux's novels live on but, without his bizarre charismatic living presence, his intellectual reputation has dwindled, tainted by self-invention. Romain, conversely, never set himself up as a cultural savant and his career was as fractured as his early life was peripatetic. He didn't use his wartime past to enhance his status; rather the reverse, in fact, where Tonton Macoute was concerned. He spent his last years in terror of exposure for fraud. Yet the uncomfortable truths about humanity which he learnt early in life and which sustained all his fiction, have come to earn honour and respect for his oeuvre in his adopted homeland. Again in contrast to Malraux, succeeding posthumous revelations about his outlandish personal history, far from damning his reputation, have paradoxically burnished the legend, enhancing the cult standing of Gary-Ajar in France and Eastern Europe, if not worldwide.

Although Romain had rarely been backward in talking about himself, he scrupulously avoided two subjects. He never made literary capital out of his war record and after their divorce he never mentioned his first wife. His silence about Lesley was no doubt profoundly offensive to her, but less obviously it was also a mark of respect: he knew he could trust her to handle his dark materials. They might stab each other to the heart before they would reveal the other's secrets. Beyond the grave he left her free to mythologize him as she chose. She reverted to calling herself Madame Gary, or Madame Blanch Gary, lightly asserting that 'in France it improves my place at table', and returned to another great love: Pierre Loti.

14

Loti-Land

It is good to know the truth and to speak it; but it is better to know the truth and to speak about the palm trees.

Arab proverb

LESLEY WAS ALWAYS inclined to swim against the tide of fashion. When she told Philip Ziegler who would be the subject of her next biography, he sampled Loti's books with growing dismay and warned her that this sort of period charm would leave the British public cold, while French readers disliked having their own writers explained to them by the English. Loti's perfumed tales of exotic doomed romance had been immensely popular during his lifetime in the fin de siècle era of the Third Republic. Proust could quote him by the page; writers more worldly than 'le sublime illettré', as Anatole France described him, envied the rapturous innocence of his prose. But in post-colonial times his novels were derided for their romantic excess and kitsch exoticism (although Philip Mansel, introducing a later edition of Lesley's biography, absolves Loti from imperialism, the cardinal offence of orientalism).

Lesley refused to be deterred. Loti was her avatar: an earlier explorer of the terrain that would be identified as hers, 'the role of the heart in "the kingdom of the mind"'. His exotic landscapes could have served as maps for her imagination. His wanderlust, his voluptuous sensitivity to *genius loci*, the longing for the Orient and the Islamophilia that made him believe he had been born half Arab, the fusion of his passion for a woman and the city of Istanbul which inspired no less than three novels (*Les Désenchantées*, the third and by common consent the worst, ran to 400 editions), were all qualities that she might almost have inherited from him. She shared his passionate nostalgia for the past, his way of using travel to free his imagination (reversing Dr Johnson's maxim), and his descriptive artistry (like Lesley, he was as dextrous with a paintbrush as with words).

Fantasy and escape were the two driving forces she identified in Loti's character: who else does that bring to mind? The lonely child, half stifled by his adoring female household, daydreamed incessantly of running away to sea like his elder brother. Eventually Loti got what he wanted, as he usually would. During a long career in the French navy he began to write his delirious romances, set in the far places to which his voyages had taken him: Tahiti, Turkey, Japan, Senegal. Pierre Loti was a pseudonym adopted for Rarahu, his Tahitian lover, who found it easier to pronounce than his real name, Julien Viaud. Lesley's phrase 'the wilder shores of love' could have been coined with him in mind, although his formula became so repetitive that one critic protested, 'Mais les mariages de Loti se font partout.' His adoring public devoured them all, as they did his later novels about Brittany and his travelogues of expeditions to Morocco, India, Persia and Angkor Wat.

When *Pierre Loti: A Portrait of an Escapist* was published in France, Lesley insisted in a rare appearance on French television that she had undertaken it for her mother, who had never travelled except through Loti's books and had bequeathed her love of them to Lesley. Her dedication, though, was to Sacheverell Sitwell, another exoticist, whose equally outmoded status concerned Lesley no more than Loti's. She spent weeks of research at the Bibliothèque Nationale in Paris. In pursuit of her labour of love she persuaded Susan Train to be her chauffeur and companion; Train readily agreed to a road trip around the countryside of the Charente Maritime and Saintonge where Loti had lived. At the family house in Rochefort Lesley met his relatives, who still occupied private quarters there, and established a close rapport with Madame Samuel Loti-Viaud, his daughter-in-law, who rightly detected that Loti's secrets would be safe with this unlikely elderly visitor whose clipped English accent belied her perceptive understanding and sympathy for the man. Lesley was invited to spend a week at Bakhar Etchea, The Solitary House, at Hendaye in the Basque country where Loti lived in later life, and was allotted a table to work there.

Mme Loti-Viaud readily unburdened herself about her gifted, conflicted father-in-law and her frank talk about him ignited Lesley's enthusiasm: Loti's granddaughter, Christiane Pierre-Loti Viaud, remembered the 'louanges de Loti', their rapturous praise. At the same time Loti's family appreciated that despite Lesley's age (she was nearly eighty) they were dealing with an unusual intelligence. Christiane, returning to the room where Lesley sat working at her table, glanced into her clear blue eyes and was unnerved by a gaze of such shrewdness and depth that she never forgot it: 'She wanted to *capture* something in me,' she remembered. 'She was looking at me but assessing me at the same time.'

At the Rochefort house Lesley marvelled at the Turkish, Arab and Japanese rooms, the Chinese pavilion, the Renaissance hall, the Louis XVI salon and the private mosque in which Loti indulged his oriental fantasies. She empathized with the cult of *things* whereby he fetishized his past (the tombstone of his Turkish love was shipped home with crateloads of mementoes, overwhelming his dismayed family). She pored over frenzied love letters from his fans, his paintings, pictures of his adored cats whom he regarded as people, just as she did: some of them had sailed round the world with him, others he photographed in bonnets and frocks and had their own printed visiting cards.

Loti's rage for life made him an intoxicating subject, always bursting the bounds of his literary persona. Lesley treated his manifest peculiarities with indulgence. His intense dislike of his tiny, weedy figure ('I was not my type') led him to take several months' leave from his distinguished naval service for body-building training as a circus acrobat (years later Frank Harris saw him turning perfect backward somersaults for Princess Alice in the palace at Monaco). His use of high heels, rouge and kohl eyeliner were all apparently tolerated by his superior officers, along with his custom of dressing up in ethnic costume or even as a naval rating. When calling on his friend Sarah Bernhardt in the intervals of her performances he preened himself in her enormous headdresses. Yet he was surprisingly attractive to the opposite sex, according to Lesley fell in love with one woman after another, and fathered at least two families.

Loti was a sexual Houdini whose ambivalent identity was as contradictory as so much else in his character. By today's standards it seems perverse *not* to surmise that he was gay, given his habit of bringing along a handsome silent rating to receptions in the chic Paris salons, not to mention his lingering sketches of the virile bare-chested seamen who sailed round the world with him. Yet notwithstanding Gide's and

Cocteau's emphatic conclusion that Loti had been exclusively homosexual and that his Turkish love, Aziyadé, was a boy, Lesley (like his later French biographer) found no proof in the letters, intimate journals and eye-witness accounts. She accepted Loti, not so much at face value (given the heavy make-up), but *as he wanted to be seen*. With Lesley it was ever thus.

His horror of passing time and the inevitability of death emerged in the ingenuous expression of perverse desires (his 'charnel' fantasy of being united with his loved one in the grave, buried on top of one another so that their bodies would mingle in decomposition). Yet as Lesley pointed out, his wallowing regret for lost loves and exotic haunts hardly deserved sympathy, since looking back in an ecstasy of melancholy was his greatest pleasure.

Living for so long with Loti, she could reflect on the insights that his complex persona offered to the mystery of Romain, whose suicide had jolted him to the forefront of her thoughts. Not only did Loti obsessively escape from himself in pseudonyms and physical disguises, but she also revealed a parallel in his close friend Lucien Jousselin's aperçu about his sexual character. When Loti agonized about a new amorous escapade that had plunged him from ecstasy into rejection and despair, Jousselin ('Plumkett' in Loti's fiction) argued that, having worked himself into a frenzy with his own verbal outpourings, he should *use* his tumultuous emotions in his writing, then take refuge in his family's unconditional loyalty. Loti craved a state of high emotion to feed his work, yet in order to write he also needed a background of stability. The fleeting intensity of his love affairs, Plumkett added, was a result of his multiple personality; a woman would respond passionately to one identity, only to retreat when he showed her another that was not at all the same. Although Lesley was describing Loti, she surely had another model and her own experience in mind.

After Romain's suicide Christiane Pierre-Loti Viaud made a sympathetic phone call to Lesley at Menton. 'Laissez-moi parler sur ce temps!' Lesley told her fiercely. The urge to talk about Romain was overwhelming and Viaud listened to her stories for as long as the force of memory drove her. Nearly two decades later Viaud read Lesley's *Romain, un regard particulier* and recognized in it the exact same anecdotes that she had heard on the phone after his death.

As always Lesley overran in length on Loti and laboured for weeks to bring her manuscript down to size. Most of the cutting was done in London, where she stayed with Pat Creed in Tite Street, wheeling her unwieldy progeny in and out of the flat on a porter's trolley for painful sessions with Philip Ziegler at Collins. Ziegler was ruthless on the tangential detail that Lesley was addicted to: 'She would come back in tears, weeping, because he had just struck through page after page after page.' Often she worked in bed, consoling herself with Mars Bars and other treats that she missed in France. Pat, who was out at work all day, left Lesley to come and go as she pleased; sometimes she would visit Eden and Marston Fleming, staying overnight in their garden studio. Pat held small dinner parties, inviting 'Lesley's Arabists' or mutual friends and acquaintances from English or American *Vogue*.

Although the effort of cutting the text by a third left her exhausted, Lesley was still game for a celebratory junket for *Sheba* in 1982 with Henry Clarke to Muscat and Oman (where she was still on hobnobbing terms with heads of state, 'perfect darlings'). The commission fell through at the last minute because the Sultan was away, leaving Clarke to rage that he had lost a thirty-page assignment for *Vogue*. Lesley resigned herself to recovering from bronchitis and writing an introduction for the book, which still needed more work. She continued to labour over a final draft at Garavan, taking it with her to London in early March 1983.

Harcourt Brace published her *Pierre Loti: A Portrait of an Escapist* in the United States, where it won plaudits in the *New York Times* and *Washington Post*. In London the few reviews were favourable if bemused by Lesley's intentions: in the *TLS* the Rev. Philip Thody observed that her 'excellent biography' often read 'like a very good novel about an unhappy man', adding that Loti was fortunate indeed in having such a sympathetic biographer. For Ziegler this response was not unexpected. 'Lesley was not much of a one about digging below the surface to extract the truth,' he conceded, 'or not the *factual* truth – it was the essential truth she was looking for.' (The French were more interested in Loti's non-literary aspects; when the translation was published in 1966 she was asked to write about his mother for *Le Figaro* and about his house for *Paris Match*.)

After seeing the English and American editions into print in 1983, mindful of the occasion Lesley took a trip to Loti-land. Fifteen years after her previous visit she found Istanbul much changed and his beloved Broussa transformed into a suburb, but she still loved the tempo and manners that she met there.

Nonetheless, at almost eighty Lesley was bound to accept that her energy had limits. She shelved a project on Richard Lovelace that she had been entertaining. Despite her robust constitution her brittle bones made her physically fragile; that November she tripped on an uneven paving stone in Ventimiglia and shattered her knee, which had to be wired together. She was immobilized for weeks and briefly wondered whether she would ever walk again.

To distract herself from this morbid prospect she started gathering bits of writing and recollections for a travel/food book, which was taken by her old publisher John Murray. The result, brought out in 1989, was *From Wilder Shores: The Tables of My Travels* (a wag at Murray's wanted to call it *The Wilder Shores of Lunch*), described as a sketchbook of 'the dishes, places and people . . . encountered while on the move through life'. Half a dozen chapters were worked up from recent features for assorted magazines – well into her eighties Lesley was still contributing to *Food and Wine*, *Gourmet*, *House and Garden* and *Architectural Digest*.

The result was a hotchpotch of Edwardian breakfasts and suet puddings, bland 'eating for France' in the diplomatic corps, Hollywood banquets, the Istanbul idyll sweetened by sticky Turkish pastries, ecstatic memories of Afghanistan (goat stew), and a twenty-four-hour dalliance with a shaggy Yugoslav partisan who held up the train to Istanbul (she forgot what they ate). What it did evoke was the keen appetite for experience that had allowed her to savour hunger as well as satiation. She magicked a three-course meal from her frugal Roquebrune larder and the village shop, starting with a 'rich, swarthy' tapenade and building to a finale of sugary yellow courgette-flower fritters; she recommended the 'careless luxury' of picnics served with assorted silver christening mugs and cutlery. Following the book's publication a few cross readers wrote to complain that some of the recipes were inaccurate, and she blamed Murrays for marketing it as a recipe book instead of a food memoir.

Lesley did not fade with age. She was selfish and not at all a nice little old lady, she warned visitors. Her solipsism sometimes made her peremptory with 'lower orders', because she didn't think about them. Answering a Proust's Questionnaire, she said she most easily forgave the sin of rudeness, since she was so often rude herself. Once she had made up her mind, she never went back on her decision. She had christened her house 'Kuçuk Teppe', Turkish for little hill, to chime with the street name, Chemin de Vallaya (little valley), and majestically ignored the fact that the Mairie had renamed the road after Katherine Mansfield, whom she disliked; she either used the old name or misspelt the new one as Catherine.

Like the Cheshire cat she would surge into sharp focus in an unforgettable interview or profile, usually to publicize her books, then vanish for months or years. Journalists who interviewed her were almost invariably enchanted and sometimes devastated later. The writer Valerie Grove, then a frenetically busy profile writer for the *Sunday Times*, was sent to Menton to talk to Lesley about *From Wilder Shores*. After a 'ghastly journey' of delays to and at the airport, she eventually stepped off the 6 p.m. train from Nice and went straight to Lesley's house. 'All beautiful', her diary notes recorded, 'food, aroma, quotes, atmosphere. Mosquito bites.'

'It was one of the most memorable interviews of my life,' she remembered, like many others before and since. 'I was captivated. I immediately wanted to live in a house cluttered by memories. It was completely beguiling.' The following weekend, still bewitched by her visit, Valerie laboured over a brandade of cod, '*humming* with garlic', to Lesley's recipe, for guests to Sunday lunch. In early July, in between interviewing the railway union leader Jimmy Napp and Benazir Bhutto, she wrote and polished a joyous piece on Lesley's new cookbook (someone who described cheeses as *emotional* and publishers as *inert* deserved special attention) and handed it in to the paper, for publication that Sunday. A few days later she hurried to the publisher's launch party to be frigidly dismissed by Lesley, who was outraged to have been relegated to a half-page about her book in the food section, instead of a lengthy interview.

Nobody got past the exterior, but Maureen Cleave's profile for Lesley's (official) eightieth birthday in 1987 nicely registered the full wattage of her robust appetites and wayward charm. First the atmosphere:

> The house itself is invisible, submerged in a sea of green, for she leaves the cultivation of the more garish Mediterranean blooms to her neighbours. She lives here with her two cats and a small white dove but

whatever cosy image these words bring to mind does not survive long in her company. The fact that she is now 80 is better reason to relish the spice of life.

That morning a builder working on the house next door had gone mad. 'Leaping into my garden shaking like castanets and yelling "Murder, Murder" – naked but for a gold necklace and a small pouch in front containing his treasure. . . The doctor was somewhere on a yacht so we had to call the *pompiers* and oh, the fussation! Here you see me, human wreckage.'

She paused for effect and because the evening train to Strasbourg shot past yards from where we sat concealed behind thickets of bamboo and cypress, olive and fig. The white dove fluttered in alarm. A toad croaked in the garden and from the house came the strains of Turkish flutes and mingled smells of incense and roasting meat.

Mrs Blanch wore a Tunisian caftan of silk the blue of a thrush's egg and a necklace of lapis lazuli. The French Riviera is, of course, no longer smart and her elegant friends have moved inland to build houses with what she calls swimming baths, but she herself has a teasing allure and ineffable style and she is just as much fun as a roomful of exotic people.

Then the writing:

A reviewer once conceded that her prose might be purple but it glowed, and indeed it does; *it burns into the kindred soul* [my italics] . . . It is hard to classify her as a writer, unless as a scholarly romantic in a school of her own. She has a way of bringing the past and the present together that is peculiarly exciting.

One of the worst things to endure was the death of old friends, human or animal. George Cukor died in 1983 and Rebecca West, another prized occasional friend, the same year; Gerald de Gaury in 1984. Henry Clarke, increasingly irascible, refused to acknowledge his leukaemia and held out until the age of seventy-seven in 1996. When mourning a much loved companion she retreated into savage despair and was inconsolable.

However, she had many devoted friends, was venerated by scholarly admirers and could rarely resist exotic oriental guests even when they imported tensions to the household, bringing the cats out in eczema. Her 'peasant dwelling in a bamboo grove', as she was apt to describe it, attracted a flow of visitors. Her godson Morgan Mason would visit with his family. Lorna Sage stopped off to see her on her way to Italy.

The Persian writer and singer Shusha Guppy interviewed her for the *Paris Review* and became a devoted friend. Susan Train and Georgia de Chamberet saw her often and eased her existence, as did Beatrix Miller, her former editor at Brogue. Alice Wooledge Salmon, another American journalist, Bettina McNulty of *House and Garden*, and Bettina's husband Henry were among many visitors. Her agent was the late Pat Kavanagh whose husband Julian Barnes's affinity with France, 'embedded in another country' as she herself had been, aroused her sympathy. Pat Creed stayed only once, deterred by Lesley's (deliberately?) ingenuous remarks about the 'darling little rat running across the ceiling carrying an egg'.

She knew so many people over the years that she was inundated with requests to recall the recently departed: 'I tell them I met everyone and knew no one.' Lesley was fiercely partisan in her loyalties and her friends responded in kind. She cultivated Arabists, Russian historians, textile connoisseurs and other specialists in arcane fields who could feed her omnivorous interests. They returned the compliment, relishing her wit, diverse knowledge and originality, the scholars among them defending her from dissenters' grumbles that she was an orientalist who sometimes made things up.

Lesley always had plenty of people to catch up with: she never lost her gift for cultivating the right people and meeting new ones. Philippa Scott, traveller, Turkey hand and oriental textiles connoisseur, was enlisted by a phone call from Lesley to find her a violet Persian *khalat*. She arrived at the address in Chelsea to find that her new client had come down with flu and had tried but failed to cancel the appointment. Lesley answered the door in a bedroom *déshabille* of men's long-johns dyed orange, a short Persian dressing gown covered with blowsy roses, and a shocking-pink turban shot through with tinsel thread, which disarmed her visitor.

Her visits to London were events to celebrate and in her eighties her presence could still turn a meeting into a party. Her Lebanese friend Nabil Saidi, then Sotheby's special adviser on oriental manuscripts and Islamic art, hosted lunches at the Ritz for Lesley with Philippa Scott and Countess 'Patsy' Jellicoe, also an Islamic art historian. Once Saidi smuggled an Ottoman candlestick to the table to enhance the oriental theme, prompting Lesley to contribute her enormous Ottoman brooch, pinned to a bread roll, for extra glitter.

Although hostile to the concept of children in general she was very good with individual offspring, making no concession to the age difference and indeed somehow becoming their age herself. Philip Ziegler's children, found her 'enchanting and strange and rather dotty. . . . She was wonderful with children provided that she didn't have to do anything about them. The thought of Lesley changing a nappy is too grisly to conceive,' he added. She consulted the Erlanger boys, who called her 'Les', about moving to Tunisia: too cold in winter, they advised. She was fond of the young sons of Adam Munthe, grandson of Axel Munthe, and his French wife Nelly, Élie de Rothschild's daughter, who specialized in oriental textiles. The story went that the Munthe parents, who had left Lesley to babysit, returned home to find the little boys wide awake and sitting on her lap, enthralled by an unexpurgated tale of herself and a sheikh on a sand dune: 'Again! Again!' they cried.

'Staff' problems were an ongoing saga. Lesley could accommodate a couple (chauffeur-gardener and cook-maid), but one or other invariably turned out to be unsuitable. Alice, from Hull, was a long-standing if fiery helpmeet, despite a cooling-off period when her English husband was replaced by a French carpenter who monopolized her attention. Mireille Goërand, daughter of Ida d'Agostin, remained a friend and ally in Roquebrune. Yvonne Molinari, in Ventimiglia, typed for her. When all else failed, Darling Self found consolation in the sustaining presence of her beautiful things.

Sic transit gloria mundi. At about two in the morning on the night of 6–7 April 1994, Lesley was awoken by a crash: the house was on fire and burning roof timbers were falling through her living-room ceiling. A netting cage for her doves outside prevented her escape through the bedroom window. Somehow she managed to get out through the smoke-filled living room to the garden, where from a safe distance she watched the house ignite like a torch. Soon afterwards the front wall collapsed. The fire brigade arrived quickly and directed two hoses on to the blaze, but it was too late to save the villa, which was 'effectively one hundred per cent destroyed', according to the report in *Nice-Matin*. Lesley and her housekeeper were treated for smoke inhalation by ambulance paramedics, but not hospitalized.

The next morning she stood ankle-deep in the ashes of her roofless living room, still in her nightdress with a borrowed shawl clutched

over it. The cats, her greatest anxiety, had survived. She had burnt
Romain's letters long before. But the gorgeous nest of colours and
textures and patterns and learning that had been an extension of herself
was so much smut and floating ashes. She mourned her irreplaceable
library of oriental books willed to New College, Oxford; her icons
and rugs and samovars; her gros-point cushions, oriental robes and
jewellery – all the treasured relics from her travels. Among the few
remnants were her wedding rings (three, she insisted, deliberately not
explaining); inside the remains of a tin, rare photographs of Romain as
a little boy and his mother when she was young and glamorous; and
Lesley's painted portrait of Mortimer, the ginger cat who had lived
with them in St Leonard's Terrace.

'Everybody was awfully kind, they rushed round and did what they
could. The first [thing] they said to me was what do you want? I said
I want a handbag. You can't live without one.' A crocodile-skin handbag was duly supplied by the Rothschilds. Some of Lesley's friends
commented that they could at least have afforded a bed.

She briefly considered moving to England before rejecting the
option because of the quarantine ban on her cats. It was exile for life,
then. At ninety Lesley installed herself in a flat near by and, after endur-
ing the mind-numbing procedure of getting all her documents replaced
('and of course they're very paper-minded here'), embarked on lengthy
negotiations concerning her insurance claims on the reconstruction of
her house over the ruins of the old one. There ensued long months of
supervision on the building site where the work was carried out to
minimum insurance standards by workmen from across the frontier,
who took scant pride in the results. Her lost Turkish fireplace was irreplaceable and the disproportions of the new rooms nagged at her.
Replacement furniture was vamped up with a paintbrush or dressed
with throws and cushions. She transferred a few treasures from
Roquebrune, followed by more when her summer eyrie had to go; she
could no longer manage the steep alleys and steps, unreachable by cars.

Through force of will she had summoned her house back into existence. At John Murray they packed up parcels of books which were
sent out to substitute for some of her lost library, and once her desk
was back in the alcove she returned to work (motto: 'Get up and get
on with it'). The subject she chose to console herself with after her loss
was none other than Romain. Since his death his reputation had

continued to inflate and expand, so she hoped that a short memoir might stem the flow of requests for information from students, scholars and (much more to her liking) enthusiasts for his work.

Romain, un regard particulier (1998) was published only in France, where his readership was growing exponentially, but her English text dominated the idiomatic French translation. Her contribution to the Gary canon was a sequence of scenes, reflections and minutiae of their life together: a telling insider's account of Romain before he found fame and as he adjusted to it, when the man she knew was in a state of perpetual flux until the legend gelled. The overall impression is of an album of impish, finely drawn cartoon sketches of Romain and herself, like her Christmas cards illustrations while they were married. She readily cites his Bluebeard propensities (from Los Angeles he sent her, while in the throes of writing *The Sabres of Paradise*, to inspect the French embassy in Venice before he applied for his next post, but by the time she got back he had already changed his mind. . . he vetoed postings to Tunis or Damascus because he wouldn't have access to a ready supply of mistresses). On the many mysteries that Romain left to billow around himself, she was elusive or pleaded ignorance: leave him to his myths, Lesley insisted, just as she had insisted about Loti and would always insist about herself.

The book about Romain was the last she ever completed, though not her final subject, which was Darling Self. Her memoirs were still in progress when she died.

After the millennium, her earlier books began to seep back into print, first quietly, then to growing acclaim. There was confusion about Lesley's approaching centenary since in her entry for *Who's Who* she had made herself three years younger than she really was. As the date approached she discreetly reverted to her actual age without referring to the disparity. In 2001, *Journey into the Mind's Eye* was reissued by Sickle Moon Books, then transferred to Eland's list of travel classics. Lesley made a fuss when she discovered that the phrase 'fragments of an autobiography' had been dropped off the cover. But she treasured Philip Mansel's glowing tribute, which consecrated the myth of the Traveller while ranking this as 'one of the finest English books about Russia', appealing to 'the heart, the mind and the senses'. The same year she was awarded the MBE for services to literature ('Too little too late,' she commented laconically). More of her books were reissued; *Harriette Wilson's Memoirs* came next in 2003, followed by *The Wilder Shores of Love.*

A momentum was building, bringing the deep satisfaction of being picked up by a new generation and carried forward towards the only end of age. A year later the first ever translation of *Journey into the Mind's Eye* appeared in France, beautifully rendered into French by Guillaume Villeneuve who became a friend and a Lesley Blanch convert. Billed as 'at once autobiographical account, travelogue and tragicomic novel', *Voyage au coeur de l'esprit* made a splash partly on account of the glamorous wartime wedding photo of herself, alone but victorious, on the cover, despite Lesley's protests that the picture had nothing to do with the book. At last Madame Blanch Gary was applauded in France as a writer as well as Romain's wife. In Britain of course it was the other way round, Romain's books having vanished entirely.

Héloise d'Ormesson, Lesley's publisher at Denoël, said she had backed the book not only for its fine writing but also on the hunch that Lesley would appeal to French readers as a certain stereotype of the eccentric English female traveller, never mind if the template wasn't an accurate fit. Her age was newsworthy in itself and at ninety-nine Lesley was prepared to do her own promotion. D'Ormesson was proved correct: a succession of interviewers made the pilgrimage to Garavan and all returned with a similar respectful portrait of a *grande dame* (the French stereotype required grandeur), recalling the scandalous life of the 'high-born, well-brought-up libertine' from an 'affluent London suburb' whose rebellious course had been set forever by her childhood passion for the Traveller. The Run-Away Game that Lesley had played as a little girl, as one interviewer acutely remarked, was the art of living on two planes that existed in friendly rivalry with one another – reality and dreams – and in her hundredth year Lesley was still a champion at the game. Although maintaining the legend had become important to her, it was out in the world, self-sustaining and irresistible, and she rarely mentioned it herself. In any case that was only a fragment of a rich and racy past from which she could summon so many others. She had gone beyond the limits of art, in Romain's phrase, to become her own living masterpiece, enframed within her chosen landscape.

Lesley was delighted to see her books coming back into print, despite the work involved. Her young friend Turi Munthe, commissioning briefly for I.B. Tauris, was responsible for new editions of *The Sabres of Paradise* next, and *Pierre Loti*, each with a respectful and knowledgeable introduction by a specialist in the field (Philip Marsden and Philip Mansel respectively). On the other hand, interviews and photographs required a tremendous amount of scene-setting beforehand, bringing conflicting views about her 'rediscovery'. She braced herself for visitors, fretting about the state of the house or garden; to a clumsy reassurance that one had come to see Lesley, not her plants, she responded sharply: 'I *am* my plants.' Photographers were a special torture: Lesley, a familiar of Horst, Beaton and Clarke, expected hours of styling beforehand and was shocked when press photographers expected to snap her in thirty minutes without helping to arrange her turban and beads. After a vicious attack of shingles (St Anthony's Fire, she called it, making even that dread condition sound romantic), she was self-conscious about her hair, which she now wore short and fringed; it suited her aquiline features better than the lacquered curls of earlier decades.

Profiles continued to appear at intervals, the writers carefully vetted beforehand. Even when confusion began to set in, her quick-witted answers would begin before the questions had finished. She never lost her subversive edge or sense of the ridiculous. She deftly avoided repeating herself, and her commanding manner and self-mocking name-dropping completed the disarming effect. Occasionally she allowed herself stabs of regret at the memory of roads not taken: she should have found a little house in the Hollywood hills and stayed on in Los Angeles, or married the descendant of Shamyl, or the Turkish ambassador she had met through the Rothschilds, whose lovely house in the Levant full of beautiful things chimed exactly with her taste, before he so inconveniently died. However, she was just as likely to dismiss men as useless: 'They're awfully babyish, you know, and vain. They're a lot of dead weight half the time.' She was as opinionated and interested in the world as ever: disgusted by the Bush–Blair Coalition invasion of Iraq, impressed by the Islamic world's respect for the aged. She readily admitted that she despised everything in the modern world except anaesthetics, and had come to prefer animal to human company.

Her memoirs continued slowly, with many interruptions. Perpetually approached by researchers to recall the great and the good, she became understandably jealous of her time. Naturally she was opposed to a biography in any normal sense of the term, although at one stage she considered a collaborative effort. The only person beside herself capable of bequeathing her an acceptable past was Romain, who had already done that in *Lady L.*

Romain, meanwhile, was rising from the dead yet again, his flickering genie summoned ominously this time by an enormous new biography whose author didn't respect 'image'. It appeared in February 2004, casting a shadow over Lesley's approaching centenary. The author had done formidable research and spoken to everybody. In *Le Nouvel Observateur* Anne Crignon, who had recently interviewed Lesley about *Coeur de l'esprit*, listed her among the half-dozen people closest to Romain and raised the valid question: 'Were they aware, in entrusting to her [the biographer] letters, documents and journals kept hidden from the curious until this day, that they would be complicit in this operation of demystification?' 'The biographer's métier is pitiless,' she concluded of this assault by a thousand pinpricks.

Lesley, who had generously given time to all of Romain's biographers when asked, was appalled by the dissection of her marriage and divorce, spattering blood over her carefully composed chiaroscuro. She might have been less saddened by the relentless itemizing of his love affairs, having herself been open about Romain's womanizing, than by the revelation of his birthplace as Vilnius, not Moscow: this was a stab at the heart of the preordained Russian kismet that he represented to her. In addition the book had gone into print apparently missing a fact-checking stage, which rendered much of the research unstable (a last jinx thrown by Romain, perhaps?). Lesley had been quoted without cross-checks on dates and remembered detail, not always her forte, leaving her awkwardly placed to protest about muddles.

Lesley's triumphant revival, gallantly overseeing the reissue of her books and presiding over interviews, was interrupted. Her agitation was such that she was distracted from preparations for the centenary party that was thrown for her in the gardens of the Clos du Perronet in Menton three weeks after her birthday. Nonetheless she dressed regally in a scarlet and gold silk robe, draped a pink tasselled scarf round her head *à la turque* and, seated on a wicker throne, held court for her distinguished guests who had travelled across Europe to pay homage. In London a window of the Travellers' Bookshop in

Notting Hill was dressed with photographs and books devoted to her centenary.

From then on, the prospect receded of a biography of Lesley authorized by herself and this project was singled out for cannon-shot in one of her last interviews.

The French government appointed her an Officier de l'Ordre des Arts et des Lettres in her centenary year. She still held potent sway over her scattered dominion of courtiers and vassals who loved, feared and obeyed her. She was as choosy as ever about her visitors. Those who were admitted wooed her with gifts as they would an oriental sultana, racking their brains beforehand about what to take: it needn't be expensive, but it must be *special*. In the same spirit, friends pooled their presents for a Christmas stocking, to be carried out to her.

At the end of her life as at the beginning, she awoke to and was lulled to sleep by railway sounds close by. The flight of garden steps became difficult and her fragile bones made sorties a hazard. After two attacks of pneumonia the garden was decreed out of bounds for her in winter. She hated the immobility that encroached with being old: 'Old age is not for cissies,' she said, quoting Bette Davis. As her horizons dwindled the thought of her mother's lonely last years in London weighed on her. She admitted to missing London, especially in winter when visitors stopped coming.

On 4 May 2007, Lesley Blanch fell ill and sank into a coma. She died during the night of Sunday 6 and Monday 7 May 2007, a month short of her 103rd birthday. Until the last she maintained the same standards that she had accorded to herself and to others throughout her life, getting dressed and applying lipstick for a physiotherapist's visit almost on the eve of her last decline. Not long before, she had refused an invitation to appear in a television programme about Cecil Beaton on the grounds that she was too old, adding: 'A year ago, at a hundred and one, I would have done it.'

The funeral was held in the village church at Roquebrune, next door to the Aladdin's cave she had cherished. In September Shusha Guppy, Philip Ziegler and Philip Mansel were among the speakers at the memorial celebration held for her at the Lawrence Kellys' house in London, and the former Shahbanou of Iran sent a recorded message of sympathy.

A plaque was installed outside the door that had once let in the Mediterranean light for her and Romain at Roquebrune. In the obituaries Romain Gary and the Traveller competed as her greatest influence.

Notes

LB = Lesley Blanch
RG = Romain Gary
JM = John Murray London, Albemarle Street, publishers' archives
GCC = George Cukor Collection, Department of Special Collections, Academy of Motion Picture Arts and Sciences' Margaret Herrick Library, Los Angeles
BLJD = Bibliothèque Littéraire Jacques Doucet, Paris

Epigraphs

xi The story of a life: Muriel Spark, *Loitering with Intent*, London: Virago, 2007, p. 41.
xi And what Russian: Nikolai Gogol, *Dead Souls*, trans. David Magarshack, London: Penguin Classics, 1961, p. 258.
xi Admittedly the truth: André Malraux, *Antimemoirs*, trans. Terence Kilmartin, London: Penguin, 1967, p. 14.

Preface and Acknowledgements

xiv secrecy and gap: Rose Baring, interview with author, 27 April 2004.
xvi a wife-shaped void: Germaine Greer, *Shakespeare's Wife*, London: Bloomsbury, 2007, p. 4.
xvi In the biography: Fabrice Larat, *Romain Gary: Un itinéraire européen*, Chêne-Bourg: Editions Médecine et Hygiène, 1999, p. 5.

Prologue

3 the faculty of uttering facts: V.S. Pritchett, 'The Spanish Bed' in *On the Edge of the Cliff*, London: Chatto & Windus, 1979, p.49.

Chapter 1: The Run-Away Game

7 46 Grove Park Gardens: my thanks to Eileen Marino for showing me round the house.

8 still partly countryside: maps and ratepayers' lists, Parish of St Paul's Grove Park, Chiswick Public Library.

8 Culverden, one of the first houses: ibid.

8 moved in after their marriage, live-in maid: 1901 Census.

8 Because I couldn't get my own way: Alice Wooledge Salmon, obituary.

9 Mabel Martha Thorpe was born in Hackney: 1881 Census. Mabel Thorpe (aged five) was registered at 24 Lorne Terrace, Stoke Newington, with her mother Jenny Thorpe (thirty-two) from Bow, John (two) and Jenny (ten months).

9 Marriage to Walter: Mabel Martha Thorpe married Walter Blanch in Islington on 8 July 1900: marriage certificate.

9 James Blanch was a builder: James Blanch was registered as 'Junior Builder' in the 1863 Post Office London Directory and as 'Master Builder' in 1881.

10 the family still lived at 30 East Street: 1881 Census.

10 James Blanch's death took place at home on 3 August 1883: last will and testament.

10 an extremely capable businesswoman: ratepayers' lists for the Parish of St-George-the-Martyr, Holborn, February 1885, Holborn Public Library. Under the entry for 30/31 East Street, 'James' is crossed out and 'Miss Rhoda' inserted above the surname Blanch.

10 Rhoda was collecting the rent: ibid. By 1922 Rhoda Blanch owned nos. 21, 22, 30, 31 and 33 East Street. She also owned 18 Robert Street, a house and workshop at 2 and 4 Johns Mews and 16 Chapel Street. Emily Blanch had the leasehold on a house and shop at no. 11, and eventually bought the freehold.

11 a bit of a Gradgrind: Barnaby Rogerson, interview with author, 27 April 2004.

11 The family moved to Burlington Court: Ratepayers' lists, Parish of St Paul's Grove Park, Chiswick Public Library.

11 Rateable values: ibid.

11 horrid caged-in Victorian life: LB, interview with author, January 2003.

12 Ermyntrude the rabbit: ibid.

12 wherever the sky was all around: LB, *From Wilder Shores: The Tables of My Travels*, p. 60.

12 a very brilliant brain: LB, telephone interview with author, 31 July 2002.

12 threw his dinner jacket on the fire: Andrew Lycett, 'Seduced by Eastern Promise', *The Times* Review.

13 only one domestic servant: ratepayers' lists, Chiswick Public Library.

13 did almost everything in the kitchen: LB, interview with author, January 2003.

13 whose tray meals I enjoy: LB, *Round the World in Eighty Dishes*, dedication.

13 The solitary breakfast ritual: LB, *From Wilder Shores*, p. 5.

14 who could only travel through Loti: LB, interview with author, January 2003.

14 kindergarten school . . . the Misses Peeke: LB, *Journey into the Mind's Eye*, p. 23.

15 But to make everything that you will see and hear: Italo Calvino, *Hermit in Paris*, London: Jonathan Cape, 2003, p. 130.

16 Compared with the imperial territories: Virginia Nicholson, *Among the Bohemians*, p. 227.

16 Frances Partridge: ibid. Fantastically moving: ibid.

16 The new Trans-Siberian Railway: Eric Newby, *The Great Red Train Ride*, London: Weidenfeld & Nicolson, 1968, pp. 214–15.

17 picture of Imam Shamyl: LB, interview with author, January 2003.

18 Lesley's schooldays: St Paul's Girls' School archives. LB's personal file; bound copies of *Minutes of Meetings*; *The Paulina* (school magazine); Howard Bailes, *Once a Paulina . . . A History of St Paul's Girls' School*.

18 Miss Volkhovsky: LB, *Mind's Eye*, p. 31. She was the Callisthenics mistress, on St Paul's payroll list from January 1915.

18 muddle with brushes: LB, interview with author, January 2003.

18 some very nice pencil drawings: *The Paulina*, December 1918.

18 'Studio News' in *The Paulina* lists Lesley in the Royal Drawing Society Examination Honours for December 1916, July 1917 (bronze star 'for an original composition in colour') and December 1917.

19 Some Folk-Songs were also sung: ibid., December 1916.

19 a library you had to ask to get into: LB, interview with author, January 2003.

19 half of Lesley's fees transferred: *Minutes of Meetings*, 1917–22, 21 February 1919.

20 She had a best friend, Edna: Lesley's profile of 'Eden Box', aka Edna Fleming (*Harper's Bazaar*, Dec. 1949), recalled their thirty-year

friendship. This clashes with scanty information concerning Edna Fleming's chronology. Possibly the artist, like Lesley, made herself younger than she actually was.

20 her appreciation of Lee: LB, 'Vernon Lee's Italy', in *Under a Lilac-Bleeding Star*, p. 153.

20 Things were always made out to be so much worse: LB, interview with author, January 2003.

20 enrolled for a Fine Art Diploma at the Slade: with thanks to Wendy Kirkby, University College London Records Office.

21 Russian bonds: in 1986 a settlement was reached with most countries except France, where the debt would have drained Soviet coffers even without interest. Eventually Russia agreed to pay $400 million, less than 1 per cent of the debt.

22 managed to be gay and charming: LB, interview with author, January 2003.

22 transferred to a commercial art college: Andrew Lycett, interview with LB, *The Times*.

23 *Racecourse and Hunting Field* with drawings in colour by LB, Constable, 1931.

23 Becky Sharp was her favourite heroine: LB, Proust's Questionnaire (unpublished), interview with author, January 2003.

23 she was herself: LB (ed.), *The Game of Hearts: Harriette Wilson and Her Memoirs*, p. 6.

23 Harriette . . . was born witty. . .: ibid., p. 7.

24 I was very pretty, I will say that: LB, telephone interview with author, July 2002.

24 picnic in Cornwall: LB, *From Wilder Shores*, p. 62.

24 the most completely feminine person: Philip Ziegler, interview with author, 18 February 2004.

24 the smart arty set: Cecil Beaton, quoted in Michael Prodger, *Sunday Telegraph*, 8 February 2004.

24 The mid-1920s was an age of extravagant parties: Peter Quennell, *The Marble Foot: An Autobiography*, p. 162.

26 Lesley met Diaghilev in Paris: LB, 'Private View', *Daily Mail*, 7 September 1945.

26 her friend and ally: Hélène Hoppenot, journals, 19 October 1954.

27 Lesley's marriage to Robert Alan Wimberley Bicknell: marriage certificate.

27 outside the charmed Slav circle: LB, *Mind's Eye*, p. 166.

28 naughty marriage: Andrew Lycett, interview with LB, *The Times*.

28 Robert Bicknell was its tenant: *Kelly's Directories* for Richmond,

1929–40; Borough of Richmond Register of Voters, 1929–40, Richmond Public Library.

29 by 1932 Bicknell had left: ibid. Lesley and Robert Alan Wimberley Bicknell were divorced in 1941. He subsequently remarried, had three children and died in 1967.

29 radiant unreal horizon: LB, 'My Day', *Vogue* UK, January 1973, p. 4.

29 but his face is shadowy: LB, *Mind's Eye*, p. 175.

Chapter 2: The Promised Land

31 Feodor Komisarjevsky: my chief source was Victor Borovsky, *A Triptych from the Russian Theatre*, on the lives of Fyodor Petrovich (father), Vera (half-sister) and Fyodor/Feodor Komisarjevsky.

31 trained as an architect: Komisarjevsky designed a number of cinemas and theatres in London and the Home Counties, notably the Phoenix Theatre in Charing Cross Road and the Granada in Tooting.

31 arrived in England: Michael Billington, *Peggy Ashcroft*, London: John Murray, 1988, p. 20.

31 *régisseur*: Borovsky, *A Triptych*, p. 413.

31 symphonic control: he wrote several books about his 'synthetic' system for theatre production.

32 he entered the room: Borovsky, phone call with author, April 2003.

32 Mysterious and cynical: John Gielgud, obituary of Komisarjevsky, *The Times*, 21 April 1954.

32 Edith Evans, one of few: Borovsky, *A Triptych*, p. 319.

32 Who was the shadowy figure: LB, 'Private View', *Daily Mail*, 7 September 1945.

32 she met Komisarjevsky in Paris: LB, *Mind's Eye*, p. 181.

33 Rachmaninov's house, Chaliapin: LB, *Mind's Eye*, pp. 67–8.

34 The Settings designed by Komisarjevsky: Shakespeare Memorial Theatre Summer Festival programme, 27 June to 10 September 1932.

34 too slowly and too often: Ivor Brown, review, *Observer*, 31 July 1932.

34 but there is invention: ibid.

34 Just as a new theatrical idea: Borovsky, *A Triptych*, p. 340.

34 the vagabond: Borovsky, phone call with author, April 2003.

35 marry three times: LB, *Mind's Eye*, p. 166.

35 the outward form of self-sufficiency: Peter Ustinov, *Dear Me*, London: Heinemann, 1977, p 36.

35 another grief: Walter Blanch's death certificate.

36 love and *entrechats*: LB, *Mind's Eye,* pp. 212–13.

36 florid Caucasian: LB, 'Vogue's Spotlight', *Vogue,* 6 July 1938.

37 Euclidian drama: review by 'H.H.', unidentified newspaper cutting, 15 August 1934, London Theatre Museum.

37 Constant Lambert, 'Nought + Nought = Nought': (unidentified) newspaper cutting, 5 August 1934, ibid.

37 may now be said to end: 'Last Night of the Ballet', *Observer,* 12 August 1934, ibid.

38 She made the trip: Marie Rambert, *Quicksilver,* pp. 152–3.

39 badly off: ibid., p. 153.

39 the real blood and bones, strange birds: LB, *Mind's Eye,* pp. 201–2.

40 *Lady Macbeth of Mstensk,* Shusha Guppy, 'Lesley Blanch' in *Looking Back,* p. 16.

40 darling Mim: LB, letter to Marie Rambert, 20 February 1968, Rambert Archives.

40 Marie Rambert and LB, 'Some Impressions of the Ballet in Russia – 1934' in *Playtime in Russia,* p. 83.

40 A step into the past: ibid., p. 91.

40 She said she made two: LB, phone call with author, 31 July 2002.

41 Some of All the Russias: LB, *Vogue,* March 1942, p. 30.

41 replaced as tenants by Frieda Harris: Borough of Richmond Register of Voters.

41 this modish cloister: Lesley said she was the only woman resident, but the writer G.B. Stern was among several other women living in Albany in the 1930s. A galaxy of writers lived there in the 1940s and 1950s: J.B. Priestley, Graham Greene, Terence Rattigan, Harold Nicolson, Kenneth Clark, Patrick Hamilton, Edgar Lustgarten, Malcolm Muggeridge. *Albany 1803–2003,* ed. Elizabeth Oliver, London: The Trustees of Albany; J.C. Ray, unpublished PhD thesis, Royal Holloway and Bedford New College, University of London, 1997.

42 *Schalète*: LB, *Round the World,* p. 100.

42 Anti-Beige: LB, *Harper's Bazaar,* June 1935, p. 18.

42 The manager asked: LB, interview with author, January 2003.

42 They threw me into it: LB, phone call with author, 31 July 2002.

43 She got the hang of it: Audrey Withers, interview with author, 1997.

43 the most completely: ibid.

43 something I did: LB, interview with author, January 2003.

43 With illustration: ibid.

44 She was a bohemian: Anne Scott-James, *Sketches from a Life,* p. 69.

45 'My Cook is a Catastrophe': LB, *Vogue*, 26 May 1937, p. 111.

45 'First Night Hocus Focus': LB, *Vogue*, 10 November 1937, p. 59.

45 An early column: LB, 'Vogue's Spotlight', *Vogue*, 14 April 1937, p. 98.

45 Her first signed column: LB, 'Vogue's Spotlight', *Vogue*, 28 October 1936, p. 68.

45 'Women of Achievement': *Vogue*, 31 March 1937, p. 64.

46 good-gracious living: LB, *Mind's Eye*, p. 213.

47 her most revealing sketch: *Daily Mail*, 27 August 1945.

47 'Unaccustomed as I am': LB, *Vogue*, April 1941, p. 52.

47 She was still living in Albany: Anne Scott-James, phone call with author, 16 August 2004.

48 colleagues remembered her: Withers, interview with author, 1997.

48 Amy herself: Anne Scott-James, *In the Mink*, p. 62.

49 Martha became a favourite: Jane Stockwood, phone call with author, 4 November 2003.

50 I felt that Lee's features: Withers, *Lifespan*, p. 52.

50 *boiling* at the time: LB, interview with author, January 2003.

50 Cinemas now flash: LB, *Vogue*, October 1940, p. 47.

51 There were these oil bombs: LB, interview with author, January 2003.

51 Lightness is too often triteness: LB, 'Vogue's Spotlight', *Vogue*, May 1943, p. 50.

52 Pascal lives nomadically and Alas; Nonn!: LB, 'Titans' Triumph', *Vogue*, November 1940, p. 44. Giraffes in prams: ibid.

53 The imaginary panel of thinkers: LB, 'Brains to Trust', *Vogue*, July 1942, p. 42.

53 As always she took liberties: LB, 'Vogue's Spotlight', *Vogue*, July 1943, p. 42.

53 did eventually track him down: 'Re: Bob Hope', *Vogue*, September 1943, p. 55. Hope's noisy party one night in his bedroom at Claridge's with Adolphe Menjou and Clark Gable kept awake their neighbours, Sacheverell and Georgia Sitwell, who had just heard that their eccentric father had died: S. Bradford, *Sacheverell Sitwell*, London: Sinclair-Stevenson, 1993, p. 312.

53 'The true story of Lili Marlene': LB, *Vogue*, April 1944, p. 52.

54 a stage set: Scott-James, *Sketches from a Life*, p. 70.

54 He was wearing battle dress: Scott-James, interview with author, 17 January 1997.

54 An old and famous name: LB, 'Vogue's Spotlight', *Vogue*, November 1942, p. 46.

54 charming pastry-cook: LB, *Round the World*, p. 45.

55 It was their total lack: Peter Quennell, *The Wanton Chase*, p. 24.

55 the Wrens: LB, 'Seaworthy and Semi-seagoing', *Vogue*, September 1943, p. 50.

55 art occupies in society: Cyril Connolly, quoted in John Lehmann, *A Nest of Tigers*, London: Macmillan, 1968, p. 204.

56 Escapism takes many forms: LB, 'Vogue's Spotlight', *Vogue*, March 1943, p. 52.

56 Harriette Wilson amused her during air raids: LB, phone call with author, July 2002.

56 a book about making the most: Constance Spry, *Come into the Garden, Cook*, illustrated by LB.

56 a piece about Pushkin: LB, 'Pushkin the Dandy became Hero of the Russians', *Evening Standard*, 10 February 1944, p. 6.

56 By the spring of 1944: James Lees-Milne, *Ancestral Voices and Prophesying Peace*, London: John Murray, 1995, pp. 284-5.

56 Lesley's meeting with Romain: LB, *Romain, un regard particulier*, pp. 9-12; LB, *Mind's Eye*, p. 274.

57 bowl of olives: in *Mind's Eye* Lesley describes Romain as sitting hunched over a bowl of salted almonds when she first saw him; either way, the hostess was still cross with him.

Chapter 3: 'Lesley's Frog'

58 In the Free French capital, life was intense: Jean Pierre-Bloch, *Londres Capitale de la France Libre*, Paris: Carrère/Michel Latou, 1986, p. 58.

58 Romain's war: biographies of Romain.

59 he sat silently writing: René Gatissou, interview with author, 29 August 2003.

59 shaking awake his protesting . . . comrade: Pierre-Louis Dreyfus, interview with author, September 2003.

59 On operations with the Lorraine Squadron: RG, *Forest of Anger*, trans. Viola Gerard Garvin.

60 Alternative version of first meeing: 'Vogue's Eye View', *Vogue*, 15 October 1966, p. 81.

60 *Forest of Anger* was published at the end of 1944, six months after its acceptance, which would therefore have been in June, just before Romain met Lesley.

60 in possession of the flat at Swan Court: Scott-James, *Sketches from a Life*, p. 70; interviews with author, January 1997, June 2002.

61 Lesley and Romain at St Leonard's Terrace: LB, *Romain*, p.23. Lesley's memoir was my chief source for her recollections of Romain in Chapters 3 and 5.

62 Lesley's Frog: LB, *Romain*, p. 25. Mortimer: ibid., p. 35.

62 vague about when they met: Lesley also said she met Romain soon after he had been injured, but their meeting would have been months later. Although Romain applied to return to active service after his injury in January 1944, aside from his stomach injury he had already flown more than twenty-five missions (official notes, Ordre de la Libération website). From May he was retired to administrative duties at the Free French HQ in Carlton Gardens. That, plus the VI reprisal raids starting after D-Day, places their meeting in June or July.

62 Romain's misleading chronology and no mention of Lesley: according to *Promise at Dawn* (1960, written shortly before Romain left Lesley), his life-defining event in mid-1944 was his novel's acceptance for publication, heralding his birth as a writer. By this account the publisher's telegram was handed to him on the airstrip on his return from a bombing raid. But Free French bombers were otherwise deployed by then, and Romain had left active service months earlier.

62 Secret gathering of invasion forces, newsreels of the landings, VIs targeting Greater London, etc.: Angus Calder, *The People's War*.

63 Whimsical reading list, Beatrix Potter etc.: LB, *Romain*, pp. 26–9, 63; LB, interview with author, January 2003.

64 rough Warsaw schoolboy's tongue: Feliks Topolski, *Autobiography*.

65 a chapter to be published in *La France Libre*: David Bellos, 'Le Malentendu: l'histoire cachée d'Education européenne', in Hangouët and Audi (eds), *L'Herne, Cahier 85: Romain Gary*, p. 150.

65 seething with spies: ibid.

66 incredible beauty: LB, *Romain*, p. 43.

66 Not a word of this was true: although Romain did later refer to passing a diploma in Slav languages at Warsaw university in 1934–5 (RG, *La Nuit sera calme*, pp. 234–5). His friend Sigurd Norberg produced a photograph of them both as teenagers in Warsaw, with Romain's father: Myriam Anissimov, *Romain Gary, le caméléon*, Paris: Denoël, 2006 (paperback).

66 *The Outskirts of Stalingrad*: Ralph Schoolcraft, *Romain Gary*, p. 30.

67 goy wife: LB, *Romain*, p. 37.

67 Romain's nationality: LB, *Mind's Eye*, p. 274.

68 supreme *précieuse*: Topolski, *Autobiography*, unpaginated. This lovely sensitive brute: ibid.

68 a certain form: RG, *Lady L.*, book jacket designed by LB, London: Michael Joseph, 1959.

NOTES TO PAGES 68–79

68 took Romain to meet her mother: LB, *Romain*, pp. 33–5.

68 the flat in Richmond: Scott-James, interview with author, January 1997.

69 Quit the wailing wall: LB, interview with author, January 2003.

69 *Oh, Lesley est un numéro*: ibid.

70 do make an effort and account of wedding: LB, *Romain*, p. 38.

70 the face of a woman who knew what she wanted: LB, 'Laurence Hope', in *Lilac-Bleeding Star*, p. 189.

71 their witnesses: René Gatissou, interview with author, 29 August 2003.

71 Marriage certificate: recorded at Chelsea Register Office, 4 April 1945.

71 a deprived quarter of Eastern Europe: LB, *Romain*, p. 154.

71 Romain's origins: Agranovsky and Baranova, 'Winner of the "Prix Goncourt" Romain Gary', trans. from Russian by Rachel Bugler.

72 Leave him to his legend: LB, *Romain*, p. 21.

Chapter 4: The Columnist

73 It is impossible to overestimate: Scott-James, *Sketches from a Life*, p. 54.

73 'Red Tape and Blue Pencil': *The Leader*, 28 April 1945.

74 obsessive Russian bias: 'Politics behind Films', 30 June; 'Film Children', 3 March; 'Children's Cinema', 21 July; 'Russian Cinema', 24 February, *The Leader*, 1945.

74 Profiles: Eric Ambler, 24 March; Billy Wilder, 23 June; Anatole de Grunwald, 10 February; Beatrice Lillie, 13 October, *The Leader*, 1945.

75 a second weekly column: LB, 'Private View', *Daily Mail*, Monday 6 August to 12 November 1945, p. 2.

76 a new world order: LB, ibid., 20 August; DDT and Shetland ponies, 2 September; Macdonald Hastings, 9 September 1945.

76 towards the end of the war: Scott-James, *In the Mink*, p. 65.

77–9 LB, *Daily Mail* columns, 1945: Whitechapel Gallery, 21 September; divorce rates, 28 September; female diplomats and the food renaissance, 8 October; 'Hashish Corner', 21 September; Rodney Ackland, 15 October; pogrom-minded letters, 22 October; social diary, 5 November; Helena Rubinstein, 12 November.

79 Romain's novel overtaken by historical events: for background to the literary awards, see Schoolcraft, *Romain Gary*; David Bellos,

'Le Malentendu', in Hangouët and Audi (eds), *L'Herne, Cahier 85: Romain Gary*.

80 This is a literary event: Louis Lambert, *Le Pays*; Not a novel of the Resistance: Maurice Nadeau, *Combat*, n.d., quoted in Anissimov, *Romain Gary*, pp. 191–2.

80 In the last ten years: praise from Joseph Kessel, quoted in Schoolcraft, *Romain Gary*, p. 33.

80 Gaston Palewski vetoed Romain's London appointment: Raymond Aron, *Memoirs: Fifty Years of Political Reflection*, trans. George Holoch, London: Holmes & Meier, 1990, pp. 148–9.

82 Mortimer's portrait: shown to author, January 2003.

Chapter 5: *En Poste*

83 And indeed the most coldly: Robert Musil, *The Man Without Qualities*, London: Picador, 1974, p. 11.

83 I wonder, does Paris reflect: LB, 'The Geography of Time', *Vogue*, May 1945, p. 52.

83 terrible discretion: Beevor and Cooper, *Paris after the Liberation*, p. 153. Baron Élie de Rothschild's return: ibid.

84 Romain's meeting with Sartre and de Beauvoir: ibid., p. 66.

84 Hôtel Bristol: LB, *Romain*, pp. 45–6.

84 existentiel, existentialisme: RG to Raymond Aron, London, 8 August 1945: R. Aron, personal archive, quoted in Mireille Sacotte, 'Correspondance Romain Gary–Raymond Aron', in Hangouët and Audi (eds), *L'Herne, Cahier 85: Romain Gary*, p. 128.

84 His modest appointment: LB, *Romain*, p. 46. Artists' studios: ibid., p. 47.

85 The Turkish marriage trunk: Scott-James, *In the Mink*, p.66; Topolski, *Autobiography*.

86 Lesley Blanch will return in a few weeks: *The Leader*, 19 January 1946.

86 cinema-going in France and Switzerland: ibid., 16 March 1946, pp. 13–15.

86 last article: ibid., 20 April 1946, pp. 18–19.

86 She also made time: Scott-James, *Sketches from a Life*, pp. 156–7.

86 she besieged Romain with letters: LB, interview with author, January 2003.

87 Lesley's journey: ibid.

87 Turkoman jewel merchant: ibid.

87 Aimée Dubucq de Rivery: Joe Boyd, 'Lesley Blanch, Time Traveller', *Guardian* Review, 9 July 2005, p. 20.

87 sidling round under the point of the harbour: LB, interview with author, January 2003.

88 the most beautiful room in the world: LB, 'The Forbidden Treasures of Topkapi', *Architectural Digest*, 1988.

88 indulged herself in food markets: LB, *From Wilder Shores*, p. 40.

88 romantic breakfasts on the Asiatic side: LB, *Round the World*, p. 69; LB, *From Wilder Shores*, p. 40.

89 Nedi Trianova: LB, *Romain*, pp. 58, 63–5.

91 the legendary George Dimitrov: RG, *La Nuit sera calme*, p. 115.

91 picking them out of lacey bedjacket: Scott-James, *In the Mink*, p. 66.

91 a Macedonian cook-maid: LB, 'Raiina – a Balkan Cook', in *Lilac-Bleeding Star*, p. 59.

92 always curtsey to the papal nuncio: LB, phone call with author, July 2002.

93 receptions at the Soviet embassy: LB, *Round the World*, p. 73; LB, *Romain*, p. 62.

94 Dashed his brains out: LB, interview with author, January 2003.

94 She was undoubtedly narcissistic: LB, 'The Fading Garden and the Forgotten Rose', in *Lilac-Bleeding Star*, p. 83. Loved to express herself through rooms and houses: ibid. p. 89. Frame for loving: ibid., p. 93.

95 *Pussinka dousha*, don't you know: LB, *Mind's Eye*, p. 146.

95 *Des foutaises*: LB, *Romain*, p. 60.

95 Atanass and his mother: LB, 'Fragments of a Balkan Journal', in *Lilac-Bleeding Star*, p. 50. In *Round the World*, Lesley said Raiina had introduced her to the gipsy woman.

95 Lesley's travels outside Sofia: LB, interview with author, January 2003. Photograph of Vratsa, in LB, *Lilac-Bleeding Star*.

96 King Simeon was dethroned: in 2001 Simeon returned to Bulgaria as prime minister.

96 black tongue: RG, *La Nuit sera calme*, p. 117.

96 *Tulipe* sold fewer than 200 copies: Schoolcraft, *Romain Gary*, p. 38.

99 Pas-de-Confort: LB, *Romain*, p. 73. Teased by Nancy: ibid., p. 76.

99 His first banana: Yves Agid, interview with author, 11 June 2004.

99 animal portraits: LB, 'Pets in Paint', *Vogue*, January 1951, p. 80.

100 profile about a pseudonymous painter: LB, 'The Gentle Jungle', *Harper's Bazaar*, December 1949, p. 61.

100 Fear of Germany is a defeat in itself: Larat, *Romain Gary: Un itinéraire européen*, p. 86.

101 Roquebrune: LB, *Romain*, p. 81; interview with author, January 2003.

103 neither a Jew, nor a Bulgarian: Christian Carra de Vaux-Saint-Cyr quoted in Hélène Hoppenot, journals, 17 February 1950, BLJD.

103 It's a lottery: ibid.

103 A handsome boy: ibid.

103 his English wife: ibid.

104 Does he still wear his sleeves: ibid., 1 April 1950.

104 Spanish protocol: LB, *From Wilder Shores*, p. 74.

104 She still had five or six years of youth: RG, *The Colours of the Day*, trans. Stephen Becker, p. 41.

105 his tic below the belt: Huston, *Tombeau de Romain Gary*, p. 42.

105 two enormous egotists: Scott-James, phone call with author.

105 Death of Hadji: Hélène Hoppenot, journals, 13 December 1950, BLJD.

106 Strange man, this Gary: ibid., 8 October 1950.

106 with a cartoonist's precision: LB, *Romain*, p. 93.

107 Unpaid bills: LB to Nancy Mitford, 18 July 1951.

107 Lesley visited Vienna: LB to Nancy Mitford, 15 January 1951.

107 Romain's Wagner postcard: LB, *Romain*, p. 125.

107 Lesley sent 'The Fading Garden' to *Cornhill*, 6 February 1951.

107 splendid piece of travel nostalgia: John Murray's reply for Peter Quennell, 27 February 1951, JM.

107 Salammbo: LB to John Murray, 1 March 1951, ibid.

107 'The Fading Garden' accepted: John Murray to LB, 15 March 1951, ibid.

108 urged him to cut the other essays instead: LB to John Murray, 9 August 1951, ibid.

108 General Lyautey was subsequently France's Military Governor in Morocco, then Resident-General.

108 Lesley's profile of Isabelle Eberhardt accepted: John Murray to LB, 24 October 1951, JM.

108 Lesley returned to Tunis in October: Hélène Hoppenot, journals, 14 and 15 October 1951, BLJD.

109 Neither of them: ibid., 25 December 1951.

109 write a book: John Murray to LB, 4 January 1952, JM.

Chapter 6: New York

110 The Quai d'Orsay had found Romain a position: Bona, *Romain Gary*; Larat, *Romain Gary*; LB, *Romain*.

111 she succumbed to flu: LB to John (Jock) Murray, 5 January 1952, JM.

112 Ninth floor apartment: LB to Jock Murray, 10 May 1952, ibid; LB interview with author, January 2003.

112 TV would make Romain impotent: LB, *Romain*, p. 100.

112 breakfasts drenched in maple syrup: LB to Jock Murray, 30 March 1952, JM.

112 Sleepy Hollow: LB, 'The Pace that Kills', *Vogue*, September 1953, p. 150.

113 Romain's solo grand tour: RG, *La Nuit sera calme*, pp. 167–78.

113 his money ran out: Hélène Hoppenot, journals, 8 August 1952, BLJD.

113 LB's tour in a Cadillac: LB to Jock Murray, 8 August 1952, JM.

114 Lesley's handwritten outline: ibid.

114 It is only proper that the irritations of life: Jock Murray to LB, 20 August 1952, ibid.

114 the whirring wheels of industrialization: Shusha Guppy, 'Lesley Blanch' in *Looking Back*, p. 7.

114 already finished 25,000 words: LB to Jock Murray, 25 September 1952, JM.

115 hectic bouts of entertaining: LB, *Round the World*, p. 164.

115 sketched evening gown: LB to Jock Murray, 1 November 1954, JM.

115 Runyonesque restaurants: LB to Jock Murray, 13 December 1952, ibid.

115 the Hoppenots' Christmas Eve ceremony: Hélène Hoppenot, journals, 24 December 1952, BLJD.

116 Lesley's explosive material about Simenon: ibid., 14 November 1952; *New Yorker* cut in with a profile: ibid., 25 January 1953.

116 Tiepolos on the walls: LB to Jock Murray, 30 March 1952, JM; evenings at El Morocco, LB to Jock Murray, 22 March 1953, ibid.

116 Your control must be like iron: Jock Murray to LB, 7 April 1953, ibid.

117 the Far East or the Pacific: Hélène Hoppenot, journals, 21 May 1953.

117 an operation to remove his gall bladder: ibid., 16 July 1953.

117 Her early misgivings about New York: LB, interview with author, January 2003.

117 Princess Obolensky: LB, *Romain*, p. 100.

117 Count Hilarion Voronzov: LB to Osyth Leeston, 1970s (n.d.), JM.

117 Carson McCullers, Puerto Rican dance halls and Ali Khan: LB, interview with author, January 2003.

118 Malraux's interest in cats and Lesley's book: LB, *Romain*, p. 105.

118 a doubtful endpaper: Jock Murray, memo, 14 August 1953, JM.

119 empty and neglected: LB to Jock Murray, Boxing Day 1953; admitted turmoil later, LB to Jock Murray, 14 September 1954, ibid.

119 Charles Boyer: LB to Jock Murray, 22 February 1954, ibid.

119 They flew to Guatemala: LB to Jock Murray, 30 March 1954, ibid.

119 She took detailed notes: LB, 'Many Mexicos', in *Lilac-Bleeding Star*, p. 116.

119 biggest crises around his birthday: Hélène Hoppenot, journals, 10 April 1952, 21 May 1953, 6 May 1954, BLJD.

119 It's his Russian soul: ibid., 6 May 1954.

120 British sales had reached 22,000: Jock Murray to LB, 10 September 1954, JM.

120 It should be read by everyone: Stewart Perowne for BBC Radio Arabic Service, 11 December 1954; a dazzling experiment in biography: *Sunday Express*, 5 September 1954; spicy and rococo: *The Economist*, 9 October 1954; definitely reacted against progress: Elizabeth Bowen, 'The Happy Four Lost Ladies' in *Tatler*, October 1954; find it hard to swallow the idea: *Time* Magazine, US, 13 September 1954; something of a bore: Peter Quennell in *Daily Mail*, 22 September 1954; violent, strident, uncomfortable creature: *TLS*, 2 October 1954.

121 a striking piece of work: *Astrologer's Quarterly*, March/May 1955.

121 The uneven cobbled alleys: LB, *Wilder Shores*, p. 206.

122 So loving a nature: ibid., p. 56.

123 slashing hippopotamus-hide whips: ibid., p. 199.

123 There is no hard evidence: Philip Mansel, *Constantinople: City of the World's Desire, 1453–1924*, London: John Murray, 1995, p. 250.

123 Lambert found the sultana's grave: Joe Boyd, 'Lesley Blanch, Time Traveller,' *Guardian* Review.

123 In Turkey she is known: Boris Akunin, *Turkish Gambit*, London: Weidenfeld, 2005, pp. 81–2.

124 Dinner with Alexander Calder: Hélène Hoppenot, journals, 17 September 1954, BLJD.

124 Lesley is a sorceress: RG, Paris: *Elle*, 7 May 1955, p. 26.

124 *Actualité littéraire*: 32 February 1957.

124 catering night after night: LB to Jock Murray, 1 November 1954, JM.

125 Hoppenot's campaign for Romain's promotion: Anissimov, *Romain Gary*, pp. 251–3.

125 where Romain would live was uncertain: LB to Jock Murray, 2 December 1954, JM.

126 'buisness': LB's habitual misspelling of 'business', e.g. in letters referred to below.

126 Robert Lantz appointed LB's agent: LB to Jock Murray and Osyth Leeston, 14 September 1954, ibid. Awkward situation with Marie Rodell: ibid.

126 Lionel Lemon & Co.: Jock Murray to LB, 10 September 1954, ibid.

126 Osyth Leeston enlisted to look after Lesley's mother: Osyth Leeston to LB, 10 September 1954, ibid.

126 Guests at a gala dinner: LB to Jock Murray and Osyth Leeston, 1 November 1954, ibid.

126 Lord Beaverbrook, her neighbour: LB to Osyth Leeston and Jock Murray, 2 December 1954, ibid. Osbert Sitwell, Noël Coward: ibid.

127 Romain phoned Mme Hoppenot: Hélène Hoppenot, journals, 16 December 1954, BLJD.

127 Romain's travails in London and problem with the ambassador: variously in Larat, *Romain Gary*, p. 96; Anissimov, *Romain Gary*, p. 256; Hélène Hoppenot, journals, 16, 21, 29 December 1954 and 8 January 1955, BLJD.

128 due no doubt to my Jewish blood: Hélène Hoppenot, journals, 8 January 1955, ibid.

128 Lesley's revelation to Mme Hoppenot: ibid., 19 October 1954.

128 he turned down offers of posts: ibid., 8 January 1956.

129 Her success affected his morale: LB, interview with author, January 2003.

129 The hospital urged his wife to rush to his bedside: LB, *Romain*, p. 115.

129 Jock very sad: Jock Murray to LB, 15 March 1955, JM.

129 Romain's visit to Aldworth: Scott-James, interview with author, June 2002. Romain never forgot her hospitality. Years later she would call in the favour when, at crisis point with Osbert Lancaster before they married, she escaped to Paris and stayed overnight at Romain's and Jean Seberg's palatial flat in the rue du Bac. While she was out, Romain opened the door to Lancaster who, he gleefully reported afterwards, was 'in a very emotional state – as far, that is, as an Englishman is capable of emotion': ibid. and Richard Boston, *Osbert: A Portrait of Osbert Lancaster*, London: Collins, 1989, pp. 228–9.

129 une personne si tumultueuse: Hélène Hoppenot, journals, 23 December 1954, BLJD.

129 fort gaie: ibid., 8 February 1955.

130 numerous translation rights sold and considered: Jock Murray to LB, 15 March 1955, JM.

130 Lesley's stay in London: Jock Murray to LB, 20 April; JM to Wolfgang Kruger Verlag, 24 May; JM to LB, 14 June 1955, ibid.

130 Romain wrote to Jock: RG to John Murray, King Edward VII Hospital, Beaumont St, W1, 17 May 1955, ibid.

131 he contacted Lesley: Hélène Hoppenot, journals, December 1956, BLJD.

131 looking after Romain: LB to Jock Murray, 26 June 1955, JM.

131 Lesley's research trip to Turkey: LB to Jock Murray, 19 August 1955, ibid.

132 suggests a piece about Pierre Loti: LB to Jock Murray and Osyth Leeston, 10 September 1955, ibid.

132 left untouched the bank transfer: ibid.

132 Romain persuaded to help with translation: ibid.

132 Lesley wired M. Hoppenot: Hélène Hoppenot, journals, 11 October 1955, BLJD.

132 supervised more building work: LB to Jock Murray, December 1955 n.d., JM.

133 a severe reader's report: ibid.

133 she reworked her Loti piece: Jock Murray to LB, 14 October 1955, 9 December 1955, ibid.

133 anxious to see it in print: LB to Jock Murray, n.d., ibid.

133 a *moi* in every landscape: LB, 'Loti-land', *Lilac Bleeding Star*, p. 172.

Chapter 7: Los Angeles I

134 Here, if anywhere else in America: William Butler Yeats, quoted in Sam Hall Kaplan, *LA Lost and Found*, Santa Monica: Hennessey & Ingalls, 2000, p. 79.

134 RG's proposition: Elizabeth Jane Howard, *Slipstream*, London: Macmillan, 2002, pp. 287–99 and 334. Elizabeth Jane Howard, phone call with author, 24 May 2003.

135 Lesley upset by private upheavals, Romain's new post uncertain: LB to Osyth Leeston, February 1956, n.d., JM.

135 talkative cat: LB to Jock Murray, 3 November 1955, ibid.

135 Murray delighted with her drawings: Jock Murray to LB, 26 January 1956; his February deadline, JM to LB, 16 November 1955, ibid.

135 proofs of the Loti essay: Jock Murray to LB, 26 January 1956; LB to Jock Murray, 'Saturday', n.d., ibid.

135 Punctuation checked by James Lees-Milne: LB to Jock Murray, 1 February 1956, ibid.

135 1919 Outpost Drive: my thanks to Sebastian Gutierrez, film and

television director, and current owner, for showing me the house, October 2005.

136 Orange swags and canopies: Don Bachardy, interview with author, Los Angeles, 27 October 1975.

136 Romain's new post: Bona, *Romain Gary*; Anissimov, *Romain Gary*.

136 not cut from the same cloth: Charlotte Hyde, Tourist Board, telephone call with author, Los Angeles, October 2006.

138 The theme of illusion and reality: Gavin Lambert, *The Slide Area: Scenes of Hollywood Life*, London: Penguin, 1963, p. 17.

138 studio round: Romain Gary, 15 May 1960, UCLA Library Film and Television Archive.

138 James Mason's rackety parties: LB, interview with author, January 2003.

138 a whole room full of buttons: Hugo Vickers, *Cecil Beaton*, pp. 462–3.

138 exquisitely crafted costumes: LB, interview with author, January 2003.

138 Apart from the chic + elegance: Fleur Cowles Meyer to George Cukor, 16 April 1956, GCC.

139 Lesley's playing card: GCC; LB, interview with author, January 2003.

139 has not, or has passed, *ambition*: Kenneth Tynan, quoting LB, in Gavin Lambert, *On Cukor*, London: W.H. Allen, 1973, p. 6.

139 Friends are of enormous importance: Emanuel Levy, *George C: Master of Elegance*, p. 38.

139 suede-lined walls and Cukor's habitués: Don Bachardy, interview with author, Los Angeles, 27 October 1975.

140 as if it were the present: Gavin Lambert, *On Cukor*, p. 10.

140 Alan Jay Lerner, Paul Newman and Joanne Woodward: David Richards, *Played Out: The Jean Seberg Story*, pp. 92 and 158; LB, interview with author, January 2003. (Not everyone was charmed by Romain and Lesley. Anaïs Nin wrote a poisonous fictional portrait of Lesley especially in *Collages*, London: Peter Owen, 1964).

140 her whole life and being: LB, 'Isabel Burton', in *Wilder Shores*, p. 11.

141 Lesley never understood the lack of editing: LB, *Romain*, p. 122.

141 seven months' absence from Los Angeles: LB to Jock Murray and Osyth Leeston, 'Easter Sunday' (21 April 1957), JM.

141 Hilarion Voronzov's memories: LB to Osyth Leeston, 18 August (1970s), ibid.

142 Tamara Grigorievna, Princess of Georgia: LB, *The Sabres of Paradise*, p. 470.

142 The Baddeley Bequest: ibid., Acknowledgements, p. xii.

142 not in my time addicted to brigandage: J.F. Baddeley, *The Rugged Flanks of Caucasus*, vol. 1, p. 8, London Library.

142 Biographical details of Baddeley: preface by Sir Oliver Wardrop and short biography by Sir Charles Hagberg Wright, ibid.

143 Baddeley's annotated index: *Index Caucasica*, and 97 mounted photographs: Baddeley Bequest, London Library.

143 cherished project: LB, *Sabres*, p. xii.

143 Odette Arnaud urged Lesley to join Romain in Paris: Anissimov, *Romain Gary*, p. 286.

144 she had to borrow from the hotel concierge: LB, *Romain,* p. 119.

144 the mysterious Goncourt 1956: *L'Aurore*, 14 December 1956; shiny eyebrows, charme slave: Claude le Roux, *Paris-Presse*, 15 December 1956; petite moustache de guitariste, *Le Courrier Limoges*, 4 December 1956. News reports from Romain Gary cuttings folders, Editions Gallimard.

144 Sylvia Agid's cartoons: Anissimov, *Romain Gary*, pp. 480–1.

144 His mother had given him the name: Georgette Elegy, *Paris-Presse*, 5 December 1956.

145 Our needs – for justice, for freedom and dignity: RG, *The Roots of Heaven*, p. 172.

145 This season, as everyone knows: René Chabbert, *Dimanche Matin*, 18 November 1956.

145 Kléber Haedens: *France Dimanche*, 30 November 1956; Carmen Tessier: *France-Soir*, 7 December 1956.

145 We don't care: *Le Canard enchainé*, n.d.

146 arguably helped to win him the Goncourt: Schoolcraft, *Romain Gary*, p. 45.

146 Sylvia Agid's account of the party: Sylvia Agid to Christel Söderlund, 11 January 1957, quoted in Anissimov, *Romain Gary*, p. 292.

147 Hoppenot sighed at the prospect: Hélène Hoppenot, journals, 18 March 1955, BLJD.

147 Lesley knew about the apartment: LB, interview with author, January 2003.

147 the sexual impulse was his motivating force: LB, *Romain*, p. 143.

148 already broken up for good, twice: Hélène Hoppenot, journals, 21 December 1956, BLJD.

148 he wished Lesley was there to advise him: ibid., 20 April 1960.

148 the part . . . that longed to 'cling': LB, interview with author, January 2003.

149 Lesley's research at Samuelian's Oriental bookshop etc.: LB, *Sabres*, Acknowledgements, pp. xi–xii.

149 her reading room: LB to Jock Murray, February 1957, n.d., JM.

149 left for Los Angeles in early April: John Murray, memo, 2 April 1957, ibid.

150 Lesley's house maintenance: LB to Jock Murray, 'Monday'; LB to Jock Murray and Osyth Leeston, 21 April 1957, ibid.

150 Bastille Day: LB to Jock Murray, n.d., ibid. Writing in their dressing gowns: ibid.

151 On a sublime occasion hosted by Cole Porter: LB, *From Wilder Shores*, p. 90. Eating with Hollywood grandees: ibid., p. 89.

151 Being French in Hollywood: Don Bachardy, interview with author, Los Angeles, 27 October 1975.

151 the two of them ever participating: ibid.

151 Lesley's red coat at a funeral: LB, *Romain*, p. 146. Nest of fur coats: ibid.

152 Countess Morphy, *Recipes of All Nations*, London: Herbert Joseph, 1946. (Lesley acknowledged her recipe for 'Little Pigs of Heaven': *Round the World*, p. 53.)

152 Balkan brigands were sheer fantasy: Pat Creed, interview with author, 19 April 2004.

152 Chop suey does not exist in China: *Time and Tide*, 16 February 1957.

153 the finer shades: LB, *The Game of Hearts*, p. 7.

154 brisk appetites: LB, ibid., p. 7; she is her own Boswell: ibid., p. 4.

154 I shall not say why and how: ibid., p. 63.

154 New edition reviewed: Rosemary Hill, 'I am the thing itself': *London Review of Books*, 25 September 2003, pp. 19–20.

154 specialising in scandal: RG to Jock Murray, 17 May 1955, written from King Edward VII's Hospital, JM.

154 I'm not in the least interested in myself: RG to André Bourin, ten-part radio interview, 1969, France-Culture (in which he talked about himself for several hours).

155 mulling over a sort of autobiography: Bona, *Romain Gary*, p. 195.

155 further complexities in the French edition: Schoolcraft, p. 173, n. 25.

156 learning from him attitudes, mannerisms: RG, *Lady L.*, London: Michael Joseph, 1959, p. 102.

156 special English sophistication: ibid., p. 116.

157 I have a stylistic problem: Bona, *Romain Gary*, pp. 220–1.

157 such good theatre: *Lady L.*, p. 130. An exact reproduction of her room: ibid., pp. 156–7. A huge, rich slice of Turkish delight: ibid., p. 29.

158 *Lady L.* was the book in which he put most of himself: RG to André Bourin, radio interviews, 1969, France-Culture.

158 Hélène Hoppenot disliked *Lady L.*: Hélène Hoppenot, journals, 20 April 1969, BLJD.

159 he asked a Bulgarian friend: Anissimov, *Romain Gary*, pp. 295–8.

Chapter 8: Los Angeles II

160 With the swift movement: Leo Tolstoy, *The Cossacks*, trans. Rosemary Edmonds, p. 177.

160 Romain and Lesley in Mexico: LB, 'Fragments of a Mexican Journal', *Cornhill*, 1957; LB, 'Many Mexicos', in *Lilac-Bleeding Star*, p. 116; LB, *Romain,* pp. 136–41.

160 Romain's earplugs and brain tumour: LB, 'Many Mexicos', in *Lilac-Bleeding Star*, p. 116.

161 showing Lesley his progress: LB, *Romain*, p. 141.

161 In your mother's love: RG, *Promise at Dawn*, p. 27; backbreaking task: ibid., p. 33.

162 to dash off his first screenplay: *France-Soir*, 26 February 1958.

162 Zanuck dissatisfied: LB to Jock Murray, 12 March 1958, JM.

162 in the George V Hotel: *France-Soir*, 26 February 1958.

162 Fort Archambault, Chad, then Zanuckville, Cameroon: news reports, Gallimard archive.

162 Holden and Howard were cast in preference to a French star: Zanuck insisted that all French actors with passable English wore lavender lingerie. Cable from Darryl Zanuck in John Huston Collection, *Roots of Heaven* Papers, Margaret Herrick Library LA.

163 Lesley and Romain disappointed, then deny it: *Libération*, 22 September 1958; *Paris-Presse*, 24 September 1958.

163 a request by David Selznick and Jennifer Jones's bedroom: LB, interview with author, January 2003.

163 Walter Wanger offered him the role of Caesar: RG, *La Nuit sera calme*, p. 291.

163 insane Roman Emperor: LB to Jock Murray, 12 March 1958, JM.

164 the visiting ambassadress: LB to Jock Murray, 29 March 1958, ibid.

164 Romain afraid of becoming over-Americanized: Bona, *Romain Gary*, p. 234.

165 The Algerian crisis: Julian Jackson, *Charles de Gaulle*, 2003.

165 under special dispensation: Larat, *Romain Gary*, p. 123; Anissimov, *Romain Gary*, p. 312.

165 'The Man Who Stayed Lonely to Save France': RG, *Life*, 8 December 1958, p. 144.

166 *Lady L.* among the twenty most-read books: *France-Soir*, April 1959.

166 l'homme de ma vie: RG, in *De Gaulle Première*, film dir. Daniel Costello, 1975, quoted in Larat, p. 128.

166 still gaps in the narrative: LB to Jock Murray, 29 March 1958, JM.

166 she had reached Chapter 21: LB to Jock and Diana Murray, 8 December 1958, ibid.

166 alive the other side: Jock Murray to LB, 31 December 1958, ibid.

166 Played the guitar, smogs had lifted: LB to Jock and Diana Murray, 8 December 1958, ibid.

166 had not quite finished: LB to Jock Murray and Osyth Leeston, 30 April 1959, ibid.

167 Lesley in Paris, manuscript being typed: LB to Jock Murray, n.d., ibid.

167 Missed Shamyl's grandson: ibid.

167 Found Madame Drancy's journal at Samuelian's: LB, interview with author, January 2003. This incident is not mentioned in her letters or in *Sabres*.

167 fateful meeting with Ali-Akbar-Bek-Toptchibatchi: LB to Jock Murray, 2 July 1959, JM.

167 Toptchibatchi would give her letters of introduction: ibid.

167 She stayed at the old Park Hotel: LB, interview with author, January 2003.

167 The Koska house of Imam Said Shamyl: LB, Epilogue, *Sabres*, p. 476.

168 LB met the imam's great-grandchildren: ibid., p. 477.

168 Zobeida Shamyl initially suspicious: Shusha Guppy, 'Lesley Blanch' in *Looking Back*, p. 1; LB, interview with author, January 2003.

168 a rare portrait of Djemmal-Edin: LB, interview with author, January 2003.

168 Denver Lindley at Viking New York had accepted it: Denver Lindley to Jock Murray, 12 August 1959; John Murray to Denver Lindley, 14 August 1959, JM.

168 splendid over the agonizing procedure of cutting: Jock Murray to Denver Lindley, 2 September 1959; Denver Lindley to Jock Murray, 11 September 1959, JM.

169 Jock wrote to Mr Jones of Lionel Lemon: 2 September 1959, ibid.

169 Lesley visited Horst: LB to Osyth Leeston, n.d., ibid.

169 Robert Lantz planned to sell film rights: Robert Lantz to Jock Murray, 14 December 1959, ibid.

169 Brass elephant and sundry parcels: LB to Jock Murray, n.d., ibid.

169 Neglect and chaos at the consulate: LB to Osyth Leeston, 'Sunday 11', ibid.

169 The ambassador and his entourage: LB to Osyth Leeston, 27 October 1959, ibid.

170 François Moreuil left his card: David Richards, *Played Out: The Jean Seberg Story*, p. 90, p. 92.

Chapter 9: After Supper

171 We are going to speak of terrible things: Stendhal, quoted by François Truffaut in early script of *Breathless*. Michel Marie, 'It really makes you sick! Jean-Luc Godard's *A Bout de souffle*' (1959) in Susan Hayward and Ginette Vincendeau (eds), *French Film: Texts and Contexts*.

172 unspoilt: Otto Preminger, 'I made the mistake of taking a young, inexperienced girl', *The Times*, 22 November 1962.

173 Toptchibatchi wrote ominously to Murray: 4 December 1959, JM.

173 Lesley argued forcefully: LB to Osyth Leeston and Jock Murray, 27 December 1959, ibid.

173 Serializations: Jock Murray to LB, 8 January 1960, ibid.

173 Jock regretted page proofs: Jock Murray to Denver Lindley, 11 March 1960, ibid.

174 Lesley protested against jacket design: LB to no. 50, 12 January, 2 February 1960, ibid.

174 Toptchibatchi wrote to Monsieur Osyth Leeston: 25 February 1960, ibid.

174 Lesley quickly rallied: LB to Jock Murray and Osyth Leeston, undated; LB to Toptchibatchi, 3 March 1960, ibid.

   Postscript: yet as Toptchibatchi predicted, Lesley's Russian sources and spellings have been assumed by opponents of the Kremlin-backed regime in Chechnya to imply research derived from their Russian oppressors and the material therefore tainted by a pro-Russian bias. Vanessa Redgrave, conversation with author, Hampstead, summer 2008.

174 persuading her publishers . . . to change the title: Denver Lindley to Jock Murray, 7 March 1960; LB to no. 50, 9 March 1960; Osyth Leeston to LB, 11 March 1960; Jock Murray to Denver Lindley, 11 March 1960; LB to no. 50, 16 March 1960, JM.

175 Romain was working for Cukor on *Lady L.*: script dated 28 December 1959, 7 January 1960, 18 January 1960, GCC.

175 François called in at the consulate: Richards, *Played Out*, p. 94. This is

the only biography of Jean Seberg and my chief source of information about her.

175 secret short trip to Mexico: Anissimov, *Romain Gary*, p. 331.

176 It is an extraordinary book: LB, *Romain*, p. 126.

176 comparable to *War and Peace*: Hélène Hoppenot, journals, 20 April 1960, BLJD.

176 Lesley's acknowledgement to Romain: *Sabres*, p. xi.

176 Vichy for a health cure: LB to Osyth Leeston, March/April, n.d., JM.

176 applied for two months' leave: Anissimov, *Romain Gary*, p. 334.

176 *A Bout de souffle* was released on 16 March: Michel Marie, '"It really makes you sick!"', in Hayward and Vincendeau (eds), *French Film: Texts and Contexts*.

177 More than a quarter of a million people: ibid.

177 the look, simultaneously blank: David Thomson, *Independent on Sunday*, 2 July 2000.

177 As Mel Gussow in the *Times* put it: Mel Gussow, quoted in 'Character Assassination', *Jump Cut*, 28, 1983, pp. 67–71.

177 This was a new kind of woman: Lesley Cunliffe, 'The Jean Machine', *Vogue* UK, November 1993, p. 190.

178 Jean's breakdown: Richards, *Played Out*, p. 97. Jean's stay at Savigny: Anissimov, *Romain Gary*, p. 335.

178 this unheard-of family precedent: Bernard Giquel, 'Je voudrais avoir une vie ennuyeuse', *Paris Match*, 11 November 1961, p. 126.

178 Started divorce proceedings: Richards, *Played Out*, p. 98.

178 Je suis bouleversé! Hélène Hoppenot, journals, 20 April 1960, BLJD.

179 Lesley's heroic stand at Hollywood: LB to Osyth Leeston, n.d.; LB to Jock Murray and Osyth Leeston, n.d.; LB to Jock Murray, 12 April 1960, JM.

180 the book of my heart: LB to Jock Murray, 12 April 1960, ibid.

180 the project that she had decided on in New York: LB to no. 50, February 1960 n.d., ibid.

180 I opened myself up: RG to Anne-Marie de Vilaine, *L'Express*, 21 April 1960.

180 This book is . . . not an autobiography, Schoolcraft, *Romain Gary*, p. 55; p. 175, n. 38.

181 to make absolutely sure: Cass Canfield to RG, 7 June 1961, Harper & Row Papers, Columbia.

181 J'avais toujours un témoin en moi: RG, *La Nuit sera calme*, p. 27.

181 Bondy's letter to Romain: quoted in Anissimov, *Romain Gary*, p. 94.

182 *Promise at Dawn*: Robert Lantz sold the film rights for $100,000. Romain's friend Jules Dassin eventually made the movie for MGM in 1970, casting his wife, Melina Mercouri, as Romain's mother.

182 Effects of book on Lesley: LB, *Romain*, pp. 153–5.

182 plane crash in Africa: *Promise at Dawn*, p. 260; duel at the Regent's Palace Hotel: ibid., pp. 242–50.

183 the Walter Goetz imbroglio: RG to Jock Murray, 6 May; Jock Murray to RG, 9 May; LB to Jock Murray, 13 May; Jock Murray to LB, 17 May, all 1960, JM.

183 in an exhausted and rather nervy state: Jock Murray, memo, 30 May 1960, ibid.

184 back in Hollywood: LB to Osyth Leeston and Jock Murray, 21 June 1960, ibid.

185 Romain left before Bastille Day: LB, *Romain*, p. 155.

185 Lesley still felt the pain: ibid., p. 155.

185 Romain's negotiations with Harper & Row: Harper & Row Papers, Columbia.

186 Romain on leave from the Quai d'Orsay: Maurice Chapelan, *Figaro Littéraire*, 30 July 1960.

186 She was the only living thing: RG, *Talent Scout*, p. 152.

187 frozen and unable to emote: cf. Jean's petrified performance in *The Mouse that Roared* directed by Jack Arnold, the unexpected hit that made Peter Sellers famous (1959).

188 faithful to Jean for two years: Hélène Hoppenot, journals, 30 September 1960, BLJD.

188 *Paris-Soir*'s account of Jean's divorce: ibid., 28 September 1960.

188 Lesley heard from a New York journalist: ibid., 13 November 1960.

189 leaving parties in her honour: Osyth Leeston to LB, 9 September 1960, JM.

189 miniscule bungalene: LB to Jock Murray, 25 October 1960, ibid.

189 Lesley in New York, Sulgrave Palace Hotel: Robert Lantz to Jock Murray, 10 October 1960, ibid. Jack Paar show, Russian princes: LB to no. 50, 'Saturday', ibid.

189 Does it strike you: Rebecca West to LB, 12 September 1960, ibid.

191 the power of Gibbon: Brian Aldiss, *Oxford Mail*, 29 September 1960.

191 novelistic invention of dialogue: 'Conquest of the Caucasus', *Times Literary Supplement*, 14 October 1960.

191 words as thick as blackberries: Harold Nicolson, *Observer*, 23 October 1960.

191 splendid story, overwhelming partiality: *The Economist*, 12 November 1960.

191 excessive savagery: L. Collier, *Geographical Journal*, June 1961.

191 a splendid piece of romantic writing etc: Mark Frankland, 'Caucasian Romance', *Time and Tide*, 3 December 1960.

192 couldn't invent: Guppy, 'Lesley Blanch' in *Looking Back*, p. 22.

192 detection and intuition and a subconscious enlightenment: LB, 'Laurence Hope in India' in *Lilac Star*, p. 201.

192 Comparison with Kapuscinski: cf. his *Shah of Shahs*, London: Penguin Classics, 2006.

193 Romain refused to see her: LB to George Cukor, 19 November 1960, GCC.

193 C'est Venus entière à sa proie attachée: Hélène Hoppenot, journals, 13 November 1960, BLJD.

194 Cukor agreed to her delayed return: George Cukor to LB, telegram, 29 November 1960, GCC.

194 Jean's *chevalier servant*: Hélène Hoppenot, journals, 5 November 1960, BLJD.

194 apartment in the rue du Bac: *Paris-Presse*, 15 December 1960.

194 la pauvre petite: Hélène Hoppenot, journals, 10 December 1960, BLJD. It's a fashion: ibid.

195 the great disappointment of my life: ibid.

Chapter 10: Divorce

196 She well remembered: RG, *Lady L.*, p. 19.

196 new quarters in Hollywood and Countess Goulash: LB to Jock Murray, 10 March 1960, JM.

196 Lesley was not on the studio payroll: staff list on *Lady L.*, 12 April 1961, GCC.

196 they were reproducing Paris 1900: ibid.

196 Lesley's research and sketches: ibid.

197 inside Romain's portrait of herself: Test Scenes, ibid.

197 Cukor's memo: George Cukor to Sol Siegel, 11 April 1961, ibid.

197 little clot: LB, interview with author, January 2003.

197 just walked out on that one: Gavin Lambert, *On Cukor*, 1972.

197 The project folded: eventually Peter Ustinov wrote the script and directed the movie with Sophia Loren as Annette/Lady L. and Paul Newman as a disappointing Armand (who ends up as Lady L's chauffeur, not in her strongbox), in a big-budget production that flattened

Romain's lightly ironic tale. David Niven, Philippe Noiret, Marcel Dalio, Michel Piccoli and Claude Dauphin co-starred. Dire notices greeted the film in 1965; Ustinov omitted it from his memoirs.

198 flowery felicitation: LB to Jock Murray, 8 May 1960, JM.

198 several weeks in a Hollywood clinic: Hélène Hoppenot, journals, 4 November 1961, BLJD.

198 like an Arab princess and un apartement de Sheikh arabe: Yves Agid, interview with author, 11 June 1964.

199 *She had accepted him*: ibid.

199 c'est son boulot: Bernard Giquel, 'Je voudrais avoir une vie ennuyeuse', *Paris Match*, 11 November 1961, p. 26.

200 the predatory temptress in *The Blue Angel*: Hélène Hoppenot, journals, 13 November 1960, BLJD.

200 journalists . . . made him her Svengali: cf. Donald Labadie, 'Everybody's Galatea', *Show*, August 1963, p. 77.

200 grande séduction: Yves Agid, interview with author, June 1964.

200 Basically she had no refuge and which seemed logical: ibid.

201 Jean's tour of the Far East: Richards, *Played Out*, Chapter 13.

202 tetanised: Yves Agid, interview with author, June 2004.

202 Jean's film and stage offers: Richards, *Played Out*, Chapter 12.

202 Jealousy: *Paris-Jour*, 23 September 1961, Gallimard archive.

203 There has never been: Bernard Giquel, 'Je voudrais avoir une vie ennuyeuse', *Paris Match*.

203 'Love has Made a Woman of Me': Philippe Alexandre, *Jours de France*, 18 November 1961, p. 42.

203 Lesley – Madame Romain Gary: ibid.

204 that talented English writer: Sam White's Paris Diary, *Evening Standard*, 10 November 1961, p. 7. Painful lack of taste: ibid.

204 avalanche of publicity and clearly distressed: ibid., 17 November 1961.

204 Lesley stayed in rue de Varenne: Hélène Hoppenot, journals, 4 November 1961, BLJD.

204 In the daily *Paris-presse Intransigeant*: Jean-François Devay, 'Mme Romain Gary ne répondra même pas', 21 November 1961, p. 3.

205 beside himself with rage: Hélène Hoppenot, journals, 20 November 1961, BLJD.

205 faux ménage: ibid.

205 Hélène advised her to see a lawyer: ibid.

205 Two hundred thousand dollars: ibid. Diable!: ibid.

205 The most extraordinary thing to me: Scott-James, interview with author, 11 June 2002.

206 Romain begged Vimont and Hoppenot: Hélène Hoppenot, journals, 9 March 1962, BLJD.

206 Eden Fleming was summoned: ibid., 12 April 1962.

206 a divorce would hardly seems [sic] worthwhile: ibid.

206 Jean told Paton Price she deliberately fell pregnant: Richards, *Played Out*, p. 124.

207 Gee, that was a funny sort of picture: Joseph Roddy, 'The Restyling of Jean Seberg', *Look* magazine, 7 March 1962.

207 Diego's birth: Richards, *Played Out*, pp. 123–6.

208 Romain's letter to René Agid: Anissimov, *Romain Gary*, p. 368.

208 claimed that Lesley had tried to stipulate: Hélène Hoppenot, journals, 20 August 1962, BLJD.

208 borrowed money from friends: LB to George Cukor, 17 February 1963; George Cukor to LB, letter and telegram, 28 February 1963; LB to George Cukor, 8 March 1963, GCC.

208 A little note of despair: ibid., 6 February 1963.

208 Paid up at the last minute: LB to Jock Murray, 14 March 1963, JM; LB to George Cukor, 8 March 1963, GCC.

209 Story for *Show*: LB to George Cukor, 8 March 1963, ibid.

209 Martha Blanch's cat: LB to Osyth Leeston and Jock Murray, 14 March 1963, JM.

209 told the Hoppenots he would be ruined: Hélène Hoppenot, journals, 5 April 1963, BLJD.

209 Lunch guests at the Elysée Palace: Elysée Palace chief of protocol Jean-Paul Alexis, quoted in Michel Tauriac, *Vivre avec de Gaulle*, Paris: Plon, 2009, p. 273.

209 Romain and Jean's marriage in Corsica: Richards, *Played Out*, p. 140; press cuttings, Gallimard.

Chapter 11: The Siberian Book

211 The human soul's need for beauty: RG, *Lady L.* (French edition), quoted in Schoolcraft, *Romain Gary*, p. 19.

211 crimson-painted walls: Valerie Wade, 'Chez Elles', *Sunday Times Magazine*, 27 September 1970, p. 50.

211 back in circulation by early summer 1962: Hélène Hoppenot, journals, 18 June 1962, BLJD.

212 Jockey Club set: LB to George Cukor, 8 March 1963, GCC.

212 the only American Nancy found acceptable: LB to George Cukor, 17 February 1962, ibid.

212 All was lost; confused; wrong: LB to Osyth Leeston, 'Monday'; LB to Osyth Leeston and Jock Murray, 'Monday'; LB to Osyth Leeston and Jock Murray, 'Saturday'; LB to Osyth Leeston, 23 June; LB to Jock Murray and Osyth Leeston, n.d.: all between April and June 1963, JM. Lost typescript: John Murray to the Postmaster, Western District Post Office, 6 May 1963, ibid.

212 Many thanks for your letter: Osyth Leeston to LB, 11 July 1963, ibid.

213 shrieking before she was hit: Osyth Leeston to LB, 16 August 1963, ibid.

214 It never seems to have occurred: LB, 'Laurence Hope – A Shadow in the Sunlight', *Lilac-Bleeding Star*, p. 186.

214 the chimera of distance: 'Perpetuam Mobile', *Lilac-Bleeding Star*, p. 2. (Cristiani's instrument was the cello, not the violin as Lesley stated. In 1845 Cristiani gave the first public cello recital by a woman.)

215 The artist's other soul and her mileage: ibid., p. 14.

215 So quiet have we kept: Osyth Leeston to LB, 26 September 1963, ibid.

216 conifer tree dug up from the taiga: in Lesley's rooftop garden, LB, *Lilac-Bleeding Star*, p. 97. Transplanted to Eden Fleming's garden: *Mind's Eye*, p. 345.

216 that most delicate and subtle part: Osyth Leeston to LB, 13 December 1963, JM.

216 The Traveller's son: ibid.

217 Returned her contract: LB to Osyth Leeston, 31 December 1963, ibid.

217 partly enthusiastic: review, Osyth Leeston to LB, 3 January 1964, ibid.

217 That novel was a landscape: Guppy, 'Lesley Blanch' in *Looking Back*, p.1.

218 Lesley worked at Albemarle Street with Jane Boulenger: Jane Moore, interview with author, 14 April 2004.

218 injured her foot again in Tunis: LB to Jock Murray and Osyth Leeston, 12 August 1964, JM.

218 sad and disappointing news: Osyth Leeston to LB, 14 August 1964, ibid.

219 Simon Bessie was enthusiastic: Jane Boulenger to Simon Bessie, 15 October 1964; Simon Bessie to Jane Boulenger, 23 October 1964, ibid.

219 Hassan and Hilda Arfa: General Hassan Arfa, *Under Five Shahs*, 1964.

220 Lesley recommended Hilda Arfa's memoirs: LB to Osyth Leeston, 3 November 1964, JM.

220 Introduced Baronne Trenck: LB to Osyth Leeston, 8 April 1965, ibid.

220 Osyth Leeston's letter to Lesley: 17 May 1965, ibid.

220 The year of the Minarets: LB to no. 50, Christmas 1964, ibid.

221 She had reached the Afghan frontier: Hélène Hoppenot, journals, 12 December 1964, BLJD.

221 Lesley urged George Cukor to read *The Nine Tiger Man*: LB to George Cukor, 10 January 1965, GCC.

222 'Low Behaviour in High Places': *Nine Tiger Man* subtitle.

222 Delighted Dearest Lesley: George Cukor, telegram to LB, 4 February 1965, ibid.

222 *Nine Tiger Man* offered to Elizabeth Taylor, Audrey Hepburn: George Cukor to LB, 1 March 1965, ibid.

223 a smasher: George Cukor to LB, 16 March 1965, ibid.

223 photographed for *Newsweek*: LB to George Cukor, 22 March 1965, ibid.

223 My brain reels: George Cukor to LB, 30 March 1965, ibid.

223 exquisite: LB to George Cukor, 24 May 1965, ibid.

223 skittish anecdote: ibid.

223 Martha Blanch transferred to a convent: LB to George Cukor, 6 November 1965, ibid.

223 a house for sale: ibid.

224 Lesley's illness and operation: LB to George Cukor, 16 May 1966, ibid.; LB to Jock Murray, n.d. (1966), JM.

224 spent the early part of 1966 convalescing: LB to George Cukor, 16 May 1966, GCC.

224 Paperback reprint of *Wilder Shores*: Jock Murray to LB, 27 January 1966, JM.

224 always calm: LB to Nancy Mitford, 'Hospital, Monday', n.d.

225 She is the most difficult person: Nancy Mitford to James Lees-Milne, 26 September 1970, quoted in Charlotte Mosley (ed.), *Love from Nancy: The Letters of Nancy Mitford*, London: Hodder & Stoughton, 1993, p. 521.

225 Darling, must you: LB, telephone interview with author, 31 July 2002.

226 tiny twins with large bottles of drink: Maureen Cleave, 'A mystery woman lifts the veil', *Daily Telegraph*, 1987.

226 Violet Trefusis: Philippe Julian and John Phillips, *Violet Trefusis: Life and Letters*, 1976.

226 *Here Lies Mrs Trefusis*: Harold Acton, *Nancy Mitford*, p. 176.

226 Lesley and Auntie Vi: Nancy Mitford to Alvilde Lees-Milne, 1 April 1967, ibid., p. 184.

226 Lesley's presents to Violet: Julian and Phillips, *Violet Trefusis*, p. 130.

226 Nancy proposed a trade union: Selina Hastings, *Nancy Mitford*, p. 177, footnote.

227 John Mortimer worked on *The Nine Tiger Man* script: Emanuel Levy, *George C: Master of Elegance*, p. 315.

227 Fox was insisting on another lavish production: Gavin Lambert, *On Cukor*, p. 249.

227 on the last two chapters: LB to George Cukor, 2 January 1967, GCC.

227 tremendous fun: Philip Ziegler, interview with author, 18 February 2004.

227 An abrupt jump in the text: LB, *Mind's Eye*, p. 274.

228 The gap: Ziegler, interview with author, February 2004.

228 corrected proofs during the May 1968 riots: William Foster, *Scotsman*, 14 December 1968.

228 My book is not altogether autobiography: LB, *Mind's Eye*, jacket copy, 1968.

228 the love of my heart: ibid., p. 13.

229 little pink and yellow villas: ibid., p. 152.

229 What I loved about her writing: Ziegler, interview with author, February 2004.

230–1 A rather odd book: Rodney Ackland, 'Traveller's Tale', *Spectator*, 13 November 1968. Quotations courtesy of the Rodney Ackland Estate.

232 It's a dream world: Ziegler, interview with author, London, February 2004.

232 Using the means of fiction: Schoolcraft, *Romain Gary*, p. 57.

233 platonic conception: F. Scott Fitzgerald, *The Great Gatsby*, Harmondsworth: Penguin, p. 105.

233 incorruptible dream: ibid., p. 160.

234 Only one (male) reviewer: Jean-Paul Enthoven, 'La folie russe de Lady L', *Le Point*, 13 June 2003, p. 119.

234 grouped with Nancy Mitford: Valerie Wade, 'Chez Elles', photographed by Roger Gain, *Sunday Times Magazine*, 27 September 1970, p. 50.

234 'People at Home Abroad': photographed by Henry Clarke, *Vogue* UK, July 1966, p. 60.

234 a big feature on scent: LB, 'Scent: Essence of Adventure', ibid., November 1966, p. 98.

234 she revisited Bulgaria: LB, 'Bulgarian Rhapsody', ibid., April 1969, p. 98.

235 in spite of my love for Jean and America: RG, quoted in Richards, *Played Out,* p. 192.

235 I had to tell Romain: Roderick Mann, 'Why I am living in a Deep-Freeze – by Jean Seberg', London: *Sunday Express*, 17 August 1969.

235 I'll give you a hint: Joyce Haber, *LA Times*, 1969, quoted in Richards, *Played Out*, p. 192.

235 'Can a small-town girl from Ohio find happiness in Paris?': 'Newsmakers', *Newsweek*, 24 August 1970.

235 RG, 'Le grand couteau': *France-Soir*, 29 August 1970.

235 Witnesses to the lie: JS quoted in Des Wilson, 'A star is reborn', *Observer Magazine*, 10 March 1974, p. 25.

236 Jean's letter to Romain: quoted in Anissimov, p. 475.

236 Her mother's death at Hazlewell: Martha Blanch, death certificate.

Chapter 12: The Peacock Throne

237 In my teens: Shusha Guppy, *The Blindfold Horse*, p. 39.

237 Come out from behind the veil: Eve Arnold, *The Unretouched Woman*, p. 74.

237 She was a romantic, I a realist: Eve Arnold, *In Retrospect*, p. 135.

237 went to woo Lesley: Meriel McCooey, phone call with author, 2007.

237 unwilling to travel with another woman: Eve Arnold, *In Retrospect*, p. 135. Lunch at the Wig and Pen Club: ibid.

238 the mountains of Afghanistan: ibid.

238 the wild and lovely kingdom: LB and Eve Arnold, 'Behind the Veil': '1. The Seven Veils of Islam: Afghanistan', *Sunday Times Magazine*, 1 November 1970, p. 34.

238 splendour and savagery: ibid. Violent rhythms: ibid.

238 As the French say: Eve Arnold, *In Retrospect*, p. 135.

240 Lesley loved it all: ibid., p. 143.

240 extremely tenacious: LB to Osyth Leeston, n.d., JM.

240 three long instalments: LB and Eve Arnold, 'Behind The Veil': '1. The Seven Veils of Islam: Afghanistan', 1 November 1970, p.34; '2: The Trucial States', ibid., 8 November 1970, p. 18; '3. Egypt', ibid., 15 November, p. 40, *Sunday Times Magazine*.

241 tradition, protection, equality: LB, '1: Afghanistan', ibid., p. 34.

241 the necessity of *doing*: LB, '2: The Trucial States', ibid., p. 25.

241 everywhere except in bed: ibid., p. 19.

241 Women are what men make them: ibid.

241 Muslim women seemed to glow: ibid., p. 25.

241 I walked with the Sheikh: Jane Digby's diary, 5 January 1954, in Mary S. Lovell, *A Scandalous Life: The Biography of Jane Digby*, p. 178.

243 trains almost under the bed: LB, phone call with author, July 2002.

243 The Sitwells' visit: LB to Nancy Mitford, 26 March 1973.

243 I seem to have lived: LB, 'My Day . . . and what of it?', *Vogue*, January 1973, p. 4.

243 Drains, for example: ibid.

244 Slop about: ibid.

244 Ah! Needlework: LB, 'Every Cushion tells a Story', *Vogue*, January 1974, p. 84.

244 Titti-Mi died: LB to Nancy Mitford, 10 October 1972.

244 six-week visit to Iran: LB to Jock Murray, 28 September 1973; LB to Jock Murray, 20 November 1973, JM.

246 the desert she had loved: LB, *Pavilions of the Heart: The Four Walls of Love*, p. 92.

246 It was for love of her: ibid., p. 112.

246 that marvellous life force: ibid., p. 123.

247 creative artists: ibid., p. 130.

247 bourgeois stabilities: ibid., p. 131.

247 My first wife was too old: Martine Carré, 'Dix ans avec RG', interview by Gilles Martin-Chauffier, *Paris Match*, 6 November 1981.

248 as if she had cultivated her own ghost: RG, *Europa*, Paris: Editions Gallimard, 1972, p. 223.

248 Edwina emblematic of Jean: Romain's insistence in *La Nuit sera calme* (pp. 62–71) that Edwina was based on his first love Ilona Gesmay, who later became incurably insane, looks like a deliberate misdirection to avoid associations with Jean.

248 a kind of autobiographical novel: François Bondy, 'On the Death of a Friend', London, *Encounter*, August 1981, p. 33.

249 Divided between laughter and indignation: Hélène Hoppenot, journals, 12 May 1974, BLJD.

249 It's all pure fiction: ibid. Falsified too: ibid.

249 British tax was being deducted: Gordon S. Blair and Mr Bray (secretary at John Murray), correspondence, January 1975, JM.

250 sinking heart: LB to Osyth Leeston, 20 May 1975, ibid.

250 became a client of A.D. Peters: Osyth Leeston to LB, 9 April 1976, ibid.

250 Letter from acquaintance: LB to Osyth Leeston, 21 May 1974; Osyth Leeston, memo to Jock Murray, 4 June 1974, ibid.

250 Mme Shaply-Shamyl: LB to no. 50, undated postcard (early 1976), ibid.

250 this unbelievable charm: Scott-James, interview with author, January 1997.

251 fondness for the esoteric: Gerald de Gaury, *Traces of Travel Brought Home from Abroad*, p. 48.

251 sits tranquilly beside him: ibid., p. 109.

251 We were all cutting capers: LB, interview with author, January 2003.

251 I used to say, I cannot dress: ibid. A turban with a great brooch: ibid.

252 The village's Ligurian customs: LB, *From Wilder Shores: The Tables of My Travels*, p. 34.

252 Visit from Katharine Hepburn: LB to George Cukor, December 1969, GCC. Lesley described Garbo in this incident in *Romain*, p. 94.

252 delighted to renew an old acquaintance with Osbert: Scott-James, *Sketches from a Life*, p. 71; interview with author, 14 January 1997.

252 France you see to me is a country: LB, interview with author, January 2003.

252 In January 1975 she tried Morocco: LB to George Cukor, 27 January 1975, GCC.

253 Light of the Aryans: LB, *Farah, Shahbanou of Iran, Queen of Persia*, London: Collins, 1978, p. 13.

254 Lord Chamberlain figure: Ziegler, interview with author, February 2004. Last time we talked about this: ibid.

254 Savak's network of 60,000 agents: Ryszard Kapuscinski, *Shah of Shahs*, p. 46.

255 Shahbanou had invited her: LB to Osyth Leeston, 26 October 1975, JM.

255 Sir Anthony Parsons made Lesley welcome: LB, *Farah*, Acknowledgements, p. 9.

255 The Shah and his retinue were served Bloody Marys: Barnaby Rogerson and Rose Baring, interview with author, 27 April 2004. A phalanx of bodyguards swimming: ibid.

255 having to use a tape recorder: LB, *Farah*, p. 16.

256 pined in vain for the Bazaar: ibid., p. 75.

256 impertinent gossip: LB, 'The Pleasures, Palaces and Pillars of Persia', *Vogue* UK, June 1975, p. 120.

257 the elliptical courtier's approach: LB, *Farah*, p. 15.

257 The Imperial Court radiated a hard, meretricious glitter: Anthony Parsons, *The Pride and the Fall*, p. 21.

257 lovely, very feminine crown: LB, *Farah*, p. 122.

257 the size of a smallish tangerine: ibid.

257 ceremonies for fiftieth anniversary: Parsons, *The Pride and the Fall*, p. 21.

258 In 1977 she returned twice; quiet orderly Switzerland: LB to Pat Creed, two letters, n.d.; Pat Creed, interviews with author, 19 April and 6 May 2004.

258 Ziegler was to accompany Lesley to Iran: Ziegler, interview with author, February 2004.

258 Launch party cancelled: LB to Pat Creed, 13 May 1978.

259 one of the most ignoble episodes of modern history: Guppy, 'Lesley Blanch' in *Looking Back*, p. 18.

259 'Farah: The Worker Queen', *Cosmopolitan* UK, July 1978, p. 100.

259 stick to the facts: Ziegler, interview with author, February 2004.

259 returned to the biography of Pierre Loti: LB to Pat Creed, 31 May 1978; LB to Pat Creed, 12 December (1979).

259 Stayed with the Rothschilds: LB to Pat Creed, 12 December 1979.

259 more informally with Susan Train: ibid. Pat Creed, interview with author, 19 April 2004.

260 she'd read so much: Susan Train in *Une vie, une oeuvre*, radio broadcast produced by Nathalie Triandafyllides, presented by Françoise Estèbe, with Georgia de Chamberet, Christiane Pierre-Loti Viaud, Philip Mansel, Susan Train, Guillaume Villeneuve, France-Culture, 22 May 2008.

260 in a room, smoking a narguileh: ibid.

Chapter 13: The Life and Death of Emile Ajar

261 Mon 'je' ne me suffit pas: RG, *La Nuit sera calme*, p. 179.

261 A note from Romain: LB, *Romain*, p. 158.

261 a handful of confidants: but Lesley's name was not among those listed by Romain in *La Vie et mort d'Emile Ajar* (1981). RG, *The Life and Death of Emile Ajar* with *King Solomon*, trans. Barbara Wright, p. 256.

263 represents in their nature the moving moment: Emile Ajar, *Gros-Câlin*, Paris: Mercure de France, 1974, p. 105.

263 they always find themselves the same: ibid.

264 heartbreaking kid: Michel Cournot, 'Ma vérité sur l'affaire Ajar'. Cournot's article is one of three first-hand accounts of the Emile Ajar story which have been my principal sources. The second is by Paul Pavlowitch, *L'Homme que l'on croyait* (1981). The third is *The Life and Death of Emile Ajar* by Romain Gary himself (op. cit.).

265 Paul Pavlowitch couldn't remember exactly: Pavlowitch, *L'homme que l'on croyait*, p. 80, p. 85.

265 give life to this picaro: RG, *The Life and Death of Emile Ajar*, in *King Solomon*, p. 252.

265 all the pages of Ajar: Cournot, 'Ma vérité sur l'affaire Ajar'.

265 I knew that Emile Ajar was doomed: RG, *Life and Death of Emile Ajar*, p. 252.

266 a super-Queneau: Jean-Marie Catonné, *Romain Gary/Emile Ajar*, p. 13.

266 A baroque and deeply moving masterpiece: Yves Andouard, *Le Canard enchaîné*, 1 October 1975.

266 magico-poetic realism . . . a work of art: Michel Georis in *L'Eventail*, 1 October 1975.

266 total novel: RG, *Life and Death of Emile Ajar*, p. 251.

268 an uncle who I call Tonton Macoute: Emile Ajar, *Pseudo*, Paris: Mercure de France, 1976, p. 26.

268 two characters battling inside me: ibid., p. 147.

269 like a meteorite: Pavlowitch, *L'Homme que l'on croyait*, p. 258.

269 vomited: Matthieu Galey, *L'Express*, 20 December 1976.

270 This is my last book: Emile Ajar, *Pseudo*, p. 213.

271–3 Last months of Jean Seberg: Richards, *Played Out*, Chapters 37 to 39; biographies of RG.

272 A bona fide movie (*La Légion saute sur le Kolwezi*): Raoul Coutard, interview with author, January 2004.

272 Death of Jean Seberg: Richards, *Played Out*, p. 374; press reports.

273 Jean Seberg and the FBI: Romain's press conference, 10 September 1979, Journal télévisé, *Antenne 2*. 'Après la mort de Jean Seberg', *Le Monde*, 12 September 1979. Jean Seberg's FBI file, copied under Freedom of Information Act.

273 I've fulfilled my duty: RG, quoted in Bona, *Romain Gary*, p. 380.

273 The image of Jean is still intact: RG, quoted in Pavlowitch, *L'homme que l'on croyait*, p. 308.

273 The Nazis were *human*: RG, *Les Cerfs-volants*, Paris: Editions Gallimard, 1980, p. 278.

274 You have got to be mad: Gilbert Salem, *24 Heures*, 7–8 June 1980.

274 Story of war and grand passion: Daniel Adler, *La Presse Nouvelle*, 11 July 1980.

274 Finished with that shit: Pavlowitch, *L'Homme que l'on croyait,* p. 292.

274 Romain's 'suicide' call to René Agid and with panache: Yves Agid, interview with author, June 2004.

274 Romain called to see Lesley: LB, interview with author, January 2003.

275 I'm going to kill myself: Pavlowitch, *L'Homme que l'on croyait*, p. 312.

275 Nothing to do with Jean Seberg: biographics of RG.

275 Romain's funeral: biographies of RG, especially Bona, *Romain Gary*; press reports.

276 My father considered: Diego Gary quoted in Bona, *Romain Gary*, p. 396.

276 this was also the man who went to war: Yves Agid, interview with author, June 2004.

276 Romain's ashes: Anissimov, *Romain Gary*, pp. 651–2.

277 Who knows what a full bibliography: François Bondy, 'On the Death of a Friend', London, *Encounter*, August 1981, p. 33.

277 Bernard Pivot's book programme: 'Romain Gary et Emile Ajar', *Apostrophes*, 3 July 1981.

278 I've enjoyed myself very much: RG, *Life and Death of Emile Ajar*, in *King Solomon*, p. 256.

278 Jacqueline Piatier: *Le Monde*, 2 July 1981.

278 Ajar was a money-spinner, who got the profits?: *Libération*, 3 July 1981.

278 Yiddish Angst: Jean-Marie Rouart, *Le Quotidien de Paris*, 7 July 1981.

278 Two souls dwelled, Faust-like: François Bondy, 'A Man and his Doubt', *Encounter*, October 1981, p. 42.

278 Volume was the mark of success: LB, *Romain*, pp. 122–3.

279 respect for his oeuvre: see Tzvetan Todorov, 'The Achievement of Romain Gary' in *Hope and Memory*, trans. David Bellos, London: Atlantic Books, 2003, p. 213.

279 it improves my place at table: Alice Wooledge Salmon, obituary.

Chapter 14: Loti-land

280 It is good to know the truth: Arab proverb.

280 dismayed by Lesley's choice: Ziegler, interview with author, February 2004.

280 Loti absolved from imperialism: Philip Mansel, foreword to LB, *Pierre Loti: Travels with the Legendary Romantic*, 2004.

280 the role of the heart: Philip Mansel, 'Landscape of the Heart', *Spectator*, 24 November 2001, p. 52.

281 reversing Dr Johnson's maxim (which was that the object of travel was to regulate the imagination by reality): LB, interview with author, January 2003.

281 Mais les marriages de Loti: LB, 'Loti-land', *Lilac-Bleeding Star*, pp. 172–3.

281 Lesley's rare appearance on French TV: Bernard Pivot, *Apostrophes*, 13 June 1986.

282 louanges de Loti: Christiane Pierre-Loti Viaud in 'Lesley Blanch: Une Vie, une oeuvre', France-Culture.

282 she wanted to *capture* something: Christiane Pierre-Loti Viaud, ibid.

282 I was not my type: LB, *Pierre Loti* (2004 edition), p. 9.

283 his later French biographer: Alain Quella-Villéger, *Pierre Loti: Le pèlerin de la planète*, 1998.

283 Lucien Jousselin's aperçu: LB, *Pierre Loti* (2004 edition), pp. 156, 157.

283 Laissez-moi parler sur ce temps!: Christiane Pierre-Loti Viaud in 'Lesley Blanch: Une Vie, une oeuvre', France-Culture.

284 She would come back in tears: Pat Creed, interview with author, 19 April 2004.

284 celebratory trip to Muscat and Oran: LB to Pat Creed, postcard, 23 September (1983); trip called off, ibid.

284 Perfect darlings: LB, interview with author, January 2003.

284 Still working on final draft: LB to Pat Creed, 16 February 1983; planned to bring it to London, ibid.

284 excellent biography: Rev. Philip Thody, review, *Times Literary Supplement*, 18 November 1983, p. 1282.

284 Lesley was not much of a one: Ziegler, interview with author, London, February 2004.

284 Lesley's trip to Loti-land: LB to Pat Creed, postcard, 23 September 1983.

285 shattered her knee: LB to Pat Creed, 29 November 1983. Lovelace project: ibid.

285 the dishes, places and people: LB, *From Wilder Shores: The Tables of My Travels*, Foreword, p. 1.

285 rich, swarthy tapenade: ibid., p. 33. Careless luxury: ibid., p. 62.

285 Proust's Questionnaire: LB, interview with author, January 2003.

286 All beautiful: Valerie Grove, phone call with author, 13 February 1989. *Humming* with garlic: ibid.

286 to appear that Sunday: Valerie Grove, 'An appetite for exotic dishes', 'Look' pages, *Sunday Times*, 9 July 1989.

286 The house itself is invisible: Maureen Cleave, 'A mystery woman lifts the veil', *Daily Telegraph*, 11 July 1987. A reviewer once conceded: ibid. Quotations by permission of Maureen Cleave.

287 bringing the cats out in eczema: LB to Pat Creed, 'Tuesday', n.d.

287 peasant dwelling in a bamboo grove: Guppy, 'Lesley Blanch' in *Looking Back*, p. 2.

288 embedded in another country: LB, phone call with author, July 2002.

288 darling little rat: Pat Creed, interview with author, 19 April 2004.

288 I tell them I met everyone: LB, interview with author, January 2003.

288 orange longjohns: Philippa Scott, interview with author, 2 April 2009.

288 lunches at the Ritz: Nabil Saidi, phone call with author, 9 April 2009.

289 enchanting and strange and rather dotty: Ziegler, interview with author, February 2004.

289 the Erlanger boys called her 'Les': LB, interview with author, January 2003.

289 Lesley babysitting Toby and Turi Munthe: Baring and Rogerson, interview with author, 27 April 2004.

289 effectively one hundred per cent: 'Une villa détruite par le feu avenue Katherine Mansfield', Faits divers, Nice-Matin, Menton edition, 7 April 1994, p. 2.

290 Everybody was awfully kind: LB, interview with author, January 2003.

290 they're very paper-minded here: ibid.

290 John Murray packed up parcels of books: Grant McIntyre, email to author, August 2008.

290 Get up and get on with it: Anne Boston, 'Home from a wilder shore', The Times, 24 May 2003.

291 one of the finest English books about Russia: Philip Mansel, 'Landscape of the Heart', Spectator.

291 Too little too late: LB, interview with author, January 2003.

292 at once autobiographical account: LB, Voyage au coeur de l'esprit, 2003, trans. Guillaume Villeneuve.

292 Lesley's publisher at Denoël: Héloise d'Ormesson, meeting with author, 12 November 2003.

292 high-born, well brought up libertine: Dominique Bona, 'Les passions orientales de Lesley Blanch' in Le Figaro Littéraire, 8 May 2003, p. 8.

292 affluent London suburb: Anne Crignon, 'Lady L.' in Le Nouvel Observateur, 15–21 May 2003, p. 114.

293 I am my plants: LB, phone call with author, 2002.

293 past suitors: LB, interview with author, January 2003.

293 They're awfully babyish: Graham Lord, Daily Telegraph, 10 July 1993.

294 an enormous new biography: Anissimov, Romain Gary.

294 Were they aware, in entrusting to her: Anne Crignon, 'La biographie de

Romain Gary: Sa vie devant nous', *Le Nouvel Observateur*, 26 February 2004.

295 Old age is not for cissies: LB, interview with author, January 2003.

295 Lesley's last days and illness: Guillaume de Villeneuve, in 'Lesley Blanch: Une Vie, une oeuvre', France-Culture broadcast, 2008.

295 A year ago, at a hundred and one: obituary of LB, *Daily Telegraph*, 10 May 2007.

Sources

Books by Lesley Blanch

The Wilder Shores of Love, London: John Murray, 1954. Published in French as *Les Rives sauvages de l'amour*, Paris: Plon, 1956.

Round the World in Eighty Dishes, illustrations by the author, London: John Murray, 1956.

The Game of Hearts: Harriette Wilson and Her Memoirs, edited and with introduction by LB, London: Gryphon, 1957. Reprinted as *Harriette Wilson's Memoirs*, London: Phoenix Press, 2003.

The Sabres of Paradise, London: John Murray, 1960. Reprinted as *The Sabres of Paradise: Conquest and Vengeance in the Caucasus*, with introduction by Philip Marsden, London: I.B. Tauris & Co., 2004. Published in French as *Les Sabres du Paradis*, trans. Jean Lambert, Paris: Le Cercle du Nouveau Livre, 1963; Denoël, 2004.

Under a Lilac-Bleeding Star, London: John Murray, 1963.

The Nine Tiger Man, London: Collins, 1965. Published in French as *L'Homme aux neuf tigres*, trans. Jean Périer, Paris: Robert Laffont, 1966.

Journey into the Mind's Eye: Fragments of an Autobiography, London: Collins, 1968. Reprinted by Sickle Moon, London, 2001. Published in French as *Voyage au coeur de l'esprit*, trans. Guillaume Villeneuve, Paris: Editions Denoël, 2003.

Pavilions of the Heart: The Four Walls of Love, London: Weidenfeld & Nicolson, 1974. Reprinted by Tauris Parke, London, 2007.

Farah Shahbanou of Iran, Queen of Persia, London: Collins, 1978.

Pierre Loti: Portrait of an Escapist, London: Collins, 1983. Reprinted as *Pierre Loti: Travels with the Legendary Romantic*, with introduction by Philip Mansel, London: I.B. Tauris & Co., 2004. Published in French as *Pierre Loti*, trans. Jean Lambert, Paris: Seghers, 1986.

From Wilder Shores: The Tables of My Travels, London: John Murray, 1989.

Romain, un regard particulier, trans. Jean Lambert, Arles: Actes Sud, 1998 (published only in French). Reprinted by Editions Rocher, 2009.

Lesley Blanch and Marie Rambert, 'Some Impressions of the Ballet in

Russia – 1934', in *Playtime in Russia*, ed. Hubert Griffith, London: Methuen, 1935, p. 83.

Books Illustrated by Lesley Blanch

Racecourse and Hunting Field, edited and introduction by Samuel J. Looker with drawings in colour by LB, London: Constable, 1931.

Constance Spry, *Come into the Garden, Cook*, with black-and-white drawings by LB, London: J.M. Dent & Sons, 1942.

Selected Articles by Lesley Blanch

Architectural Digest

'Antiques: Amenities that Travel', 43: 9 September 1986, p. 164.
'Paintings of the Table', 44: 3 March 1987, p. 24.
'The Forbidden Pleasures of Topkapi', 45: 5 May 1988, p. 276.

Cornhill

'The Fading Garden and the Forgotten Rose', 165: 987, Summer 1951, p. 228.
'Isabelle Eberhardt', 166: 991, Spring 1952, p. 5.
'Fragments of a Balkan Journal', 166: 994, Winter 1952–3, p. 304.
'The Echo of a Voyage' (extract from *The Wilder Shores of Love*), 167: 998, Winter 1953–4, p. 125.
'Unfolded Tents' (extract from *The Wilder Shores of Love*), 167: 999, Spring 1954, p. 181.
'Loti-land', 168: 1007, Spring 1956, p. 388.
'Fragments of a Mexican Journal', 169: 1009–14, 1957, p. 277.

Daily Mail

LB, 'Private View' column, Mondays, 6 August to 12 November 1945.

Harper's Bazaar

'Anti-Beige: A Plea for Scarlet Living', June 1935, p. 18.
'The Gentle Jungle' (profile of Eden Box), December 1949, p. 60.

The Leader

Weekly column on cinema, Hulton Press, 30 December 1944 to 20 April 1946.

Lilliput

'Gooseberry Fool' (short story), 14: 5 May 1944, p. 356.
'Uncle Petya: Tchaikowsky's Niece Remembers', 16: 3 March 1945, p. 231.
'George Cruikshank', 16: 6, June 1945, p. 484.

Sunday Times Colour Magazine

'Behind the Veil', photographed by Eve Arnold, November 1970.
1: 'The Seven Veils of Islam': Afghanistan, 1 November, p. 34;
2: The Trucial States, 8 November, p. 19;
3: Egypt, 15 November, p. 19.

Vogue

Lesley Blanch wrote regularly for British *Vogue* from October 1936 to November 1944, contributing a 'Spotlight' column, profiles and features, as well as intermittent pieces afterwards. Selected articles include:

'An apotheosis of RMS Queen Mary' with illustrations by LB, 13 May 1936, p. 80.
'Spotlight' column (Rambert/Komisarjevsky/Leontovich), 28 October 1936, p. 104.
'My Cook is a Catastrophe', 26 May 1937, p. 111.
'First Night Hocus Focus' with illustrations by LB, 10 November 1937, p. 59.
'Brave New Ballet', 25 May 1938, p. 58.
'Living the Sheltered Life', October 1940, p. 47.
'Titans' Triumph' (Gabriel Pascal, *Major Barbara*), November 1940, p. 44.
'Portfolio in Perspective', 'The Years Between' (for *Vogue* twenty-five-year retrospective issue), September 1941, pp. 34, 38.
'The WAAF Way', October 1941, p. 62.
'WRNS on the Job', November 1941, p. 56.
'Ack-Ack ATS and Others', January 1942, p. 34.
'Some of All the Russias', March 1942, p. 30.
'The Cinema', September 1942, p. 46.
'Noël Coward's New Medium', October 1942, p. 54.

'Re: Bob Hope', September 1943, p. 55.

'Lord and Lady Louis Mountbatten', November 1943, p. 38.

'The True Story of Lili Marlene', April 1944, p. 52.

'To France – Here and There', July 1944, p. 43.

'Feliks Topolski', November 1944, p. 52.

'The Geography of Time', May 1945, p. 53.

'Always Travel Heavy', November 1949, p. 76.

'The Pace that Kills', September 1953, p. 150.

'Alla Turca: the romantic, decadent, grandiose seraglio', December 1966, p. 148.

'My Day and What of It?', January 1973, p. 4.

'Every Cushion Tells a Story', January 1974, p. 84.

'Pleasures, Palaces and Pillars of Persia', June 1975, p. 120.

'My First Vogue Moment', October 2004, p. 99.

Selected Books by Romain Gary

These are the books written by Romain Gary while he was married to Lesley Blanch.

Forest of Anger, trans. Viola Gerard Garvin, London: The Cresset Press, 1944. (*Education européenne*, Paris: Calmann Lévy, 1945.)

Tulipe, Paris: Calmann Lévy, 1947.

Le grand vestiaire (dedicated to Lesley Blanch), Paris: Gallimard, 1948. *(The Company of Men,* trans. Joseph Barnes, New York: Simon & Schuster, 1950.)

Les Couleurs du jour. Paris, Gallimard, 1952. (*The Colours of the Day*, trans. Stephen Becker, London: White Lion Publishers, 1976; first published by Michael Joseph, 1953.)

Les Racines du ciel, Paris: Gallimard, 1956. (*The Roots of Heaven*, trans. Jonathan Griffin, New York: Simon & Schuster, 1958.)

Lady L. (book jacket designed by LB), London: Michael Joseph, 1959. (*Lady L.,* Paris: Gallimard, 1964.)

La Promesse de l'Aube, Paris: Gallimard, 1960. (*Promise at Dawn*, trans. John Markham Beach, London: The Companion Book Club, 1961.)

Talent Scout, London: Michael Joseph, 1961. (*Les Mangeurs d'étoiles*, Paris: Gallimard, 1966.)

Select Bibliography

Acton, Harold, *Nancy Mitford*, London: Hamish Hamilton, 1975.

Agranovsky, Genrich (State Jewish Museum of Lithuania) and Baranova, Galina (State Historic Archive of Lithuania), unpublished paper: 'Winner of the "Prix Goncourt" Romain Gary – A Native of Vilnius'.

Arnold, Eve, *The Unretouched Woman*, London: Jonathan Cape, 1976.

——*In Retrospect*, London: Sinclair-Stevenson, 1996.

Bailes, Howard, *Once a Paulina . . . A History of St Paul's Girls' School*, London: James & James (Publishers) Ltd, 2000.

Beevor, Antony and Cooper, Artemis, *Paris after the Liberation*, London: Penguin 1995.

Bellos, David, 'Le malentendu: l'histoire cachée d'*Education européenne*' in Hangouët and Audi (eds), *L'Herne, Cahier 85: Romain Gary* (see below), p. 150.

Bona, Dominique, *Romain Gary*, Paris: Mercure de France, 1987.

Borovsky, Victor, *A Triptych from the Russian Theatre*, London: Hurst & Co., 2001.

Bradford, Sarah H., *The Sitwells: and the Arts of the 1920s and 30s*, London: National Portrait Gallery, 1994.

Burke, Carolyn, *Lee Miller*, London: Bloomsbury, 2005.

Calder, Angus, *The People's War: Britain 1939–45*, London: Granada, 1971.

Catonné, Jean-Marie, *Romain Gary/Emile Ajar*, Paris: Editions Belfond, 1990.

Cleave, Maureen, 'A Mystery Woman Lifts the Veil', *Daily Telegraph*, 11 July 1987.

Cournot, Michel, 'Ma vérité sur l'affaire Ajar', *Le Nouvel Observateur*, 30 August–5 September 1990, pp. 78–82, reprinted in Hangouët and Audi (eds), *L'Herne, Cahier 85: Romain Gary*, p. 68 (see below).

Emmet Long, Robert (ed.), *George Cukor: Interviews*, Jackson, Mississippi: University Press of Mississippi, 2001.

Gary, Romain, *La Nuit sera calme*, Paris: Gallimard, 1974.

——*Vie et mort d'Emile Ajar*, Paris: Editions Gallimard, 1981. (*Life and Death of Emile Ajar*, in *King Solomon*, trans. Barbara Wright, New York: Harper & Row, 1983, p. 244.)

de Gaury, Gerald, *Traces of Travel Brought Home from Abroad*, London: Quartet, 1983.

Grove, Valerie, 'An appetite for exotic dishes', 'Look' section, *Sunday Times*, 9 July 1989.

Guppy, Shusha, 'Lesley Blanch', *Looking Back*, New York: British American Publishing/ Paris Review Editions, 1991, p. 1.

Hangouët, Jean-François, *Romain Gary: A la traversée des frontières*, Paris: Gallimard, 2007.

——ed. with Paul Audi, *L'Herne, Cahier 85: Romain Gary*, Paris: Editions de l'Herne, 2005.

Hastings, Selina, *Nancy Mitford: A Life*, London: Hamish Hamilton, 1985.

Huston, Nancy, *Tombeau de Romain Gary*, Arles: Actes Sud, 1995.

Jackson, Julian, *Charles de Gaulle*, London: Haus Publishing, 2003.

Julian, Philippe and Phillips, John, *Violet Trefusis: Life and Letters*, London: Hamish Hamilton, 1976.

Lambert, Gavin, *On Cukor*, London: W.H. Allen, 1973.

Larat, Fabrice, *Romain Gary: Un itinéraire européen*, Chêne-Bourg: Editions Médecine et Hygiène, 1999.

Levy, Emanuel, *George C: Master of Elegance*, New York: William Morrow & Co. Inc, 1994.

Lovell, Mary S., *A Scandalous Life: The Biography of Jane Digby el Mezrab*, London: Richard Cohen Books, 1995.

——*A Rage to Live: A Biography of Richard and Isabel Burton*, London: Little, Brown and Company, 1998.

Lycett, Andrew, 'Seduced by Eastern Promise', *The Times* Review, 12 June 2004, p. 12.

Marie, Michel, ' "It really makes you sick!": Jean-Luc Godard's *A Bout de souffle* (1959)', in Hayward, Susan and Vincendeau, Ginette (eds), *French Film: Texts and Contexts*, London and New York: Routledge, 1990, p. 201.

Mosley, Charlotte (ed.), *Love From Nancy: The Letters of Nancy Mitford*, London: Hodder & Stoughton, 1993.

Muir, Robin and Pepper, Terence, *Horst Portraits: 60 Years of Style*, London: National Portrait Gallery, 2001.

Nicholson, Virginia, *Among the Bohemians: Experiments in Living 1900–1939*, London: Viking, 2002.

Pavlowitch, Paul, *L'homme que l'on croyait*, Paris: Librairie Arthème Fayard, 1981.

Penrose, Antony (ed.), *Lee Miller's War*, London: Condé Nast, 1992.

Quella-Villéger, Alain, *Pierre Loti: Le pèlerin de la planète*, Bordeaux: Aubéron, 1998.

Quennell, Peter, *The Marble Foot: An Autobiography 1905–1938*, London: Collins, 1976.

——*The Wanton Chase: an autobiography from 1939*, London: Collins, 1980.

Rambert, Marie, *Quicksilver*, London and Basingstoke: Macmillan, 1972.

Richards, David, *Played Out: The Jean Seberg Story*, New York: PBJ Books, 1981.

Salmon, Alice Wooledge, Obituary of Lesley Blanch, *Guardian*, 10 May 2007.

Schoolcraft, Ralph, *Romain Gary: The Man Who Sold His Shadow*, Philadelphia: University of Pennsylvania Press, 2002.

Scott-James, Anne, *In the Mink*, London: Michael Joseph, 1952.

——*Sketches from a Life*, London: Michael Joseph, 1993.

Sitwell, Sacheverell, *Southern Baroque Art*, London: G. Duckworth, 1930.

Todorov, Tzvetan, 'The Achievement of Romain Gary', in *Hope and Memory*, trans. David Bellos, London: Atlantic Books, 2003, p. 213.

Topolski, Feliks, *Autobiography*, London: Faber & Faber, 1988.

Vickers, Hugo, *Cecil Beaton*, London: Weidenfeld & Nicolson, 1985.

Withers, Audrey, *Lifespan*, London: Peter Owen, 1994.

TV, Film and Radio

Television

Apostrophes, includes LB discussing Pierre Loti, 16 June 1986.

Une vie, une oeuvre: Romain Gary, l'insaisi, directed by Nancy Huston, France-Culture, 1993.

Film

Romain Gary, directed by Variety Moszynski, Visual Lynx Productions, 1985.

Radio

'Lesley Blanch: Une vie, une oeuvre', produced by Nathalie Triandafyllides, presented by Françoise Estèbe, with Georgia de Chamberet, Christiane Pierre-Loti Viaud, Philip Mansel, Susan Train, Guillaume Villeneuve, France-Culture, 22 May 2008.

'Romain Gary', series of ten radio interviews by André Bourin, France-Culture, June–July 1969.

Background Reading

Arfa, Hassan, *Under Five Shahs*, London: John Murray, 1964.

Atkinson, Thomas Witlam, *Travels in the Regions of the Upper and Lower Amoor*, London: Hurst & Blackett, 1861.

Baddeley, J.F., *The Russian Conquest of the Caucasus*, London: Longmans, Green & Co., 1908.

———*The Rugged Flanks of Caucasus*, London: Oxford University Press, 1940.

———Index Caucasica (unpublished), 97 photographs of the Caucasus (unpublished). All part of the Baddeley Bequest at the London Library.

Elliot, Jason, *Mirrors of the Unseen: Journeys in Iran*, London: Picador, 2006.

From Russia: French and Russian Master Paintings 1870–1925 from Moscow and St Petersburg, London: Royal Academy of Arts, 2008.

Gogol, Nikolai, *Dead Souls*, trans. David Magarshack, Harmondsworth: Penguin Classics, 1961.

Guppy, Shusha, *The Blindfold Horse: Memories of a Persian Childhood*, London/New York: Tauris Parke Press, 2006.

Herzen, Alexander, *My Past and Thoughts*, trans. Constance Garnett, London: Chatto & Windus, 1974.

Kapuscinski, Ryszard, *Shah of Shahs*, trans. William R. Brand and Katarzyna Mroczkowska-Brand, London: Penguin Modern Classics, 2006.

Lermontov, Mikhail, *A Hero of our Time*, trans. Vladimir and Dmitri Nabokov, London: Everyman, 1992.

Milosz, Czeslaw, *Native Realm: a Search for Definition*, trans. Catherine S. Leach, London: Sidgwick & Jackson, 1981.

Parsons, Anthony, *The Pride and the Fall: Iran 1974–9*, London: Jonathan Cape, 1984.

Pushkin, Alexander, *The Queen of Spades and Other Stories*, trans. Rosemary Edmonds, London: Penguin Classics, n.d.

Reiss, Tom, *The Orientalist: In Search of a Man Caught Between East and West*, London: Vintage, 2006.

Said, Edward W., *Orientalism*, London: Routledge & Kegan Paul, 1978.

Sutherland, Christine, *The Princess of Siberia*, London: Methuen, 1984.

Tolstoy, Leo, *The Cossacks* with *The Death of Ivan Ilyich, Happy Ever After*, trans. Rosemary Edmonds, London: Penguin Classics, 1960.

Archives

John Murray, 50 Albemarle Street, London, publishers' archives.

George Cukor Collection, Academy of Motion Picture Arts and Sciences, Margaret Herrick Library, Beverly Hills, California.

John Huston Collection, Academy of Motion Picture Arts and Sciences, Margaret Herrick Library, Beverly Hills, California.

Hélène Hoppenot Journals, Bibliothèque Littéraire Jacques Doucet, Paris.

Harper & Row Papers, Butler Museum, Columbia University, New York (Romain Gary).

Joseph Barnes Papers, Columbia University, New York (Romain Gary).

Press Association, Cuttings Library, London.

Editions Gallimard, press clippings, Paris (Romain Gary).

Editions Mercure de France, press clippings, Paris (Romain Gary).

Index

Works by Lesley Blanch (LB) appear directly under title; works by others under author's name